21 世纪应用型本科计算机案例型规划教材

计算机专业英语(第 2 版)

主　编　张　勇　段君玮
副主编　张春华　肖萍萍
参　编　李伟光　邢　翀　李　倩
　　　　崔　钢　崔立新　宋小华

内 容 简 介

本书是一本面向 21 世纪的计算机专业英语教材，它主要涉及计算机基础知识、计算机专业知识以及计算机前沿技术，具体包括计算机硬件、计算机语言、软件工程、数据库、Internet、Windows 7 操作系统、.NET 技术、网络安全、分布式系统、数字媒体技术、游戏动画、嵌入式系统、物联网、云计算以及人工智能等领域的知识和技术。全书以最新的计算机文献和经典原版教材为基础，选材以突出新技术与实用技术且难度适当为目标，并配有同步对照的词汇注释、练习题以及实用的科技英语语法，使读者能够快速掌握计算机专业英语的特点和大量的专业词汇，并对相关的计算机领域知识有所扩展。同时为了方便查阅词汇，正文中还附有词汇表。本书在第 1 版的基础上增加了目前计算机领域的最新研究热点和前沿知识，能够拓展读者的知识面并使其迅速了解计算机应用的发展方向。

本书可供高等院校计算机专业及相关专业的本、专科学生使用，也可作为计算机水平考试的考生、计算机爱好者以及 IT 领域的工程技术人员的参考用书。

图书在版编目(CIP)数据

计算机专业英语/张勇，段君玮主编. —2 版. —北京：北京大学出版社，2012.9
(21 世纪应用型本科计算机案例型规划教材)
ISBN 978-7-301-21088-8

Ⅰ.①计… Ⅱ.①张…②段… Ⅲ.①电子计算机—英语—高等学校—教材 Ⅳ.①H31

中国版本图书馆 CIP 数据核字(2012)第 186403 号

书　　　　名：	计算机专业英语(第 2 版)
著作责任者：	张　勇　段君玮　主编
策划编辑：	郑　双
责任编辑：	郑　双　程志强
标准书号：	ISBN 978-7-301-21088-8/TP・1237
出　版　者：	北京大学出版社
地　　　址：	北京市海淀区成府路 205 号　100871
网　　　址：	http://www.pup.cn　http://www.pup6.cn
电　　　话：	邮购部 010-62752015　发行部 010-62750672　编辑部 010-62750667
电子邮箱：	编辑部 pup6@pup.cn　总编室 zpup@pup.cn
印　刷　者：	北京虎彩文化传播有限公司
发　行　者：	北京大学出版社
经　销　者：	新华书店
	787 毫米×1092 毫米　16 开本　21.25 印张　486 千字
	2008 年 8 月第 1 版　2012 年 9 月第 2 版　2025 年 1 月第 10 次印刷
定　　　价：	49.00 元

未经许可，不得以任何方式复制或抄袭本书之部分或全部内容。
版权所有　侵权必究　　举报电话：010-62752024
　　　　　　　　　　　　电子邮箱：fd@pup.cn

21世纪应用型本科计算机案例型规划教材
专家编审委员会

(按姓名拼音顺序)

主　任	刘瑞挺			
副主任	陈　钟	蒋宗礼		
委　员	陈代武	房爱莲	胡巧多	黄贤英
	江　红	李　建	娄国焕	马秀峰
	祁亨年	王联国	汪新民	谢安俊
	解　凯	徐　苏	徐亚平	宣兆成
	姚喜妍	于永彦	张荣梅	

信息技术的案例型教材建设

(代丛书序)

刘瑞挺

北京大学出版社第六事业部在 2005 年组织编写了《21 世纪应用型本科计算机系列实用规划教材》，至今已出版了 50 多种。这些教材出版后，在全国高校引起热烈反响，可谓初战告捷。这使北京大学出版社的计算机教材市场规模迅速扩大，编辑队伍茁壮成长，经济效益明显增强，与各类高校师生的关系更加密切。

2008 年 1 月北京大学出版社第六事业部在北京召开了"21 世纪应用型本科计算机案例型教材建设和教学研讨会"。这次会议为编写案例型教材做了深入的探讨和具体的部署，制定了详细的编写目的、丛书特色、内容要求和风格规范。在内容上强调面向应用、能力驱动、精选案例、严把质量；在风格上力求文字精练、脉络清晰、图表明快、版式新颖。这次会议吹响了提高教材质量第二战役的进军号。

案例型教材真能提高教学的质量吗？

是的。著名法国哲学家、数学家勒内·笛卡儿(Rene Descartes，1596—1650)说得好："由一个例子的考察，我们可以抽出一条规律。(From the consideration of an example we can form a rule.)"事实上，他发明的直角坐标系，正是通过生活实例而得到的灵感。据说是在 1619 年夏天，笛卡儿因病住进医院。中午他躺在病床上，苦苦思索一个数学问题时，忽然看到天花板上有一只苍蝇飞来飞去。当时天花板是用木条做成正方形的格子。笛卡儿发现，要说出这只苍蝇在天花板上的位置，只需说出苍蝇在天花板上的第几行和第几列。当苍蝇落在第四行、第五列的那个正方形时，可以用(4，5)来表示这个位置……由此他联想到可用类似的办法来描述一个点在平面上的位置。他高兴地跳下床，喊着"我找到了，找到了"，然而不小心把国际象棋撒了一地。当他的目光落到棋盘上时，又兴奋地一拍大腿："对，对，就是这个图"。笛卡儿锲而不舍的毅力，苦思冥想的钻研，使他开创了解析几何的新纪元。千百年来，代数与几何，井水不犯河水。17 世纪后，数学突飞猛进的发展，在很大程度上归功于笛卡儿坐标系和解析几何学的创立。

这个故事，听起来与阿基米德在浴缸洗澡而发现浮力原理，牛顿在苹果树下遇到苹果落到头上而发现万有引力定律，确有异曲同工之妙。这就证明，一个好的例子往往能激发灵感，由特殊到一般，联想出普遍的规律，即所谓的"一叶知秋"、"见微知著"的意思。

回顾计算机发明的历史，每一台机器、每一颗芯片、每一种操作系统、每一类编程语言、每一个算法、每一套软件、每一款外部设备，无不像闪光的珍珠串在一起。每个案例都闪烁着智慧的火花，是创新思想不竭的源泉。在计算机科学技术领域，这样的案例就像大海岸边的贝壳，俯拾皆是。

事实上，案例研究(Case Study)是现代科学广泛使用的一种方法。Case 包含的意义很广：包括 Example 例子，Instance 事例、示例，Actual State 实际状况，Circumstance 情况、事件、境遇，甚至 Project 项目、工程等。

我们知道在计算机的科学术语中，很多是直接来自日常生活的。例如 Computer 一词早在 1646 年就出现于古代英文字典中，但当时它的意义不是"计算机"而是"计算工人"，即专门从事简单计算的工人。同理，Printer 当时也是"印刷工人"而不是"打印机"。正是由于这些"计算工人"和"印刷工人"常出现计算错误和印刷错误，才激发查尔斯·巴贝奇(Charles Babbage，1791—1871)设计了差分机和分析机，这是最早的专用计算机和通用计算机。这位英国剑桥大学数学教授、机械设计专家、经济学家和哲学家是国际公认的"计算机之父"。

20世纪40年代，人们还用Calculator表示计算机器。到电子计算机出现后，才用Computer表示计算机。此外，硬件(Hardware)和软件(Software)来自销售人员。总线(Bus)就是公共汽车或大巴，故障和排除故障源自格瑞斯·霍普(Grace Hopper，1906—1992)发现的"飞蛾子"(Bug)和"抓蛾子"或"抓虫子"(Debug)。其他如鼠标、菜单……不胜枚举。至于哲学家进餐问题，理发师睡觉问题更是操作系统文化中脍炙人口的经典。

以计算机为核心的信息技术，从一开始就与应用紧密结合。例如，ENIAC用于弹道曲线的计算，ARPANET用于资源共享以及核战争时的可靠通信。即使是非常抽象的图灵机模型，也受益于二战时图灵博士破译纳粹密码工作的关系。

在信息技术中，既有许多成功的案例，也有不少失败的案例；既有先成功而后失败的案例，也有先失败而后成功的案例。好好研究它们的成功经验和失败教训，对于编写案例型教材有重要的意义。

我国正在实现中华民族的伟大复兴，教育是民族振兴的基石。改革开放30年来，我国高等教育在数量上、规模上已有相当的发展。当前的重要任务是提高培养人才的质量，必须从学科知识的灌输转变为素质与能力的培养。应当指出，大学课堂在高新技术的武装下，利用PPT进行的"高速灌输"、"翻页宣科"有愈演愈烈的趋势，我们不能容忍用"技术"绑架教学，而是让教学工作乘信息技术的东风自由地飞翔。

本系列教材的编写，以学生就业所需的专业知识和操作技能为着眼点，在适度的基础知识与理论体系覆盖下，突出应用型、技能型教学的实用性和可操作性，强化案例教学。本套教材将会有机融入大量最新的示例、实例以及操作性较强的案例，力求提高教材的趣味性和实用性，打破传统教材自身知识框架的封闭性，强化实际操作的训练，使本系列教材做到"教师易教，学生乐学，技能实用"。有了广阔的应用背景，再造计算机案例型教材就有了基础。

我相信北京大学出版社在全国各地高校教师的积极支持下，精心设计，严格把关，一定能够建设出一批符合计算机应用型人才培养模式的、以案例型为创新点和兴奋点的精品教材，并且通过一体化设计、实现多种媒体有机结合的立体化教材，为各门计算机课程配齐电子教案、学习指导、习题解答、课程设计等辅导资料。让我们用锲而不舍的毅力，勤奋好学的钻研，向着共同的目标努力吧！

刘瑞挺教授 本系列教材编写指导委员会主任、全国高等院校计算机基础教育研究会副会长、中国计算机学会普及工作委员会顾问、教育部考试中心全国计算机应用技术证书考试委员会副主任、全国计算机等级考试顾问。曾任教育部理科计算机科学教学指导委员会委员、中国计算机学会教育培训委员会副主任。PC Magazine《个人电脑》总编辑、CHIP《新电脑》总顾问、清华大学《计算机教育》总策划。

前　　言

计算机自诞生之日起，就一直以前所未有的速度发展着。作为未来 IT 业的技术人员，必须具有熟练阅读计算机专业英语文献的能力，以便及时了解计算机发展的新技术和新动向。因此高等院校计算机及其相关专业纷纷开设了计算机专业英语课程。《计算机专业英语》是计算机及相关专业人员重要的工具书，也是学习掌握计算机技术的桥梁。计算机专业英语的阅读理解能力是衡量一个人计算机技术水平的重要标志之一。由于计算机技术日新月异，新概念、新术语、新资料源源不断从国外引入，直接采用英文术语(或缩写语)的现象越来越普遍；伴随 Internet 应用的日益普及，网上拥有浩瀚的英文信息；计算机操作过程中所出现的菜单、提示、帮助及错误反馈信息也常用英文界面，若不能迅速理解其含义，将会严重影响上机、上网、工作。此外，英文操作手册及技术资料均包含较详细、全面、准确的技术细节，这是任何编译资料所不能代替的。

本书的编写目标是使学生不仅能学到专业英语词汇、扩大知识面，同时也能掌握用英语表达专业知识的方法，提高阅读及理解专业英文资料的能力，掌握计算机专业文章翻译的方法和技巧。

本书面向计算机应用及相关专业的本、专科学生，它主要涉及计算机基础知识、计算机硬件、计算机语言、软件工程、数据库、Internet、Windows 7 操作系统、.NET 技术、网络安全、分布式系统、数字媒体技术、游戏动画、嵌入式系统、物联网、云计算以及人工智能等领域的知识和技术。全书以最新的计算机文献和经典原版教材为基础，选材以突出最新技术与实用技术且难度适当为目标，并配有同步对照的词汇注释、练习题以及实用的科技英语语法。

本书有以下几个方面的特点：

(1) 选材涉及的计算机专业领域广泛且能够及时反映计算机发展的新技术。

(2) 介绍了必要的语法知识及科技文章的翻译方法及技巧。

(3) 具有非常详细的词汇同步注释，使那些即使英文水平一般的读者也能轻松阅读。

(4) 阅读材料难度适当，强调理解及分析。

(5) 每章配有习题、参考译文及习题参考答案，方便读者学习。

全书共分 15 章，在第 1 版的基础上对内容进了适当改动，主要增加了数字媒体技术、嵌入式系统、物联网、云计算等前沿知识。全书的具体章节内容如下：第 1 章介绍台式计算机和膝上型计算机的优缺点以及选择方式；第 2 章是计算机硬件的相关知识，包括处理器、存储器、输入/输出等技术；第 3 章是计算机语言知识部分，内容包括计算机语言的类型、流行语言 Java 及 JSP 语言简介；第 4 章介绍微软的最新操作系统 Windows 7 的新特征和使用特点；第 5 章介绍 Windows 编程的基础知识和相关技术；第 6 章是关于软件工程的介绍，包括软件工程的背景、软件生命周期及设计方法学；第 7 章是数据库技术，其内容以微软的最新数据库 SQL Server 2005 为例，介绍了数据库的可伸缩性以及数据库开发的特点；第 8 章是关于计算机网络及网络安全的相关知识，包括常见网络类型、互联网的历史和现状以及网络安全等；第9章以微软的 VB.NET 和 C#.NET 为例，介绍了.NET 框架和技术；第 10 章介绍了分布式系统的特征、面临的挑战以及分布式系统的体系结构模型；第 11 章介绍了人工智能的相关知识；第 12 章介绍了数字媒体的最新研究领域和相关技术；第 13 章介绍了嵌入式系统的相关知识和技术；第 14 章介绍了物联网的基本概念和相关技术；第 15 章介绍了云计算的基本知识和相关技术。

　　本书的第 1、3、9、10 章由张勇老师编写，第 4、5、7 章由段君玮老师编写。其余章节由张春华、肖萍萍、李伟光、邢翀、李倩、崔钢、崔立新、宋小华几位老师共同编写。

　　由于编者水平有限，不当之处敬请读者批评指正！

编　者

2012 年 3 月

目 录

Chapter 1　Choosing Your Computer 1
Section A　Choosing Your Computer: Desktop or Laptop? 1
Section B　Pros and Cons of the Desktop Computers 5
Section C　Pros and Cons of Laptop Computers 10
Grammar 1　科技英语的语言特点(Ⅰ) 15

Chapter 2　Computer Hardware 23
Section A　CPU 23
Section B　Memory 31
Section C　I/O Subsystem Organization and Interfacing 36
Grammar 2　科技英语的语言特点(Ⅱ) 39

Chapter 3　Computer Languages 48
Section A　Programming Language 48
Section B　The Java Language 53
Section C　JSP 58
Grammar 3　科技英语的写作特点(Ⅰ) 62

Chapter 4　Windows 7 70
Section A　Features New to Windows 7 70
Section B　Removed Features 74
Section C　Details of Windows 7 78
Grammar 4　科技英语的写作特点(Ⅱ) 82

Chapter 5　Windows Programming 88
Section A　Windows Programming Options 88
Section B　Using Unicode in Windows 92
Section C　Windows and Messages 97
Grammar 5　科技英语的写作特点(Ⅲ) 100

Chapter 6　Software Engineering 107
Section A　The Tar Pit 107
Section B　The Software Life Cycle 112
Section C　Design Methodologies 119
Grammar 6　科技英语翻译方法与技巧(Ⅰ) 123

Chapter 7 Get Your Arms around Microsoft SQL Server ... 131

- Section A Introduction to SQL Server 2005 ... 131
- Section B Database Scalability Revisited ... 135
- Section C Features for Database Development ... 139
- Grammar 7 科技英语翻译方法与技巧(Ⅱ) ... 143

Chapter 8 Computer Networking and Networking Security ... 150

- Section A Computer Networking ... 150
- Section B History and Present Situation of the Internet ... 154
- Section C Networking Security ... 160
- Grammar 8 科技英语翻译方法与技巧(Ⅲ) ... 165

Chapter 9 .NET Framework ... 173

- Section A What is .NET? ... 173
- Section B Using Visual Studio.NET ... 177
- Section C Using the .NET SDK ... 182
- Grammar 9 谈科技翻译中的长句的翻译 ... 186

Chapter 10 Distributed Systems ... 192

- Section A Characterization of Distributed Systems ... 192
- Section B Challenges of Distributed Systems ... 197
- Section C Architecture Models of Distributed Systems ... 203
- Grammar 10 科技文献翻译中的汉语表达 ... 208

Chapter 11 Artificial Intelligence ... 216

- Section A Expert Systems ... 216
- Section B Strategies for State Space Search ... 220
- Section C Current Challenges and Future Directions ... 226
- Grammar 11 英语科技文献的阅读技巧(I) ... 233

Chapter 12 Digital Media Technology ... 241

- Section A Introduction of Digital Media Technology ... 241
- Section B Virtual Reality Technology ... 246
- Section C Virtual Reality Modeling Language ... 249
- Grammar 12 英语科技文献的阅读技巧(Ⅱ) ... 256

Chapter 13 Embedded System ... 263

- Section A Introduction of Embedded System ... 263
- Section B History and Future ... 266
- Section C Application Area ... 270
- Grammar 13 谈谈科技英语听力的学习方法 ... 272

Chapter 14　Internet of Things ... 277
Section A　The Development History ... 277
Section B　The Key Technology ... 283
Section C　Challenges and Concerns ... 288
Grammar 14　科技英语文体的基本特点 ... 293

Chapter 15　Cloud Computing ... 299
Section A　What Cloud Computing Really Means ... 299
Section B　Mobile Cloud Computing ... 303
Section C　Clash of the Clouds ... 307
Grammar 15　其他计算机英语文体的写作技巧 ... 313

参考文献 ... 321

Chapter 1 Choosing Your Computer
(选择你的计算机)

Section A Choosing Your Computer: Desktop or Laptop?

When it's time to think about buying a new computer, the very first question you must ask yourself (and the other people who will use the new computer) is the one in this section's title: Should I buy a **desktop** computer or a **laptop**?

This section will help you make that important decision; it explains how to **evaluate** the special features of each type and describe their benefits and drawbacks. Later in this chapter, you can find a lot more detail about using each of those features, but right now it's the most important to decide whether the lightweight and compact design of a laptop is important enough to sacrifice the lower cost, **flexible construction**, and generally larger keyboard and screen in a desktop system or not.

What's the difference?

Before beginning a discussion on the **pros and cons** of each type, it might be useful to define certain terms.

A desktop computer usually has most of its **components** in a **modular** case, with a separate keyboard, video display, mouse, and speakers connected to the case through cables or wireless links. The case for a desktop computer might be either **horizontal** or **vertical**.

A few specialty **manufacturers** offer compact designs that don't meet the industry standards (such as a computer with the **processor** and related parts built into the video monitor package), but most desktop computers **resemble** the ones shown in Fig. 1.1.

desktop ['desktɔp]
n. [计]桌面，台式计算机
laptop ['læptɔp]
n. [计]膝上型计算机，便携式计算机
evaluate [i'væljueit]
vt. 评价，估计，求……的值
flexible ['fleksəbl]
adj. 柔韧性，易曲的，灵活的，柔软的，能变形的
construction [kən'strʌkʃən]
n. 建筑，建筑物，解释
pros and cons
正反
component [kəm'pəunənt]
n. 成分，部件
modular ['mɔdjulə]
adj. 模的，有标准组件的
horizontal [ˌhɔri'zɔntl]
adj. 地平线的，水平的
vertical ['və:tikəl]
adj. 垂直的，直立的，顶点的
manufacturer [ˌmænju'fæktʃərə]
n. 制造业者，厂商
processor ['prəusesə]
n. 处理器
resemble [ri'zembl]
vt. 像，类似

Fig. 1.1　A desktop computer

A laptop computer is a self-contained, lightweight, **portable** unit that can operate on battery power. The most common laptop design is sometimes described as a **clamshell** because it opens up like a big **bivalve**, with the keyboard in the bottom half and the screen in the top. Fig. 1.2 shows a typical laptop computer.

portable ['pɔ:təbl]
adj. 轻便的, 手提(式)的, 便携式的
clamshell ['klæmʃəl]
n. 蛤壳, <美>蛤壳式挖泥机
bivalve ['baivælv]
n. 双壳类

Fig. 1.2　A laptop computer

The newest portable computers, known as **tablets**, have touch-sensitive screens that are often attached to the keyboard section with rotating hinges. This allows a user to write on the screen with a special **stylus** without opening the clamshell. Microsoft has designed support for tablets into the most recent versions of the Windows **operating system**.

tablet ['tæblit]
n. 写字板, 书写板

stylus ['stailəs]
n. 铁笔
operating system
操作系统

How do you use your computer?

In most cases, the choice between a desktop and a laptop computer depends on the way you expect to use this particular machine. If you're planning to carry the computer with you when you travel for business, or if you want to take the computer on vacation with you to **surf** the Internet while your family surfs the waves on a **beach**, the choice is obvious: You need a laptop portable. On the other hand, if you are looking for an office machine that never moves away from your workspace, a desktop computer is the better choice.

To make a good decision, think about the way you expect to work with your computer:

- Will you always use it in the same location, or will you carry it from one place to another?
- Do you expect to use your computer away from your own home or office?
- If you're in business, do you expect to use the computer in your **clients**' or customers' offices or on a job site?
- If you're a student, will you take the computer to class and use the same computer at home or in your dorm room? How about taking notes in the library or **laboratory**? Will you want to take this computer home during vacations?
- If you plan to use the computer at home, do you want to carry it from one room to another? If it's portable, will your children take it to their bedrooms and bury it under their toys or **laundry**?
- Are you buying this computer to share among two or more users who don't always work at the same location?
- Do you want to use this computer in places where **AC** power is not easily accessible?
- Will you have limited space in the location where you expect to use your computer?
- Is **security** important? Do you want to make sure that nobody else can use the computer when you're not there? Do you want to protect the computer (and the data stored on its drives) from theft and damage?

In general, you need a laptop if you expect to move the

---

surf [sə:f]
vt. 在激浪上驾(船), 在……冲浪; [计] 冲浪

beach [bi:tʃ]
n. 海滩

client ['klaiənt]
n. [计]顾客, 客户, 委托人

laboratory [lə'bɔrətəri, 'læbərətəri]
n. 实验室

laundry ['lɔ:ndri]
n. 洗衣店, 要洗的衣服, 洗熨

AC
abbr. Alternating Current, 交流电

security [si'kjuəriti]
n. 安全

computer around. That might mean carrying it from one room to the next, or anywhere in between. If you plan to keep the computer in the same place all the time, a desktop computer is usually the way to go.

It's not always that easy. Sometimes, one type or the other might appear to be more **convenient**, but one or more specific features could drive your choice in the other direction. The rest of this chapter describes specific characteristics of each type that might contribute to your choice.

convenient [kən'vi:njənt]
adj. 便利的，方便的

Summary.

When you're thinking about a new computer, it's essential to decide which type meets your specific requirements.

The most important advantages of desktop computers are related to economy and the size of the components inside and outside the case. Bigger keyboards and screens make it easier to use your computer, while the modular construction and extra space inside the box allow you (or your service technician) to repair or **modify** the computer more easily. On the other hand, those big cases and **external** devices are all heavy and bulky, so they're more difficult to move around.

modify ['mɔdifai]
vt. 更改，修改
v. 修改
external [eks'tə:nl]
adj. 外部的，客观的，

Exercises

I. Fill in the blanks with the information given in the text.

1. A _____ computer usually has most of its components in a modular case.
2. A desktop computer is bigger and more _____ than a laptop.
3. The newest _____ computers, known as tablets, have touch-sensitive screens that are often attached to the keyboard section with rotating hinges.
4. Microsoft has designed support for tablets into the most recent versions of the Windows _____.
5. A _____ computer is a self-contained, lightweight, portable unit that can operate on battery power.
6. The most common laptop design is sometimes _____ as a clamshell because it opens up like a big bivalve, with the keyboard in the bottom half and the screen in the top.
7. In most cases, the choice between a desktop and a laptop computer depends on the way you expect to use this _____ machine.
8. If you are looking for an office machine that never moves away from your workspace, a _____ computer is the better choice.

II. Translate the following passages from English into Chinese.

There's a third alternative that might be worth your attention when you're trying to decide what kind of computer to buy. If you expect to use the computer in a single location most of the time, but you want the convenience of a portable when you take your twice-a-year business trips and on those rare evenings and weekends when you must take work home with you, consider using a laptop with a separate monitor, mouse, and keyboard. In the office, you have the functional benefits of a full-size keyboard and screen, but when it's necessary, you can pull a few plugs out of their sockets and take the computer with you.

Some manufacturers call this category a desktop replacement because the laptop takes the place of a conventional desktop processor case. Many laptops even include a special docking-station connector that takes the place of all those separate cables and sockets.

Section B Pros and Cons of the Desktop Computers

Desktop computers are the natural choice when a computer remains in the same place for all of its working life. The modular design of a desktop system makes it **relatively** easy to **configure** it with exactly the right set of features and functions for your specific needs. And if you expect to perform your own work, a computer in a desktop case is much easier to repair and modify than a laptop.

relatively ['relətivli]
adv. 相关地
configure [kən'figə]
vi. 配置，设定
vt. 使成形，使具有一定形式

On the other hand, a desktop computer with its separate keyboard, mouse, monitor, and speakers is big, bulky, and **awkward** to move around。

awkward ['ɔ:kwəd]
adj. 难使用的，笨拙的

Desktops cost less.

When price is the most important, a desktop computer is the better choice because a desktop computer often costs less than a laptop with comparable performance. Even after you add the price of a separate monitor, keyboard, and mouse to the basic system, the total is probably lower than a laptop with the same features. If you're looking for the least expensive computer you can buy, or the least expensive computer at a specific level of performance, a desktop system is the clear choice.

Of course, it is possible to spend more for a desktop computer than the price of a good laptop by choosing a super-fast processor and **graphics controller**, lots of memory, a large **flat-panel** monitor, and other high-end components and features, but that's not a fair comparison. The price of a desktop system is always far lower than a laptop machine with similar specifications.

graphics controller
图形控制杆
flat-panel
平板
assemble [ə'sembl]
vt. 集合，聚集，装配
Dell
戴尔，美国最大的计算机公司之一

If you can **assemble** your own computer from parts, the savings can be even greater. Major computer builders such as **Dell** and **Hewlett-Packard** may offer very inexpensive models with limited performance for less than the cost of assembling a similar

Hewlett-Packard
惠普，著名的计算机公司

machine yourself, but if you want a system with better performance, you can often find higher-quality parts for less than the cost of an off-the-shelf product. Cases, **motherboards**(as shown in Fig.1.3), **disk drives**, **expansion cards**, and other standard parts for desktop computers are easy to find.

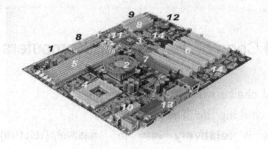

Fig. 1.3 Motherboard

So building your own system can be a practical alternative for people who have more time and assembly skills than ready cash, and who want something better than an entry-level system. But there are no **widespread** standards for the size and layout of laptop components, so it's not always practical to look for a **generic** laptop case, keyboard, video display, and motherboard that you can put together yourself.

Desktops use standard parts.

The parts inside a desktop computer usually follow one or more design standards, so it's often possible to replace a component that fails with a new one from a different manufacturer. And when you want to add more **memory**, a larger **hard drive**, or maybe a second graphics controller and monitor to your system, you can be confident that you won't have to limit yourself to products from a single manufacturer. Just because the label on the case says Compaq or Gateway, you can still go to a big-box retailer and choose from among many different brands. This combination of modular design and **competition** is one reason that the prices of most desktop computer components are lower than the **comparable**, non-standard parts in a laptop.

In addition, the common parts specifications allow a repair shop to maintain a smaller inventory because they can use the same parts in many different desktop computer makes and models.

Desktops have a flexible design.

Desktop computers are modular systems that make it easy to add or replace **individual** parts to meet each user's particular requirements. A computer intended for an **illustrator** or a **computer-aided** designer might have a higher-quality graphics controller and video display, where a purchasing **agent** may not use anything more demanding than a word processor and a spreadsheet. Most computer manufacturers let you order exactly the set of features and **specifications** that you want.

When your needs change, it's usually easy to open up a desktop case and reconfigure the system, unless your computer uses **proprietary** parts. You can be confident that the sockets on the motherboard and the mounting holes in the drive bays fit the new **expansion** card or disk drive, and the main printed **circuit board** that controls the rest of the system (the motherboard) works with the new parts.

Modular design also means that you can transfer some old parts to your new computer when you replace your Old Faithful machine that has finally become **obsolete**. For example, I wrote this book on an old Northgate keyboard that I have moved from one computer to the next for more than fifteen years; I like the way its keys respond to my typing. Northgate stopped making these keyboards many years ago (similar keyboards are still available from other makers, but they're very expensive), but the **plug** on the keyboard's cable still fits the socket on my current computer and it works just fine with a twenty-first century processor and motherboard.

Of course, there are some limits to this flexible design. You can't use a brand-new memory module or the latest disk drives with a 10-year-old motherboard because the designs have changed to **accommodate** newer and better processors and other devices.

Desktops are easy to upgrade.

You can improve the computer's performance by adding new components and replacing existing parts with new ones that have faster speed, greater capacity, or more features. Once again, the desktop computer's modular design makes it easy to work inside the case. Of course, there's a point of **diminishing** returns where

---

individual [ˌindiˈvidʒuəl]
adj. 个别的，单独的，个人的
illustrator [ˈiləstreitə(r)]
n. 插图画家，图解者，说明者
computer-aided
计算机辅助的
agent [ˈeidʒənt]
n. 代理(商)
specification [ˌspesifiˈkeiʃən]
n. 详述，规格，说明书，规范
proprietary [prəˈpraiətəri]
adj. 所有的，私人拥有的
expansion [iksˈpænʃən]
n. 扩充，开展，膨胀，扩张物，辽阔，浩瀚
circuit board
电路板
obsolete [ˌɔbsəˈliːt]
n. 废弃物，陈旧物

plug [plʌg]
n. 插头

accommodate [əˈkɔmədeit]
vi. 适应
vt. 供应，供给，使适应，调节，和解，向……提供，容纳，调和
upgrade [ˈʌpgreid]
n. 升级，上升，上坡
diminishing [diˈminiʃiŋ]
adj. 逐渐缩小的

it's better and less costly to buy a new system, but just about every desktop computer has room for **economical** improvement. The most common and effective motherboard has one or more **sockets** for memory modules, so you can increase the total amount of memory by adding one or more new modules to the memory that is already in place. You can also remove the existing memory and replace it with the same number of modules with more memory on each module. Adding memory is easier in a desktop system because there's plenty of space inside the case.

Except for a few very small cases, all desktop computers have two or more internal **drive bays**. Therefore, you can add storage **capacity** by installing another hard drive to the system simply by **mounting** the drive in a vacant drive bay and connecting a couple of cables. It's not necessary to transfer the data already stored on the existing drive first.

The **CPU** chip in a desktop system——the central processing unit that controls everything else——is also relatively easy to remove and replace with a faster CPU with similar architecture, and that fits in the same socket. A new CPU can offer faster processing and better performance than the one that was **originally** supplied with the computer. Unlike most of the other integrated circuits on the motherboard, the CPU mounts in a special socket that uses a **latching** mechanism to hold it in place, so it's not necessary (or possible) to solder a new chip directly to the printed circuit board.

All of these upgrades are easy to perform, but they often require some changes to the computer's hardware or software **configuration**. Before you try an upgrade, consult the computer manual or the motherboard manual for information about jumpers or switch settings on the motherboard, and **adjustments** to the BIOS settings (the BIOS——basic input/output system——is the set of programs the computer uses to test hardware and load Windows or some other operating system).

Desktops take up a lot of space.

Desktop computers do have some drawbacks. A desktop case with a separate keyboard occupies more physical space than a more **compact** laptop computer. For most of us, the space on our desks or worktables is prime real estate, so a computer with a

---

economical [,i:kəˈnɔmikəl]
adj. 节约的，经济的

socket [ˈsɔkit]
n. 窝，穴，孔，插座，牙槽

drive bays
驱动槽

capacity [kəˈpæsiti]
n. 容量，生产量，容量，智能，能力，才能，接受力，地位

mount [maunt]
vt. 爬上，使上马，装上，设置，安放

CPU
abbr. Central Processing Unit
中央处理单元，中央处理器

originally [əˈridʒənəli]
adv. 最初，原先

latching [ˈlætʃiŋ]
n. 闭塞，闭锁，关闭

configuration [kənˌfigjuˈreiʃən]
n. 构造，结构，配置，外形

adjustment [əˈdʒʌstmənt]
n. 调整，调节，调节器

compact [ˈkɔmpækt]
adj. 紧凑的，紧密的，简洁的

smaller footprint is highly desirable. This may be less of an issue today than it used to be, because flat-panel monitors are much less **intrusive** than the old **cathode-ray tube** displays that were often 18 inches or more from front to back.

intrusive [in'tru:siv]
adj. 打扰的，插入的
cathode-ray tube
阴极射线管

Desktops are difficult to transport.

Desktop computers are big and heavy. If you ever have to move your desktop system with all its **accessories** and **accouterments** from one room to another, you probably want to use a cart with several shelves, or at least an office chair with wheels. Then you must find and attach at least half a dozen different cables to the back of the box or convince your local computer expert to do it for you before you can use the computer again. Moving a desktop computer is a complicated and **time-consuming** exercise.

accessory [æk'sesəri]
n. 附件，零件，附加物
accouterment [ə'ku:təmənt]
n. 穿着，配备，饰物

time-consuming
adj. 耗时的

Desktops require external power.

On one hand the electrical **circuits**, fan motors, and disk drives in your computer use DC power from the power supply inside the case. On the other hand, the power supply, along with your video display and other external accessories, needs a source of **domestic** AC power (110 volts in North America and Japan, 220 volts in most other places). If there isn't a wall outlet nearby, you need some kind of **generator**, or a big battery with an inverter, or an extremely long extension cord.

circuit ['sə:kit]
n. 电路，一圈，周游，巡回电路
domestic [də'mestik]
adj. 家庭的，国内的，与人共处的，驯服的
generator ['dʒenəreitə]
n. 发电机，发生器

Exercises

Ⅰ. **Fill in the blanks with the information given in the text.**

1. A desktop computer with its separate _____, mouse, monitor, and speakers is big, bulky, and awkward to move around.

2. You can't use a brand-new memory module or the latest disk drives with a 10-year-old motherboard because the designs have changed to _____ newer and better processors and other devices.

3. when you want to add more _____, a larger _____, or maybe a second graphics controller and monitor to your system, you can be confident that you won't have to limit yourself to products from a single manufacturer.

4. A desktop case with a _____ keyboard occupies more physical space than a more compact laptop computer.

5. A new CPU can offer faster processing and better performance than the one that was _____ supplied with the computer.

II. Translate the following passages from English into Chinese.

By Wintel computers, we mean computers designed around Intel processors (and similar processors made by AMD), and the Microsoft Windows operating system. However, this is not a "How to Use Windows" book that covers every imaginable feature and function in the Windows operating system——there are other books in the Bible series for that. This book may have been specifically written about using your computer with Windows XP (with Service Pack 2 installed), but readers who run their computers with Linux or Unix and those who have upgraded to Windows Vista can also find a lot of useful information here.

Section C Pros and Cons of Laptop Computers

Laptop computers are compact, lightweight alternatives to full-size desktop machines. Your laptop is a **self-contained** system that can easily fit into a **briefcase** or backpack. When you arrive at your **destination** (or when you want to use the computer along the way), you can open up the clamshell case, turn on the power switch, and start working or playing a game just as soon as Windows completes its startup **routine**.

A laptop computer might be easy to carry around, but that **convenience** comes at a price in ease of use and repair, cost, and security. If you expect to move your computer often, a laptop is the obvious choice. But don't spend the extra money for a laptop until you consider the drawbacks of a portable system.

Laptops are portable.

The whole point of a laptop computer is easy **transport**. If you're a frequent traveler, or if you expect to use a single computer at the office or school and at home, a laptop is far more convenient than a desktop system. A laptop weighs less than a desktop machine with similar performance, and it comes in a smaller package.

Because laptop computers can use **batteries**, you can use them almost anywhere. Combined with a **wireless** Internet link, you can work on your own computer or connect to the rest of the world without the need to find a source of AC power for a few hours.

In addition to the **central processor**, memory, and data storage that are common inside a desktop case, a laptop computer also includes a keyboard, a video display, and a **substitute** for a mouse. Therefore, you don't have to buy those

self-contained ['selfkən'teind]
adj. 设备齐全的, 独立的, 沉默寡言的
briefcase ['brifkeis]
n. (扁平的, 柔韧的, 装文件, 书报的)公文包
destination [,desti'neiʃən]
n. 目的地, [计]目的文件, 目的单元格
routine [ru:'ti:n]
n. 例行公事, 常规, 日常事务, 程序
convenience [kən'vi:njəns]
n. 便利, 方便, 有益, 有用的, 方便的用具、机械、安排等
transport [træns'pɔ:t]
n. 传送器, 运输, 运输机
vt. 传送, 运输, 流放, 放逐

battery ['bætəri]
n. 电池
wireless ['waiəlis]
adj. 无线的

central processor
中央处理器
substitute ['sʌbstitju:t]
n. 代用品, 代替者, 替代品

devices separately, and you don't have to connect them to the case before you can start using your computer.

Laptops have design limitations.

If laptop computers were better than desktop machines in every way, nobody would bother with a desktop system. However, the same small size and reduced weight that makes a laptop easy to move around often makes it more difficult to use.

Smaller Screen

The screens on most laptop computers are no more than 15 inches from corner to corner, often as little as 12 or 13 inches. This compares to the most common desktop monitors, whose screens measure anywhere from 17 to 21 inches or more. When a desktop monitor and a laptop screen are set to the same **resolution**, the images on the laptop are always smaller. And the same text on the smaller laptop screen is almost always more difficult to read. A few laptops with larger screens——some more than 20 inches——are available, but they're extremely expensive, and a screen that big makes the whole computer less compact and portable.

resolution [ˌrezəˈljuːʃən]
n. 坚定, 决心, 决定, 决议

Smaller Keyboard

The size of a laptop computer's keyboard is limited by the width of its case. Except for a unique unfolding butterfly keyboard that IBM tried and **abandoned** in the mid-1990s, a laptop keyboard cannot be any wider than the lower half of the clamshell. Even though laptop keyboards don't include all of those extra keys that appear to the right of the traditional **typewriter** keys on a desktop keyboard, the individual keys on a laptop are often smaller and closer together than those on a separate keyboard.

abandon [əˈbændən]
vt. 放弃, 遗弃

typewriter
打字机

If you're a **touch-typist** who is used to a traditional keyboard, this can have a huge impact on your speed and accuracy. All those typing exercises in high school and all those years of text and data entry have conditioned your fingers to expect to find each letter in the same place on any keyboard. You don't have to think about finding a letter; your brain **automatically** takes your fingers to that key. But when the keys'

touch-typist
手动打字员

automatically [ɔːtəˈmætikli]
adv. 自动地, 机械地

locations are slightly different, you either hit the wrong key more often, or you type more slowly in order to direct each **keystroke** to the right location.

Laptops are easy to steal.

In an airport, a railway station, or a library, an **unattended** laptop computer can easily disappear within minutes. For all the same reasons that make laptop computers convenient to carry, they are also extremely attractive targets for theft. They're easy to **grab** and hide, and easy to sell to an **unscrupulous** bargain hunter.

Worse, the information stored on a laptop's hard drive can be even more valuable than the machine itself. Business records, **thesis** notes, and other information stored in data files can be difficult or impossible to **reconstruct**.

Laptops are more expensive.

When you buy a laptop computer, you pay something extra for the added convenience of a **lightweight** portable system. The price of a laptop computer is always higher than a desktop system with similar performance. That added cost is a **combination** of more expensive design, non-standard parts, and an expensive battery in every computer. A laptop also has to be more **durable** than a desktop system.

Even though you can **recharge** it when you run the computer on external power, your computer's battery won't last forever. The life of a laptop battery depends on the way you use the computer, but you probably need a new one at least every couple of years.

Laptops need repairs more often.

It's easy to understand why a laptop computer is more likely to need repairs than a desktop machine if you consider the way people treat them. The owner of a laptop grabs it off the desk, drops it into a bag or a briefcase, and throws it over a shoulder or onto a baggage cart. Then it gets shaken around for a couple of hours, until the owner stops into a coffee shop and fires up the computer to check for E-mail. Oops! Was that hot coffee and warm milk you **spilled** into the keyboard? Oh well, use some

keystroke ['kiːstrəuk]
n. (打字机等)键的一击

unattended [ˌʌnə'tendid]
adj. 没人照顾的，未被注意的，无人出席的

grab [græb]
v. 抢夺，攫取，夺取

unscrupulous [ʌn'skruːpjuləs]
adj. 肆无忌惮的，无道德的，不谨慎的

thesis ['θiːsis]
n. 论题，论文

reconstruct [ˌriːkən'strʌkt]
v. 重建，改造，推想

lightweight ['laitweit]
n. 轻量级选手，不能胜任者

combination [ˌkɔmbi'neiʃən]
n. 结合，联合，合并，化合，化合物

durable ['djuərəbl]
adj. 持久的，耐用的

recharge ['riː'tʃɑːdʒ]
vt. 再充电，再控告，再袭击

spill [spil]
vt. 使溢出，使散落，洒，使流出，使摔下，倒出

napkins to soak it up and put it back in the bag.

Even if you handle your laptop computer carefully, it may still be exposed to more **hazards** than a desktop system: laptops run hotter, they are turned on and off more often, and they're subjected to more physical **abuse**.

Laptops use proprietary parts.

If a manufacturer controls the market for replacement parts, they can charge whatever they want. A few laptop parts such as memory modules and hard drives are common among more than one manufacturer, but case parts, motherboards, mounting hardware, keyboards, and screens are all **unique** in just about every make and model.

Spare parts are often expensive, but if you stick to well-known brands, they should be easy to find. In order to **identify** the exact part your computer needs, you must consult a service manual, where you probably have to consult an **exploded** parts diagram. Your local computer parts **emporium** probably doesn't keep parts for every popular laptop type in stock, so you have to order the thing directly from the factory.

Laptops are difficult to repair or modify.

It sometimes seems as if the design of laptop computers is based on the Trash Compactor method. That's the one where you lay out all the parts on a big table and then **squeeze** everything down until it all fits into the case. The parts inside a laptop clamshell are tightly stacked and combined in order to fit all the same features and functions that are **available** inside a much larger desktop case.

The parts are smaller and closer together, and they are often held together with teeny tiny **screws** and connectors that are easy to lose. It's often difficult to locate a disconnected cable or a loose screw because there's another component in the way. Without a detailed set of instructions from a service manual or a manufacturer's Web Site, you might not even get the cover open without damaging something.

---

napkin ['næpkin]
n. 餐巾，餐巾纸
hazard ['hæzəd]
n. 冒险，危险，冒险的事
abuse [ə'bjuːz]
n. 滥用，虐待，辱骂，陋习，弊端
proprietary [prə'praiətəri]
adj. 所有的，私人拥有的

unique [juː'niːk]
adj. 唯一的，独特的
identify [ai'dentifai]
vt. 识别，鉴别，把……和……看成一样
exploded [iks'pləudid]
adj. 爆破了的，被打破的
emporium [im'pɔːriəm]
n. 商场，商业中心，大百货商店

squeeze [skwiːz]
v. 压榨，挤，挤榨

available [ə'veiləbl]
adj. 可用到的，可利用的，有用的，有空的
screw [skruː]
n. 螺钉，螺旋，螺杆

Exercises

Reading the text and talking about how to buy a new computer.

Whether you ultimately decide to buy a desktop computer or a laptop (see Chapter 1 for help making that choice), your strategy for selecting exactly the right machine to fit your particular needs is the same: looking for the best combination of features, quality, performance, support, and price. This chapter tells you how to identify the features and options that your computer should include and how to evaluate the less tangible characteristics that make the difference between a cheap computer and a true bargain.

Cost

As in most retail, computer vendors do charge what the market can take. New features tend to cost more upon their first introduction to the public and decrease in price as the novelty wears off; fancy yet useless designs can also rack up the price a bit. But the largest part of a computer's cost is directly related to its performance and the quality of its components. Because the retail computer business is extremely competitive, computers with similar performance and features almost always have similar prices. A cheaper computer contains slower, cheaper parts. When you buy a new computer, you usually get what you pay for.

Unless you can find a special sale or rebate, it's probably not productive to choose a computer based exclusively on price. It's better to identify the features and options that make a difference to the way you use the machine. Let the performance and features drive your choice.

Quality

Quality in a computer is partially reflected in more durable, more reliable parts. Although it's possible to assemble a computer from premium-quality components, most manufacturers and screwdriver shops use less expensive parts that are still entirely adequate for most users. Most of the components inside your computer can last long after advances to the technology make them obsolete.

The Internet is full of detailed reviews and anecdotal reports about every imaginable piece of computer gear, from fully assembled systems to individual cases, motherboards, and plug-in cards. If a particular item has a history of failure or terrible factory support, you can be sure that a bunch of unhappy people have described their experiences online. A Web search on the make and model name or number plus the word "review" can probably direct you to sites that offer praise or warnings about the piece of equipment you're considering. Don't pay much attention to the glowing reports in the manufacturer's own site or those of their dealers, but look for independent reports, especially the ones in user forums and blogs. Don't worry as much about one or two negative stories among a lot more positives——even the best products get those. If you find a 10-page technical review, look for the subjective evaluations on the first and last pages.

Brand name or white box?

A handful of major computer makers such as Dell, Hewlett-Packard, and Lenovo (formerly IBM) add value to their products with custom software and special design features, but they and the vast majority of other desktop-computer makers use parts and components from the same suppliers. Many smaller companies assemble computers entirely from generic parts that are often equal in quality to the ones used by the big brand-name companies. Their products are often known as white-box computers because the package that surrounds the assembled computer does not always identify the company that put it together.

White-box computers (which are really beige or black more often than not) are assembled from standard cases, motherboards, and other parts by wholesalers and retailers as their house brands, and by Internet and mail-order dealers. They often carry an adhesive label with the assembler's name in an inch-square indentation on the front of the case and maybe a serial number on the back panel, but those are usually the only things that aren't completely generic. Assuming the computer has been assembled from high-quality parts, a white-box system is likely to be at least as reliable and perform as well as or better than one from a major manufacturer.

The biggest differences between a generic computer and a computer from one of the big international brands are the additional software supplied with the system and the quality of before-and-after-purchase support. The big manufacturers often include their own proprietary utilities for things like disaster recovery and online technical support preloaded onto the computer's hard drive, along with a customized version of Microsoft Windows that displays the manufacturer's name instead of a generic Windows logo every time you turn on the computer. Some of these programs are actually useful, but others just take up space. It's up to you to decide whether they're worth enough to justify a higher price.

Grammar 1 科技英语的语言特点(Ⅰ)

科技英语的特点由它主要描述的内容来决定的，我们知道，科技英语主要的描述内容就是科技领域中的科学技术。这就决定了科技英语务必要叙述准确，推理严谨，用词准确。所以，科技文献资料的叙述以抽象性、概念性和高度的逻辑性为其主要特征，形成了科技语言所特有的语言表达方式。在学习之前，了解科技应用的语言特征，掌握其基本的语言风格和语言特点对于我们的学习是十分必要的。

任何一种语言(language)均是由语音(pronunciation))、词汇 (vocabulary)和语法(grammar)三大部分构成的。词汇是构成句子的基础，句子则是构成文章的基础。因此，下面我们将从科技英语的"词的特点"和"句的特点"来解析科技英语的语言特点。

科技英语词的特点

1. 多用技术性词汇

专业类词汇的特点就是词义狭窄、单一，应用范围基本都是在各自的专业英语。有些专业类词汇在文中出现的频率不高，其字母拼写一般较长，并且拼写越长其词义往往越狭窄。

例如：

bandwidth (带宽);

hexadecimal (十六进制);

flip-flop(触发器)。

2. 次专业词汇在科技英语中的特殊用法

次专业词汇是指不受上下文限制，在科技英语中出现频率很高的词汇。这类词汇的特点就是，语意环境不同，往往意思也不同。

例如：

conductor：在日常生活中可表示售票员和乐队指挥，在电学中却表示导体；

register：在计算机中表示寄存器，在电学中可表示计数器、记录器，在乐器中表示音区，日常生活中则表示登记簿、名册、挂号信等。

Bus：在日常用语中表示公共汽车，但是在科技英语中是总线的意思。

3. 常用派生的名词

专业英语词汇大部分都是用派生法构成的，即通过对词根加上各种前缀和后缀来构成新词。加前缀构成新词一般只改变词义，不改变词类。

例如：

词缀	词缀含义	例词
Inter-	between, among	international, interface
Counter-	against	counteract, counterpart
sub-	beneath, less than	subway, submarine
in-		intake, inlet
out-		output, outlet
tele-	far away	telescope
micro-	small	microcomputer
super-	to an unusually high degree	superman, supermarket
-ics	subject	dynamics, statistics
-ist		dentist, artist
-phone	sound	microphone

加后缀构成新词可能改变也可能不改变词义，但一定会改变词类，
例如：

reality   n. ———— real (*a.*) + ity;
discussion   n. ———— discuss (*v.*) + ion;
sailor   n. ———— sail (*v.*) + or。

4. 词性转换多

英语单词有不少是多性词，即既是名词，又可作为动词、形容词、介词或副词，字形无殊，功能各异，含义也各不相同，如不仔细观察，必定会出错。

例如： light

名词： (启发)in (the)light of 由于，根据；
　　　(光)high light(s) 强光，精华； (灯)safety light 安全指示灯。
形容词：(轻)light industry 轻工业；
　　　(明亮)light room 明亮的房间；
　　　(淡)light blue 淡蓝色；
　　　(薄)light coating 薄涂层。
动词： (点燃)light up the lamp 点灯。
副词： (轻快)travel light 轻装旅行；
　　　(容易)light come, light go 来得容易去得快。

诸如此类的词性转换，在科技英语中十分常见，几乎每个技术名词都可转换为同义的

形容词。词性转换增加了科技英语的灵活性和表现力,所以必须根据上下文判定用词在句中的词性和含义,才能够做到对全句正确无误的理解。

5. 广用缩略词及专用名词

在科技英语文章中,常常看到缩略词,这些词已经固化成为科技英语专业中的专业词。例如:

CD(change directory) 改变目录　　RD(remove directory) 删除目录

LEA (load effective address offset) 装入有效地址偏移量

还有一些常见的专用名词,例如:

Access	数据库软件(MS)
FoxPro	数据库软件
Java	网络编程语言(Sun)
Ethernet	以太网
Navigator	环球网浏览软件(Netscape)
NetWare	局域网络操作系统(Novell)
Delphi	视窗系统开发工具(Borland)
Excel	电子表格软件(MS)

科技英语属于正式书面文体,在词汇方面,除了科技专门术语外,科技英语使用的所有词语,包括普通词汇和技术性词汇,大多数属于正式书面语体的范畴。大家在学习科技英语过程中,对词汇的掌握方法不要机械记忆,那样效果并不理想,推荐的方法是采用归类记忆(触景生情)和象形记忆(顺藤摸瓜),这样容易做到举一反三和灵活应用。

 **参考译文**

Section A　选择你的计算机:台式计算机还是膝上型计算机?

当你考虑要买一台新的计算机时,首先你必须问问自己 (和其他想要用这台计算机的人)如同本节标题一样的问题:我应该买一台台式计算机还是膝上型计算机?

本章将要帮助你做出这个重要的决定。它能够告诉你怎样评价每一种类型计算机的重要特征,并描述其优缺点。在本章的后面,你能找到更多的关于每种类型计算机的细节特征,但是现在最重要的是要决定一件事情,即是不是选择具有更轻巧的和更精密设计的膝上型计算机,比选择价格低廉、灵活的构造以及更大的键盘和屏幕的台式计算机更加重要?

区别

在开始探讨每种计算机的优缺点之前,有必要对一些术语进行解释。

通常,一台台式计算机的大部分部件都放到一个模块箱中,包括一个独立的键盘、视频设备、鼠标,以及通过电缆或无线设备连接的扬声器。一个台式计算机的机箱可能是水平的或者是垂直的。

一些专业制造商也会提供不符合业界标准的紧凑型设计(如一台计算机的处理器和相关部件被构建在视频显示包中),但是多数台式计算机与图 1.1 显示的类似。

膝上型计算机具有独立、轻巧、灵便,并通过蓄电池就能使用等特点。大多数膝上型计算机有时看起来像一个大牡蛎,因为它打开后像一个大的蛤壳,其键盘在底半部,而屏幕在上半部。图 1.2 展示了一个典型的膝上型计算机。

最新型的便携式计算机,就是写字板,它拥有经常与带有转动铰链的键盘部分相连的敏感的触摸屏。这时用户无需打开"蛤壳"就可以用一支特别的笔在屏幕上书写。微软已经设计了支持写字板的最新版本的 Windows 操作系统。

怎样用你的计算机

在大多数情况下,到底选择台式计算机还是膝上型计算机取决于你希望用这个特殊的机器去做什么。如果你计划着携带你的计算机出差,或者当你度假时,你的家人在海滩上冲浪,而你却想在 Internet 冲浪,这时你的选择是显然的:你需要便携式的膝上型计算机。另一方面,如果你寻找从来不需远离你工作区的一台办公用的计算机,一台台式计算机就是更好的选择。

为了做出适当的决定,请思考下面关于你对计算机的工作期望:
- 你是准备一直让你的计算机在同一个地方工作,还是想将它从一个地方搬到另一个地方?
- 你是否期望使用远离家或办公室的计算机?
- 你在处理公务时,是否期望在你的客户或顾客的办公室或在工作的地点使用计算机?
- 如果你是一名学生,你是否希望将计算机带到班级,并且在家或在你的宿舍里使用同一台计算机?或者用它在图书馆或实验室做笔记?在假期期间,你是否想要使用这台计算机?
- 如果你准备在家使用计算机,你是不是需要将它从一个房间搬到另一个房间?如果它是便携式的,你的孩子们是否会将它放到他们的卧室,并且会把它埋在他们的玩具里或洗衣房?
- 你买这台计算机是不是由两个或多个不在同一个地点的用户来共享?
- 你买的这台计算机所使用的地方是不是不容易找到交流电电源?
- 在你期望使用计算机的地方空间是不是有限?
- 安全性是不是重要的?你是否要确信当你不在的时候,没有其他人能够使用这台计算机?你是否需要防止存储在计算机磁盘上的数据被窃取和破坏?

通常,如果你希望经常将计算机移动,你需要买膝上型计算机。那将意味着经常需要将它从一个房间移动到另一个房间,或者在任何地点间移动等。如果你准备让你的计算机一直在同一个地点,那么台式计算机通常是你的选择。

当然,选择不总是那么容易的。有时候,某一种类型或另一种类型计算机可能更加方便,但是一个或某个具体的特征会驱使你选择另一种类型的计算机。本章接下来将介绍每种类型计算机的特点,或许对你的选择会有帮助。

总结

当你考虑买一台新的计算机时,决定选择哪种类型计算机的关键在于你的具体需求。

台式计算机的最重要的好处是经济性,以及它内部和外部的部件的尺寸。更大的键盘和屏幕使你使用计算机更加容易,而模块化的结构以及机箱内部额外的空间让你(或你的服务技术员)更加容易修理或改装计算机。另一方面,那些大机箱和外部设备都很笨重并且体积较大,因此移动起来会更加困难。

Section B 台式计算机的优缺点

当一台计算机在其整个使用期间一直都被放在一个地方,台式计算机是一个理所当然的选择。台式计算机的模块化设计使得你能更加容易地根据其具体特点、功能和你的需求进行配置。而且你如果修理和维修自己的计算机,台式机箱要比膝上型计算机更容易些。

另一方面,台式计算机由于带有独立的键盘、鼠标、显示器和扬声器,因此体积较大、较笨重,移动起来比较费劲。

台式计算机价格更低廉

当价格成为首要问题时，一台台式计算机则是更好的选择。因为一台台式计算机通常比一台膝上型计算机便宜。即使你在基本的系统之外增加了独立的显示器、键盘和鼠标，整个价格上还是要比同样配置的膝上型计算机便宜。如果你正在寻找价格最低廉的计算机，或者在某一个具体性能要求下相对较便宜的计算机，一台台式计算机是一个不错的选择。

当然，花费比膝上型计算机更多的价钱去购置一个台式计算机，使其具有超快的处理器和图形控制器、超大的内存、大尺寸的液晶显示器，以及其他的高端部件和配置，这不是不可能的，但这不是一个公平的对比。具有相似配置的台式计算机的价格要远远低于膝上型计算机。

如果你要自己来装配计算机的话，可能能节省更多。主要计算机制造商，如戴尔和惠普，可能会提供一个非常便宜但功能有限的计算机，这要比你自己装配同样配置的计算机便宜。但是，如果你想要一台更好性能的系统，你经常能容易地找到比现成的产品更便宜的优质的配件。例如，机箱、主板(如图 1.3 所示)、磁盘驱动器、扩展卡，以及其他的台式计算机的标准配件。

因此，对于那些有较多的时间和好的装配技术而现金较少，同时又要求计算机比基本系统具有更高性能的人来说，自己装配计算机是一个更实际的选择。但是由于膝上型计算机没有配件的统一尺寸和布局标准，你在搜寻普通的能够组合在一起的膝上型计算机机箱、键盘、视频设备以及主板时会发现，这并不现实。

台式计算机使用标准配件

在一台台式计算机内部通常有一个或更多的设计标准，因此用一个其他制造商的配件去替换一个损坏的配件通常是可能的。并且当你要为系统增加内存、换一个更大的硬盘驱动器或者一个二代的图形控制杆，再或者一个显示器，你不用担心非要在一个制造商那里购买。如果你的机箱品牌是 Campaq 或者 Gateway，你仍然可以去一些大的机箱零售商那里进行选择一些不同品牌的部件。这种模块化的组合设计和市场竞争使得大多数台式计算机配件比那些相应的非标准的膝上型计算机配件更低廉。

另外，常见的零件规格可以使一个维修商店保持一个小的库存量，因为他们可以将相同规格的零件用于许多不同品牌和型号的台式计算机上。

台式计算机拥有灵活的设计

台式计算机采用模块化系统，使得在满足每位用户的特殊需求时能够容易地增加或替换单个部件。如果一台计算机要求能够画图或带有计算机辅助设计系统，就要配置一个高质量的图形控制器以及显示设备，而一个采购人最多也不过就是使用文字处理软件和报表系统。大多数计算机制造商会让你准确地提出对零件特点和规范的需求。

当你需要改变它时，除非你的计算机使用的是享有专利的部件，否则打开机箱来重新配置系统通常并不是很容易的。你必须确信主板上的插座以及电源的插孔和新的扩展卡或硬盘之间，以及控制其他系统的印制电路板和新的部件之间都是匹配的。

模块化设计也意味着当你要扔掉已经废弃的计算机时，你可以将一些旧的配件放到新计算机上。例如，我写这本书时，用的 Northgate 键盘已经用了 15 年，其间更换了一台又一台的计算机。我很喜欢敲打该键盘的感觉。Northgate 公司许多年前已经停止生产这些键盘了(一些类似的键盘仍然可以从其他的制造商那里买到，但价格比较贵)，但是这个键盘的电缆插头仍然能和我目前计算机的插座匹配，而且它与这个 21 世纪生产的处理器和主板匹配得也非常好。

当然，这种灵活的设计也有一些局限。你不能使用一个新品牌的内存或者近期生产的硬盘去匹配 10 年前生产的主板，因为设计者已经要求它们匹配更新的和更好的处理器和其他设备。

台式计算机容易升级

你可以通过用新部件替换旧部件的方式提高你的计算机的性能，使其具有更快的速度、更大容量、更多的功能。在此又不得不提，模块化设计使其变得更加容易。当然，虽然购买新的、更好的系统更便宜了，使得收益有所减少，但是，台式计算机仍然有可改善的空间。大多数普通的主板都有一个或更多的扩展槽用于扩展内存，因此你可以通过买一个或更多的内存条来增加内存的容量。你也可以用每个容量都更大的内存条来替代现有的内存条。在台式计算机中，增加内存容量是非常容易的，因为在机箱中有很多的空间。

除了一些非常小的机箱外，所有的台式计算机都有两个或更多的内部磁盘驱动槽。因此，你可以在系统中一个空的驱动槽上通过电缆的连接简单地安装另一块硬盘，从而增加存储容量。先将现有的磁盘上的数据进行转移是没有必要的。

CPU 芯片即中央处理器，用来控制系统中的每件事情。在台式计算机系统中，用一个相似结构的、能够匹配同样插槽的 CPU 来替换或者移走旧的 CPU，相对来讲也是容易的。一个新的 CPU 要比原始计算机提供的 CPU 能够提供更快的处理速度和更好的性能。不像主板上的其他集成电路，CPU 安装在一个特殊的插槽上，这个特殊的插槽用一个封闭的机关固定在一个地方，因此在印制电路板上直接焊接一块新的芯片是没有必要的(或者说不可能的)。

所有这些升级都是容易实现的，但是它们经常需要改变计算机的硬件和软件配置。在升级之前，应该查阅一下计算机手册或者主板手册，了解关于主板上跳线或开关的设置，以及 BIOS 的设置(即基本输入/输出系统，是一系列程序，用来测试硬件和装载 Windows 或其他的操作系统的)。

台式计算机占用更多的空间

台式计算机确实有一些缺点。一个带有独立键盘的台式计算机的机箱要比一台紧凑的膝上型计算机占用更多的空间。对于大多数人来说，书桌或工作台才是我们宝贵的"财产"，因此一台能占据更小空间的计算机才是理想的。跟过去相比，如今这也许是一个无足轻重问题，因为一个液晶显示器要比那些旧的、通常为 18 英寸的阴极射线管显示器占用更少的空间，尤其是前后的空间。

台式计算机运输起来较困难

台式机又大又重。如果你必须将你的台式计算机以及所有它的辅助部件和配件从一个房间移动到另一个房间，大概要使用带有几个架子的推车或至少一把带轮子的办公椅。在你能再次使用它之前，你必须搜寻至少六条不同的电缆连接到机箱的后面，或者你可以说服你的本地计算机专家来做这件事情。 移动一台台式计算机是一项复杂和费时的锻炼。

台式计算机需要额外的电源

一方面，计算机上的电子线路、风扇系统以及磁盘驱动器都需使用机箱内部电源提供的直流电。另一方面，内部电源、视频显示器以及其他的外部设备都需要一个本地的交流电源(在北美和日本，都是 110 伏，其他地方是 220 伏)。如果附近没有壁装电源插座，你需要发电器或者带有转换器的蓄电池，也可以是一条非常长的延长线。

Section C 膝上型计算机的优缺点

膝上型计算机是紧凑型的，质量较轻的，而足够尺寸的台式计算机正好相反。你的膝上型计算机本身是一个独立的系统，能够很容易装进公文包或背包。当你达到目的地(或者你在途中要用计算机)时，你可以打开机壳，打开电源，一旦 Windows 操作系统正常启动完，你就可以开始工作或游戏。

膝上型计算机可能很容易地搬运，但这种便利更多来自于使用轻松、修理方便、价格合理及其安全性。如果你经常搬动计算机，一台膝上型计算机是明智的选择。除非你认为它有缺陷，否则不必在你的计算机上花费额外的费用。

膝上型计算机方便携带

膝上型计算机整体上是容易搬运的。如果你经常旅行，或者你希望在办公室、学校和家中使用一台单独的计算机，膝上型计算机要比台式计算机方便得多。一台膝上型计算机要比一台具有相似性能的台式计算机质量轻，而且可以方便地放到一个较小的包里面。

因为膝上型计算机可以使用蓄电池，所以你几乎可以在任何地方使用它。如果配置一个无线的 Internet 连接设备，你可以几个小时内在你的计算机上工作或和世界各地联系，而不需要寻找交流电电源。

除了 CPU、存储器和数据存储等内部构造与台式计算机机箱一样，膝上型计算机也包含键盘、显示器及鼠标替代品。因此在你开始使用计算机之前，不必分别买这些设备，也不必去连接它们。

膝上型计算机有设计上的限制

如果膝上型计算机在每一方面都比台式计算机要好，那么就没有人会买台式计算机了。然而，小尺寸和轻质量使得膝上型计算机容易搬动，却同样会使它使用起来困难。

更小的显示屏

大多数膝上型计算机的显示屏从一个角到另一个角不足 15 英寸，通常是 12 或 13 英寸。这一点对比台式计算机来说，台式计算机的显示屏无论如何测量都会达到 17~21 英寸，或者更大。当一个台式显示器和膝上型显示器被设置成同样的分辨率时，膝上型计算机的图像总是更小的，而且同样的文本在膝上型计算机上看起来会更难阅读。一些膝上型计算机拥有超过 20 英寸的显示屏，但它们都极其昂贵，而且大的显示屏使得整个计算机缺少紧凑感并且携带不够方便。

更小的键盘

膝上型计算机的键盘因为它的机体的宽度而受到限制。除了 IBM 在 20 世纪 90 年代中期尝试并且放弃的一个独特的展开型蝴蝶键盘，膝上型计算机键盘不可能比机壳的下半部分宽。即使膝上型计算机的键盘不包括那些在台式计算机中拥有的传统键盘上能看到的额外的一些键，每个膝上型计算机的键盘上的键还是比分体式键盘的键更小、更紧凑。

如果你是一个用惯了传统键盘的打字员，这将对你的速度和准确性有很大的影响。所有学校的打字练习软件以及这些年的文本和数据输入习惯会使你的手指条件反射地寻找键盘上的字符位置。你根本不必去找字母，你的大脑已经自动控制你的手指放在那个位置了。但是当你键盘上的键的位置稍微不同了，要么会增加你敲错键的几率，要么会为了每次正确敲击键盘，迫使打字速度变慢。

膝上型计算机更容易被偷窃

在飞机场、火车站，或者在图书馆，一台膝上型计算机可能会在几分钟内，一不注意就消失了。膝上型计算机容易携带，同样也是吸引小偷目标的原因。他们容易被窃取并隐藏起来，而且也较容易被卖到肆无忌惮的小贩手中。

更糟糕的是，在膝上型计算机的硬盘中存储的数据可能比机器本身更有价值。一些数据文件中的商业纪录、论文笔记或其他的信息是难以甚至根本不可能重新建立。

膝上型计算机更加昂贵

当你购买一台膝上型计算机时，你还要为这个便携式的系统花费一些额外的开销。膝上型计算机的价格通常都要比具有相似性能的台式计算机更昂贵。这些额外的开销支付的是一些昂贵的设计、非标准设计的部件，以及在每台膝上型计算机上都需要的、价格昂贵的电池。膝上型计算机必须比台式计算机更耐用些。

即使你在利用额外的电源给你的计算机充电,你的电池也不会永远好用。电池的寿命依赖于你如何使用计算机,但是你可能每两年就需要一个新的电池。

膝上型计算机需要更频繁的维修

如果你考虑一下人们使用膝上型计算机的方式,你可能更容易理解为什么一台膝上型计算机要比台式计算机需要更频繁的维修。膝上型计算机的主人将它从办公桌抓起并塞入背包或公文包,然后它就会被扔到肩上或一个背包箱里面。接下来,它会被摇晃几个小时,直到主人进入咖啡厅或突然想起检查一下电子邮件才能停止。是把那么热的咖啡和牛奶撒到键盘上了吗?不过还好,主人用纸巾擦干净后又重新将它放入包里。

即使你非常小心地对待你的膝上型计算机,但仍然要比台式计算机有更多的危险。膝上型计算机运行时会更热,它们被开关得更频繁,并且更易受到破坏。

膝上型计算机使用私有式配件

如果一个制造商想控制替换的配件市场,他们可以想要什么就有什么。有些膝上型计算机的配件如内存、硬盘驱动器是不只一个制造商有的,但是像机箱、主板、硬件配置、键盘,以及显示屏在每一个制造商那里都是唯一的。

一些配件通常较昂贵,但是如果你坚持要用著名品牌的,可以很容易找到它们。为了能够找到你的计算机所需要的精确配件,你必须查阅服务手册,在那里你还有可能必须查阅一下分解部件的图解。你所在的地区的配件零售商不可能在仓库中存放每种流行的膝上型计算机的配件,因此你还必须从工厂直接预订。

膝上型计算机维修较困难

有时候,膝上型计算机就好像是基于垃圾压缩机的原理进行设计的,即把所有的部件放到一张桌子上,然后将每件东西都挤到机箱里面。膝上型计算机的每个部件都被紧紧地放在一起,为的是能够实现一个比它大得多的台式计算机同样可用的功能。

这些更小的部件连接得更紧密,并且它们通常是通过容易丢失的极微小的螺钉和连接器连接的。通常想要放置一个分开的电缆或大的螺钉是很困难的,这是因为往往有另一个部件已经在那个位置上了。如果没有一套详细的指导手册或者制造商的网站服务说明,在没有破坏任何东西的情况下,你几乎不可能打开机盖。

Chapter 2　Computer Hardware
(计算机硬件)

Section A　CPU

We build computer to solve problems. Early computer solved mathematical and engineering problems, and later computers emphasized information processing for business applications. Today, the computer also control machines as diverse as automobile, engines, robots, and **microwave** ovens. A computer system solves a problem from any of these **domains** by accepting input, processing it, and producing output.

Computer systems consist of **hardware** and **software**. Hardware is the physical part of the system. Once designed, hardware is difficult and expensive to change. Software is the set of programs that instruct the hardware and is easier to modify than hardware. Computers are valuable because they are general-purpose machines that can solve many different kinds of problems, as opposed to special-purpose machines that can each solve only one kind of problem. Different problems can be solved with the same hardware by supplying the system with a different set of **instructions**. That is, with different software.

Most computer systems, from the **embedded** controllers found in automobiles and consumer appliances to personal computers and mainframes, have the same basic **organization**. Every computer has four basic hardware components:

- Central processing unit(CPU).
- Main memory.
- Input devices.
- Output devices.

Fig.2.1 shows these components in a block diagram. The lines between the blocks represent the flow of information flows from one component to another on the bus, which is simply a group of wires connecting the components. Processing occurs in the CPU and main memory. The organization in Fig. 2.1, with the components connected to each other by the bus, is common.

microwave ['maikrəuweiv]
n. 微波
domain [dəu'mein]
n. (活动、学问等的)范围，领域
hardware ['hɑːdwɛə]
n. 硬件，部件
software ['sɔftwɛə]
n. 软件

instruction [in'strʌkʃən]
n. 指令，指示
embed [im'bed]
vt. 嵌入，嵌套
organization
[ˌɔːgənai'zeiʃən]
n. 组织，机构

However, the other **configurations** are possible as well.

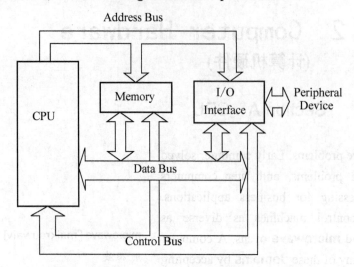

Fig. 2.1 The basic architecture of microcomputer

Computer hardware is often classified by its relative physical size:

- Small microcomputer;
- Medium minicomputer;
- Large mainframe.

Just the CPU of a mainframe often occupies an entire **cabinet**. Its input/output(I/O) devices and memory might fill an entire room. Microcomputers can be small enough to fit on a desk or in a briefcase. As technology advances, amount of processing previously possible only on large machines becomes possible on smaller machines. Microcomputers now can do much of the work that only minicomputers or mainframes could do in the past.

The **classification** just described is based on physical size as opposed to **storage** size. A computer system user is generally more concerned with storage size because that is a more direct indication of the amount of useful work that the hardware can perform. The speed of computation is another **characteristic** that is important to the user. Generally speaking, users want a fast CPU and large amounts of storage, but a physically small machine for the I/O devices and main memory.

The CPU

The part of the computer that runs the program (executes program instructions) is known as the **processor** or central

configuration
[kən,figju'reiʃən]
n. 构造, 结构, 配置, 外形

cabinet ['kæbinit]
n. 柜, 壳, 箱

classification
[,klæsifi'keiʃən]
n. 分类, 分级
storage ['stɔridʒ]
n. 存储, 储藏(量), 储藏库
characteristic
[,kæriktə'ristik]
n. 特性, 特征

processor ['prəusesə]
n. 处理机, 处理器

processing unit (CPU). In a microcomputer, the CPU is a single electronic component. Microprocessor is a processor whose elements have been **miniaturized** into one or a few **integrated** circuits. It is a **semiconductor** CPU and one of the principal components of the microcomputer. The elements of the microprocessor are frequently contained on a single chip or within the same package, but are sometimes distributed over several separate chips.

The central processing unit has 2 components——the **control unit** and the **arithmetic-logic unit**. The control unit tell the rest of the computer system how to carry out a program's instructions. It directs the movement of electronic signals between memory——which **temporarily** holds data, instructions, and processed information——and the arithmetic-logic unit. It also directs these control signals between the CPU and input and output devices. In a microcomputer with a micro programmed instruction set, it contains an additional control-memory unit.

The arithmetic-logic unit, usually called the ALU, **performs** two types of operations——arithmetic and logical. Arithmetic operations are, as you might expect, the fundamental math operations: addition, subtraction, multiplication, and division. Logical operations consist of comparisons. That is, two pieces of data are compared to see whether one is equal to (=), less than (<), or greater than (>) the other.

The CPU controls the computer. It fetches instructions from memory, supplying the address and control signals needed by memory to **access** its data. The CPU **decodes** the instruction and controls the **execution** procedure. It performs some operations **internally**, and supplies the address, data, and control signals needed by memory and I/O devices to execute the instruction. Nothing happens in the computer unless the CPU causes it to happen.

Internally, the CPU has three sections. The **register** sections, as its name implies, includes a set of registers and a bus or other communication mechanism. The registers in a processor's instruction set **architecture** are found in this section of the CPU. The system address and data buses interact with this section of the CPU. The register section also contains other registers that are not directly accessible by the programmer. The relatively simple CPU

---

miniaturize ['miniətʃəraiz]
vt. 使小型化
integrate ['intigreit]
vt. 集成，使成整体，使一体化
semiconductor ['semikən'dʌktə]
n. 半导体
control unit
控制单元
arithmetic-logic unit
算术逻辑单元
temporarily ['tempərərili]
adv. 暂时地，临时地

perform [pə'fɔ:m]
vt. 履行，执行

access ['ækses]
vt. 存取，接近
decode [,di:'kəud]
vt. 解码，译解
execution [,eksi'kju:ʃən]
n. 实行，完成，执行
internally [in'tənəli]
adv. 在内，在中心
register ['redʒistə]
n. 寄存器
architecture ['ɑ:kitektʃə]
n. 体系结构

includes registers to latch the address being accessed in memory and a temporary storage register, as well as other registers that are not a part of its instruction set architecture.

During the fetch portion of the instruction **cycle**, the processor first outputs the address of the instruction onto the address bus. The processor has a register called the program counter; the CPU keeps the address of the next instruction to be fetched in this register. Before the CPU outputs the address onto the system's address bus, it **retrieves** the address from the program counter register. At the end of the instruction fetch, the CPU reads the instruction code from the system data bus. It stores this value in an internal register, usually called the instruction register or something similar.

The control unit also generates the signals for the system control bus, such as the READ, WRITE, and the other signals. A microprocessor **typically** performs a sequence of operations to fetch, decode, and execute an instruction. By **asserting** these internal and external control signals in the proper **sequence**, the control unit causes the CPU and the rest of the computer to perform the operations needed to correctly process instructions.

This description of the CPU is incomplete. Current processors have more complex **features** that improve their **performance**. One such mechanism, the **instruction pipeline**, allows the CPU to fetch one instruction while simultaneously executing another instruction.

In this section we have introduced the CPU from a system perspective, but we have not discussed its internal design. We examine the registers, data paths, and control unit, all of which act together to cause the CPU to properly fetch, decode, and execute instructions. **Microsequenced CPUs** have the same registers, ALUs and data paths as hardwired CPUs, but completely different control units.

System Buses

Physically, a bus is a set of wires. The components of the computer are connected to the buses. To send information from one component to another, the source component outputs data onto the bus. The **destination** component then inputs this data from the bus. As the complexity of a computer system increases, it

cycle ['saikl]
n. 周期,循环

retrieve [ri'tri:v]
v. 重新得到

typically ['tipikəli]
adv. 代表性地,典型地
assert [ə'sə:t]
v. 断言
sequence ['si:kwəns]
n. 次序,顺序,序列
feature ['fi:tʃə]
n. 特征,特色,特写
performance [pə'fɔ:məns]
n. 性能,履行,执行,成绩
instruction pipeline
n. 指令流水线

microsequenced CPUs
微序列 CPU

destination [,desti'neiʃən]
n. 目的地,目的文件,目的单元格

becomes more efficient (in terms of minimizing connections) at using buses rather than direct connections between every pair of devices. Buses use less space on a circuit board and require less power than a large number of direct connections. They also require fewer pins on the chip or chips that comprise the CPU.

The system shown in Fig. 2.1 has 3 buses. The **uppermost** bus in this figure is the address bus. When the CPU reads data or instructions from or writes data to memory, it must **specify** the address of the memory location it wishes to access. It outputs this address to the address bus; memory inputs this address from the address bus and uses it to access the proper memory location. Each I/O devices, such as a keyboard, monitor, or disk drive, has a **unique** address as well. When accessing an I/O device, the CPU places the address of the device on the address bus. Each device can read the address off of the bus and determine whether it is the device being accessed by the CPU. Unlike the other buses, the address bus always receives data from the CPU; the CPU never reads the address bus.

Data is **transferred** via the data bus. When the CPU fetches data from memory, it first outputs the memory address on its address bus. Then memory outputs the data onto the data bus; the CPU can then read the data from the data bus. When writing data to memory, the CPU first outputs the address onto the address bus, then outputs the data onto the data bus. Memory then reads and stores the data at the proper location. The processes for reading data from and writing data to the I/O devices are **similar**.

The control bus is different from the other two buses. The address bus consists of n lines, which combine to **transmit** one n-bit address value. Similarly, the lines of the data bus work together to transmit a single **multi-bit** value. In contrast, the control bus is a collection of individual control signals. These signals indicate whether data is to be read into or written out of the CPU, whether the CPU is accessing memory or an I/O device, and whether the I/O device or memory is ready to transfer data. Although this bus is shown as **bidirectional** in Fig. 2.1, it is really a collection of (mostly) **unidirectional** signals. Most of these signals are output from the CPU to the memory and I/O subsystems, although a few are output by these subsystems to the CPU.

uppermost ['ʌpəməust]
adj. 最上的，最高的
specify ['spesifai]
vt. 指定

unique [juːˈniːk]
adj. 唯一的，独特的

transfer [trænsˈfəː]
vt. 传递，转移

similar ['similə]
adj. 相似的，类似的
transmit [trænzˈmit]
vt. 传输，转送，传达
multi-bit
多位

bidirectional
双向的
unidirectional
单向的

A system may have a hierarchy of buses. For example, it may use its address, data, and control buses to access memory, and an I/O controller. The I/O controller, in turn, may access all I/O devices using a second bus, often called an I/O bus or a **local** bus.

local ['ləukəl]
adj. 局部的

Instruction Cycle

The instruction cycle is the procedure a microprocessor goes through to process an instruction. First the microprocessor fetches, or reads, the instruction from memory. Then it decodes the instruction, determining which instruction it has fetched. Finally, it performs the operations necessary to execute the instruction. (Some people also think there is an additional element in the instruction cycle to store results. Here, we include that operation as part of the execute function.) Each of these functions——fetch, decode, and execute——consists of a sequence of one or more operations.

Let's start where the computer starts, with the microprocessor fetching the instruction from memory. First, the microprocessor places the address of the instruction on to the address bus. The memory subsystem inputs this address and decodes it to access the sired **memory location**.

memory location
存储单元

After the microprocessor allows **sufficient** time for memory to decode the address and access the requested memory location, the microprocessor asserts a READ control signal. The READ signal is a signal on the control bus, which the microprocessor asserts when it is ready to read data from memory or an I/O device. (Some processors have a different name for this signal, but all microprocessors have a signal to perform this function.) Depending on the microprocessor, the READ signal may be active high (asserted - 1) or active low (asserted - 0).

sufficient [sə'fiʃənt]
adj. 充分的, 足够的

When the READ signal is asserted, the memory subsystem places the instruction code to be fetched onto the computer system's data bus. The microprocessor then inputs this data from the bus and stores it in one of its internal registers. At this point, the microprocessor has fetched the instruction.

Next, the microprocessor decodes the instruction. Each instruction may require a different sequence of operations to execute the instruction. When the microprocessor decodes the instruction, it determines which instruction is in order to select the correct sequence of operations to perform. This is done entirely within the microprocessor; it does not use the system buses.

Finally, the microprocessor executes the instruction. The sequence of operations to execute the instruction varies from instruction to instruction. The execute **routine** may read data from memory, write data to memory, read data from or write data to an I/O device, perform only operations within the CPU, or perform some combination of these operations.

routine [ruːˈtiːn]
n. 程序，常规

Read Cycle

To read data from memory, the microprocessor performs the same sequence of operations it uses to fetch an instruction from memory. After all, fetching an instruction is simply reading it from memory. Fig. 2.2 shows the timing of the operations to read data from memory.

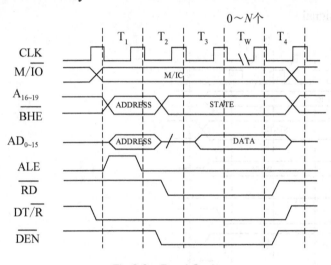

Fig.2.2 Read Cycle

In Fig. 2.2, notice the top **symbol**——CLK. This is the computer system clock; the microprocessor uses the system clock to **synchronize** its operations. The microprocessor places the address onto the bus at the beginning of a clock cycle, a 0/1 sequence of the system clock. One clock cycle later, to allow time for memory to decode the address and access its data, the microprocessor asserts the READ signal. This causes memory to place its data onto the system data bus. During this clock cycle, the microprocessor reads the data off the system bus and stores it in one of its registers. At the end of the clock cycle, it removes the

symbol [ˈsimbəl]
n. 符号，记号，象征
synchronize [ˈsiŋkrənaiz]
v. 同步

address from the address bus and cancel the READ signal. Memory then removes the data from the data bus, completing the memory read operation.

Write Cycle

The timing of the memory WRITE operation is shown in Fig. 2.3. The processor places the address and data onto the system buses during the first clock cycle. The microprocessor then asserts a WRITE control signal (or its equivalent) at the start of the second clock cycle. Just as the READ signal causes memory to read data, the WRITE signal **triggers** memory to store data. Some time during this cycle, memory writes the data on the data bus to the memory location whose address is on the address bus. At the end of this cycle, the processor completes the memory write operation by removing the address and data from the system buses and canceling the WRITE signal.

trigger ['trigə]
n. 触发器
vt. 引发, 引起, 触发

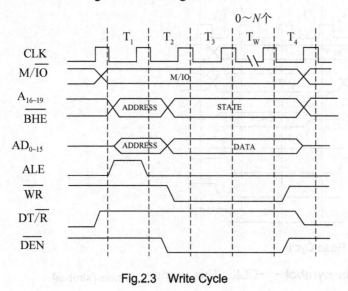

Fig.2.3 Write Cycle

Exercises

I. Fill in the blanks with the information given in the text.

1. Just as the CPU controls the computer (in addition to its other functions), the control unit controls the CPU. This unit generates the internal _____ that cause registers to load data, increment or clear their contents, and output their contents, as well as cause the _____ to perform the correct function.

2. The internal working of every computer can be broken down into four parts: CPU, memory, input and output devices. The function of the _____ is to execute (process) information stored in memory. The function of _____ devices such as the keyboard and video monitor is to provide a means of communicating with the CPU.

3. The _____ inside a computer carries information from place to place just as a street bus carries people from place to place. In every computer, there are three types of buses: address bus, data bus, and _____.

4. The CPU uses _____ to store information temporarily. The information could be two values to be processed, or the address of the value needed to be fetched from _____.

5. These studies have motivated the key characteristics of _____ machines: ①a limited instruction set with a fixed format; ②a large number of registers or the use of a compiler that optimizes register usage; ③an emphasis on optimizing the instruction pipeline.

II. **Translate the following passages from English into Chinese.**

One method of increasing the complexity of an integrated circuit is simply to scale the chip down. For example, if every line etched into the silicon die could be shrunk in half, the same circuit could be built in one-fourth the area. The evolution of dynamic memory chips (DRAMs) follows this rule exactly. The original IBM PC used 16 KB DRAMs. These were soon replaced with 64KB chips, then 256 KB chips, and now 16 MB, and even 64 MB chips.

The "trick", of course, is being able to improve processing skills sufficiently to allow this scaling to continue. In 1969, the minimum feature size (the smallest detail that can be etched into a chip) was 10 microns (10×10^{-6} meter). By 1997, this had shrunk to 0.25 micron——40 times smaller!

The Pentium uses a superscalar architecture. This means that the chips capabilities go beyond those achieved simply by scaling down its size. In particular, the Pentium is the first microprocessor in the Intel family to support two instruction pipelines, each with its own arithmetic——logic unit, address generation circuitry, and data cache interface. The result is a processor that can actually execute two different instructions simultaneously.

Section B   Memory

Memory Terminology

In the design of all computers, semiconductor memories are used as **primary storage** for code and data. Semiconductor memories are connected directly to the CPU and they are the memory that the CPU first asks for information (code and data). For this reason, semiconductor memories are sometimes referred to as primary memory. The main requirement of primary memory is that it must be fast in responding to the CPU; only semiconductor memories can do that. Among the most widely used semiconductor memories are **ROM** and **RAM**. Before we discuss different types of ROM and RAM, we discuss some important terminology common to all semiconductor memories first, such as capacity, organization, and speed.

Memory Capacity

The number of **bits** that a semiconductor memories chip can store is called its chip **capacity**. It can be units of Kbits(**kilobits**),

terminology [ˌtəːmiˈnɔlədʒi]
n. 术语学
primary storage
主存

ROM
只读存储器
RAM
随机存取存储器
bit [bit]
n. 位，比特
capacity [kəˈpæsiti]
n. 容量，生产量
kilobits [ˈkiləubait]
n. 千字节，1024字节

Mbits(**megabits**), and so on. This must be distinguished from the storage capacity of computers. While the memory capacity of a memory **IC** chip is always given in bits, the memory capacity of a computer is given in bytes. For example, an article in a technical journal may state that the 16M chip has become **popular**. In that case, although it is not mentioned that 16M means 16 megabits, it is understood since the article is referring to an IC memory chip. However, if an advertisement state that a computer comes with 16M memory, since it is referring to a computer it is understood that 16M means 16 megabytes.

Memory Organization

Memory chips are organized into a number of locations within the IC. Each location can hold 1 bit, 4 bits, 8 bits, or 16 bits, depending on how it is designed internally. The number of bits that each location within the memory chip can hold is always equal to the number of data pins on the chip. How many locations exist inside a memory chip? That depends on the number of address pins. The number of locations within a memory IC always equals 2 to the power of the number of address pins. Therefore, the total number of bits that a memory chip can store equals to the number of locations times the number of data bits per location. To **summarize**:

(1) Each memory chip contains 2^x locations, where x is the number of address pins on the chip.

(2) Each location contains y bits, where y is the number of data pins on the chip.

(3) The entire chip will contain $2^x \times y$ bits, where x is the number of address pins and y is the number of data pins on the chip. Table 2-1 serves as a reference for the calculation of memory organization.

Table 2-1 Powers of 2

x	2^x
10	1Kb
11	2Kb
12	4Kb
13	8Kb
14	16Kb

megabits [ˌmegəbit]
n. 百万位, 兆位
IC
集成电路, 指令计数器
popular ['pɔpjulə]
adj. 普及的, 流行的

summarize ['sʌməraiz]
v. 概述, 总结, 摘要而言

Speed

One of the most important characteristics of a memory chip is the speed at which data can be accessed from it. To access the data, the address is presented to the address pins, and after a certain amount of time has elapsed, the data shows up at the data pins. The shorter this elapsed time, the better, and consequently, the more expensive the memory chip. The speed of the memory chip is commonly referred to as its access time. The access time of memory chips varies from **nanoseconds** to hundreds of nanoseconds, depending on the IC technology used in the design and **fabrication**. The three important memory characteristics of capacity, organization, and access time will be used extensively.

ROM and RAM

ROM (read-only memory) is the type of memory that does not lose its contents when the power is turned off. For this reason, ROM is also called **nonvolatile** memory. There are different types of ROM, such as PROM, EPROM, EEPROM, and flash EPROM.

RAM, also called read/write memory, can be used to store data that changes. RAM memory is called **volatile** memory since cutting off the power to the IC will mean the loss of data. There are three types of RAM: static RAM (SRAM), dynamic RAM (DRAM), and NV-RAM(nonvolatile RAM). Many computer systems, including personal computers, include both ROM and RAM.

Internal Chip Organization

The internal organizations of ROM and RAM chips are similar. To **illustrate** the simplest organization, a linear organization, consider an 16×4 ROM chip. (For simplicity, programming components are not shown.) This chip has three address inputs and two data outputs, and 16 bits of internal storage arranged as eight 2-bit locations.

The three address bits are decoded to select one of the eight locations, but only if the chip enable is active. If CE=0, the decoder is disabled and no location is selected. The **tri-state** buffers for that location's **cells** are enabled, allowing data to pass to the output buffers. If both CE and OE set to 1, these buffers are

---

nanosecond ['nænəu,sekənd]
n. 十亿分之一秒
fabrication [,fæbri'keiʃən]
n. 制作，构成

nonvolatile ['nɔn'vɔlətail]
adj. 非易失性的

volatile ['vɔlətail]
adj. 易失性的，可变的，不稳定的

illustrate ['iləstreit]
vt. 举例说明，图解，加插图于，阐明

tri-state
三态
cell [sel]
n. 单元，细胞

enabled and the data is output from the chip; otherwise the outputs are tri-stated.

As the number of locations increases, the size of the address decoder needed in a linear organization becomes **prohibitively** large. To **remedy** this problem, the memory chip can be designed using multiple dimensions of decoding.

In larger memory chips, this savings can be significant. Consider a 4096×1 chip. The linear organization will require a 12 to 4096 decoder, the size of which is proportional to the number of outputs. (The size of an n to 2^n decoder is thus said to be $O(2^n)$.) If the chip is organized as a 64×64 two dimensional arrays instead, it will have two 6 to 64 decoders: one to select one of the 64 rows and the other to select one of the 64 cells within the row. The size of the decoders is proportional to 2×64, or $O(2 \times 2^n /2) = O(2^n /2 +1)$. For this chip, the two decoders together are about 3 percent of the size of the one larger decoder.

prohibitively [prə'hibitivli]
adv. 禁止地，抑制地
remedy ['remidi]
vt. 校正，补救，治疗

Memory Subsystem Configuration

It is very easy to set up a memory system that consists of a single chip. We simply connect the address, data, and control signals from their system buses and the job is done. However, most memory systems require more than one chip. Following are some methods for combining memory chips to form a memory subsystem.

Two or more chips can be combined to create memory with more bits per location. This is done by connecting the **corresponding** address and control signals of the chips, and connecting their data pins to different bits of the data bus. For example, two 1K×4 chips(2114) can be combined to create an 1K×8 memory, as shown in Fig. 2.4. The chips receive the same ten address inputs from the bus, as well as the same CS and WR signals. The data pin of the first chip is connected to $D_0 \sim D_3$ and another is connected to $D_4 \sim D_7$ of the data bus.

corresponding [ˌkɔris'pɔndiŋ]
adj. 相应的，通信的

When the CPU reads data, it places the address on the address bus. Two chips read in address bits A_0, A_1, and A_9 and perform their internal decoding. If the CS and WR signals are activated, the chips input the data from data bus. Since the address and enable signals are the same for eight chips, either all chips or neither chip is active at any given time. The computer never has only one of the two active. For this reason, they act just as a single $1K\times 8$ chip, at least as far as the CPU is concerned. Instead of creating wider words, chips can be combined to create more words. The same two $1K\times 8$ chips could instead be configured as a $2K\times 8$ memory subsystem.

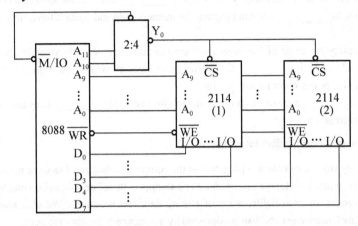

Fig.2.4 The lines of memory

Beyond the Basics

The memory subsystem described in this chapter is sufficient for small, embedded computers. Personal computers and mainframes, however, require more complex **hierarchical** configurations. These computers include small, high-speed **cache** memory. The computer loads data from the physical memory into the cache; the processor can access data in the cache more quickly than it can access the same data in physical memory. Many microprocessors include some cache memory right on the processor chip. A computer that includes cache memory must also have a cache controller to move data between the cache and physical memory.

hierarchical [ˌhaiəˈrɑːkikəl]
adj. 分等级的
cache [kæʃ]
n. 高速缓冲存储器

At the other extreme, modern computers include **virtual memory**. This mechanism uses a hard disk as a part of the computer's memory, expending the memory space of the computer while minimizing cost, since a byte of hard disk costs less than a byte of RAM. As with the cache, virtual memory needs a controller to move data between physical memory and the hard disk.

virtual memory
虚拟存储器

Exercises

I. Fill in the blanks with the information given in the text.

1. There are two well-known types of memory chips. One types is called _____. The other is _____.

2. ROM is the type of memory that does not lose its contents when the power is turned off. For this reason, ROM is also called nonvolatile memory. There are different types of ROM. _____ refers to the kind of ROM that the user can burn information into. In _____, one can program the memory chip and erase it thousands of times.

3. Storage cells in _____ memory are made of flip-flops and therefore do not require refreshing in order to keep their data. The other kind of RAM is _____, the major advantages of which are high density (capacity), cheaper cost per bit, and lower power consumption per bit.

4. In the design of all computers, _____ are used as primary storage for code and _____. They are the memory that the CPU first asks for information.

II. Translate the following passages from English into Chinese.

RAM is the internal and temporary storage of data and programs in the computer's memory. Once the power is turned off or interrupted, everything in internal storage disappears. Such storage is therefore said to be volatile. Thus, we need external, more permanent, or nonvolatile, ways of storing data and programs. We also need external storage because users need much more capacity than is possessed by a computer's primary memory.

The most widely used external storage media are floppy disks, hard disks, optical disks, and magnetic tape. It is important for users to understand the advantages, disadvantages, and typical users for each. Any particular microcomputer could use all of the different media. However, a typical system has a hard-disk drive and one or two other drivers. The hard-disk drive is designated as the C driver and is typically used for storing system and application programs.

III. Translate the following terms or phrases from English into Chinese and vice versa.

1. decode
2. ROM(Read-Only Memory)
3. capacity
4. cache
5. buffer
6. 半导体存储器
7. 非易失性存储器
8. 尺度，维(数)
9. 随机存取存储器
10. 虚拟存储器

Section C　I/O Subsystem Organization and Interfacing

Input devices take data and programs people can read or understand and convert them to a form the computer can process. This form consists of the machine-readable electronic signals of 0s and 1s. On the contrary, output devices convert machine-readable information into people-readable form. Next we will introduce the input/output (I/O) **subsystem** organization and **interfacing**.

The CPU treats memory as **homogeneous**. From the CPU's perspective, each location is read from and written to in

subsystem ['sʌb,sistim]
n. 子系统，辅助系统
interfacing ['intəfeisiŋ]
n. 界面连接，接口连接
homogeneous
[,hɔməu'dʒi:njəs]
adj. 同类的，相似的，均一的，均匀的

exactly the same way. Each memory location performs the same function——it stores a data value or an instruction for use by the CPU. I/O devices, on the other hand, are very different. A personal computer's keyboard and hard disk perform vastly different functions, yet both are part of the I/O subsystem. Fortunately for the system designer, the interfaces between the CPU and the I/O devices are very similar.

Each I/O device is connected to the computer system's address, data, and control buses. Each I/O device includes I/O interface circuitry; it is actually this circuitry that interacts with the buses. The circuitry also interacts with the actual I/O device to transfer data.

As for the generic interface circuitry for an input device, the data from the input device goes to the tri-state buffers. When the values on the address and control buses are correct, the buffers are enabled and data passes on to the data bus. The CPU can then read in this data. When the conditions are not right, the logic block does not enable the buffers; they are tri-stated and do not place data onto the bus.

The key to this design is the enable logic. Just as every memory location has a unique address, each I/O device also has a unique address. The enable logic must not enable the buffers unless it receives the correct address from the address bus. It must also get the correct control signals from the control bus. For an input device, an RD (or RD') signal must be asserted. (as well as the I/O signal, or equivalent, in systems with isolated I/O.)

The design of the interface circuitry for an output device, such as a computer monitor, is somewhat different than that for the input device. Tri-state buffers are replaced by the register. The tri-state buffers are used in input device interfaces to make sure that no more than one device writes data to the bus at any time. Since the output devices read data from the bus, rather that write data to it, they don't need the buffers. The data can be made available to all output devices; only the device with the correct address will read it in.

The load logic plays the role of the enable logic in the input device interface. When this logic receives the correct address and control signals, it asserts the LD signal of the register, causing it to read data from the systems data bus. The output device can then read the data from the register at its **leisure** while the CPU performs other tasks.

A **variant** of this design replaces the register with tri-state buffers. The same logic used to load the register is used to enable the tri-state buffers instead. Although this can work for some designs, the output device must read in data while the buffers are enabled. Once they are disabled, the outputs of the buffers are tri-stated and the data is no longer available to the output device.

Some devices are used for both input and output. A personal computer's hard disk drive falls into this **category**. Such a device requires a combined interface that is essentially two interfaces, one for input and the other for output. Some logic elements, such as the gates that check the address on the address bus, can be used to generate both the buffer enable and register load signals.

I/O devices are much slower than CPUs and memory. For this reason, they can have timing problems when interacting with the CPU. To illustrate this, consider what happens when a CPU wants to read data from a disk. It may take the disk drive several **milliseconds** to **position** its heads properly to read the desired value. In this time, the CPU could have read in invalid data and fetched, decoded, and executed thousands of instructions.

Most CPUs have a control input signal called READY (or something similar). Normally this input is high. When the CPU outputs the address of the I/O device and the correct control signals, enabling the tri-state buffers of the I/O device interface, the I/O device sets READY low. The CPU reads this signal and continues to output the same address and control signals, which cause the buffers to remain enabled. In the hard disk drive example, the drive **rotates** the disk and positions its read heads until it reads the desired data.

The CPU then reads the data from the bus and continues its normal operation. The extra clock cycles generated by having READY set low are called wait states. CPUs can also use the READY signal to synchronize data transfers with the memory subsystem.

These I/O interfaces are fine for small computers, such as the microwave oven controller, but they suffer from poor performance in larger computer systems. In all but the smallest

leisure ['leʒə; 'li:ʒə]
n. 空闲, 闲暇
variant ['vɛəriənt]
n. 变量

category ['kætigəri]
n. 种类, 类别

millisecond ['mili,sekənd]
n. 毫秒
position [pə'ziʃən]
vt. 安置, 决定……的位置

rotate [rəu'teit]
v. (使)旋转

systems, it is not acceptable for the CPU to have to wait thousands of clock cycles for data from an I/O device. Many systems use **interrupts** so they can perform useful work while waiting for the much slower I/O devices.

interrupt [ˌintəˈrʌpt]
vt. 中断

These I/O interfaces are also not suited to large data transfers. In the systems in this chapter, each byte of data transferred between an I/O device and memory must pass through the CPU. This is **inefficient** for many common operations, such as loading a program from disk into memory. Direct memory access (DMA) is a method used to bypass the CPU in these transfers, thus performing them much more quickly.

inefficient [ˌiniˈfiʃənt]
adj. 效率低的, 效率差的

Exercises

I. Fill in the blanks with the information given in the text.

1. Each I/O devices, such as input devices _____, _____, or disk drive, has a unique address as well. When accessing an I/O device, the CPU places the address of the device on the address bus. Each device can read the address off of the bus and determine whether it is the device being accessed by the CPU.

2. Each I/O device is connected to the computer system's _____, data, and control buses. Each I/O device includes I/O _____ circuitry that interacts with the buses.

3. The key to this design is the enable logic. Just as every memory location has a unique address, each I/O device also has a _____ address. The enable logic must not enable the buffers unless it receives the correct address from the address bus.

4. For a I/O devices to be recognized by the CPU, it must be assigned an address. No two devices are allowed to have the _____ address. The CPU puts the address on the address bus, and the decoding circuitry finds the device. Then the CPU uses the _____ either to get data from that device or to sent data to it.

II. Translate the following passages from English into Chinese.

The term I/O is used to describe any program, operation or device that transfers data to or from a computer and to or from a peripheral device. Every transfer is an output from one device and an input into another. Devices such as the keyboard and the mouse are input-only devices while devices such as printers are output-only. A writable CD-ROM is both an input and an output device. A computer device, such as a printer is not part of the essential computer, i.e., the memory and microprocessor. Peripheral devices can be external——such as a mouse, keyboard, printer, monitor, external Zip driver or scanner——or internal, such as a CD-ROM driver, CD-R driver, or internal modem. Internal peripheral devices are often referred to as integrated peripherals.

Grammar 2 科技英语的语言特点(Ⅱ)

科技英语用句的特点

科技英语是正式书面文体, 和平时所接触的日常英语不同, 它常常是描述客观的事实,所以用句本身有自己的特点。下面详细说明其用句的特点。

1. 复杂长句多，且多用陈述句

科技文章要求叙述准确，推理严谨，因此一句话里包含三四个，甚至五六个分句的现象，并非少见。译成汉语时，必须按照汉语习惯分解成适当数目的分句，才能条理清楚，避免洋腔洋调。这种复杂长句居科技英语难点之首，要学会运用语法分析方法来加以解剖，以便以短代长，化难为易。

例如：

Factories will not buy machines unless they believe that the machine will produce goods that they are able to sell to consumers at a price that will cover all cost.

这是由一个主句和四个从句组成的复杂长句，只有进行必要的语法分析，才能正确理解和翻译。现试译如下：

除非相信那些机器造出的产品卖给消费者的价格足够支付所有成本，否则厂家是不会买那些机器的。

节译：

要不相信那些机器造出的产品售价够本，厂家是不会买的。

后一句只用了 24 个字，比前句 40 个字节约用字 40%，而对原句的基本内容无损。可见，只要清楚原文的结构和内涵，翻译时再在汉语上反复推敲提炼，复杂的英语长句也是容易驾驭的。

2. 常用被动句

英语使用被动语态大大多于汉语，这是因为被动语态结构与主动语态结构相比，更少主观色彩，更富于客观性，这很适合描述客观事物。例如，莎士比亚传世名剧《罗密欧与朱丽叶》中的一句就两次用了被动语态：

Juliet was torn between desire to keep Romeo near her and fear for his life, should his presence be detected.

朱丽叶精神上受到折磨，既渴望和罗密欧形影不离，又担心罗密欧万一让人发现，难免有性命之忧。

科技英语更是如此，有三分之一以上用被动语态。

例如：

1) No work can be done without energy.

译文：

没有能量决不能做功。

2) All business decisions must now be made in the light of the market.

译文：

所有企业现在必须根据市场来做出决策。

3. 句中出现的非谓语动词多

在英语中，每个简单句只能用一个谓语动词，如果读到几个动作，就必须选出主要动作作为谓语，而将其余动作用非谓语动词形式，这样才能符合英语语法要求。

例如：

要成为一个名副其实的内行，需要学到老。

在这句话中，有"成为"、"需要"和"学"三个表示动作的词，译成英语后为

To be a true professional requires lifelong learning.

可以看出,选择"需要"(require)作为谓语,其余两个动作:"成为"用不定式形式 to be,而"学"用动名词形式 learning,这样才能符合英语语法要求。

4. 句中大量使用非限定性动词

在科技英语中,关系代词 that 和 which 以及非人称代词 it 的使用频率较高,同时为了能将问题简明地说明清楚,在科技英语文章中常使用结构简单的动词不定式、动名词和分词这些非谓语结构来表达各种从句或分句。

例如:

When a program is finished, a new one can take its place in memory, allowing the computer to process completely different data.

当一个程序结束时,一个新程序可以在内存中取得其位置,这就可以允许计算机处理完全不同的数据。

 参考译文

Section A CPU

人们为解决问题而制造计算机。早期的计算机解决的是数学和工程问题,后来计算机着重解决商业应用中的信息处理问题。如今,计算机还用来控制如汽车、发动机、机器人和微波炉等各式各样的机器。计算机系统解决上述这些领域中的任何一个问题都是通过接收输入、处理问题和生成输出来实现的。

计算机系统由硬件和软件组成。硬件是系统的物理部分。硬件一旦设计完毕,要修改是困难的,并且花费也大。软件是控制硬件的程序集合,比硬件容易修改。计算机之所以有用,是因为它们能解决很多不同类型的问题,是通用的机器。相对而言,每种专用机只能解决一类问题。通过为系统配备不同的指令系统,即配备不同的软件,能用同一硬件去解决不同的问题。

大多数计算机系统,从汽车和日用电器中的嵌入式控制器到个人计算机和大型主机,都具有相同的基本组成。每台计算机都有如下 4 种基本硬件部件:
- 中央处理器(CPU);
- 主存储器;
- 输入设备;
- 输出设备。

图 2.1 以一个框图的形式展示了这几种部件。各框之间的连线代表信息流在总线上从一个部件流向另一个部件,简单地说,总线就是连接各部件的一组线缆。处理是在 CPU 和主存储器中进行的。图 2.1 中通过总线相互连接的各部件的组成是很常见的。当然,也可能有其他配置。
- 计算机硬件常以相对体积大小来分类:
- 小型计算机;
- 中型计算机;
- 大型计算机。

一台大型计算机的 CPU 往往要占用一个机柜,它的输入/输出(I/O)设备和存储器可能占据整个房间。微型计算机则可以小到能放在桌子上或公文包里。随着技术的进步,以前只能在大型计算机上进行的大量处理工作,现在可以在更小的机器上进行。很多过去只能在小型或大型计算机上做的工作现在微型计算机都能完成。

上面所述的计算机是按照物理尺寸的大小而不是按存储器的容量大小来分类的。计算机系统用户通常

更关心存储器的容量大小,因为这更直接地表明硬件所能完成的有效工作量。运算速度对于用户来说是另一个重要特性。一般来讲,用户需要快速的 CPU 和大容量存储器,而 I/O 设备和主存储器的体积则要小。

CPU

处理器或中央处理单元(CPU)是计算机中运行程序(执行程序指令)的部件。在微型计算机中,CPU 是一个独立的电子部件。微处理器是一种小型化处理器,其所有元件都集成在一块或数块集成电路内。它是半导体 CPU,是微型计算机的主要部件。微处理器的元件通常安装在一个芯片上或在同一组件内,有时也分布在几个芯片上。

中央处理单元由控制逻辑部件和算术逻辑部件组成。中央处理单元控制计算机系统中的其他部件执行指令。它指示存储器(暂时存储数据、指令、处理信息)和算术逻辑单元之间的信号传递。它还要控制 CPU 和输入/输出设备之间的信息传递。在具有微程序控制的指令集的微型计算机中,它包含附加的控制-存储部件。

算术逻辑单元通常称为 ALU,通常能够完成算术运算和逻辑运算两种运算。算术运算和你想到的一样,就是一些基本的算术运算:加、减、乘和除。逻辑操作主要是比较,即将两组数据进行比较,确定它们是相等(=)、小于(<)或大于(>)的关系。

CPU 控制整个计算机。它从存储器中获取指令,提供存储器存取数据需要的地址和控制信号。CPU 对指令进行译码并且控制整个执行过程。它执行一些内部操作,并且为存储器和 I/O 设备执行指令提供必要的地址、数据和控制信号。除非 CPU 激发,否则,计算机什么事情都不会发生。

CPU 内部有三大分区。寄存器区,顾名思义,包括一组寄存器、一条总线或其他通信机制。微处理器指令集结构中的寄存器就属于 CPU 的这一分区,系统的地址和数据总线与寄存器区交互,此分区还包括程序员不能直接访问的一些寄存器。相对简单的 CPU 含有寄存器,用以锁存正在访问的存储器地址,还有暂存器以及指令集结构中没有的其他寄存器等。

在指令周期的取指阶段,处理器首先将指令的地址输出到地址总线上。处理器有一个叫做程序计数器的寄存器,CPU 将下一条要取的指令的地址存放在程序计数器中。在 CPU 将地址输出到系统的地址总线之前,必须从程序计数器中取出该地址。在取指阶段结束前,CPU 从系统数据总线上读取指令码。它把该指令码存储在某个内部寄存器中,该寄存器通常被称为指令寄存器或其他相似的名字。

控制单元也产生系统控制总线上的信号,如读(READ)、写(WRITE)和其他信号等。典型的微处理器执行取指令、对指令译码和执行指令等一系列的操作。通过以正确的顺序激发这些内部或外部控制信号,控制单元使 CPU 和计算机的其余部分完成正确处理指令所需要的操作。

以上对 CPU 的描述并不完整,现在的处理器拥有更加复杂的特征以提高其性能。这些机制中有一种是指令流水线技术,它允许 CPU 在执行一条指令的同时取出另一条指令。

本节我们从系统的角度介绍了 CPU,但我们还没有讨论它的内部设计。我们介绍了 CPU 的寄存器、数据通路、控制单元等所有能使 CPU 正确地读取、译码和执行指令的部件。微程序 CPU 具有同硬连线 CPU 一样的寄存器、ALU 和数据通路,但二者控制单元完全不同。

系统总线

从物理角度而言,总线就是一组导线。计算机的部件就是连在总线上的。为了将信息从一个部件传到另一个部件,源部件先将数据输出到总线上,然后目标部件再从总线上接受这些数据。随着计算机系统逐渐变得复杂,使用总线比每个设备对之间直接连接要有效得多(就减少连接数量而言)。与大量的直接连接相比,总线使用较少的电路板空间,耗能更少,并且在芯片或组成 CPU 的芯片组上需要较少的引脚。

图 2.1 所示的系统包括 3 组总线。最上面的是地址总线。当 CPU 从存储器读取数据或指令,或写数据到存储器时,必须指明将要访问的存储器单元地址。CPU 将该地址输出到地址总线上,而存储器从地址总

线上读取该地址,并且用它来访问正确的存储单元。每个 I/O 设备,如键盘、显示器或者磁盘驱动器,同样都有一个唯一的地址。当访问某个 I/O 设备时,CPU 将此设备的地址放到地址总线上。每一个设备均从总线上读取地址并且判断自己是否就是 CPU 正要访问的设备。与其他总线不同,地址总线总是从 CPU 上接收信息,而 CPU 从不读取地址总线。

数据是通过数据总线传送的。当 CPU 从存储器中读取数据时,它首先把存储器地址输出到地址总线上,然后存储器将数据输出到数据总线上,这样 CPU 就可以从数据总线上读取数据了。当 CPU 向存储器中写数据时,它首先将地址输出到地址总线上,然后把数据输出到数据总线上,这样存储器就可以从数据总线上读取数据,并将它存储到正确的单元中。对 I/O 设备读写数据的过程与此类似。

控制总线与以上两种总线都不相同。地址总线由 n 根线构成,n 根线联合传送一个 n 位的地址值。类似地,数据总线的各条线组合起来传输一个单独的多位值。相反,控制总线是单根控制信号的集合。这些信号用来指示数据是要读入 CPU 还是要从 CPU 写出,CPU 是要访问存储器还是要访问 I/O 设备,是 I/O 设备还是存储器已就绪要传送数据等。虽然图 2.1 所示的控制总线看起来是双向的,但它实际上(大多数)是单向信号的集合。大多数信号是从 CPU 输出到存储器与 I/O 子系统的,只有少数是从这些子系统输出到 CPU 的。

一个系统可能具有分层次的总线。例如,它可能使用地址、数据和控制总线来访问存储器和 I/O 控制器。I/O 控制器可能依次使用第二级总线来访问所有的 I/O 设备,第二级总线通常称为 I/O 总线或者局部总线。

指令周期

指令周期是微处理器完成一条指令处理的步骤。首先,微处理器从存储器读取指令,然后将指令译码,辨明它读取的是哪一条指令。最后,它完成必要的操作以执行指令。(有人认为在指令周期中还要包括一个附加的步骤来存储结果,这里我们把该操作当作执行功能的一部分。)每一个功能——读取、译码和执行都包括一个或多个操作。

当微处理器为存储器留出充足的时间来对地址译码和访问所需的存储单元之后,微处理器发出一个读(READ)控制信号。当微处理器准备好可以从存储器或是 I/O 设备读数据时,它就在控制总线上发一个读信号。(对于这个信号,一些处理器有不同的名字,但所有处理器都有这样的信号来执行这个功能。)根据微处理器的不同,读信号可能是高电平有效(信号=1),也可能是低电平有效(信号=0)。

发出读信号后,存储器子系统就把要读取的指令码放到计算机的数据总线上,微处理器就从数据总线上输入该数据,并且将它存储在其内部的某个寄存器中。至此,微处理器已经取得了指令。

接下来,微处理器对这条指令译码。每一条指令可能要由不同的操作序列来执行。当微处理器对该指令译码时,它确定处理的是哪一条指令以便选择正确的操作序列去执行。这一步完全在微处理器内完成,不需要使用系统总线。

最后,微处理器执行该指令。指令不同,执行的操作序列也不同。执行过程可以是从存储器读取数据、写数据到存储器、读或写数据到 I/O 设备,执行 CPU 内部操作,或者执行多个上述操作的组合。

微处理器从存储器读取数据所执行的操作序列,同从存储器中读取一条指令是一样的。毕竟读取指令就是简单地从存储器中读取它。图 2.2 显示了从存储器中读取数据的操作时序。

读周期

在图 2.2 中,注意最上面的符号——CLK,它是计算机的系统时钟,微处理器用系统时钟使其操作同步。在一个时钟周期(系统时钟的 0/1 序列)的开始位置,微处理器将地址放到总线上。一个时钟周期(允许存储器对地址译码和访问数据的时间)之后,微处理器才发出读信号。这使得存储器将数据放到数据总线上。在这个时钟周期之内,微处理器从系统总线上读取数据,并存储到它的某个寄存器中。在这个时钟周期结束时,微处理器撤销地址总线上的地址,并撤销读信号,然后存储器从数据总线上撤销数据,也就完成了存储器的读操作。

写周期

存储器写操作的时序如图 2.3 所示。在第一个时钟周期，处理器将地址和数据放到总线上，然后在第二个时钟周期开始时发出一个写(WRITE)控制信号(或与之等价的信号)。像读信号促使存储器读取数据一样，写信号促使存储器存储数据。在这个时钟周期的某个时刻，存储器将数据总线上的数据写入地址总线指示的存储单元内。当这个时钟周期结束，微处理器从系统总线上撤消地址、数据及写信号后，就完成了存储器的写操作。

Section B 存储器

存储器术语

在计算机设计中，半导体存储器曾被用做主存，用以存储代码和数据。半导体存储器直接与 CPU 相连，CPU 首先从存储器中获取信息(代码和数据)。因此，半导体存储器有时指的就是主存。主存必须快速地对 CPU 做出反应，只有半导体存储器才能够做到这种快速反应。广泛使用的半导体存储器是 ROM 和 RAM。在讨论不同种类的 RAM 和 ROM 之前，我们先来讨论一下有关半导体存储器的一些重要术语，如存储容量、组成和速度。

存储容量

半导体存储器芯片能够存储的数位的数量称为芯片的容量，它的单位可以是 Kb(千位)或 Mb(兆位)等，这些必须与计算机的辅助存储器容量加以区别。计算机存储器的容量通常以字节为单位，而存储器 IC(集成电路)芯片的存储以位为存储单位。例如，某科技期刊的一篇文章中提到 16M 芯片使用得非常普遍。这种情况下，虽然没有提到 16 兆意味着 16M 位，但这是显而易见的，因为文章中指的是 IC 芯片的存储容量；而如果一个广告中提到一台计算机具有 16M 的存储器，因为指的是计算机的存储器容量，所以 16M 意味着 16 兆字节。

存储器的组成

在 IC 中，存储器芯片构成了一定数量的存储单元。根据芯片内部的设计，每个单元能够存储 1 位、4 位、8 位，甚至 16 位数位。存储器芯片内每个存储单元存储的位数与芯片的数据引脚的数量相同。在存储器芯片中有多少个单元呢？这取决于地址引脚的数量。存储器芯片中单元的数量等于 2 的地址引脚数量的乘方。因此，存储器芯片能够存储的位数为单元数与每个单元中能够存储的数据位数的乘积。总结如下：

(1) 每个存储器芯片具有 2^x 个单元，x 是芯片地址引脚的数量。
(2) 每个单元存储 y 位，y 是芯片数据引脚的数量。
(3) 每个芯片将存储 $2^x \times y$ 位，x 是芯片地址引脚的数量，y 是芯片数据引脚的数量。表 2-1 是存储器组成的相关计算。

速度

存储器芯片的一个非常重要的特征参数就是数据的存取速度。为了存取数据，首先将地址信息传送到地址引脚上，一段时间以后，要存取的数据就会出现在数据引脚上。使用的时间越短，相应地，效果越好，存储芯片的价格也越高。存储器芯片的存取速度通常是指它的存取时间。根据在设计和制作过程中的 IC 的技术情况的不同，存储器芯片的存取时间分布从几纳秒到几百纳秒不等。存储器的 3 个重要特性，即容量、组成和存取速度，具有广泛的应用。

ROM 与 RAM

ROM 是一种存储器，当电源关闭时，ROM 内的信息不会丢失。因此，ROM 又被称为非易失性存储器。

ROM 又可以分为许多种，如 PROM、EPROM、EEPROM 和闪速 EPROM。

RAM 也称为可读写存储器，用来存储可以改变的数据。因为断电后 IC 芯片中的信息丢失，所以 RAM 又称为易失性存储器。RAM 分为三类：静态 RAM(SRAM)、动态 RAM(DRAM) 和 NV-RAM(非易失性 RAM)。许多计算机系统，包括个人计算机，都同时拥有 ROM 和 RAM。

芯片的内部组成

ROM 和 RAM 芯片的内部组成是相似的。为了说明一个最简单的组成——线性组成，以一个 16×4 的 ROM 芯片为例。(为了简化，在此并未画出编程器件。) 这个芯片有 3 个地址输入端和两个数据输出端，以及 64 位的内部存储元件，它排列成 16 个单元，每个单元 4 位。

3 个地址位经过译码，可以选择 8 个单元中的一个，但只有芯片的使能端有效才行。如果 CE=0，译码器被禁止，则不选择任何单元。该单元上的三态缓冲器是有效的，允许数据输出到缓冲器中。如果 CE=1 且 OE=1，则这些缓冲器有效，数据从芯片中输出；否则，输出是高阻态。

随着单元数量的增加，线性组成中地址译码器的规模变得相当大。为了补救这一问题，存储器芯片可以设计成使用多维译码方式。

在大型存储器芯片中，这种节省显得至关重要。以一个 4096×1 芯片为例，其线性组成将需要一个 12:4096 译码器，译码器大小与输出的数量成正比。(假定一个 $n:2^n$ 译码器的大小是 $O(2^n)$。) 如果芯片排列成 64×64 的二维数组，它将有两个 6:64 译码器：一个用来选择 64 行中的一行，另一个用来在选定行中选择 64 个单元中的一个单元，该译码器的大小正比于 $2×64$，或写成 $O(2×2^n/2) = O(2^{n/2+1})$。对于这个芯片，两个译码器总的大小约是那个大译码器大小的 3%。

存储器子系统的构成

构造包含一个简单芯片的存储器系统是非常容易的，我们只需要简单地从系统总线上连接地址信号线、数据信号线和控制信号线就完成了。然而，大多数的存储器系统需要多个芯片。下面是通过存储器芯片组合来形成存储器子系统的一些方法。

两个或多个芯片可以组合起来构造一个每单元有多位的存储器。这可以通过连接芯片相应的地址信号线和控制信号线，并将它们的数据引脚连到数据总线的不同位上来完成。例如，两个 1K×4 芯片(2114)可以组合产生一个 1K×8 存储器，如图 2.4 所示。两组芯片从总线上接收相同的十位地址输入，所有芯片有共同的 CS 和 WR 信号。第一组芯片的数据引脚连接到数据总线 $D_0 \sim D_3$，另一组芯片的数据引脚连接到数据总线 $D_4 \sim D_7$。

当 CPU 读取数据时，它将地址放在地址总线上。两组芯片读取地址位 A_0、A_1 到 A_9，并执行内部译码操作。如果 CS 和 WR 信号是有效的，则两个芯片从到数据总线输入数据。因为八个芯片的 CS 和 WR 信号是相同的，因此在任一时刻所有芯片要么同时有效，要么同时无效。正因如此，它们的行为就像一个单一的 1K×8 芯片，至少就 CPU 而言是这样的。除了构造更宽的字以外，芯片组合还可以构造出更多的字。同样的两个 1K×8 芯片能够组成一个 2K×8 存储子系统。

基本功能的拓展

本章描述的存储器子系统对于较小的、嵌入式计算机而言是足够的。然而，个人计算机和大型主机需要更加复杂的层次结构。这些计算机包含体积小的、高速的高速缓冲存储器。计算机将数据从物理存储器中装载到高速缓冲存储器中；处理器在高速缓冲存储器中访问数据比在物理存储器中快得多。许多微处理器就在处理器芯片中含有一些高速缓冲存储器。含有高速缓冲存储器的计算机同时也要有一个高速缓冲控制器，用来在高速缓冲和物理存储器间传输数据。

在另一端，现代计算机还具有一个虚拟存储器。这种机制使用硬盘充当计算机存储器的一部分，扩大了计算机的存储空间，而且降低了价格，因为一个字节的硬盘价格比一个字节的 RAM 要便宜得多。同高速缓冲一样，虚拟存储器也需要一个控制器以便在物理存储器和虚拟存储器之间传输数据。

Section C I/O 子系统的组成和接口

输入设备获取人们能够读懂或理解的数据，并转换成计算机能够处理的形式，该形式为由多个 0 和 1 组成的计算机能够识别的电子信号。相反，输出设备主要是将机器能够识别的信息转换成人能够识别的信息形式。接下来我们将介绍 I/O 子系统的组成和接口。

CPU 把存储器看做是同构的。从 CPU 的角度来看，每一个单元的读操作和写操作都是一样的，每一个单元执行同样的功能，即存储 CPU 使用的数据或指令。另一方面，I/O 设备是很不一样的。个人计算机的键盘和硬盘执行的是千差万别的功能，但它们同是 I/O 子系统的一部分。对系统设计者而言，幸运的是 CPU 和各 I/O 设备之间的接口是非常相似的。

每一个 I/O 设备与计算机系统的地址总线、数据总线和控制总线相连接，它们都包括 I/O 接口电路，与总线交互的实际上正是这一电路，同时，它与实际的 I/O 设备交互来传输数据。

对于一个输入设备的一般接口电路，从输入设备来的数据传送到三态缓冲器。当地址总线和控制总线上的值正确时，缓冲器设为有效，数据传到数据总线上，然后 CPU 可以读取数据。当条件不正确时，逻辑块不会使缓冲器有效，它们保持高阻态，而且不把数据传到总线上。

这一设计的关键在于使能逻辑。正如每一个存储单元都有一个唯一的地址一样，每一个 I/O 设备也有一个唯一的地址。除非使能逻辑从地址总线得到了正确的地址，否则不能置缓冲器为有效状态。同时，它还必须从控制总线上得到正确的控制信号。对于一个输入设备，RD(或者 RD')信号必须有效(在独立 I/O 系统中，I/O 信号，或其他等效的信号也如此)。

输出设备(如显示器)接口电路的设计与输入设备的设计有所不同，寄存器代替了三态缓冲器。输入设备中使用三态缓冲器是为了确保在任何时刻都只有一个设备向总线写数据，而输出设备是从总线读取数据，不是写数据，因此不需要缓冲器。所有的输出设备都可获得数据，但只有具有正确地址的设备才能读取它。

装载逻辑发挥着输入设备接口中使能逻辑的作用。当此逻辑获得正确的地址信号和控制信号后，它发出寄存器的 LD 信号，促使它从系统数据总线上读取数据。然后输出设备可以在其空闲的时候从寄存器中读取该数据，同时 CPU 可以执行其他的任务。

该设计中的一个变量也可以用三态缓冲器代替寄存器。装载寄存器的逻辑同样用于使能三态缓冲器。虽然对于某些设计，这是可行的，但是输出设备必须在缓冲器有效时读入数据。一旦缓冲器被禁止，其输出就是高阻态，该数据也就不能够再供输出设备使用。

有些设备既用于输入又用于输出，个人计算机中的硬盘驱动器就属于这一类。这样的设备需要一个组合接口，本质上是两个接口，一个用于输入，另一个用于输出。一些逻辑元件，如检查地址总线上的地址是否正确的门电路，既可以产生缓冲器的使能信号，也可以产生寄存器的装载信号。

I/O 设备比 CPU 和存储器慢得多。基于这个原因，当它们与 CPU 交互时，就可能存在时序上的问题。为了说明这一点，考虑当 CPU 想要从硬盘中读取数据时会发生的情况，这可能要消耗磁盘驱动器几毫秒来正确地定位磁头，以便读取想要的数值。而在这段时间里，CPU 可能已经读入了无效数据，并且读取、译码和执行了成千上万条指令。

大多数 CPU 都有一个控制输入信号，叫做就绪信号(READY)(或其他意思相近的名称)，通常其输入为高电平。当 CPU 输出某 I/O 设备的地址和正确的控制信号，促使 I/O 设备接口的三态缓冲器有效时，该 I/O 设备置 READY 信号为低电平。CPU 读取这一信号，并且继续输出同样的地址信号和控制信号，使缓冲器保持有效。在硬盘驱动器的例子中，驱动器旋转磁头，并且定位读写磁头，直到读到想要的数据为止。

然后 CPU 通过缓冲器将数据输出到数据总线上，并重新设置 READY 为高电平。这时 CPU 才从总线上读入数据，之后继续它的正常操作。设置 READY 为低电平而生成的附加时钟周期叫做等待状态。CPU

Chapter 2 Computer Hardware

同样也可以使用 READY 信号来同步与存储器子系统之间的数据传输。

这些 I/O 接口对于小型计算机而言已经很好了，如微波炉控制器，但是在大型的计算机系统中，它们的性能则很差。在除最小系统以外的所有系统中，让 CPU 等待成千上万个时钟周期从 I/O 设备中得到数据是不能接收的。为此，许多系统都使用了中断机制，以便 CPU 在等待慢得多的 I/O 设备时，可以执行其他有用的工作。

这些 I/O 接口不适合大量的数据传输。在本章的系统中，I/O 设备和存储器之间传输的每一个字节都必须通过 CPU，这对于许多常见的操作(如从磁盘向主存装载一个程序)来说效率低下。直接存储器访问(DMA)就是在数据传输中绕过 CPU 的一种方法，因此执行起来速度很快。

Chapter 3 Computer Languages
(计算机语言)

Section A Programming Language

Introduction

Programming languages, in computer science, are the artificial languages used to write a sequence of **instructions** (a computer program) that can be run by a computer. Similar to **natural languages**, such as English, programming languages have a vocabulary, grammar, and syntax. However, natural languages are not suited for programming computers because they are **ambiguous**, meaning that their vocabulary and grammatical structure may be interpreted in **multiple** ways. The languages used to program computers must have simple logical structures, and the rules for their grammar, spelling, and **punctuation** must be precise.

Programming languages vary greatly in their **sophistication** and in their degree of **versatility**. Some programming languages are written to address a particular kind of computing problem or for use on a particular model of computer system. For instance, programming languages such as **FORTRAN** and **COBOL** were written to solve certain general types of programming problems——FORTRAN for scientific applications, and COBOL for business applications. Although these languages were designed to address specific categories of computer problems, they are highly **portable**, meaning that they may be used to program many types of computers. Other languages, such as machine languages, are designed to be used by on specific model of computer system, or even by one specific computer in certain research applications. The most commonly used programming languages are highly portable and can be used to effectively solve diverse types of computing problems. Languages like C, **Pascal**, and BASIC fall into this category.

Instruction [in'strʌkʃən]
n. 指示, 用法说明(书), 教育, 指导, 指令
natural languages
自然语言
ambiguous [,æm'bigjuəs]
adj. 暧昧的, 不明确的
multiple ['mʌltipl]
adj. 多样的, 多重的
punctuation [pʌŋktju'eiʃ(ə)n]
n. 标点, 标点符号
sophistication [sə,fisti'keiʃən]
n. 强词夺理, 诡辩, 混合
versatility [,vɜ:sə'tiləti]
n. 多功能性
FORTRAN ['fɔ:træn]
n. 公式翻译程序语言
COBOL ['kəubəul]
[计]abbr. Common Business Oriented Language
面向商业的通用语言
portable ['pɔ:təbl]
adj. 轻便的, 手提式的, 便携式的; [计] 可移植的
Pascal
n. [计]Pascal 语言

Chapter 3 Computer Languages

Language Types

Programming languages can be classified as either low-level languages or high-level languages. Low-level programming languages, or machine languages, are the most directly by a computer. Machine languages differ depending on the manufacturer and model of computer. High-level languages are programming languages that must first be translated into a machine language before they can be understood and processed by a computer. Examples of high-level languages are C, C++, Pascal, and FORTRAN. **Assembly languages** are intermediate languages that are very close to machine languages and do not have the level of **linguistic** sophistication exhibited by other high-level languages, but must still be translated into machine language.

assembly languages
n. 汇编语言
linguistic [liŋ'gwistik]
adj. 语言上的，语言学上的

1. Machine Languages

In machine languages, instructions are written as sequences 1s and 0s, called bits, that a computer can understand directly. An instruction in machine language generally tells the computer four things:

1) where to find one or two numbers or simple pieces of data in the main computer memory (RAM).

2) a simple operation to perform, such as adding the two numbers together.

3) where in the main memory to put the result of this simple operation.

4) where to find the next instruction to perform.

While all **executable** programs are eventually read by the computer in machine language, they are not all programmed in machine language. It is extremely difficult to program directly in machine language because the instructions are sequences of 1s and 0s. A typical instruction in a machine language might read 10010 1100 1011 and mean add the contents of storage **register** A to the contents of storage register B.

executable ['eksikju:təbl]
adj. 实行的，执行的

register ['redʒistə]
n. [计]寄存器

2. High-level Languages

High-level languages are directly sophisticated sets of **statements** utilizing words and syntax from human language. They are more similar to normal human languages than assembly

statements ['steitmənt]
n. 声明，陈述，综述

or machine languages and are therefore easier to use for writing complicated programs. These programming languages allow larger and more complicated programs to be developed faster. However, high-level languages must be translated into machine language by another program called a **compiler** before a computer can understand them. For this reason, programs written in a high-level language may take longer to execute and use up more memory than program written in an assembly language.

compiler [kəm'pailə]
n. [计] 编译器

3. Assembly Languages

Computer programs use assembly languages to make machine-language programs easier to write. In an assembly language, each statement corresponds roughly to one machine language instruction. An assembly language statement is composed with the aid of easy to remember **commands**. The command to add the contents of the storage register A to the contents of storage register B might be written ADD B, A in a typical assembly language statement. Assembly languages share certain features with machine languages. For instance, it is possible to **manipulate** specific bits in both assembly and machine Languages. Programmers use assembly languages when it is important to minimize the time it takes to run a program, because the translation from assembly language to machine language is relatively simple. Assembly languages are also used when some part of the computer has to be controlled directly.

command [kə'mɑːnd]
n. 命令,掌握,司令部

manipulate [mə'nipjuleit]
vt. (熟练地)操作,使用(机器等)

Classification of High-level Languages

High-level languages are commonly classified **procedure-oriented, functional, object-oriented**, or logical languages. The most common high-level languages today are procedure-oriented languages. In these languages, one or more related blocks of statements that perform some complete function are grouped together into a program module, or procedure, and given a name such as "procedure A". If the same sequence of operations is needed elsewhere in the program, a simple statement can be used to refer back to the procedure. In essence, a procedure is just a mini-program. A large program can be constructed by grouping together procedures that perform different tasks. Procedural languages allow programs to be shorter and easier for the computer to read, but they require the programmer to design

procedure-oriented
面向过程的
functional ['fʌŋkʃənl]
adj. 功能的,函数的
object-oriented
面向对象的

each procedure to be general enough to be used in different situations.

Functional languages treat procedures like mathematical functions and allow them to be processed like any other data in a program. This allows a much higher and more **rigorous** level of program construction specified and changed by the user as the program is running to be given values only once. This simplifies programming by reducing the need to be concerned with the exact order of statement execution, since a variable does not have to be **redeclared** or restated each time it is used in a program statement. Many of the ideas from functional languages have become key parts of many modern procedural languages.

Object-oriented languages are **outgrowths** of functional languages. In object-oriented languages, the code used to write the program and the data processed by the program are grouped together into units called objects. Objects are further grouped into classes, which define the **attributes** objects must have. A simple example of a class is the class Book. Objects within this class might be Novel and Short Story. Objects also have certain functions associated with them, called methods. The computer accesses an object through the use of one of the object's methods. The method of performs some action to the data in the object and returns this value to the computer. Classes of objects can also be further grouped into **hierarchies**, in which objects of one class can **inherit** methods from another class. The structure provided in object-oriented languages makes them very useful for complicated programming tasks.

Logic languages use logic as their mathematical base. A logical program consists of sets of facts and if-then rules, which specify how one set of facts may be deduced from others, for example:

If the statement X is true, then the statement Y is false.

In the statement of such a program, an input statement can be logically deduced from other statements in the program. Many **artificial intelligence** programs are written in such languages.

Programming Languages History

Programming languages date back almost to the invention of the digital computer in the 1940s. The first assembly languages **emerged** in the late 1950s with the introduction of commercial

rigorous ['rigərəs]

adj. 严格的，严厉的，严酷的，严峻的

redeclared ['ridi'klɛəd]

n. [计]重新声明

outgrowths ['autgrəuθ]

n. 长出，派出，结果，副产物

attribute [ə'tribju(:)t]

n. 属性，品质，特征，加于，归结于

hierarchies ['haiərɑːki]

n. 层次，层级
inherit [in'herit]

vt. 继承，遗传而得

artificial intelligence

n. 人工智能

emerge [i'məːdʒ]

vi. 显现，浮现，暴露，形成

computers. The first procedural languages were developed in the late 1950s to early 1960s: FORTRAN, created by John Backus, and then COBOL, created by Grace Hopper. The first functional language was **LISP**, written by John McCarthy in the late 1950s. Although heavily updated, all three languages are still widely used today.

In the late 1960s, the first object-oriented languages, such as **Simula**, emerged. Logic languages became well known in the mid 1970s intelligence software. During the 1970s with the instruction of **PROGLOG**, a language used to program artificial intelligence software. During 1970s, procedural languages continued to develop with **ALGOL**, BASIC, Pascal, C and **Ada**. **Smalltalk** was a highly influential object-oriented language that led to the merging of object-oriented and procedural languages in C++ and more recently in Java. Although pure logic languages have declined in popularity, variations have become vitally important in the form of relational languages for modern databases, such as **SQL**.

LISP
[计]LISP 语言，表处理语言
Simula
[计]Simula 语言，仿真语言，模拟语言
PROGLOG
[计]PROGLOG 语言，一种逻辑程序设计语言
ALGOL
[计]ALGOL 语言，一种算法语言
Ada
[计]Ada 语言
Smalltalk
[计]Smalltalk 语言，IBM 开发的面向对象的语言
SQL
[计]结构化查询语言

Exercises

I. Fill in the blanks with the information given in the text.

1. The most commonly used programming languages are highly _____ and can be used to effectively solve diverse types of _____ problems.
2. Programming languages can be classified as either _____ languages or _____ languages.
3. High-level languages must be translated into _____ language by another program called a _____ before a computer can understand them.
4. High-level languages are commonly classified _____, _____, _____, or _____.
5. In the late 1960s, the first object-oriented languages, such as _____, emerged.

II. Translate the following passages from English into Chinese.

A computer program is a set of instructions that directs a computer to perform some processing function or combination of functions. For the instructions to be carried out, a computer must execute a program, that is, the computer reads the program, and then follows the steps encoded in the program in a precise order until completion. A program can be executed many different times, with each execution yielding a potentially different result depending upon the options and data that the user gives the computer.

Programs fall into two major classes: application programs and operating systems. An application program is one that carries out some function directly for a user, such as word processing or game playing. An operating system is a program that manages the computer and the various resources and devices connected to it, such as RAM, hard drives, monitors, keyboards, printers, and modems, so that they may be used by other programs. Examples of operating systems are DOS, Windows 9x, OS/2, and UNIX.

Section B The Java Language

Why is Java so hot?

There's no getting around the fact that Java is the most exciting thing to hit the Internet since the World Wide Web. That's because it fills a need-several needs, in fact. With Java, programmers are able to deliver what everyone who uses the Web has been **clamoring** for-true interactivity.

First of all, Java is a programming language. Languages are used to compose a set of instructions which a computer follows. These groups of instructions are called programs, applications, executables, or, in the case of Java, applets. Java can also be used to build **stand-alone** programs, called applications, just like any other programming language. It's the applets that are the most **innovative** thing about Java.

Java applets, add life to the World Wide Web. By "life" I mean that with Java you can add **animation**, local data searches, and a wide variety of other functions and features that just weren't possible without the Java environment.

In order to look at the Web, you need a **browser**. A browser is an application which runs over the Internet and interprets HTML code. There are graphical and non-graphical browsers, but we're only interested in the graphical ones (the ones that can display pictures on your screen). There are a lot of browsers available. Currently there are only two which support Java: **Netscape** 2.0 and **HotJava**.

What is Java?

The folks who designed Java hoped to solve some of problems they saw in modern programming. As we said, Java's core principles developed out of a desire to build software for consumer electronics. Like those devices, the language needed to be compact, reliable, portable, distributed, **real-time**, and **embedded**. Sun Microsystems' official definition Java is:

A simple, object-oriented, distributed, interpreted, robust, secure, **architecture neutral**, portable, high-performance, **multithreaded**, and dynamic language.

clamoring ['klæmərəs]
adj. 大喊大叫的

stand-alone
n. 单机, 卓越
innovative [inəuveitiv]
adj. 创新的, 革新(主义)的
animation [ˌæni'meiʃən]
n. 活泼, 有生所
browser [brauzə(r)]
n. 浏览器, 吃嫩叶的动物, 浏览书本的人
Netscape
美国 Netscape 公司, 以开发 Internet 浏览器闻名
HotJava
美国 Sun 公司开发的, 支持Java 开发环境的 Internet 浏览器

real-time
adj. [计] 实时的, 接到指示立即执行的
embedded [em'bedid]
adj. 植入的, 深入的, 内含的
architecture neutral
adj. [计]结构中立的
multithreaded
adj. [计]多线程的

Java is simple.

Even though the Java developers decided that C++ was unsuitable for their purposes, they designed Java as closely to C++ as possible. This was done in order to make the system more familiar, more **comprehensible**, and to shorten the time necessary to learn the new language. One of Java's greatest appeals is that, if you're a programmer, you already know how to use it. Ninety percent of the programmers working these days use C, and almost all object-oriented programming is done in C++.

Another goal of the designers was to eliminate support for multiple class **inheritance**, **operator overloading**, and extensive automatic **coercion** of data types; several of the poorly understood, confusing and rarely used, features of C++. Also omitted from Java were header files, pre-processor, pointer arithmetic, structures, unions, or multi-dimensional arrays. They were selective, and **retained** features that would ease development, **implementation**, and maintenance of software, while omitting things that would slow a developer down. For example, even though operator overloading was eliminated they kept method overloading.

Another problem faced by C and C++ programmers is storage management, which is the allocation and freeing of memory. Ordinarily, a C programmer needs to keep a careful eye on how much memory their program is using. When a **chunk** of memory is no longer being utilized, the programmer needs to make sure the program frees it up so it can be re-used. This is even harder than it sounds, especially in large programs, and is the main cause for memory leaks and bugs. When programming in Java, you don't need to worry about those problems.

The Java system has an embedded auto garbage collection. The **garbage collector** simplifies Java programming, but at the expense of making the system more complicated. Because it has automatic garbage collection, Java not only makes programming easier, it also dramatically cuts down on the number of bugs and eliminates the **hassle** of memory management.

Java is small.

One of the features of Java which Sun neglected to mention

---

comprehensible
[,kɔmpri'hensəbl]
adj. 可理解的，易于了解的

inheritance [in'heritəns]
n. 遗传，遗产

operator overloading
操作符重载

coercion [kəu'ə:ʃən]
n. 强迫，威压，高压政治

retained [ri'tein]
vt. 保持，保留

implementation
[,implimen'teiʃən]
n. 执行

chunk [tʃʌŋk]
n. 大块、矮胖的人或物

garbage collector
垃圾回收器

hassle ['hæsl]
n. 激战

in its definition was Java's size——or lack of it. As a side effect of being simple, Java is a very small. Remember that one of the original goals of Java was to **facilitate** the construction of software that ran stand-alone in small machines.

The size of the basic **interpreter** and class support is about 40KB of RAM; adding the basic standard libraries and thread support (essentially a self-contained **microkernel**) adds an additional 175KB. The combined total of approximately 215KB is significantly smaller than comparable programming languages and environments.

Java is object-oriented.

Java is an object-oriented language. That means that it's part of a family of languages that focuses on defining data as objects and the methods that may be applied to those objects. As we've said, Java and C++ share many of the same **underlying** principles, they just differ in style and structure.

As part of the effort to keep Java simple, not everything in this object-oriented language is an object. Booleans, numbers, and other simple types are not objects, but Java does have **wrapper** objects for all simple types. Wrapper objects allow all simple types to be implemented as though they were classes.

Java is distributed.

An essential characteristic of client/server (CLS)applications like Java is the ability to share both information and the data processing workload. The term "distributed" describes the relationship between system objects, whether these objects are on remote or local systems. One of the great things about Java applets and applications is that they can open and access objects across the Web via **URLs** as easily as they can access a local file system.

Java is interpreted (and compiled).

Strictly speaking, that's true, although in reality Java is both interpreted and compiled. In fact, only about twenty percent of the Java code is interpreted by the browser——but this is a crucial twenty percent. Both Java's security and its ability to run on multiple **platforms** stem from the fact that the final steps of compilation are handled locally.

facilitate [fə'siliteit]
vt. 使容易，使便利，推动，帮助，使容易，促进
interpreter [in'tə:pritə]
n. 解释程序，解释者，注释器
microkernel
n. 微核

underlying [ˌʌndə'laiiŋ]
adj. 在下面的，根本的，潜在的

wrapper ['ræpə]
n. 包装材料，包装纸，书皮

URL
abbr.uniform resource locator，在 Internet 的 www 服务程序上用于指定信息位置的表示方法

platform ['plætfɔ:m]
n. (车站)月台，讲台，讲坛，平台

Java is robust.

"Robust" is simply computer speak for how reliable a language is. The more robust a language is, the less likely that programs written in this language will crash and the more likely it is that they will be bug-free. Strongly typed languages (like Java or C++) allow extensive compile-time checking, meaning any bugs can be found early. "Strongly typed" means that most of the data type checking isn't performed at run-time, rather it's performed during **compilation**.

Java is secure.

Java's security is still something which remains to be proven. The concept of allowing another site to **download executables** sight unseen to your machine is something which just doesn't sit right with many computer and Internet professionals. The simple truth is, viruses are out there, and no one wants to infect their machine by downloading a binary from the Net.

Some of the other features, such as robustness and the fact that Java is both interpreted and compiled, are aids to security.

Java is architecture neutral.

The team that designed Java was well aware that if Java was to support applications on networks it would have to support a variety of systems with a variety of CPU and operating system architectures. A Java application can execute anywhere on the network, or on the Internet, because the compiler generates an architecture neutral object file format——the compiled code is executable on many processors, provided that processor is running a Java-**savvy** browser.

Java is portable.

Java's architecture neutrality makes the concept of porting from one platform to another a little **redundant**. But even beyond platform independence, Java's use of standards for data types eliminates the "implementation dependent" aspects of the specification that are found in C and C++.

Java is high performance.

Java's not high performance in the sense of "faster than a

---

robust [rə'bʌst]
adj. 精力充沛的，健壮的

compilation [ˌkɔmpi'leiʃən]
n. 编辑

download
[计]下载
executables ['eksikjuːtəbl]
adj. 实行，执行的

savvy ['sævi]
v. 知道，了解
n. 机智，头脑，理解，悟性

redundant [ri'dʌndənt]
adj. 多余的

comparable C++ routine". In fact, it's almost the same speed. In **benchmark** tests run by Sun Microsystems on one of their SPARC Station 10 machines, the performance of byte codes converted to machine code is almost **indistinguishable** from native C or C++. Of course, that doesn't take into account the time of runtime compilation.

Interpreted byte code performance is fine for most usual tasks, there are certainly situations which call for higher performance. In those instances, the interpreted byte codes may not be the way to go. The process of generating machine code from byte code is pretty simple and produces reasonably good code.

Java is multithreaded.

The human brain is multithreaded. It can easily handle thousands of tasks simultaneously. You can be talking on the telephone while listening to the radio while pouring yourself a glass of orange juice while pinning the telephone to your ear with your shoulder while thinking about your plans for the weekend while noticing that the dishes need to be done while.

What multithreading means to Java users, is that they don't have to wait for the application to finish one task before beginning another. For example, if you were playing a **dungeon** adventure game, one thread could be handling the mathematics of the combat you were in, while another was taking care of the graphics. Multithreading eliminates a lot of **lag** time when compared to **single-threading**. On a personal computer, it means you see a lot less of the **hourglass** or **wristwatch** icon which we all know if the computer's way of saying "Don't rush me".

---

benchmark
[计] 基准
indistinguishable
[ɪndɪs'tɪŋgwɪʃəbl]
adj. 不能辨别的，不能区别的

dungeon ['dʌndʒən]
n. 地牢
lag
adj. 最后的
single-threading
[计]单线程
hourglass ['aʊəglɑːs]
n. 沙漏
wristwatch ['rɪstwɒtʃ]
n. 手表

Exercises

Ⅰ. **Fill in the blanks with the information given in the text.**

1. There are a lot of browsers available. Currently there are only two which support Java: _____ and _____.

2. Sun Microsystems' official definition Java is: A _____, _____, _____, _____, _____, _____, _____, _____, _____, and dynamic language.

3. Because it has automatic _____, Java not only makes programming easier, it also dramatically cuts down on the number of bugs and eliminates the hassle of memory management.

4. Some of the other features, such as robustness and the fact that Java is both _____ and _____, are

aids to security.

5. The size of the basic interpreter and class support is about _____ of RAM; adding the basic standard libraries and thread support (essentially a self-contained microkernel) adds an additional _____.

II. Translate the following passages from English into Chinese.

Java is a more dynamic language than C or C++. Unlike either of those languages, Java was designed to adapt to an evolving environment.

One of the major problems in development which uses C++, is that you can unwittingly or unwillingly become dependent on someone else. This is due to class libraries, a collection of plug and play components. Since C++ code has to be implemented in class libraries, if you license and use a second party's class library in your software, and that company subsequently alters or upgrades that library, you're more than likely going to have to respond. This response could be almost anything up to and including recompiling and redistributing your own software.

Section C JSP

Introduction

You probably have already noticed that most of the code in our **servlets** generated output that consisted of the **HTML** elements that composed the response to the client. Only a small portion of the code dealt with the business logic. Generating responses from servlets requires that Web application developers be familiar with Java. However, many people involved in Web application development, such as Web site designers, do not know Java. It is difficult for people who are not Java programmers to implement, maintain and extend a Web application that consists of primarily of servlets. The **solution** to this problem is Java Server Pages (JSP)——an **extension** of servlet technology that separates the presentation from the business logic. This lets Java programmers and Web-site designers focus on their strengths writing Java code and designing Web pages, respectively.

JSP simplify the delivery of **dynamic Web content**. They enable Web application programmers to create dynamic content by reusing **predefined** components and by interacting with components using server-side scripting. JSP programmers can use special software components called JavaBeans and custom **tag** libraries that encapsulate complex, dynamic functionality. A JavaBean is a reusable component that follows

servlet
[计]Servlet 是使用 Java Servlet 应用程序设计接口（API）及相关类和方法的 Java 程序
HTML
abbr. Hyper Text Markup Language
solution [səˈljuːʃən]
n. 解答，解决办法，溶解，解决方案
extension [iksˈtenʃən]
n. 延长，扩充，范围

dynamic Web content
动态网页内容
predefined [ˈpriːdiˈfain]
vt. 预先确定

tag [tæg]
n. 标签，标记符

certain conventions for class design that are discussed in the JavaBeans **specification**, which is available at java.sun.com/products/javabeans/glasgow/index.html. Custom-tag libraries are a powerful feature of JSP that allows Java developers to hide complex code for database access and other useful services for dynamic Web pages in custom tags. Web sites use these custom tags like any other Web page element to take advantage of the more complex functionality hidden by the tag. Thus, Web-page designers who are not familiar with Java can enhance Web pages with powerful dynamic content and processing **capabilities.**

The classes and interfaces that are specific to JSP programming are located in packages javax.servlet.jsp and javax.servlet.jsp.tagext. We discuss many of these classes and interfaces throughout this section as we present JSP **fundamentals**. For complete JSP details, see the JSP 2.0 specification, which can be downloaded from java.sun.com/products/jsp/download.html.

The four key components to JSPs

There are four key components to JSPs: directives, actions, scripting elements and tag libraries. **Directives** are messages to the JSP container that enable the programmer to specify page settings, to include content from other resources and to specify custom tag libraries for use in a JSP. Actions encapsulate **functionality** in predefined tags that programmers can embed in a JSP. Actions often are performed based on the information sent to the server as part of a particular client request. They also can create Java objects for use in **JSP scriptlets**. **Scripting elements** enable programmers to insert Java code that interacts with components in a JSP (and possibly other Web application components) to perform request processing. Scriptlets, one kind of scripting element, contain code fragments that describe the action to be performed in response to a user request. **Tag libraries** are part of the **tag extension mechanism** that enables programmers to create custom tags. Such tags enable Web page designers to manipulate JSP content without prior Java knowledge.

In some ways, JSP look like standard **XHTML** or **XML** documents. In fact, JSPs normally include XHTML or XML

---

specification [ˌspesifiˈkeiʃən]
n. 详述, 规格, 说明书, 规范

capability [ˌkeipəˈbiliti]
n. (实际)能力, 性能, 容量, 接受力

fundamental [ˌfʌndəˈmentl]
n. 基本原则, 基本原理

directive [diˈrektiv, daiˈrektiv]
n. 指示

functionality [ˌfʌŋkəʃəˈnæliti]
adj. 功能性, 泛函性

JSP scriptlets
一个包含任何在 JSP 中合法的脚本语言的代码片断的 JSP 脚本元素

scripting elements
脚本元素

tag libraries
标记库

tag extension mechanism
标签扩展装置

subsequent [ˈsʌbsikwənt]
adj. 后来的, 并发的

XHTML
扩展式超文本汇编语言

markup. Such **markup** is known as **fixed-template data** or **fixed-template text.** Fixed-template data often helps a programmer decide whether to use a servlet or a JSP. Programmers tend to use JSPs when most of the content sent to the client is fixed-template data and little or none of the content is generated dynamically with Java code. Programmers typically use servlets when only a small portion of the content sent to the client is fixed-template data. In fact, some servlets do not produce content. Rather, they perform a task **on behalf of** the client, then invoke other servlets or JSPs to provide a response. Note that in most cases servlet and JSP technologies are **interchangeable**. As with servlets, JSPs normally execute as part of a Web server.

When a JSP-enabled server receives the first request for a JSP, the JSP container translates the JSP into a Java servlet that handles the current request and future requests to the JSP. Literal text in a JSP becomes string literals in the servlet that represents the translated JSP. Any errors that occur in compiling the new servlet result in **translation-time errors**. The JSP container places the Java statements that implement the JSP's response in method _jspService at translation time. If the new servlet compiles properly, the JSP container invokes method _jspService to process the request. The JSP may respond directly or may invoke other Web application components to assist in processing the request. Any errors that occur during request processing are known as **request-time errors.**

Implicit Objects

Implicit objects provide access to many servlet capabilities in the context of a JSP. Implicit objects have four scopes: application, page, request and session. The JSP container owns objects with application scope. Any JSP can manipulate such objects. Objects with page scope exist only in the page that defines them. Each page has its own instances of the page-scope implicit objects. Objects with request scope exist for the duration of the request. For example, a JSP can partially process a request, then forward it to a servlet or another JSP for further processing. Request-scope objects go out of scope when request processing completes with a response to the client. Objects with

---

XML
扩展式标记语言
markup ['mɑːkʌp]
n. 涨价, 涨价幅度
[计]标记
fixed-template data
固定模式数据
fixed-template text
固定模式文本
on behalf of
代表
interchangeable
[intə'tʃeindʒəb(ə)l]
adj. 可互换的

translation-time errors
翻译时错误

request-time errors
请求时错误

Implicit objects
默认对象，固有对象

session scope exist for the client's entire browsing session.

The JSP Scripting Components

JSP often present **dynamically** generated content as part of an XHTML document that is sent to the client in response to a request. In some cases, the content is static but is output only if certain conditions are met during a request (e.g., providing values in a form that submits a request). JSP programmers can insert Java code and logic in a JSP using scripting.

The JSP scripting components include **scriptlets**, comments, expressions, declarations and escape sequences. In these components, scriptlets are blocks of code delimited by <% and %>. They contain Java statements that the container places in method jspService at translation time.

The JSP Support Comment Styles

JSPs support three comment styles: JSP comments, XHTML comments and **scripting**-language comments. **JSP comments** are delimited by <%-- and --%>. These can be placed throughout a JSP, but not inside scriptlets. XHTML comments are delimited with <!-- and -->. These, too, can be placed throughout a JSP, but not inside scriptlets. Scripting language comments are currently Java comments, because Java currently is the only JSP scripting language. Scriptlets can use Java's end-of-line comments (//) and traditional comments (delimited by /* and */). JSP comments and scripting-language comments are ignored and do not appear in the response to a client. When clients view the source code of a JSP response, they will see only the XHTML comments in the source code. The different comment styles are useful for separating comments that the user should be able to see from those that document logic processed on the server.

Exercises

I. Fill in the blanks with the information given in the text.

1. It is difficult for people who are not Java programmers to implement, maintain and extend a Web application that consists of primarily of servlets. The solution to this problem is _____——an extension of servlet technology that separates the presentation from the business logic.

2. A JavaBean is a reusable component that follows certain conventions for _____ that are discussed in the JavaBeans specification, which is available at java.sun.com/products/ javabeans/glasgow/index.html.

3. The classes and interfaces that are specific to JSP programming are located in packages _____ and _____.

4. The JSP scripting components include _____, _____, _____, _____ and escape sequences.

5. JSPs support 3 comment styles: _____, _____, _____.

Ⅱ. **Translate the following passages from English into Chinese.**

The JSP specification is the product of industry-wide collaboration with industry leaders in the enterprise software and tools markets, led by Sun Microsystems. Sun has made the JSP specification freely available to the development community, with the goal that every web server and application server will support the JSP interface. JSP pages share the "Write Once, Run AnywhereTM" characteristics of Java technology. JSP technology is a key component in the Java 2 Platform, Enterprise Edition, Sun's highly scalable architecture for enterprise applications.

Grammar 3 科技英语的写作特点(Ⅰ)

写作是运用语言技巧来表达清楚其完整的思想。科技英语因为其应用目的不同，而体现出其于众不同的特点。由于科技英语文体的主要功能是叙述科技事实、记录科技知识和描述科技新发现，因此，科技英语语言特征是结构严谨，客观准确。专业英语的客观性指其所讨论的内容是客观的，专业英语的准确性指意思表达要求准确，这是专业英语最基本的要求。所以，我们必须要了解科技英语的写作特点，这对我们理解和翻译文章是十分有利的。

以主题句为直线发展的文体特点

主题句就是能够说明文章或者段落主要思想的句子，其特点如下。

(1) 其他内容常常是对主题句的补充和解释。

(2) 根据英语的表达习惯，主题句常常出现在句子的开头，但是有时候也出现在文章的末尾。

例如：

In contrast to a stack in which both insertions and deletions are performed at the same end, a queue is a list in which all insertions are performed at one end while all deletions are made at the other. We have already met this structure in relation to waiting lines, where we recognized it as being a first-in, first-out (FIFO) storage system. Actually, the concept of a queue is inherent in any system in which objects are served in the same order in which they arrive.

栈的插入与删除操作都是在表的相同端进行的。而与此不同，队列是插入和删除操作分别在两端进行的表。我们已经遇到过这种与等待队列相关的结构，在这种情况中，我们把它当作一种先进先出的存储系统。实际上，在那些对象输入与输出顺序相同的系统中，队列的概念是与生俱来的。队列的结尾从等待队列的关联中得到名字。

其中，"In contrast to a stack in which both insertions and deletions are performed at the same end, a queue is a list in which all insertions are performed at one end while all deletions are made at the other."是主题句,在段落推进中,作者对队列和栈的实际情况进行了描述。

实际上,要想快速地掌握一段科技英语的大致内容,应该具备抓住重点的能力,在抓住重点后,对其他内容的理解就很容易了。

叙述内容逐层递进的文体特点

在科技英语中,常常是用大量的短句令描述的内容逐渐递进,所以读者在领略其主要思想内容的时候,应该从头至后,依次领会。

例如:

The ends of a queue get their names from this waiting-line relationship. The end at which entries are removed is called the head (or sometimes the front) of the queue just as we say that the next person to be served in a cafeteria is at the head (or front) of the line. Similarly, the end of the queue at which new entries are added is called the tail (or rear).

结尾处,也就是条目被移出队列的地方,被称为队列的队首(有时候也称为队前),这就好像我们在快餐厅中以下一个将点餐的顾客为一队的队首一样。同样,队列的尾部,也就是条目被添加的地方,被称为队尾(或者队后)。

例如:

We can implement a queue in a computer's memory within a block of contiguous cells in a way similar to our storage of a stack. Since we need to perform operations at both ends of the structure, we set aside two memory cells to use as pointers instead of just one, as we did for a stack. One of these pointers, called the head pointers keeps track of the head of the queue; the other, called the tail pointer, keeps track of the tail.

我们可以像存储栈那样通过连续单元组成的存储块在计算机主存储器中实现队列。因为我们需要在此结构的两端都进行操作,我们分配出两个存储单元用来作为指针,而非栈中那样仅仅需要一个单元来存储指针。其中的一个指针被称为头指针,用来保持队列头的轨迹;另一个指针被称为尾指针,用来保持队尾的轨迹。

 参考译文

Section A 编程语言

简介

在计算机科学中,编程语言是一种人工语言,用于编写可以由计算机负责操行的指令序列(即计算机程序)。 类似于自然语言,如英语、编程语言有词汇、语法以及句法。然而,自然语言并不适用于计算机编程,因为他们是模糊的,即他们的词汇和语法结构可能有多种解释方式。用于计算机编程的语言必须只有简单的逻辑结构,并且其语法、拼写和标点的规则必须是精确的。

编程语言在复杂度和功能性上有很大的不同。一些编程语言为解决一个特殊种类的计算问题或在计算机系统一个特殊模型使用。例如,编程语言 FORTRAN 和 COBOL 用于解决某些类型的编程问题,其中,FORTRAN 语言用于科学计算,而 COBOL 语言用于解决一般商业应用问题。虽然这些语言被设计成解决一定类型的计算问题,但它们是非常灵活的,即它们可以被用于许多类型的计算机。其他语言,如机器语言被用于计算机系统具体模型,甚至由一台具体计算机在某些研究应用领域内使用。最常用的编程语言,像C、Pascal、BASIC语言，是非常灵活的，可以有效地解决各种类型的计算问题。

编程语言的类型

编程语言可以分为低级语言和高级语言。低级语言，或者说机器语言，是最接近计算机的语言。机器语言基于计算机制造商和计算机模型的不同而有所区别。高级语言在可以由计算机理解和处理之前必须首先翻译成机器语言的编程语言。高级语言的例子有C、C++、Pascal和Fortran。汇编语言是非常接近机器语言的中间语言，没有其他高级语言的复杂语法，但仍然需要翻译成机器语言。

1. 机器语言

在机器语言中，指令是由一些被称为比特的0和1序列组成，它们能够被计算机直接理解。在机器语言中，通常一条指令要告诉计算机4件事情。

1）到内存(RAM)的什么地方去取一个或两个数据，或者一个简单的数据块。
2）一个简单的数据操作，如将两个数相加。
3）这个简单操作的结果放到内存的什么位置。
4）到哪里去找要执行的下一个指令。虽然计算机最终用机器语言读取了所有可执行程序，但这并不是机器语言编程的全部。编程直接使用机器语言实际上是极其困难的，因为指令是由0、1序列组成。一个典型的机器语言指令的例子是10010 1100 1011，它的含义是将寄存器A的内容和寄存器B的内容相加。

2. 高级语言

高级语言直接运用来自人类语言中的单词和句法的一些精炼语句。它们比汇编或机器语言更类似自然语言，因此更加容易编写复杂的程序。这些编程语言允许快速地开发更大和更加复杂的程序。然而，高级语言必须由另一个被称为编译器的程序翻译成机器语言后，才能被计算机理解。为此，高级语言编写的程序要比汇编语言编写的程序可能会花费更多的时间执行，并使用更多的内存。

3. 汇编语言

使用汇编语言来编程会使机器语言的程序更加容易编写。在汇编语言中，每个语句大致对应一个机器语言的指令。一个汇编语言的语句是由一个容易记忆的命令组成。在一个汇编语言语句中，将寄存器A的内容和寄存器B的内容相加可以写成 ADD B,A。汇编语言与机器语言具有某些共同特点。例如，在汇编和机器语言中，操作具体"位"是可以的。但程序员如果想要使运行程序的时间最少，可以使用汇编语言，因为将汇编语言翻译成机器语言是相对简单的。当计算机的某一零件必须直接被控制时，可以使用汇编语言。

高级语言的分类

高级语言一般被分为面向过程的、函数式的、面向对象的或者逻辑语言。当前最常见的高级语言是面向过程的语言。在这类语言中，一个或多个语句块组成一个程序模块或过程，用于执行一些完整的功能，并被赋予一个名字"过程A"。如果在程序的其他地方需要同样的操作序列，可以用一个简单的语句指向该过程。实际上，一个过程就是一个小程序。一个大的程序可以由一些完成不同任务的过程来组成。过程化语言能够让程序更短小，而且容易被计算机理解，但是需要程序员能够设计出足够的过程用于不同的情况。

函数式语言像数学函数一样对待过程，允许过程像程序的其他数据一样被处理。当程序仅通过给定的值运行一次时，用户必须以更高和更加严谨的水平指定和改变程序的构造方法。这种简化编程通过减少与语句确切的顺序有关的需要来实现，因为一个变量不必每次用于一个程序语句就重新声明。许多函数式语言的编程想法已经成为许多现代的过程式语言的关键部分。

面向对象语言是函数式语言的派生。在面向对象语言中，用于编写程序的代码和被程序处理的数据组成了被称为对象的单元。对象进而组成类，类描述了对象必须具有的属性。一个类的简单例子是Book类。

在这个类中，对象可以是小说或短故事。对象也可以包含和它们有联系的某些被称为方法的函数。计算机通过调用对象的一个方法访问对象。这个方法操纵对象中的数据并返回一个返回值给计算机。对象的类进而组成分层，在分层中，一个类的对象可以继承另一个类的方法。这种在面向对象中提供的结构在复杂的编程任务中很有用。

逻辑语言采用逻辑作为其数学基础。一个逻辑程序是由一些事实和 if-then 规则组成，它们指定一系列事实是怎么从其他的事实演绎出来的。例如：

如果语句 X 为真，则语句 Y 为假。

在这样的程序中，一个输入语句可能由程序中其他的语句演绎出来的。许多人工智能程序就是由这样的逻辑语言组成的。

程序语言的历史

编程语言的产生几乎可以追溯到数字计算机的发明，即 20 世纪 40 年代。第一个汇编语言出现在商业计算机产生的 20 世纪 50 年代末期。第一个过程语言在 20 世纪 50 年代末 60 年代初被开发：FORTRAN，由 John Backus 创造，然后是 COBOL，由 Grace Hopper 创造。第一个函数式语言是 LISP，由 John McCarthy 于 20 世纪 50 年代末编写。尽管这 3 种语言已被更新，但今天仍然被广泛使用。

在 20 世纪 60 年代末，第一个面向对象的语言 Simula 诞生了。逻辑语言在人工智能软件流行的 70 年代中期非常著名。PROGLOG 语言，一种用于人工智能软件编程的语言就是在 70 年代诞生的。在此期间，一些过程化语言如 ALGOL、BASIC、Pascal、C 和 Ada 语言相继也出现了。Smalltalk 语言是一个非常有影响力的面向对象的语言，它使面向对象语言和过程语言融合在一起，如 C++或较近的 Java 语言。尽管纯逻辑语言已经不够流行，但它的变形已经成为现代关系数据库语言非常重要的一种形式，如 SQL。

Section B　Java 语言

为什么 Java 如此热门？

毫无争议，Java 语言对于 Internet 是自从万维网出现以来最扣人心弦的事情。因为它几乎满足我们需要的一切。利用 Java 语言，程序员能够实现每个人都大声呼吁的所谓真实的互动。

首先，Java 是一种编程语言。这种语言用于形成计算机遵守的一套指令。这组指令被叫做程序、应用、执行体或者 applet 小程序。Java 也可以用于建立独立程序，像其他编程语言一样被称应用程序。关于 Java 语言中的 applet 是最具有创新性的成果。

Java applets 增加了万维网的生命力。这里的"生命力"指的是利用 Java 语言能够增加动画、本地数据查询，以及各种各样的功能和特征，而这些如果没有 Java 运行环境根本是不可能实现的。

为了浏览 Web 网站，你需要一个浏览器。浏览器是一个运行在 Internet 并且解释 HTML 代码的应用程序。浏览器分为支持图形的和不支持图形的。但我们仅对支持图形的浏览器感兴趣（即能够在你的屏幕上显示图片的浏览器）。现在有许多版本的浏览器可以使用，但目前 Java 仅支持两种浏览器：Netscape 2.0 和 HotJava。

Java 语言是什么？

人们设计 Java 语言是希望它能够解决在现代编程中所遇到的一些问题。正像人们所说的那样，Java 语言建立的核心原则是要为一些消费电器形成软件。像其他的设备一样，这种语言必须是简洁的、可靠的、可移植的、分布的、实时的和嵌入式的。Sun 微系统公司对 Java 的正式定义是：

Java 是一种具有简单、面向对象的、分布式、解释型、稳健、安全、结构中立、可移植的、高性能的、多线程的和动态执行等特征的语言。

Java 语言很简单

即使 Java 语言的开发者认为 C++ 不是很适合他们最初的目的，他们还是尽可能将 Java 语言设计成与 C++ 语言最接近。之所以这么做，是为了让系统更熟悉，更加容易理解，并且缩短对一门新的语言的学习时间。Java 语言最新吸引人的原因之一在于，如果你是一个程序员，你就能知道怎么使用它。因为如今，90%的程序员使用 C 语言，且几乎所有的程序员使用的面向对象语言都是 C++。

Java 语言的设计者的另外一个目标是要去除类的多重继承、操作符重载、数据类型的强制转换，以及许多很难理解和很少使用的并且容易混淆的 C++ 中的一些特征。同时也去除了头文件、预处理、指针运算、结构体、共用体以及多维数组。设计者有选择性地保留一些容易开发、实现、维护软件的特征，而删除那些使开发进程变慢的那些特征。例如，即使操作符重载被去除了，但他们保留了方法重载。

另外一个必须让 C 和 C++ 程序员面对的问题是存储管理，即内存的分配和回收问题。通常，一个 C 程序员必须仔细地察看其程序到底用了多少内存空间。当一块内存不再使用了，程序员必须保证他的程序能够释放它们，以备再次利用。这件事情做起来更困难，尤其在一个大型程序中，这也是内存泄漏和错误的主要原因。然而当使用 Java 语言编程时，你就不必担心这些问题了。

Java 系统中嵌入一个垃圾搜集机制。这个垃圾搜集机制能够简化 Java 编程，但是是以增加系统的复杂性为代价的。因为 Java 有自动的垃圾搜集机制，它不仅使编程更加容易，也能够大量地减少错误并排除内存管理上的一些困难。

Java 语言是很小巧的

Java 语言的一个特征是它的小巧，这一点在 Sun 微系统公司的定义中被忽略了或没有给出。作为简单性的一个方面，Java 语言是非常小巧。要知道 Java 语言的原始目的之一就是方便地构造单机上运行的软件。

基本的解释器和类支持环境需要大约 40KB 的 RAM 空间；若增加一个基本的标准库和线程支撑系统（必要的一个自包含的微内核）也只需增加 175KB 的空间。总共约 215KB 的内存空间需求相对其他的高级语言和支撑环境是较小的。

Java 语言是面向对象型的

Java 语言是一个面向对象的语言。也就是说它属于面向对象语言家族的一分子，而面向对象语言的着眼点主要在于将数据定义为对象和应用于对象的方法。正像我们说过的那样，Java 与 C++语言在原理上有很多的共性，他们仅在风格和结构上有所区别。

为了使 Java 语言简单化，并不是每件东西都被定义为一个对象。布尔类型、数值类型及其他的简单类型就没有被定义为对象，但是 Java 语言对于所有简单类型都有包装对象。包装对象允许所有简单类型像类一样执行。

Java 语言是分布的

Java 语言作为一个客户机/服务器(C/S)模式应用，其典型特征就是有能力完成信息和数据处理的共享等多种工作负荷。术语"分布式"描述的是系统对象之间的关系，不管这些对象是远程的还是本地系统的。Java 语言的 applets 程序和应用程序的最大好处在于它们能够通过 URLS 打开和进入 Web 页的对象，而且和进入本地文件系统一样容易。

严格地说，Java 语言既是解释型的，又是编译型的。实际上，只有大约 20%的 Java 代码被浏览器解释，但这是关键的 20%。Java 语言的安全性及能够跨平台性源于其最后的编译步骤是本地处理的。

Java 语言是稳健的

"稳健"一词在计算机领域指一种语言是否可靠。一种语言越稳健，用它编写的程序就越少发生"崩溃"以及越少可能产生错误。稳健型的语言（像 Java 或 C++）允许编译时进行检查，这意味着许多错误能够及早发现。"稳健型"意思是说绝大多数数据类型检查不是在运行期间执行的，而是在编译时进行的。

Java 语言很安全的

Java 语言的安全性仍旧是需要证明的事情。在不知情的情况下从另外一个站点下载一些可执行的程序到你的机器上是许多计算机和网络专家不能接受的。这是因为一个简单的事实：病毒有可能就在那里，没有人想让他们的机器从网络上下载病毒。

Java 语言的一些其他特征，如稳健性以及 Java 的解释型和编译型都能够增加 Java 语言的安全性。

Java 语言是结构中立的

Java 语言的设计小组非常关注的事情是，如果 Java 语言要支持网络应用，它必须要支持那些拥有不同 CPU 和操作系统的各种机器系统。一个 Java 的应用程序能够在网络或 Internet 上的任何地方执行，因为编译器会产生一个与体系结构无关的对象文件格式。这个编译后的代码可以在许多处理器上执行，假设处理器正在运行 Java 智能浏览器。

Java 是可移植的

Java 语言与体系结构的无关性使得从一个平台到另一个平台的接口的概念显得有点多余。但是除了平台独立性之外，Java 语言中数据类型的使用标准去除了 C 和 C++ 中的"执行依赖"问题。

Java 语言是高性能的

Java 语言的高性能并不能表现在"比 C++ 语言运行的更快"，事实上，它们几乎具有同样的执行速度。Sun 微系统公司在 10 个 SPARCStation 机器上执行的基准测试中，字节码被转换成机器代码和从标准 C 或 C++ 转换成机器码的时间几乎难以区分。当然，这没有考虑到编译时的运行时间。

字节码的解释执行对于大多数在一定情况下要求高性能的普通任务来说是非常不错的。在这样的例子中，字节码可能不是固定的方式。从字节码产生机器码的过程是非常简单的，并且产生的是非常好的、合理的代码。

Java 语言是多线程的

人类的大脑就是多线程的，能同时处理成千上万个任务。当你打电话的同时能够听收音机，同时往杯子中倒入橘汁，同时还可以把电话夹在肩膀和耳边，还可以思考你的周末计划并注意到还有盘子需要清洗等。

那么对于 Java 的使用者来说，多线程意味着它们在一个任务开始之前，不必等待另一个任务完成。例如，如果你在玩一个地狱冒险游戏时，一个线程能够处理你的战斗任务相关的数学问题，而同时另一个线程关心的却是图形问题。与单线程相比，多线程能够避免许多时间滞后问题，在一台个人计算机上，它意味着你将看到很少的鼠标呈沙漏或者腕表形状，这些形状就是我们所知道的那样："不要催我"。

Section C   JSP

简介

你可能已经注意到在我们的 servlets 中的大多数代码产生的输出包括 HTML 元素，这些元素是客户端的反馈信息，而仅有一小部分代码是处理逻辑事务的。从 servlets 产生反馈信息需要 Web 开发者熟悉 Java 语言。然而，许多 Web 程序开发人员，如 Web 站点开发人员，并不了解 Java 语言。对于那些不是 Java 程序员的开发者来说，执行、维护和扩展一个主要由 servlets 组成的 Web 应用程序是一件困难的事情。这个问题的解决方法是采用 JSP 来扩展 servlets 技术，从而将它同逻辑事务分开。这让 Java 程序员和 Web 网站的设计人员的工作重点分别放在设计 Java 代码和设计 Web 网页上。

JSP 技术简化了动态网页内容的传送。它们能够使 Web 应用程序员通过重新利用预定义的组件和使用服务器方脚本的交互来制作动态的网页。JSP 程序员可以使用那些特殊的封装了复杂、动态的功能的被称做 JavaBeans 的组件和标记库。JavaBeans 是一个能够重复利用的组件，这些组件包含了某些类设计的例程，这些将在 JavaBeans 的规范说明中讨论，而规范说明可以从 java.sun.com/products/ javabeans/glasgow/index.html 网页中获取。常用的标记库是 JSP 的一个重要的部分，它允许 Java 开发人员在访问数据库时将复杂的代码隐藏起来，而将其他有用的动态网页的服务放到标记库中。Web 网站用这些常用的标记库可以像其他的 Web 元素一样获得被标签隐藏起来的更为复杂的功能。这样，那些不熟悉 Java 语言的 Web 网页设计人员就能够设计出具有动态效果和处理能力的 Web 网页了。

那些具体的 JSP 页面编程的类和接口被放到 javax.servlet.jsp 和 javax.servlet.jsp.tagext 两个包里面。本节通过介绍 JSP 的基本原理，讨论了关于 JSP 的许多类和接口。想了解 JSP 的细节，可以参看 JSP 2.0 规范说明，读者可以从 java.sun.com/products/jsp/download.html 下载。

JSP 的 4 个关键组件

JSP 有 4 个非常关键的组件，即向导元素、执行元素、脚本元素和标签库。向导元素对于 JSP 容器来说就是信息，能够使编程者制定具体的页面设置，包括从其他资源获取的内容以及指定的在 JSP 中使用的常用标签库。执行元素在那些程序员能够嵌入 JSP 中的预定义标签中封装了一些功能。执行元素的执行经常基于信息作为一个特殊客户请求的一部分发送给服务器。它们也能在 JSP 脚本语言片断中创建 Java 的对象。脚本元素能够使程序员在一个 JSP 中（也可能是其他的 Web 应用组件）插入 Java 代码以执行请求处理。Scriptlets 是一种脚本元素，其中包含那些用来描述回应用户请求的被执行的元素。标签库作为标签扩展机制的一部分，能够使程序员去创建常用的标签。那样的标签能够使 Web 设计者在没有 Java 语言知识的前提下操纵 JSP 的内容。

从某方面看，JSP 看起来像标准的 XHTML 或 XML 文档。事实上，JSP 通常包括 XHTML 或 XML 标记。那样的标记即人们所知道的固定模板数据或文本。固定模板数据经常能够帮助一个程序员决定用 servlet 还是 JSP。当发送给客户端的大多数数据是固定模板数据，或有很少由 Java 代码产生的数据时，程序员往往要用 JSP；而当发送给客户端的数据只有很小部分内容是固定模板数据时，程序员往往用 servlets。实际上，一些 servlets 不产生内容，而是执行一个代表客户端的任务，然后引起其他的 servlets 或 JSP 产生一个回应。注意，在许多情况下，servlets 和 JSP 技术是能够互换的。与 servlets 相比，JSP 通常是作为一个 Web 服务器运行的。

当一个有效的 JSP 服务器接受第一个 JSP 请求时，JSP 容器将 JSP 翻译成一个 Java 的 servlet，用来处理对 JSP 的当前请求和将来的请求。JSP 中的逐字文本被翻译成 servlet 中的字符串，表示 JSP 被翻译了。任何在编译新的 servlet 时的错误都会导致翻译时发生错误。JSP 容器在方法 _jspService 插入一些用来执行 JSP 回应的 Java 的声明。 如果新的 servlet 适当地编译，JSP 容器会让方法 _jspService 来处理请求。在处理请求的过程中，JSP 可以直接回应或者唤起其他的 Web 应用组件去帮助完成。任何在处理请求时发生的错误就是众所周知的请求错误。

固有对象

固有对象在 JSP 的上下文中提供访问许多 servlet 的可能。固有对象有 4 个范围：应用程序、页面、请求、会话。JSP 容器拥有应用程序的对象。任何 JSP 都能操纵这些对象。页面的对象仅存在于定义它们的页面中。每个页面有自己的页面固有对象的实例。请求对象存在于请求的整个过程。例如，JSP 能够部分地处理一个请求，紧跟着一个 servlet 或另一个 JSP 进行后面的处理。当处理完客户端的请求后，请求对象就消失了，而会话对象存在于客户整个浏览过程中。

JSP 的脚本组件

作为发送到客户端以回应请求的 XHTML 文件的一部分，JSP 经常动态地产生内容。在这样的情况下，这个页面内容是静态的，但是如果某种条件下发生一个请求仅产生一个输出（如以发送一个请求的形式提供一些值）。JSP 程序员可以在 JSP 中以脚本形式插入 Java 代码或逻辑。

JSP 脚本组件包括脚本片断、注释、表达式、声明和换码序列。在这些组件中，以<%和%>形式出现的就是 scriptlet 代码段。它们包含 Java 在编译时有关容器存放在方法_jspService 中位置的声明。

JSP 的注释风格

JSP 支持 3 种注释的风格：JSP 注释、XHTML 注释与脚本语言注释。JSP 注释是通过<%-- 和 --%>括起来的，它们可以放在 JSP 程序的任何位置，但不能出现在 scriptlets 中；XHTML 注释是通过<!--和-->括起来的，也可以放在 JSP 程序的任何位置，但也不能出现在 scriptlets 中；而脚本语言注释就是目前的 Java 注释，因为 Java 当前是 JSP 中的唯一脚本语言。Scriptlets 可以采用 Java 的 end-of-line 注释形式(//)和传统注释形式(通过/*和*/括起来)。JSP 注释和脚本语言注释在对客户端进行回应时是不显示的。当客户端想要查看一个 JSP 回应的源代码时，他们也只能看到 XHTML 注释。不同的注释风格对于区别注释是有用的，用户通过它们能够看到那些在服务器上被处理的逻辑文档。

Chapter 4 Windows 7
(Window 7 操作系统)

Section A Features New to Windows 7

Windows 7 is the current **release** of Microsoft Windows, a series of operating systems produced by Microsoft for use on personal computers, including home and business desktops, laptops, netbooks, tablet PCs, and media center PCs. Windows 7 was released to manufacturing on July 22, 2009, and reached general retail availability worldwide on October 22, 2009, less than three years after the release of its predecessor, Windows Vista. Windows 7's server **counterpart**, Windows Server 2008 R2, was released at the same time.

Unlike Windows Vista, which introduced a large number of new features, Windows 7 was intended to be a more focused, incremental upgrade to the Windows line, with the goal of being compatible with applications and hardware with which Windows Vista was already compatible. Presentations given by Microsoft in 2008 focused on **multi-touch support**, a redesigned Windows shell with a new taskbar, referred to as the Super bar, a home networking system called Home Group, and performance improvements. Some standard applications that have been included with prior releases of Microsoft Windows, including Windows Calendar, Windows Mail, Windows Movie Maker, and Windows Photo Gallery, are not included in Windows 7; most are instead offered separately at no charge as part of the Windows Live Essentialssuite.

Windows 7 includes a number of new features, such as advances in touch and handwriting recognition, support for virtual hard disks, improved performance on multi-core processors, improved boot performance, DirectAccess, and **kernel** improvements. Windows 7 adds support for systems using multiple heterogeneous graphics cards from different vendors (Heterogeneous Multi-adapter), a new version of Windows Media Center, a Gadget for Windows Media Center, improved media

---

release [ri'li:s]
n. 释放，让渡，发行
vt. 释放，让与，准予发表，发射

counterpart ['kauntəpɑ:t;'kauntə,pɑ:t]
n. 职务相当的人，对应物，相似之物，副本

multi-touch support
多媒体触摸式支持

kernel ['kə:nl;kə:nəl]
n. 核心，仁，中心，精髓

features, the XPS **Essentials** Pack and Windows PowerShell being included, and a redesigned Calculator with multiline capabilities including Programmer and Statistics modes along with unit conversion for length, weight, temperature, and several others.

Many new items have been added to the Control Panel, including ClearType Text Tuner, Display Color Calibration Wizar, Gadgets, Recovery, Troubleshooting, Workspaces Center, Credential Manager, System Icons, and Display. Windows Security Center has been renamed to Windows Action Center (Windows Health Center and Windows Solution Center in earlier builds), which encompasses both security and **maintenance** of the computer. Ready Boost on 32-bit editions now supports up to 256 gigabytes of extra allocation. The default setting for User Account Control in Windows 7 has been criticized for allowing untrusted software to be launched with elevated privileges without a prompt by exploiting a trusted application. Microsoft's Windows kernel engineer Mark Russinovich acknowledged the problem, but noted that malware can also compromise a system when users agree to a prompt. Windows 7 also supports images in RAW image format through the addition of Windows Imaging Component——enabled image decoders, which enables raw image thumbnails, previewing and metadata display in Windows Explorer, plus full-size viewing and slideshows in Windows Photo Viewer and Windows Media Center.

The taskbar has seen the biggest visual changes, where the Quick Launch toolbar has been replaced with the ability to pin applications to the taskbar. Buttons for pinned applications are integrated with the task buttons. These buttons also enable the Jump Lists feature to allow easy access to common tasks. The revamped taskbar also allows the reordering of taskbar buttons. To the far right of the system clock is a small rectangular button that serves as the Show desktop icon. This button is part of the new feature in Windows 7 called Aero Peek. Hovering over this button makes all visible windows transparent for a quick look at the desktop. In touch-enabled displays such as touch screens, tablet PCs, etc., this button is slightly wider to **accommodate** being pressed with a finger. Clicking this button minimizes all windows, and clicking it a second time restores them. Additionally, there is a

Essentials
n. 要件，概要

maintenance ['meintinəns;meintənəns]
n. 维修，维护，保持，生活费用
n. 抚养费

accommodate [ə'kɔmədeit]
vt. 供给住宿，使适应，容纳，提供，顾及，调解
vi. 适应，调节

feature named Aero Snap, which automatically maximizes a window when it is dragged to the top of the screen. Dragging windows to the left/right edges of the screen allows users to snap documents or files on either side of the screen for comparison between windows, such that the windows vertically take up half the screen. When a user moves windows that were maximized using Aero Snap, the system restores their previous state automatically. This functionality is also accomplished with keyboard shortcuts. Unlike in Windows Vista, window borders and the taskbar do not turn **opaque** when a window is maximized with Windows Aero applied. Instead, they remain translucent.

For developers, Windows 7 includes a new networking **API**(application program interface) with support for building SOAP-based Web services in native code (as opposed to .NET-based WCF Web services), new features to shorten application install times, reduced UAC prompts, simplified development of installation packages, and improved globalization support through a new Extended **Linguistic** Services API. At WinHEC 2008 Microsoft announced that color depths of 30-bit and 48-bit would be supported in Windows 7 along with the wide color gamut scRGB (which for HDMI 1.3 can be converted and output as xvYCC). The video modes supported in Windows 7 are 16-bit sRGB, 24-bit sRGB, 30-bit sRGB, 30-bit with extended color gamut sRGB, and 48-bit scRGB. Microsoft has also implemented better support for solid-state drives, including the new TRIM command, and Windows 7 is able to identify a solid-state drive uniquely. Microsoft is planning to support USB 3.0 in a subsequent patch, support not being included in the initial release due to delays in the **finalization** of the standard.

Internet Spades, Internet Backgammon and Internet Checkers, which were removed from Windows Vista, were restored in Windows 7. Windows 7 includes Internet Explorer 8 and Windows Media Player 12. Users are also able to disable many more Windows components than was possible in Windows Vista. New additions to this list of components include Internet Explorer 8, Windows Media Player, Windows Media Center, Windows Search, and the Windows Gadget Platform. Windows 7 includes 13 additional sound schemes, titled Afternoon, Calligraphy, Characters, Cityscape, Delta, Festival, Garden, **Heritage**,

opaque [əu'peik]
adj. 不透明的，难懂的

API
abbr. Application Program Interface
应用程序接口

Linguistic [liŋ'gwistik]
adj. 语言的，语言学的

finalization
n. 结束
=finalisation(英)

heritage ['heritidʒ; 'herətidʒ]
n. 遗产，继承物

Landscape, Quirky, Raga, Savanna, and Sonata. A new version of Microsoft Virtual PC, newly renamed as Windows Virtual PC was made available for Windows 7 Professional, Enterprise, and Ultimate editions. It allows multiple Windows environments, including Windows XP Mode, to run on the same machine. Windows XP Mode runs Windows XP in a virtual machine and redirects displayed applications running in Windows XP to the Windows 7 desktop. Furthermore, Windows 7 supports the mounting of a virtual hard disk (VHD) as normal data storage, and the boot loader delivered with Windows 7 can boot the Windows system from a VHD; however, this ability is only available in the Enterprise and Ultimate editions. The Remote Desktop Protocol (RDP) of Windows 7 is also enhanced to support real-time multimedia application including video playback and 3D games, thus allowing use of DirectX 10 in remote desktop environments. The three application limit, previously present in the Windows Vista Starter Edition, has been removed from Windows 7. **Recommendations** for Windows 7 are to be on Windows Vista (Longhorn) before upgrading to any version of Windows 7, and to have 16GB on the hard drive.

recommendation
[ˌrekəmen'deiʃən]
n. 推荐，建议

Exercises

Ⅰ. **Reading materials.**

Bill Gates

William Henry "Bill" Gates III (born October 28, 1955) is an American business magnate, investor, philanthropist, and author. Gates is the former CEO and current chairman of Microsoft, the software company he founded with Paul Allen. He is consistently ranked among the world's wealthiest people and was the wealthiest overall from 1995 to 2009, excluding 2008, when he was ranked the third, in 2011 he was the wealthiest American and the second wealthiest person. During his career at Microsoft, Gates held the positions of CEO and chief software architect, and remains the largest individual shareholder, with 6.4 percent of the common stock. He has also authored or co-authored several books.

Gates is one of the best-known entrepreneurs of the personal computer revolution. Gates has been criticized for his business tactics, which have been considered anti-competitive, an opinion which has in some cases been upheld by the courts. In the later stages of his career, Gates has pursued a number of philanthropic endeavors, donating large amounts of money to various charitable organizations and scientific research programs through the Bill & Melinda Gates Foundation, established in 2000.

Gates stepped down as chief executive officer of Microsoft in January 2000. He remained as chairman and created the position of chief software architect. In June 2006, Gates announced that he would be transitioning from full-time work at Microsoft to part-time work, and full-time work at the Bill & Melinda Gates Foundation. He gradually transferred his duties to Ray Ozzie, chief software architect, and Craig Mundie, chief research and strategy officer. Gates' last full-time day at Microsoft was June 27, 2008. He remains at Microsoft as non-executive chairman.

Section B Removed Features

Certain capabilities and programs that were a part of Windows Vista are no longer present or have been changed, resulting in the removal of certain functionalities. These include the classic Start Menu user interface, some taskbar features, Windows Explorer features, Windows Media Player features, Windows **Ultimate** Extras and InkBall. Four applications bundled with Windows Vista —— Windows Photo Gallery, Windows Movie Maker, Windows Calendar and Windows Mail—— are not included with Windows 7, but applications with close functionality are instead available for free in a separate package called Windows Live Essentials which can be downloaded on the Microsoft **website**. Although Windows Ultimate Extras was removed, many of the extras can be installed separately. Most popular extras were Microsoft Texas Hold, Microsoft Tinker, and Windows DreamScene. Ink Ball may also be installed into Windows 7.

Originally, a version of Windows codenamed Blackcomb was planned as the successor to Windows XP (codename Whistler) and Windows Server 2003. Major features were planned for Blackcomb, including an emphasis on searching and querying data and an advanced storage system named WinFS to enable such scenarios. However, an interim, minor release, codenamed "Longhorn", was announced for 2003, delaying the development of Blackcomb. By the middle of 2003, however, Longhorn had acquired some of the features originally intended for Blackcomb. After three major viruses exploited flaws in Windows **operating systems** within a short time period in 2003, Microsoft changed its development priorities, putting some of Longhorn's major development work on hold while developing new service packs for Windows XP and Windows Server 2003. Development of Longhorn (Windows Vista) was also restarted, and thus delayed, in August 2004. A number of features were cut from Longhorn. Blackcomb was renamed Vienna in early 2006 and again renamed

ultimate ['ʌltimit;'ʌltəmit]
adj. 根本的，极限的，最后的，终极的
n. 终极，极品，根本

website ['web,sait, wəb,sait]
n. 网站

operating system
操作系统

Chapter 4 Windows 7

Windows 7 in 2007. In 2008, it was announced that Windows 7 would also be the official name of the operating system. There has been some confusion over naming the product Windows 7, while versioning it as 6.1 to indicate its **similar** build to Vista and increase compatibility with applications that only check major version numbers, similar to Windows 2000 and Windows XP both having 5.x version numbers.

The first external release to select Microsoft partners came in January 2008 with **Milestone** 1, Build 6519. At PDC 2008, Microsoft demonstrated Windows 7 with its reworked taskbar. Copies of Windows 7 Build 6801 were distributed at the end of the conference; however, the demonstrated taskbar was disabled in this build.

On December 27, 2008, the Windows 7 Beta was leaked onto the Internet via BitTorrent. According to a performance test by ZDNet, Windows 7 Beta beat both Windows XP and Vista in several key areas; including boot and shutdown time and working with files, such as loading documents. Other areas did not beat XP; including PC Pro benchmarks for typical office activities and video editing, which remain identical to Vista and slower than XP. On January 7, 2009, the 64-bit version of the Windows 7 Beta (Build 7000) was leaked onto the web, with some torrents being infected with a trojan. At CES 2009, Microsoft CEO Steve Ballmer announced the Windows 7 Beta, build 7000, had been made **available** for download to MSDN and TechNet subscribers in the format of an ISO image. The Beta was to be publicly released January 9, 2009, and Microsoft initially planned for the download to be made available to 2.5 million people on this date. However, access to the downloads was delayed because of high traffic. The download limit was also extended, initially until January 24, then again to February 10. People who did not complete downloading the beta had two extra days to complete the download. After February 12, unfinished downloads became unable to complete. Users could still obtain product keys from Microsoft to **activate** their copies of Windows 7 Beta, which expired on August 1, 2009.

The release candidate, build 7100, became available for MSDN and TechNet **subscribers** and Connect Program participants on April 30, 2009. On May 5, 2009 it became

similar ['similə, simələ]
adj. 类似的

milestone
['mailstəun, mail‚stəun]
n. 里程碑

available
[ə'veiləbl, ə'veiləbəl]
adj. 可利用的，可得到的，有空的，有效的

activate
['æktiveit, 'æktə‚veit]
v. 激活，使活动

subscriber [səb'skraibə]
n. 签署者，捐献者，订户

available to the general public, although it had also been leaked onto the Internet via BitTorrent. The release candidate was available in five languages and **expired** on June 1, 2010, with shutdowns every two hours starting March 1, 2010. Microsoft stated that Windows 7 would be released to the general public on October 22, 2009. Microsoft released Windows 7 to MSDN and Technet subscribers on August 6, 2009, at 10:00 a.m. PDT. Microsoft announced that Windows 7, along with Windows Server 2008 R2, was released to manufacturing on July 22, 2009. Windows 7 RTM is build 7600.16385.090713-1255, which was compiled on July 13, 2009, and was declared the final RTM build after passing all Microsoft's tests **internally**.

An estimated 1000 developers worked on Windows 7. These were broadly divided into "core operating system" and "Windows client experience", in turn organized into 25 teams of around 40 developers on average.

Bill Gates, in an interview with *Newsweek*, suggested that this version of Windows would be more "user-centric". Gates later said that Windows 7 would also focus on performance improvements. Steven Sinofsky later expanded on this point, explaining in the Engineering Windows 7 blog that the company was using a variety of new tracing tools to measure the performance of many areas of the operating system on an ongoing basis, to help locate inefficient code paths and to help prevent performance **regressions**.

Senior Vice President Bill Veghte stated that Windows Vista users migrating to Windows 7 would not find the kind of device compatibility issues they encountered migrating from Windows XP. Speaking about Windows 7 on October 16, 2008, Microsoft CEO Steve Ballmer confirmed compatibility between Windows Vista and Windows 7, indicating that Windows 7 would be a refined version of Windows Vista.

As with other Microsoft operating systems, Windows 7 is being studied by United States federal regulators who oversee the company's operations following the 2001 United States v. Microsoft **settlement**. According to status reports filed, the three-member panel began assessing prototypes of the new operating system in February 2008. Michael Gartenberg, an analyst at Jupiter Research said that, "Microsoft's challenge for

expire [iks'paiə, ik'spaiə]
vi. 终止，期满，失效，呼气，断气

internally [in'tə:nəli]
adv. 内部地，国内地

regression [ri'greʃən]
n. 复原，退步

settlement ['setlmənt,'setəlmənt]
n. 解决，结算，协议，安置，殖民，定居

Chapter 4 Windows 7

Windows 7 will be how can they continue to add features that consumers will want that also don't run afoul of regulators."

In order to comply with European antitrust regulations, Microsoft has proposed the use of a "ballot" screen, allowing users to download a competing **browser**, thus removing the need for a version of Windows completely without Internet Explorer, as **previously** planned. In response to criticism involving Windows 7 E and concerns from manufacturers about possible consumer confusion if a version of Windows 7 with Internet Explorer were shipped later after one without Internet Explorer, Microsoft announced that it would scrap the separate version for Europe and ship the standard upgrade and full packages worldwide.

As with the previous version of Windows, an N version, which does not come with Windows Media Player, has been released in Europe, but only for sale directly from Microsoft sales websites and selected others.

browser ['brauzə]
n. [计]浏览器，浏览(书本等)的人，草食动物
previously ['priːvjuːslɪ]
adv. 先前，在此之前

Exercises

Ⅰ. Reading materials.

Microsoft

Microsoft Corporation (NASDAQ: MSFT) is an American multinational corporation headquartered in Redmond, Washington, United States that develops, manufactures, licenses, and supports a wide range of products and services predominantly related to computing through its various product divisions. Established on April 4, 1975 to develop and sell BASIC interpreters for the Altair 8800, Microsoft rose to dominate the home computer operating system market with MS-DOS in the mid-1980s, followed by the Microsoft Windows line of operating systems.

Microsoft would also come to dominate the office suite market with Microsoft Office. The company has diversified in recent years into the video game industry with the Xbox and its successor, the Xbox 360 as well as into the consumer electronics and digital services market with Zune, MSN and the Windows Phone OS. The ensuing rise of stock in the company's 1986 initial public offering (IPO) made an estimated three billionaires and 12,000 millionaires from Microsoft employees (Forbes 400 list revealed that in March 2011 both Jon Shipley and Nathan Myhrvold lost their billionaire status). In May 2011, Microsoft Corporation acquired Skype Communications for $8.5 billion.

Primarily in the 1990s, critics contend Microsoft used monopolistic business practices and anti-competitive strategies including refusal to deal and tying, put unreasonable restrictions in the use of its software, and used misrepresentative marketing tactics; both the U.S. Department of Justice and European Commission found the company in violation of antitrust laws. Known for its interviewing process with obscure questions, various studies and ratings were generally favorable to Microsoft's diversity within the company as well as its overall environmental impact with the exception of the electronics portion of the business.

Section C   Details of Windows 7

In July 2009, in only eight hours, pre-orders of Windows 7 at amazon.com.uk **surpassed** the demand which Windows Vista had had in its first 17 weeks. It became the highest-grossing pre-order in Amazon's history, surpassing sales of the previous record holder, the seventh Harry Potter book. After 36 hours, 64-bit versions of Windows 7 Professional and Ultimate editions sold out in Japan. Two weeks after its release its market share had surpassed that of Snow Leopard, released two months previously as the most recent update to Apple's Mac OS X operating system. According to Net Applications, Windows 7 reached a 4% market share in less than three weeks. (**In comparison**, it took Windows Vista seven months to reach the same mark).

On March 4, 2010, Microsoft announced that it had sold more than 90 million Windows 7 licenses. By April 23, 2010, Windows 7 had sold more than 100 million copies in six months, which made it Microsoft's fastest-selling operating-system. As of June 23, 2010, Windows 7 has sold 150 million copies which made it the fastest selling operating system in history with seven copies sold every second. Based on worldwide data taken during June 2010 from Windows Update 46% of Windows 7 PCs run the 64-bit edition of Windows 7. According to Stephen Baker of the NPD Group during April 2010 in the United States 77% of PCs sold at retail were pre-installed with the 64-bit edition of Windows 7. As of July 22, 2010, Windows 7 had sold 175 million copies. On October 21, 2010, Microsoft announced that more than 240 million copies of Windows 7 had been sold. Three months later, on January 27, 2011, Microsoft announced total sales of 300 million copies of Windows 7. On July 12, 2011, the sales **figure** was refined to over 400 million end-user licenses and business installations. As of January 19, 2012, over 525 million copies have been sold.

Reviews of Windows 7 have been mostly positive, noting the increased usability and functionality when compared to its predecessor, Windows Vista. CNET gave Windows 7 Home Premium a rating of 4.5 out of 5 stars, stating that it "is more than what Vista should have been, [and] it's where Microsoft needed to go". *PC Magazine* rated it a 4 out of 5 saying that Windows 7 is a "big improvement" over Windows Vista, with fewer compatibility problems, a retooled taskbar, simpler home networking and faster start-up. Maximum PC gave Windows 7 a rating

surpass [sə'pɑ:s]
vt. 超越，胜过

In comparison
adj. 比较起来(比较地)

figure ['figə,'figjə]
n. 图形，数字，外形，体型，形状，人物，塑像，图表，(冰上表演动作的)花样
v. 是重要部分，认为，演算，领会到

of 9 out of 10 and called Windows 7 a "massive leap forward" in usability and security, and praised the new Taskbar as "worth the price of admission alone". *PC World* called Windows 7 a "worthy successor" to Windows XP and said that speed benchmarks showed Windows 7 to be slightly faster than Windows Vista. PC World also named Windows 7 one of the best products of the year. In its review of Windows 7, Engadget said that Microsoft had taken a "strong step forward" with Windows 7 and reported that speed is one of Windows 7's major selling points——particularly for the netbook sets. LAPTOP Magazine gave Windows 7 a rating of 4 out of 5 stars and said that Windows 7 makes computing more **intuitive**, offered better overall performance including a "modest to dramatic" increase in battery life on laptop computers. Techradar gave it a 5 star rating calling it the best version of Windows yet. The New York Times, USA Today, The Wall Street Journal, and The Telegraph also gave Windows 7 **favorable** reviews.

Some Vista Ultimate users have expressed concerns over Windows 7 pricing and upgrade options. Windows Vista Ultimate users wanting to upgrade from Windows Vista to Windows 7 must either pay $219.99 to upgrade to Windows 7 Ultimate or perform a clean install, which requires them to reinstall all of their programs.

Windows 7 is available in six different editions, of which the Home Premium, Professional, and Ultimate editions are available for retail sale to consumers in most countries. The other editions are not available in retail. The Starter edition is only available preinstalled by OEMs on new PCs, the Enterprise edition only by volume licensing, and Home Basic only to certain developing countries' markets. Each edition of Windows 7 includes all of the capabilities and features of the edition below it. All editions support the IA-32 processor architecture and all editions except Starter support (x86-64) processor architecture. The installation media is the same for all the consumer editions of Windows 7 that have the same processor architecture, with the license determining the features that are activated, and license upgrades permitting the subsequent unlocking of features without re-installation of the operating system. This is the first time Microsoft has **distributed** 2 DVDs (1 DVD for IA-32 processor architecture, the other DVD for x86-64 processor architecture) for each edition of Windows 7 (Except for Starter and Home Basic; some OEM copies have only DVD for IA-32 **architecture**; the installation DVD of Windows 7 Home Basic 64-bit edition is not included but can be obtained from Microsoft.). Users who

intuitive
[in'tju:itiv,in'tjuitiv]
adj. 直觉的

Favorable
['feivərəbl,'feivərəbəl]
adj. 有利的，顺利的，良好的，赞同的

distribut [di'stribjut]
v. 分配，散发，分布

architecture
['ɑ:kitektʃə]
n. 建筑学，结构，一座建筑物，总称建筑物，建筑风格

wish to upgrade to an edition of Windows 7 with more features can then use Windows Anytime Upgradeto purchase the upgrade, and unlock the features of those editions. Some copies of Windows 7 have restrictions, in which it must be distributed, sold, or bought and activated in the **geographical** region specified in its front cover box.

Microsoft is offering a family pack of Windows 7 Home Premium (in select markets) that allows installation on up to three PCs. The "Family Pack" costs US$149.99 in the United States. On September 18, 2009, Microsoft said they were to offer temporary student discounts for Windows 7. The offer ran in the US and the United Kingdom, with similar schemes available in Canada, Australia, Korea, Mexico, France and India. Students with a valid .edu or .ac.uk email address could apply for either Windows 7 Home **Premium** or Professional, priced at $30 or £30.

Windows 7 is also currently available as an embedded version to developers (previously Windows Embedded 2011).

The different editions of Windows 7 have been designed and marketed toward people with different needs. Out of the different editions (Starter, Home Basic, Home Premium, Professional, Enterprise, and Ultimate), the Starter edition has been designed and marketed for lower cost notebooks, Home Basic for emerging markets, Home Premium for normal home users, Professional for businesses, Enterprise for larger businesses and corporations, and Ultimate for **enthusiasts**.

Microsoft has published the minimum specifications for a system to run Windows 7(Table 4-1). Requirements for the 32-bit version are similar to that of premium editions of Vista, but are higher for 64-bit versions. Microsoft has released an upgrade advisor that determines if a computer is compatible with Windows 7.

geographical [ˌdʒiə'græfikəl]
adj. 地理的，地理学的
=geographic

Premium ['priːmiəm]
n. 额外费用，奖金，保险费
n. [商]溢价
adj. 高价的，优质的

enthusiast [in'θjuːziæst]
n. 热心人，热衷者

Table 4-1 Minimum hardware requirements for Windows 7

Architecture	32-bit	64-bit
Processor	1 GHz IA-32 processor	1 GHz x86-64 processor
Memory (RAM)	1GB	2GB
Graphics card	DirectX 9 graphics processor with WDDM driver model 1.0 (Not absolutely necessary；only required for Aero)	
HDD free space	16GB of free disk space	20GB of free disk space
Optical drive	DVD-ROM drive (Only to install from DVD-ROM media)	

Additional requirements to use certain features:

Windows XP Mode (Professional, Ultimate and Enterprise): Requires an additional 1GB of RAM and additional 15GB of available hard disk space. The requirement for a **processor** capable of hardware virtualization has been lifted.

processor ['prəusesə]
n. 加工者，处理器

Windows Media Center (included in Home Premium, Professional, Ultimate and Enterprise), requires a TV tuner to receive and record TV.

Windows 7 Service Pack 1 (SP1) was announced on March 18, 2010. A beta was released on July 12, 2010. The final version was released to the public on February 9, 2011. At the time of release, it was not made **mandatory**. Technet has information on blocking it; or getting it via Windows Update, direct download, or by ordering the Windows 7 SP1 DVD. Microsoft confirmed that the service pack is to be on a much smaller scale than those released for previous versions of Windows, particularly Windows Vista.

mandatory ['mændətəri]
adj. 法定的，义务的，强制性的，受委托的
n. 受托管理者

Windows 7 Service Pack 1 adds support for Advanced Vector Extensions (AVX), a 256-bit instruction set extension for processors, and improves IKEv2 by adding additional identification fields such as E-mail ID to it. In addition, it adds support for Advanced Format 512e as well as additional Identity **Federation** Services. Windows 7 Service Pack 1 also resolves a bug related to HDMI audio and another related to printing XPS documents.

federation [,fedə'reiʃən]
n. 联邦，联合，联盟

Exercises

I. Talking about the following translation.

Future of Windows

Windows 8, the successor to Windows 7, is currently in development. Microsoft posted a blog entry in Dutch on October 22, 2010 hinting that Windows 8 would be released in roughly 1 year. Also, during the pre-Consumer Electronics Show keynote, Microsoft's CEO announced that Windows 8 will also run on ARM CPUs. This Windows version will also be more suitable for tablets and netbooks, featuring a more touch-friendly interface. Several new features will also be introduced, such as support for USB 3.0 and the ability to run Windows from USB devices (like USB Hard Disks or USB Flash drives) with Windows To Go.

Windows 8 是一个尚未发布的 Windows 版本，预计有六个版本，分别是 Starter、Home Basic、Home Premium、Professional、Enterprise、Ultimate，其中 Ultimate 拥有最多功能，而 Starter 则最少，并且减少或限制了许多功能，但是这个版本现在只在微软内部测试。微软发表会已经决定即将在 2012 年公开使用，现在只完成内建程式的 1/12，而这是 Windows 7 SP1 和 Windows Server 2008 SP1 的后续。

Grammar 4 科技英语的写作特点(Ⅱ)

以专业词汇来完成的文体特点

科技英语的词汇一般由派生词、复合词、混成词、缩略词和借用词组成,由这些词构成的专业词汇在文体中有自身的特点。

1. 普通词汇的专业化

普通词汇获得了固定的专业意义。
例如:

woofer	低音喇叭	tweeter	高音喇叭	flag	标志,状态
cache	高速缓存	semaphore	信号量	firewall	防火墙
mailbomb	邮件炸弹	scratch pad	高速缓存	fitfall	专用程序入口

在现代科技英语中借用了大量的公共英语词汇、日常生活中的常用词汇,而且以西方特有的幽默和结构讲述科技内容。这时,读者必须在努力扩大自己专业词汇的同时,也要掌握和丰富自己的生活词汇,并在阅读和翻译时正确采用适当的含义。

2. 大量借用相邻学科中的词汇

计算机专业词汇借用了大量的相邻学科中的词汇,如通信工程技术、机械自动化学科等,其含义无任何变化。
例如:

out-gate	输出门[电路]	autocontrol	自动控制
process	过程,处理	input	输入
DIMM (Dual Inline Memory Module)		双排直插式存储器组件	
DIP (Dual-In-Line Package)		双列直插式封装组件	

3. 计算机的新词语

例如:

AKA (also known as)	正如你所知道的
AOL (American on line)	美国在线网络
BTW (By the way)	顺便
CU (see you)	再见
FAQ (frequency asked questions)	常见问题
F2F (face to face)	面对面

这些新词语除了有计算机新技术后出现的词汇外,还包括随着网络的日新月异的发展,出现的新新人类的网络用语。

4. 计算机专业词汇中多用复合词

复合词是科技英语中另一大类词汇,其组成面广,通常分为复合名词、复合形容词、复合动词等。复合词通常以小横杠"-"连接单词构成,或者采用短语构成。有的复合词进一步发展,去掉了小横杠,并经过缩略成为另一类词类,即混成词。

例如:

-based	基于,以……为基础	-centric	以……为中心的
rate-based	基于速率的	client-centric	以客户为中心的
credit-based	基于信誉的	user-centric	以用户为中心的
file-based	基于文件的	host-centered	以主机为中心的
-oriented	面向……的	-free	自由的,无关的
object-oriented	面向对象的	lead-free	无线的
market-oriented	市场导向	jumper-free	无跳线的
process-oriented	面向进程的	paper-free	无纸的

5. 计算机中有大量的专业词组

例如:

time-consuming operation	耗时操作
videotape	录像带
popup	弹出
format effector	格式控制符
graph table	装入图形表命令
graphic data processing	图形数据处理

 参考译文

Section A Windows 7 的新功能

Windows 7是微软公司发布的可用于个人计算机的,最新版本的操作系统,在此之前,微软已经推出了一系列供个人计算机、家用和商务台式计算机、笔记本式计算机、上网本、平板计算机和多媒体中心计算机使用的操作系统。Windows 7于2009年7月22日正式发布,于2009年10月22日分发到零售商,和前一个版本Vista的发布时间相隔不到3年。Windows 7的Server服务器和Windows server 2008 R2也同期发布了。

和Vista不一样,Vista介绍了大量的新性能,Windows 7则更专注于功能集中,将升级提升到窗口级标准,目标就是为了兼容Vista已经兼容的应用软件和硬件。通过微软在2008年提供的展示可以看到,Windows 7致力于多点式触摸支持系统,重新设计的窗口、任务栏(即超级工具条)和家庭网络系统(即家庭群组),此外还有其他一些性能的改进。之前发布的Windows系统包含了一些标准的应用软件,如日历、邮件、电影制作和图片处理等,但是Windows 7不包含这些,这些应用软件大多数作为Windows在线组件的一部分无偿单独提供。

Windows 7包括了许多新性能,如先进的触摸和手写识别,支持虚拟硬盘,以及性能提升的多核处理器系统,在启动、直接访问和内核方面也提升了性能。Windows 7还增加了支持系统使用多异构显卡功能,以及提供了一个新版本的多媒体的中心和供这个新媒体中心使用的桌面小工具,增强了音讯功能,内建的XPS和Windows PowerShell以及一个包含了新模式且支援单位(长度、重量、温度等)转换的新版计算器。

控制面板也增加了不少新项目,如ClearType文件调整工具,显示器色彩校正精灵、桌面小工具、系

统还原、疑难解答、工作空间中心、认证管理员、系统图标和显示指示灯等。原有的 Windows 安全中心被更名为 Windows 操作中心(在早期建设中称为 Windows 健康中心或 Windows 解决问题中心)，它有保护计算机资讯安全的功能，可以由现在支持的 32 位版本到支持高达 256MB 的额外配置。在 Windows 7 默认设置中，用户账户控制设置为允许不信任软件加以授权提升到可信的软件。微软的内核工程师意识到了这个问题，但指出如果用户授权同意，恶意攻击软件也可以进入系统。Windows 7 也支持原始图像通过图形解码器处理后，在浏览器上以缩略图的形式预览，并可以实现全尺寸视窗和在幻灯及媒体中心中查看图片。

任务栏在外观上改变较大，原有的"快速启动"已经被"钉"在任务栏上的缩小程式图标取代，并和任务按钮集成。这些按钮也让列表具有跳转功能，可以方便地获取共同任务。改组后的任务栏也允许重新排列任务栏按钮。最右边的系统时钟是一个小矩形按钮，作为显示桌面图标。这个按钮是 Windows 7 新功能的一部分，叫做 Aero Peek。悬停在该按钮上的透明窗口能够快速查看桌面。在触摸式显示器中，如触摸屏幕、平板计算机等，这个按钮在手指按压时可以稍微扩大，单击按钮可以最小化所有窗口，再次单击可以一次恢复。此外，还有一个名为 Aero Snap 的管理单元功能，当其被拖动到屏幕顶端时能够自动最大化一个窗口。将窗口拖动至屏幕左/右侧，文件或文件夹可自动调整大小，便于用户进行窗口间的对比，这样垂直窗口可以占一半的显示单元。当用户移动这个使用 Aero Snap 最大化的窗口时，系统恢复之前的自动状态。这个功能也可以实现键盘的快捷方式。和 Windows Vista 不同，在 Aero 的改进部分，当一个窗口被最大化时，该窗口的边缘以及最下方的任务栏仍将保持半透明。

对开发者来说，Windows 7 提供了一套全新的网络 API(应用程序接口)。这些 API 支持使用机器语言创建基于 SOAP 的网络服务(而非基于.NET 的 WCF 网络服务)。此外，新的操作系统缩短了应用程式安装所需的时间，对 UAC 进行了改进，简化了安装时的安装过程，并对 API 增加了不同语言的支持。

Internet 黑桃王、Internet 双陆棋以及 Internet 跳棋等 3 个在 Windows Vista 中被取消的游戏在 Windows 7 中又重新出现了。Windows 7 内建了 Internet Explorer 8 和 Windows Media Player 12。和之前的操作系统相比较起来，Windows 7 允许使用者停用更多的 Windows 内建元件。Internet Explorer 8、Windows Media Player、Windows Media Center、Windows Search 以及 Windows Gadget Platform 等都可以被使用者停用。Windows 7 新增了 13 种声音主题，分别是 Afternoon(午后)、Calligraphy(笔迹)、Characters(特色)、Cityscape(城市景色)、Delta(三角洲)、Festival(庆典)、Garden(花园)、Heritage(遗迹)、Landscape(风景)、Quirky(反复无常)、Raga(拉迦音乐)、Savanna(大草原)和 Sonata(奏鸣曲)。在 Windows 7 Professional、Enterprise 和 Ultimate 3 个版本中会含有一个类似虚拟微机 Windows Virtual PC 的功能。这种虚拟微机能让使用者在运行 Windows 7 的同时执行不同的 Windows 环境，包括 Windows XP 模式。Windows XP 模式可让使用者在一台虚拟机上运行 Windows XP，并将其正在运行的程序显示于 Windows 7 的桌面上。Windows 7 允许使用者安装一个虚拟硬盘(VHD)作为一般的数据储存介质，并可利用 Windows 7 内建的引导装置从虚拟硬盘中读取并执行 Windows 系统，但是只有 Enterprise 和 Ultimate 版本才能使用这种性能。Windows 7 的远程桌面控制功能也有改善，它支持运行视频播放、3D 游戏等实时多媒体程序，同时 DirectX 10 也可以在远程桌面环境使用。另外，原本的 Windows Vista Starter 限制使用者只能同时运行 3 个程序，但在 Windows 7 Starter 中，这个限制已经取消。Windows Vista 或 Longhorn 在升级至任何 Windows 7 版本前，都会推荐 Windows 7，并建议硬盘驱动空间达到 16GB。

Section B WINDOWS 7 移除了的功能

通过删除一些功能，Windows Vista 中的一些功能或程序已经不复存在或被更改了，如传统开始菜单样式、任务栏功能、浏览器、媒体播放器、Windows Ultimate Extras 和墨球。Windows 7 去除了 Windows Vista 中捆绑的 4 个软件——Windows Photo Gallery、Windows Movie Maker、Windows Calendar 和 Windows Mail，以名为 Windows Live Essentials 的可选软件包方式单独提供，这可从微软网站下载。尽管 Windows Ultimate Extras 被删除，但很多 Windows 7 可以单独安装。流行的有 Microsoft Texas Hold、Microsoft Tinker 和

Windows DreamScene。墨盒也可以安装在 Windows 7 中。

最初，微软是把一个代号为 Blackcomb 的 Windows 版本作为 Windows XP 和 Windows Server 2003 的替代者。主要特点是把研发的重心放在搜索查询数据和以 WinFS 命名的先进的存储系统。然而，2003 年突然发布了以 "Longhorn" 命名的系统，推迟了 Blackcomb 的发展。截至 2003 年中期，Longhorn 已经获得了原本要在 Blackcomb 中应用的功能。之后因为在 2003 年很短时间里 Windows 操作系统经历了 3 次大的病毒入侵，微软改变发展的方向，把 Longhorn 的主要开发工作放在为 Windows XP 和 Windows Server 2003 开发新的服务包上。在 2004 年 8 月，重新启动 Longhorn(Windows Vista)的开发，而后又被延迟。Longhorn 也将部分功能舍掉。2006 年年初，Blackcom 被命名为 Vienna，2007 年被命名为 Windows 7。2008 年，Windows 7 也成为操作系统的正式名称。Windows 7 产品的命名出现了一些混乱，6.1 版本和 Vista 非常相似，增加了检查主要版本号码的兼容性，类似于 Windows 2000 和 Windows XP 都有 5.x 版本号。

2008 年 1 月，微软首次对外发布合作伙伴，这是第一个里程碑 Build 6519。在 2008 年 PDC，微软发布 Windows 7 重新设计的任务栏。会议结束后 Windows 7 的备份 Build 6801 发布。然而，显示任务栏并未被完善。

2008 年 12 月 27 日，Windows 7 Beta 版本通过 BitTorrent 被泄露到 Internet 上。根据 ZDNet 性能测试，Windows 7 Beta 在几个关键领域击败 Windows XP 和 Vista，包括脚本、开关机时间和工作文件，如加载文件；其他地方还没法超越 XP，包括典型办公活动基准和视频编辑等，这和 Vista 相近，但低于 XP。2009 年 1 月 7 日，64 位版本的 Windows 7 Beta 版本(Build 7000)被泄露，有些种子感染了木马。在 2009 年的消费电子展上，微软首席执行官史蒂夫·鲍尔默宣布 Windows 7 Beta，提供可供下载到 MSDN 和 TechNet 用户的一个标准化的图像格式。2009 年 1 月 9 日测试版被公开发布，微软最初计划在这个日期提供 250 万人下载。然而，因为高流量，下载被推迟。下载限制也增加了，最初到 1 月 24 日，然后再于 2 月 10 日。不能完整地下载测试版的用户可以再附加 2 天完成下载。2 月 12 日后，就无法完成未完成的下载。用户还可以从微软获得产品密钥激活 Windows 7 Beta 副本，在 2009 年 8 月 1 日过期。

在 2009 年 4 月 30 日，微软发布候选测试软件，用户在 MSDN 和 TechNet 上可以下载。2009 年 5 月 5 日它被公众开始使用，尽管它也通过 BT 被泄露到 Internet 上。测试软件有 5 种语言，在 2010 年 6 月 1 日终止，从 2010 年 3 月 1 日开始每 2 小时关闭一次。微软表示，在 2009 年 10 月 22 日 Windows 7 将面向所有公众发布。2009 年 8 月 6 日太平洋夏令时上午 10 点，微软发布了面向 MSDN 和 TechNet 用户的 Windows 7。微软宣布 2009 年 7 月 22 日发布 Windows 7 和 Windows Server 2008 R2。Windows 7 RTM 也在 2009 年 7 月 13 日编译完成，并宣布最终通过了微软内部的测试。

估计有 1000 多个研发工作人员致力于 Windows 7 的研发。这些大致分为"核心操作系统"和"Windows 客户体验"，又平均分于 40 开发商的 25 个小组。

比尔·盖茨曾在《新闻周刊》的采访中说，这个版本的 Windows 绝对是"以用户为核心的"。盖茨最后说 Windows 7 致力于性能的提升。史蒂芬后来在 Windows 7 工程博客上对这一点进行了扩充解释，强调公司使用了新的技术手段来评测操作系统在多个领域的表现，最终目的就是为了找出低效的代码和路径以及阻止性能低下。

高级副总裁比尔·维迪指出，Vista 用户转而使用 Windows 7，不会遇到像当初从 Windows XP 系统转到 Vista 那样兼容设备的问题困扰。在 2008 年 10 月 16 日谈到 Windows 7 时候，微软首席执行官史蒂夫·鲍尔默也证实了兼容性，指出 Windows 7 是 Vista 完美的兼容产品。

Windows 7 如同微软其他操作系统一样，也被美国的反垄断专家监察根据 2001 美国 v.微软协议监督公司运作。2008 年 2 月，3 人座谈小组开始对新运行系统原型进行评估。来自 Jupiter Reasearch 分析师迈克尔·加腾伯格表示："微软的挑战将是如何在没有抵触当地相关法规的情况下，把消费者想要的新功能添加到 Windows 7 上。"

为了遵守欧盟的反垄断法，微软公司推出了一个"选择投票"窗口，允许用户自行下载浏览器，以此改变了当初计划的 Windows 版本不附带浏览器的初衷，也用此回应了 Windows 7 机器生产商将机器和浏览器捆绑一起的质疑，微软公司也宣布，将取消单独版本为欧洲其他地区升级提供全服务包服务。

随着微软其他版本的发行，一个新的不包含媒体播放软件的 N 版本也开始在欧洲发行。但是这个版本仅仅在微软网站和指定零售商发售。

Section C Windows 7 的细节

2009 年 7 月，在仅仅 8 小时内，Windows 7 在亚马逊上预售数量就超过了 Vista 17 周的数量。它成为了在亚马逊网上预订数量最多的商品，超过了之前的销售记录保持者——第七版的《哈利波特》。36 小时后，Windows 7 的 64 位专业版和终极版在日本开始销售。两个星期后公布，它的市场份额超过了苹果的 Snow Leopard，该操作系统是苹果公司 2 个月前投放在市场的最新版本。根据网络调查显示，Windows 7 在短短 3 周内就达到了 4%的市场份额。(相比之下，Vista 则是投放到市场 7 个月后才达到。)

2010 年 3 月 4 日，微软宣布，它已售出超过 9000 万个 Windows 7 使用许可证。截至 2010 年 4 月 23 日，Windows 7 已经在 6 个月内销售超过 1 亿份，成为了微软史上销售最快的操作系统。截至 2010 年 6 月 23 日，该系统已经销售了超过 1 亿 5 千万份，也成就了每秒钟销售 7 套软件的销售记录。根据全球数据调查显示，46%运行 Windows 7 的计算机使用的是 64 位 Windows 7 系统。根据史蒂芬·贝克专案组在 2010 年 4 月的调查显示，美国个人计算机零售的 77%都安装了 64 位版本的 Windows 7。截至 2010 年 7 月 22 日，Windows 7 已经销售了 1.75 亿份，2010 年 10 月 21 日，超过了 2.4 亿份，在 3 个月后，即 2011 年 1 月 27 日，超过了 3 亿份。而到了 2011 年 7 月 12 日，其销售数字攀升到了 4 亿份。截至 2012 年 1 月 19 日，超过了 5.25 亿份。

回顾 Windows 7 的开发历程可以看到，和它的前身 Vista 相比，它主要是积极地增加功能的可用性。CNET 给 Windows 7 家庭版 4.5-5 级的积极评价，并指出 Windows 7 "在应该做什么方面强于 Vista，同时这也是微软发展的方向所在"。《个人电脑》评价它较之 Vista 有很大的改进，兼容性问题更少了，任务栏重组后更精彩，简化了家庭网络设置，提升了启动的速度。Maximum PC 杂志给 Windows 7 的评价级别是 9-10 级，评价它在可用性和安全性上有"巨大的飞跃"，并称赞新的任务栏"价值值得首肯"，PC Worldcalled 称赞 Windows 7 是 Windows XP 的"成功替代者"，并承认从速度基准角度看 Windows 7 略高于 Vista。《微电脑世界》也称 Windows 7 是一年中最好的产品，在评价过程中，Engadget 说微软通过 Windows 7 "迈出了强有力的一步"，并指出速度是 Windows 7 的主要卖点，特别在笔记本式计算机领域。LAPTOP 杂志给 Windows 7 的评价也是 4-5 级，指出了 Windows 7 让计算机更直观，并称赞其提供了更好的整体性能，包括增加了笔记本式计算机的电池使用寿命。Techradar 给它 5 级评价，称它是最好的 Windows 版本。纽约时报、美国今日杂志、华尔街和电报也给 Windows 7 好评。

一些 Vista 老用户很关注 Windows 7 的定价和升级价格。Vista 用户想升级到 Windows 7 版本必须支付 219.99 美元，但是必须要求他们重新安装所有的程序。

Windows 7 有六个不同版本，其中家庭高级版、专业版和最终版本的消费者可以在多数国家的零售商那里买到，其他版本则是不可以零售的，入门版只是提供给原始设备制造商预装在新计算机上，企业版则必须批量购买，或在某些发展中国家市场可以买到。每个版本的 Windows 7 包括不同的能力和特点，所有版本支持 IA-32 处理器架构和除了启动支持(x86-64)处理器架构以外的处理器架构。

安装媒体对所有的 Windows 7 版本软件是相同的，都支持相同处理器架构，许可证决定了激活后的特征，通过许可证升级允许随后的开锁功能，不必再次安装操作系统。这是微软第一次通过两张光盘来控制不同版本的 Windows 7。希望升级到更高的 Windows 7 版本的用户可以通过窗口购买升级、解锁软件，一些 Windows 7 具有复制限制，必须通过销售和购买后，才能激活指定区域内的特定代码。

微软提供 Windows 7 的家庭包，可以提供安装三个个人计算机的软件。家庭包在美国的成本售价为 149.99 美元。2009 年 9 月 18 日，微软表示他们可以为学生提供七折的 Windows 7 系统，范围在美国和英国。之后，类似的销售计划也出现在了加拿大、澳大利亚、韩国、墨西哥、法国和印度，学生持有效证件或者通过学校的电子邮箱地址就可以申请有折扣的 Windows 7 系统，价值为 30 美元或 30 法郎。

Windows 7 目前也可作为嵌入式版本的开发者(以前嵌入式 2011)。

不同版本的 Windows 7 针对不同的市场和人群而设计。在以上版本中，入门版为低价笔记本式计算机而设计，家庭版满足普通家庭用户，专业版为各大中型企业而开发，终极版为软件爱好者而开发。

微软已经发布了运行 Windows 7 系统的最低配置(表 4-1)，要求 32 位或者相似版本的机器，但是对 64 位版本要求更高，现在微软已经发布了升级顾问，用户可以通过顾问咨询计算机是否兼容 Windows 7。

部分功能的附加要求如下。

Windows XP 模式(专业、高级或者企业版) 需要一个额外的 1GB 的 RAM 内存和额外 15GB 的可用硬盘空间且取消虚拟硬盘。

Windows Media Center(包括在家庭高级、专业、高级与企业版)，需要一个电视调谐器接收和录放机。

Windows 7 的第一个服务包 Service Pack 1(SP1)正式版于北京时间 2011 年 2 月 23 日凌晨通过 Windows Update 推送给普通用户，用户也可在之后于微软下载中心下载此服务包。

该服务包传承了当年 Windows Vista 和 Windows Server 2008 的惯例，将 Windows 7 和 Windows Server 2008 R2 的更新程序捆绑于同一个包内。其中 32 位的服务包大小约为 530MB，而 64 位 Windows 7 和 Windows Server 2008 R2 的服务包大小高达 903MB(以上程序大小数据来自简体中文版本的服务包)。

Windows 7 服务包 Service Pack 1 在 2010 年 3 月 18 日发布。测试版在 2010 年 7 月 12 日发布，最终版本于 2011 年 2 月 9 日发布。在发布之初，服务包不属于强制范围，可以通过提示信息阻止或者通过更新直接下载，也可以通过订购来获得。微软公司证实，服务包比此前的 Vista 版本要小的多。

Windows 服务包增加了支持高级矢量扩展(AXV)，一个 256 位的处理器指令扩展集，并可以通过额外领域的邮件来识别它。此外，服务包还支持先进的格式和其他身份联合服务。服务包也解决了一个音频的相关错误和其他相关的打印 XPS 文档问题。

Chapter 5 Windows Programming
(Windows 编程)

Section A Windows Programming Options

To a programmer, an **operating system** is defined by its API. An **API** encompasses all the function calls that an application program can make of an operating system, as well as **definitions** of **associated** data types and structures. In Windows, the API also implies a particular program architecture that we'll explore in the section.

Generally, the Windows API has remained quite **consistent** since Windows 1.0. A Windows programmer with experience in Windows 98 would find the source code for a Windows 1.0 program very familiar. One way the API has changed has been in **enhancements**. Windows 1.0 supported fewer than 450 function calls; today there are thousands.

The biggest change in the Windows API and its syntax came about during the switch from a 16-bit architecture to a 32-bit architecture. Versions 1.0 through 3.1 of Windows used the so-called segmented memory mode of the 16-bit Intel 8086, 8088, and 286 **microprocessors**, a mode that was also supported for **compatibility** purposes in the 32-bit Intel microprocessors beginning with the 386. The microprocessor register size in this mode was 16 bits, and hence the C int data type was also 16 bits wide. In the segmented memory model, memory addresses were formed from two components——a 16-bit segment pointer and a 16-bit **offset** pointer. From the programmer's perspective, this was quite **messy** and involved differentiating between long or far pointers (which involved both a segment address and an offset address) and short or near pointers (which involved an offset address with an assumed segment address).

Beginning in Windows NT and Windows 95, Windows supported a 32-bit flat memory model using the 32-bit modes of the Intel 386, 486, and Pentium processors. The C int data type was promoted to a 32-bit value. Programs written for 32-bit

---

operating system
操作系统
API
abbr.application program interface
应用程序接口
definition [,defi'niʃən]
n. 定义, 解说, 精确度
associate [ə'səuʃieit]
vt. 使发生联系, 使联合
consistent [kən'sistənt]
adj. 一致的, 调和的, 坚固的, 相容的
enhancement [in'hɑːnsmənt]
n. 增进, 增加
microprocessor [maikrəu'prəusesə(r)]
n. [计]微处理器
compatibility [kəm,pæti'biliti]
n. [计]兼容性
offset ['ɔːfset]
n. 偏移量, 抵消
messy ['mesi]
adj. 肮脏的, 凌乱的, 杂乱

Chapter 5 Windows Programming

versions of Windows use simple 32-bit **pointer** values that address a flat **linear** address space.

The API for the 16-bit versions of Windows (Windows 1.0 through Windows 3.1) is now known as Win16. The API for the 32-bit versions of Windows (Windows 95, Windows 98, and all versions of Windows NT) is now known as Win32. Many function calls remained the same in the transition from Win16 to Win32, but some needed to be enhanced. For example, graphics **coordinate** points changed from 16-bit values in Win16 to 32-bit values in Win32. Also, some Win16 function calls returned a two-**dimensional** coordinate point packed in a 32-bit integer. This was not possible in Win32, so new function calls were added that worked in a different way.

All 32-bit versions of Windows support both the Win16 API to ensure compatibility with old applications and the Win32 API to run new applications. Interestingly enough, this works differently in Windows NT than in Windows 95 and Windows 98. In Windows NT, Win16 function calls go through a translation layer and are converted to Win32 function calls that are then processed by the operating system. In Windows 95 and Windows 98, the process is opposite that: Win32 function calls go through a translation layer and are converted to Win16 function calls to be processed by the operating system.

At one time, there were two other Windows API sets (at least in name). Win32s ("s" for "subset") was an API that allowed programmers to write 32-bit applications that ran under Windows 3.1. This API supported only 32-bit versions of functions already supported by Win16. Also, the Windows 95 API was once called Win32c ("c" for "compatibility"), but this term has been **abandoned.**

At this time, Windows NT and Windows 98 are both considered to support the Win32 API. However, each operating system supports some features not supported by the other. Still, because the **overlap** is considerable, it's possible to write programs that run under both systems. Also, it's widely **assumed** that the two products will be merged at some time in the future.

Using C and the native APIs is not the only way to write programs for Windows. However, this **approach** offers you the best performance, the most power, and the greatest **versatility** in

pointer ['pɔintə]
n. 指示器，指针
linear ['liniə]
adj. 线的，直线的，线状的，长度的

coordinate [kəu'ɔ:dinit]
adj. 同等的，并列的
dimensional [di'menʃənəl]
adj. 空间的

abandon [ə'bændən]
vt. 放弃，遗弃
overlap ['əuvə'læp]
v. (与……)交叠
assume [ə'sju:m]
vt. 假定，设想，采取，呈现
approach [ə'prəutʃ]
n. 接近，逼近，走近，方法，步骤，途径，通路
versatility [,və:sə'tilətɪ]
n. 多功能性

exploiting the features of Windows. Executables are relatively small and don't require external libraries to run (except for the Windows DLLs themselves, of course). Most importantly, becoming familiar with the API provides you with a deeper understanding of Windows **internals**, regardless of how you eventually write applications for Windows.

Among professional programmers——particularly those who write **commercial** applications——Microsoft Visual C++ with the Microsoft Foundation Class Library (MFC) has been a popular alternative in recent years. MFC **encapsulates** many of the messier aspects of Windows programming in a collection of C++ classes. Jeff Prosise's *Programming Windows with MFC, Second Edition* (Microsoft Press, 1999) provides tutorials on MFC.

Most recently, the popularity of the Internet and the World Wide Web has given a big boost to Sun Microsystems' Java, the processor-independent language inspired by C++ and incorporating a **toolkit** for writing graphical applications that will run on several operating system **platforms**. A good Microsoft Press book on Microsoft J++, Microsoft's Java development tool——*Programming Visual J++ 6.0* (1998), by Stephen R. Davis.

Obviously, there's hardly any one right way to write applications for Windows. More than anything else, the nature of the application itself should probably **dictate** the tools. But learning the Windows API gives you vital insights into the workings of Windows that are essential regardless of what you end up using to actually do the coding. Windows is a complex system; putting a programming layer on top of the API doesn't **eliminate** the complexity——it merely hides it. Sooner or later that complexity is going to jump out and bite you in the leg. Knowing the API gives you a better chance at **recovery**.

Any software layer on top of the native Windows API necessarily restricts you to a subset of full functionality. You might find, for example, that Visual Basic is ideal for your application except that it doesn't allow you to do one or two **essential chores**. In that case, you'll have to use native API calls. The API defines the universe in which we as Windows programmers exist. No approach can be more powerful or versatile than using this API directly.

internal [in'tə:nl]
adj. 内在的，国内的
commercial [kə'mə:ʃəl]
adj. 商业的，贸易的
encapsulate [in'kæpsjuleit]
vt. 装入胶囊，压缩

toolkit
n. [计] 工具包，工具箱
platform ['plætfɔ:m]
n. (车站)月台，讲台，讲坛，平台

dictate [dik'teit]
v. 指令，指示，命令，规定

eliminate [i'limineit]
vt. 排除，消除
recovery [ri'kʌvəri]
n. 恢复，痊愈，防御
essential [i'senʃəl]
adj. 本质的，实质的，基本的，提炼的，精华的
chore [tʃɔ:]
n. 家务杂事

MFC is particularly problematic. While it **simplifies** some jobs **immensely** (such as **OLE**), I often find myself **wrestling** with other features (such as the Document/View architecture) to get them to work as I want. MFC has not been the Windows programming **panacea** that many hoped for, and few people would characterize it as a model of good **object-oriented** design. MFC programmers benefit greatly from understanding what's going on in class definitions they use, and find themselves frequently consulting MFC source code. Understanding that source code is one of the benefits of learning the Windows API.

The Microsoft Visual C++ package includes more than the C compiler and other files and tools necessary to compile and link Windows programs. It also includes the Visual C++ Developer Studio, an environment in which you can edit your source code; interactively create resources such as icons and dialog boxes; and edit, compile, run, and debug your programs.

The **MSDN** portion of the Microsoft URL above stands for Microsoft Developer Network. This is a program that provides developers with frequently updated CD-ROMs containing much of what they need to be on the cutting edge of Windows development. You'll probably want to **investigate** subscribing to MSDN and avoid frequent downloading from Microsoft's Web site.

simplify ['simplifai]
vt. 单一化,简单化
OLE
对象链接和嵌入
immensely [ɪ'menslɪ]
adv. 无限地,广大地,庞大地,非常
wrestle ['resl]
vt. 与(对手)摔跤,使劲搬动
panacea [,pænə'siə]
n. 万能药
object-oriented
面向对象的

MSDN
abbr. Microsoft developer Network
微软的开发商网络
investigate [in'vestigeit]
v. 调查,研究

Exercises

Ⅰ. **Fill in the blanks with the information given in the text.**

1. To a programmer, an _____ is defined by its API. An API encompasses all the function calls that an application program can make of an operating system, as well as definitions of associated data types and structures.

2. Generally, the Windows _____ has remained quite consistent since Windows 1.0. A Windows programmer with experience in Windows 98 would find the source code for a Windows 1.0 program very familiar.

3. All 32-bit versions of Windows support both the Win16 API to ensure _____ with old applications and the Win32 API to run new applications.

4. The msdn portion of the Microsoft _____ above stands for Microsoft Developer Network.

5. MFC has not been the Windows programming panacea that many hoped for, and few people would characterize it as a model of good _____.

Ⅱ. **Translate the following passages from English into Chinese.**

When you install Visual C++ 6.0, you'll get an online help system that includes API documentation. You can get updates to that documentation by subscribing to MSDN or by using Microsoft's Web-based online help system. Start by linking to http://www.microsoft.com/msdn/, and select MSDN Library Online.

In Visual C++ 6.0, select the Contents item from the Help menu to invoke the MSDN window. The API documentation is organized in a tree-structured hierarchy. Find the section labeled Platform SDK. I'll show the location of documentation using the nested levels starting with Platform SDK separated by slashes. (I know the Platform SDK looks like a small obscure part of the total wealth of MSDN knowledge, but I assure you that it's the essential core of Windows programming.) For example, for documentation on how to use the mouse in your Windows programs, you can consult /Platform SDK/User Interface Services/User Input/Mouse Input.

Section B Using Unicode in Windows

Very simply, **Unicode** is an extension of ASCII character encoding. Rather than the 7 bits used to represent each character in strict **ASCII**, or the 8 bits per character that have become common on computers, Unicode uses a full 16 bits for character encoding. This allows Unicode to represent all the letters, **ideographs**, and other symbols used in all the written languages of the world that are likely to be used in computer communication. Unicode is intended initially to **supplement** ASCII and, with any luck, eventually replace it. Considering that ASCII is one of the most dominant standards in computing, this is certainly a tall order.

Unicode impacts every part of the computer industry, but perhaps most profoundly operating systems and programming languages. In this respect, we are almost halfway there. Windows NT supports Unicode from the ground up. (Unfortunately, Windows 98 includes only a small amount of Unicode support.) The C programming language as **formalized** by ANSI inherently supports Unicode through its support of wide characters, which I'll discuss in detail below.

It is uncertain when human beings began speaking, but writing seems to be about six thousand years old. Early writing was pictographic in nature. **Alphabets**—in which individual letters correspond to spoken sounds—came about just three thousand years ago. Although the various written languages of the world served fine for some time, several nineteenth-century inventors saw a need for something more. When Samuel F. B. Morse developed the telegraph between 1838 and 1854, he also devised a code to use with it. Each letter in the alphabet **corresponded** to a series of short and long pulses (dots and dashes). There was no distinction between uppercase and

Unicode
统一的字符编码标准，采用双字节对字符进行编码

ASCII
abbr. american standard code for information interchange
美国信息交换用标准代码（ANSI 制定）

ideograph ['ɪdɪəgrɑːf]
n. 象形(表意)文字

supplement ['sʌplɪmənt]
v. 补充

formalize ['fɔːməlaɪz]
vt. 使正式，形式化

alphabet ['æːlfəbɪt]
n. 字母表字母表，初步，入门

correspond [kɔrɪs'pɔnd]
vi. 符合，协调，通信，相当，相应

Chapter 5 Windows Programming

lowercase letters, but numbers and **punctuation** marks had their own codes.

Morse code was not the first **instance** of written language being represented by something other than drawn or printed **glyphs**. Between 1821 and 1824, the young Louis Braille was inspired by a **military** system for writing and reading messages at night to develop a code for **embossing** raised dots into paper for reading by the blind. Braille is essentially a 6-bit code that encodes letters, common letter **combinations**, common words, and punctuation. A special escape code indicates that the following letter code is to be interpreted as uppercase. A special shift code allows subsequent letter codes to be interpreted as numbers.

Telex codes, including Baudot (named after a French engineer who died in 1903) and a code known as CCITT #2 (standardized in 1931), were 5-bit codes that included letter shifts and figure shifts.

Early computer character codes evolved from the coding used on Hollerith ("do not fold, spindle, or mutilate") cards, invented by Herman Hollerith and first used in the 1890 United States census. A 6-bit character code known as BCDIC ("Binary-Coded Decimal Interchange Code") based on Hollerith coding was progressively extended to the 8-bit EBCDIC in the 1960s and remains the standard on IBM mainframes but nowhere else.

The American Standard Code for Information Interchange (ASCII) had its origins in the late 1950s and was finalized in 1967. During the development of ASCII, there was considerable **debate** over whether the code should be 6, 7, or 8 bits wide. Reliability considerations seemed to **mandate** that no shift character be used, so ASCII couldn't be a 6-bit code. Cost ruled out the 8-bit version. (Bits were very expensive back then.) The final code had 26 lowercase letters, 26 uppercase letters, 10 digits, 32 symbols, 33 control codes, and a space, for a total of 128 codes. ASCII is currently documented in ANSI X3.4-1986 Coded Character Sets—— 7-bit American National Standard Code for Information **Interchange** (7-bit ASCII), published by the American National Standards **Institute**.

There are a lot of good things you can say about ASCII. The 26 letter codes are **contiguous**, for example. (This is not the case with **EBCDIC**.) Uppercase letters can be converted to lowercase

punctuation [pʌŋktjuˈeɪʃ(ə)n]
n. 标点, 标点符号
instance [ˈinstəns]
n. 实例, 场合
glyph [glif]
n. [计]字形, 字的轮廓
military [ˈmilitəri]
adj. 军事的, 军用的
embossing [imˈbɔsiŋ]
n. 压纹, 轧花, 压花
combination [ˌkɔmbiˈneiʃən]
n. 结合, 联合, 合并, 化合, 化合物

debate [diˈbeit]
n. 争论, 辩论
mandate [ˈmændeit]
n. (书面)命令, 训令, 要求
interchange [ˌintəˈtʃeindʒ]
vt. (指两人等)交换
v. 相互交换
institute [ˈinstitju:t]
n. 学会, 学院, 协会
ANSI
abbr. American National Standards Institute 美国国家标准协会
contiguous [kənˈtigjuəs]
adj. 邻近的, 接近的, 毗边的
EBCDIC
abbr. Extended Binary-Coded Decimal Interchange Code 扩充的二进制编码的十进制交换码(亦略为 EBCDC 和 EBDIC)

and back by flipping one bit. The codes for the 10 digits are easily derived from the value of the digits. Best of all, ASCII is a very dependable standard. No other standard is as **prevalent** or as ingrained in our keyboards, video displays, system hardware, printers, **font files**, operating systems, and the Internet.

The big problem with ASCII is indicated by the first word of the **acronym**. ASCII is truly an American standard, and it isn't even good enough for other countries where English is spoken. Where is the British pound symbol (£), for instance.

English uses the Latin (or Roman) alphabet. Among written languages that use the Latin alphabet, English is unusual in that very few words require letters with accent marks (or "diacritics"). Even for those English words where diacritics are traditionally proper, such as cooperate or résumé, the spellings without diacritics are perfectly acceptable.

But north and south of the United States and across the Atlantic are many countries and languages where **diacritics** are much more common. These accent marks originally aided in adopting the Latin alphabet to the differences in spoken sounds among these languages. Journey farther east or south of Western Europe, and you'll encounter languages that don't use the Latin alphabet at all, such as Greek, Hebrew, Arabic, and Russian (which uses the Cyrillic alphabet). And if you travel even farther east, you'll discover the ideographic Han characters of Chinese, which were also adopted in Japan and Korea.

By the time the early small computers were being developed, the 8-bit byte had been firmly **established.** Thus, if a byte were used to store characters, 128 additional characters could be invented to supplement ASCII. When the original IBM PC was introduced in 1981, the video adapters included a **ROM**-based character set of 256 characters, which in itself was to become an important part of the IBM standard.

To a C programmer, the whole idea of 16-bit characters can certainly **provoke** uneasy chills. That a char is the same width as a byte is one of the very few certainties of this life. Few programmers are aware that ANSI/ISO 9899-1990, the "American National Standard for Programming Languages——C" (also known as "ANSI C") supports character sets that require more than one byte per character through a concept called

prevalent ['prevələnt]
adj. 普遍的，流行的
font files
字体文件
acronym ['ækrənim]
n. 只取首字母的缩写词

diacritic [,daiə'kritik]
adj. 可区别的，读音符号的

establish [is'tæbliʃ]
vt. 建立，设立，安置，确定

ROM
abbr. read only memory 只读存储器

provoke [prə'vəuk]
vt. 激怒，挑拨，煽动，惹起，驱使

"wide characters". These wide characters **coexist** nicely with normal and familiar characters.

ANSI C also supports **multibyte** character sets, such as those supported by the Chinese, Japanese, and Korean versions of Windows. However, these multibyte character sets are treated as strings of single-byte values in which some characters alter the meaning of successive characters. Multibyte character sets mostly impact the C run-time library functions. In contrast, wide characters are uniformly wider than normal characters and involve some **compiler** issues.

Wide characters aren't necessarily Unicode. Unicode is one possible wide-character encoding. However, because the focus is Windows rather than an abstract **implementation** of C, I will tend to speak of wide characters and Unicode **synonymously**.

Presumably, we are all quite familiar with defining and storing characters and character strings in our C programs by using the char data type. But to **facilitate** an understanding of how C handles wide characters, let's first review normal character definition as it might appear in a Win32 program. The following statement defines and **initializes** a **variable** containing a single character:

```
char c = 'A' ;
```

The variable c requires 1 byte of storage and will be initialized with the **hexadecimal** value 0x41, which is the ASCII code for the letter A.

You can define a pointer to a character string like so:
```
char * p ;
```
Because Windows is a 32-bit operating system, the pointer variable *p* requires 4 bytes of storage. You can also initialize a pointer to a character string:
```
char * p = "Hello!" ;
```
The variable *p* still requires 4 bytes of storage as before. The character string is stored in static memory and uses 7 bytes of storage——the 6 bytes of the string in addition to a **terminating** 0.

You can also define an array of characters, like this:
```
char a[10] ;
```
In this case, the compiler reserves 10 bytes of storage for the array. The expression "sizeof (a)" will return 10. If the array is global (that is, defined outside any function), you can initialize an

---

coexist [kəuig'zist]
vi. 共存
multibyte ['mʌltibait]
n. [计]多字节

compiler [kəm'pailə]
n. 编辑者, [计] 编译器

implementation
[,implimen'teiʃən]
n. 执行
synonymous [si'nɔniməs]
adj. 同义的
facilitate [fə'siliteit]
vt. 使容易, 使便利, 推动, 帮助, 使容易, 促进
initialize [i'niʃəlaiz]
vt. 初始化
variable ['vɛəriəbl]
adj. 可变的, 不定的, 易变的, [数]变量的
hexadecimal
[heksə'desɪm(ə)l]
adj. 十六进制的

terminating ['təːmi,neitiŋ]
v. 使终结

array of characters by using a **statement** like so:

```
char a[] = "Hello!" ;
```

statement ['steitmənt]
n. 声明, 陈述, 综述

If you define this array as a local variable to a function, it must be defined as a *static* variable, as follows:

```
static char a[] = "Hello!" ;
```

In either case, the string is stored in static program memory with a 0 appended at the end, thus requiring 7 bytes of storage.

Exercises

Reading materials:

Nothing about Unicode or wide characters alters the meaning of the char data type in C. The char continues to indicate 1 byte of storage, and sizeof (char) continues to return 1. In theory, a byte in C can be greater than 8 bits, but for most of us, a byte (and hence a char) is 8 bits wide.

Wide characters in C are based on the wchar_t data type, which is defined in several header files, including WCHAR.H, like so:

```
typedef unsigned short wchar_t ;
```

Thus, the wchar_t data type is the same as an unsigned short integer: 16 bits wide. To define a variable containing a single wide character, use the following statement:

```
wchar_t c = 'A' ;
```

The variable *c* is the two-byte value 0x0041, which is the Unicode representation of the letter A. (However, because Intel microprocessors store multibyte values with the least-significant bytes first, the bytes are actually stored in memory in the sequence 0x41, 0x00. Keep this in mind if you examine memory storage of Unicode text.)

You can also define an initialized pointer to a wide-character string:

```
wchar_t * p = L"Hello!" ;
```

Notice the capital L (for long) immediately preceding the first quotation mark. This indicates to the compiler that the string is to be stored with wide characters—that is, with every character occupying 2 bytes. The pointer variable *p* requires 4 bytes of storage, as usual, but the character string requires 14 bytes—2 bytes for each character with 2 bytes of zeros at the end.

Similarly, you can define an array of wide characters this way:

```
static wchar_t a[] = L"Hello!" ;
```

The string again requires 14 bytes of storage, and "sizeof (a)" will return 14. You can index the a array to get at the individual characters. The value a[1] is the wide character `e', or 0x0065.

Although it looks more like a typo than anything else, that L preceding the first quotation mark is very important, and there must not be space between the two symbols. Only with that L will the compiler know you want the string to be stored with 2 bytes per character. Later on, when we look at wide-character strings in places other than variable definitions, you'll encounter the L preceding the first quotation mark again. Fortunately, the C compiler will often give you a warning or error message if you forget to include the L.

You can also use the L prefix in front of single character literals, as shown here, to indicate that they should be interpreted as wide characters:

```
wchar_t c = L'A' ;
```

But it's usually not necessary. The C compiler will zero-extend the character anyway.

Section C Windows and Messages

Creating a window is as easy as calling the CreateWindow function.

Well, not really. Although the function to create a window is indeed named CreateWindow and you can find documentation for this function at /Platform SDK/User Interface Services/Windowing/Windows/Window *Reference/Window Functions*, you'll discover that the first argument to CreateWindow is something called a "window class name" and that a window class is connected to something called a "window **procedure**". Perhaps before we try calling CreateWindow, a little background information might prove helpful.

When programming for Windows, you're really engaged in a type of object-oriented programming. This is most **evident** in the object you'll be working with most in Windows, the object that gives Windows its name, the object that will soon seem to take on **anthropomorphic characteristics**, the object that might even show up in your dreams: the object known as the "window".

The most obvious windows **adorning** your desktop are application windows. These windows contain a title bar that shows the program's name, a menu, and perhaps a toolbar and a scroll bar. Another type of window is the dialog box, which may or may not have a title bar.

Less obvious are the various push buttons, radio buttons, check boxes, list boxes, scroll bars, and text-entry fields that adorn the surfaces of dialog boxes. Each of these little visual objects is a window. More specifically, these are called "child windows" or "control windows" or "child window controls".

The user sees these windows as objects on the screen and interacts directly with them using the keyboard or the mouse. **Interestingly** enough, the programmer's perspective is **analogous** to the user's **perspective**. The window receives the user input in the form of "messages" to the window. A window also uses messages to communicate with other windows. Getting a good feel for messages is an important part of learning how to write programs for Windows.

procedure [prə'siːdʒə]
n. 程序，手续

evident ['evidənt]
adj. 明显的，显然的
anthropomorphic [ˌænθrəpəu'mɔːfik]
adj. 神、人同形同性论的
characteristic [ˌkæriktə'ristik]
n. 特性，特征
adorn [ə'dɔːn]
v. 装饰

interesting ['intristiŋ]
adj. 有趣味的，引起好奇(或注意)的
analogous [ə'næləgəs]
adj. 类似的，相似的，可比拟的
perspective [pə'spektiv]
n. 观点，看法，观点，观察

Here's an example of Windows messages. As you know, most Windows programs have **sizeable** application windows. That is, you can grab the window's border with the mouse and change the window's size. Often the program will **respond** to this change in size by **altering** the contents of its window. You might guess (and you would be correct) that Windows itself rather than the application is handling all the messy code involved with letting the user resize the window. Yet the application "knows" that the window has been resized because it can change the format of what it displays.

How does the application know that the user has changed the window's size? For programmers accustomed to only **conventional** character——**mode programming**, there is no mechanism for the operating system to convey information of this sort to the user. It turns out that the answer to this question is central to understanding the **architecture** of Windows. When a user resizes a window, Windows sends a message to the program indicating the new window size. The program can then adjust the contents of its window to reflect the new size.

"Windows sends a message to the program". I hope you didn't read that statement without blinking. What on earth could it mean? We're talking about program code here, not a telegraph system. How can an operating system send a message to a program.

When I say that "Windows sends a message to the program" I mean that Windows calls a function within the program——a function that you write and which is an essential part of your program's code. The **parameters** to this function describe the particular message that is being sent by Windows and received by your program. This function in your program is known as the "window procedure".

You are **undoubtedly accustomed** to the idea of a program making calls to the operating system. This is how a program opens a disk file, for example. What you may not be accustomed to is the idea of an operating system making calls to a program. Yet this is **fundamental** to Windows' architecture.

Every window that a program creates has an associated window procedure. This window procedure is a function that could be either in the program itself or in a **dynamic-link**

sizeable ['saizəbl]
adj. 相当大的, 大的
respond [ris'pɔnd]
v. 回答, 响应, 做出反应
alter ['ɔ:ltə]
v. 改变

conventional [kən'venʃənl]
adj. 惯例的, 常规的, 习俗的, 传统的
mode programming
模块化编程
architecture ['ɑ:kitektʃə]
n. 建筑, 建筑学, 体系机构

parameter [pə'ræmitə]
n. 参数, 参量
undoubtedly [ʌn'dautɪdlɪ]
adv. 毋庸置疑地, 的确地
accustomed [ə'kʌstəmd]
adj. 通常的, 习惯的, 按照风俗习惯的
fundamental [,fʌndə'mentl]
adj. 基础的, 基本的

dynamic-link
动态链接

library. Windows sends a message to a window by calling the window procedure. The window procedure does some processing based on the message and then returns control to Windows.

More **precisely**, a window is always created based on a "window class". The window class **identifies** the window procedure that processes messages to the window. The use of a window class allows **multiple** windows to be based on the same window class and hence use the same window procedure. For example, all buttons in all Windows programs are based on the same window class. This window class is associated with a window procedure located in a Windows dynamic-link library that processes messages to all the button windows.

In object-oriented programming, an object is a **combination** of code and data. A window is an object. The code is the window procedure. The data is information retained by the window procedure and information retained by Windows for each window and window class that exists in the system.

A window procedure processes messages to the window. Very often these messages inform a window of user input from the keyboard or the mouse. For example, this is how a push-button window knows that it's being "clicked". Other messages tell a window when it is being resized or when the surface of the window needs to be redrawn.

When a Windows program begins **execution**, Windows creates a "message queue" for the program. This message queue stores messages to all the windows a program might create. A Windows application includes a short **chunk** of code called the "message loop" to **retrieve** these messages from the queue and dispatch them to the **appropriate** window procedure. Other messages are sent directly to the window procedure without being placed in the message queue.

If your eyes are beginning to **glaze** over with this **excessively** abstract description of the Windows architecture, maybe it will help to see how the window, the window class, the window procedure, the message queue, the message loop, and the window messages all fit together in the context of a real program.

precisely [prɪˈsaɪslɪ]
adv. 正好
identify [aɪˈdentɪfaɪ]
vt. 识别，鉴别，把……和……看成一样
multiple [ˈmʌltɪpl]
adj. 多样的，多重的

combination [ˌkɔmbɪˈneɪʃən]
n. 结合，联合，合并，化合，化合物

execution [ˌeksɪˈkjuːʃən]
n. 实行，完成，执行，死刑，制作
chunk [tʃʌŋk]
n. 大块，矮胖的人或物
retrieve [rɪˈtriːv]
v. 重新得到
appropriate [əˈprəʊprɪɪt]
adj. 适当的
glaze [gleɪz]
v. 使表面光滑
excessively [ɪkˈsesɪvlɪ]
adv. 过分地，非常地

Exercises

I. Translate the following passage into Chinese.

The most common text output function is the one I've used in many sample programs so far:

```
TextOut (hdc, xStart, yStart, pString, iCount) ;
```

The xStart and yStart arguments are the starting position of the string in logical coordinates. Normally, this is the point at which Windows begins drawing the upper left corner of the first character. TextOut requires a pointer to the character string and the length of the string. The function does not recognize NULL-terminated character strings.

The meaning of the xStart and yStart arguments to TextOut can be altered by the SetTextAlign function. The TA_LEFT, TA_RIGHT, and TA_CENTER flags affect how xStart is used to position the string horizontally. The default is TA_LEFT. If you specify TA_RIGHT in the SetTextAlign function, subsequent TextOut calls position the right side of the last character in the string at xStart. With TA_CENTER, the center of the string is positioned at xStart.

Similarly, the TA_TOP, TA_BOTTOM, and TA_BASELINE flags affect the vertical positioning. TA_TOP is the default, which means that the string is positioned so that yStart specifies the top of the characters in the string. Using TA_BOTTOM means that the string is positioned above yStart. You can use TA_BASELINE to position a string so that the baseline is at yStart. The baseline is the line below which descenders, such as those on the lowercase p, q, and y, hang.

If you call SetTextAlign with the TA_UPDATECP flag, Windows ignores the xStart and yStart arguments to TextOut and instead uses the current position previously set by MoveToEx or LineTo, or another function that changes the current position. The TA_UPDATECP flag also causes the TextOut function to update the current position to the end of the string (for TA_LEFT) or the beginning of the string (for TA_RIGHT). This is useful for displaying a line of text with multiple TextOut calls. When the horizontal positioning is TA_CENTER, the current position remains the same after a TextOut call.

You'll recall that displaying columnar text in the series of SYSMETS programs required that one TextOut call be used for each column. An alternative is the TabbedTextOut function:

```
TabbedTextOut (hdc, xStart, yStart, pString, iCount,
iNumTabs, piTabStops, xTabOrigin) ;
```

II. Translate the following sentences into English.

所谓动态链接是指 Windows 把一个模块中的函数呼叫链接到动态链接库模块中的实际函数上的程序。在程序开发中,您将各种目标模块(.obj)、执行时期链接库(.lib)文件,以及经常是已编译的资源(.res)文件链接在一起,以便建立 Windows 的.exe 文件,这时的链接是静态链接。动态链接与此不同,它发生在执行时期。

KERNEL32.dll、USER32.dll 和 GDI32.dll、各种驱动程序文件(如 KEYBOARD.drv、SYSTEM.drv 和 MOUSE.drv 和视讯及打印机驱动程序)都是动态链接库。这些动态链接库能被所有 Windows 应用程序使用。

Grammar 5　科技英语的写作特点(Ⅲ)

1. 大量使用名词化结构(nominalization)

Archimedes first discovered the principle that water is displaced by solid bodies.

Archimedes 最先发展固体排水的原理。

Archimedes first discovered the principle of displacement of water by solid bodies.

名词化结构，一方面简化了同位语从句，另一方强调 displacement 这一事实。

Television is the transmission and reception of images of moving objects by radio waves.

电视通过无线电波发射和接受活动物体的图像。

名词化结构 the transmission and reception of images of moving objects by radio waves 强调客观事实。

2. 广泛使用被动语句(the passive)

比较下面两段短文：

We can store electrical energy in two metal plates separated by an insulating medium. We call such a device a capacitor, or a condenser, and its ability to store electrical energy capacitance .It is measured in farads.

Electrical energy can be stored in two metal plates separated by an insulating medium. Such a device is called a capacitor, or a condenser, and its ability to store electrical energy is termed capacitance. It is measured in farads.

电能可储存在由一绝缘介质隔开的两块金属板内。这样的装置称之为电容器。其储存电能的能力称为电容。电容的测量单位是法拉。

根据英国利兹大学 John Swales 的统计，科技英语中的谓语至少三分之一是被动态结构。

3. 非限定动词 (the nonrestrictive verb)

(1) A direct current is a current which flows always in the direction.

(2) A direct current is a current flowing in the same direction.

在科技英语中，不常使用非限制定语从句，而使用非限定动词，即非谓语动词。

在科技文中，一般将 how,wh-词引导的从句转换成 how,wh-词引导的不定式短语，从而使句子结构更加简洁、紧凑。

(1) In the communications, the problem of electronics is how information is conveyed from one place to another.

(2) In the communications, the problem of electronics is how to convey from one place to another.

使用分词短语代替定语从句或状语从句，使用分词独立结构代替状语从句或并列分句，使用不定式短语代替各种从句，介词+动名词短语代替定语从句或状语从句。

4. 后置定语(the postposition)

1) 介词短语

The forces due to friction are called frictional forces. 由于摩擦而产生的力称之为摩擦力。介词短语 due to 的使用避免了 because 从句的使用。

2) 形容词及形容词短语的使用

In radiation, thermal energy is transformed into radiant energy, similar in nature to light.

热能在辐射时，转换成性质与光相似的辐射能 。

3) 副词

The force uptown equals the force downward so that the balloon stays at the level.

向下的力与向上的力相等，所以气球就保持在这一高度。

副词成对出现，大多表示相反的意思。

4) 分词

The heat produced is equal to the electrical energy wasted.

产生的热能等于浪费了的热能。

过去分词表被动在科技文中被广泛应用，尤其在一些并列结构的句子中。

5) 定语从句

During construction, problems often arise which require design changes.

在施工过程中，常会出现需要改变设计的问题。

 参考译文

Section A Windows 程序设计选项

对于程序员来说，操作系统是由本身的 API 定义的。API 包含了所有应用程序能够使用的操作系统的函数调用，同时包含了相关的数据类型和结构。在 Windows 中，API 还意味着一个特殊的程序架构，我们将在本节进行研究。

一般而言，Windows API 自 Windows 1.0 以来一直保持一致，没什么重大改变。具有 Windows 98 程序写作经验的 Windows 程序员会对 Windows 1.0 程序的源代码感觉非常熟悉。API 改变的一种方式是进行增强。Windows 1.0 支持不到 450 个函数调用，现在已有了上千种函数调用。

Windows API 及其语法的最大变化是从 16 位架构向 32 位架构转化的过程。Windows 从版本 1.0 到版本 3.1 使用 16 位 Intel 8086、8088 和 286 微处理器上所谓的分段内存模式，由于兼容性的原因，从 386 开始的 32 位 Intel 微处理器也支持该模式。在这种模式下，微处理器寄存器的大小为 16 位，因此 C 的 int 数据类型也是 16 位。在分段内存模式下，内存地址由两个部分组成——16 位段指针和 16 位偏移量指针。从程序员的角度看，这显得非常凌乱，也带来了 long 或 far 指针(包括段地址和偏移量地址)和 short 或 near 指针(包括带有假定段地址的偏移量地址)的区别。

从 Windows NT 和 Windows 95 开始，Windows 支持使用 Intel 386、486 和 Pentium 处理器 32 位模式下的 32 位平坦内存模式。C 语言的 int 数据类型也扩展为 32 位的值。用 32 位 Windows 编写的程序使用的是简单的平坦线性空间寻址的 32 位指针值。

所有 32 位的 Windows 都支持 Win16 API(以确保和旧有应用程序兼容)和 Win32 API(以运行新应用程序)。非常有趣的是，Windows NT 与 Windows 95 及 Windows 98 的工作方式不同。在 Windows NT 中，Win16 函数调用通过一个转换层被转化为 Win32 函数调用，然后被操作系统处理。在 Windows 95 和 Windows 98 中，该操作正好相反：Win32 函数调用通过转换层转换为 Win16 函数调用，再由操作系统处理。

在同一时刻有两个不同的 Windows API 集(至少名称不同)。Win32s（"s" 代表 "子集"）是一个 API，允许程序员编写在 Windows 3.1 上执行的 32 位应用程序。该 API 仅支持已被 Win16 支持的 32 位函数版本。此外，Windows 95 API 一度被称为 Win32c（"c" 代表 "兼容性"），但该术语已经不用了。

此时，一般认为 Windows NT 和 Win98 都支持 Win32API。然而，每个操作系统所支持的一些特性其他系统未必支持。但是，功能的重叠是肯定的，可以编写在两个系统上都运行的程序。因此，两种产品很有可能在将来合并。

使用 C 语言和原始的 API 不是编写 Windows 程序的唯一方法。然而，这种方法却提供给你最佳的性能、最强大的功能并在发掘 Windows 特性方面获得最大的灵活性。可执行文件相对较小且运行时不要求外部链接库(当然，Windows DLL 自身除外)。最重要的是，不管你最终以什么方式开发 Windows 应用程序，熟悉 API 会使你对 Windows 内部有更深入的了解。

在专业程序员中——特别是那些开发商业应用程序的程序员——Microsoft Visual C++ 和 Microsoft

Chapter 5　Windows Programming

Foundation Class Library(MFC)是近年来流行的选择。MFC 在一组 C++对象类中封装了许多 Windows 程序设计中的琐碎细节。Jeff Prosise 的 *Programming Windows with MFC* 第二版(Microsoft Press,1999 年)提供了 MFC 程序的写作指南。

最近，Internet 和 World Wide Web 的流行极大地推动了 Sun 微系统公司的 Java 语言的发展，这是一个受 C++启发却与微处理器无关的程序设计语言，而且结合了可在几个操作系统平台上执行的图形应用程序开发工具组。Microsoft Press 有一本关于 Microsoft J++(Microsoft 的 Java)开发工具的好书 *Programming Visual J++ 6.0*(1998)，由 Stephen R. Davis 编著。

显然，很难说哪种方法更有利于开发 Windows 应用程序。更主要的是，也许是应用程序自身的特性决定了所使用的工具。不管你最后实际上使用什么工具写程序，学习 Windows API 将使你更深入地了解 Windows 工作方式。Windows 是一个复杂的系统，在 API 上增加一个程序层并未减少它的复杂性，仅仅是掩盖了它，早晚你会碰到它。了解 API 会给你更好的补救机会。

在原始的 Windows API 之上的任何软件层都必定将你限制在全部功能的一个子集内。你也许发现，如你会发现使用 Visual Basic 编写应用程序非常理想，然而它不允许你做一个或两个很简单的基本工作。在这种情况下，你将不得不使用原始的 API 调用。API 定义了作为 Windows 程序员所需的一切。没有什么方法比直接使用 API 更万能的了。

MFC 更是问题层出。虽然它大幅简化了某些工作(如 OLE)，我却经常发现要让它们按我所想的去工作时，会在其他特性(如 Document/View 架构)上碰壁。MFC 并排 Windows 程序设计者所追求的灵丹妙药，很少有人认为它是一个好的面向对象设计的模型。MFC 程序员从他们使用的对象类定义如何工作中受益颇深，并会发现他们经常参考 MFC 源代码。搞懂这些源代码是学习 Windows API 的好处之一。

Microsoft Visual C++ 软件包包括 C 编译器和其他编译及链接 Windows 程序所需的文件和工具等。它还包括 Visual C++ Developer Studio，一个可编辑源代码、以交互方式建立资源(如图标和对话框)以及编辑、编译、执行和测试程序的环境。

Microsoft URL 上的 MSDN 部分代表 Microsoft Developer Network(Microsoft 软件开发者网络)。这是一个向程序员提供了经常更新的 CD-ROM 的计划，这些 CD-ROM 中包含了程序员在 Windows 开发中所需的最新东西。你也可以订阅 MSDN，这样就避免经常从 Microsoft 的网站下载文件。

Section B　Windows 环境下使用 Unicode

简单地说，Unicode 来自 ASCII 扩展的字符集。在严格的 ASCII 中，每个字符用 7 位表示，或者计算机上普遍使用的每个字符有 8 位宽；而 Unicode 使用全 16 位字符集，这使得 Unicode 能够表示世界上所有的书写语言中可能用于计算机通信的字符、象形文字和其他符号。Unicode 最初打算作为 ASCII 的补充，可能的话，最终将代替它。考虑到 ASCII 是计算机中最具支配地位的标准，这的确是一个很高的目标。

Unicode 影响到了计算机产业的每个部分，但也许对操作系统和程序设计语言的影响最大。从这方面来看，我们已经接近目标了。Windows NT 从底层支持 Unicode(不幸的是，Windows 98 只是小部分支持 Unicode)。先天即被 ANSI 束缚的 C 程序设计语言通过对宽字符集的支持来支持 Unicode。下面将详细讨论这些内容。

虽然不能确定人类开始讲话的时间，但书写已有大约 6000 年的历史了。实际上，早期书写的内容是象形文字。每个字符都对应于发声的字母表则出现于大约 3000 年前。虽然人们过去使用的多种书写语言都很实用，但 19 世纪的几个发明者还是看到了更多的需求。Samuel F. B. Morse 在 1838～1854 年间发明了电报，与此同时他还发明了一种电报上使用的代码。字母表中的每个字符对应于一系列短的和长的脉冲(点和破折号)。虽然其中大小写字母之间没有区别，但数字和标点符号都有了自己的代码。

Morse 代码并不是以其他图画的或印刷的象形文字来代表书写语言的第一个例子。1821～1824 年，年轻的 Louis Braille 受到在夜间读写信息的军用系统的启发，发明了一种代码，它用纸上突起的点作为代码来帮助盲人阅读。Braille 代码实际上是一种 6 位代码，它把字符、常用字母组合、常用单字和标点进行编码。一个特殊的 escape 代码表示后续的字符代码应解释为大写。一个特殊的 shift 代码允许后续代码被解释为数字。

Telex 代码，包括 Baudot (以一个法国工程师命名，该工程师卒于 1903 年)以及一种被称为 CCITT #2 的代码(1931 年被标准化)，都是包括字符和数字的 5 位代码。

早期计算机的字符码是从 Hollerith 卡片(不能被折叠、卷曲或毁伤)发展而来的，该卡片由 Herman Hollerith 发明并首次在 1890 年的美国人口普查中使用。6 位字符码系统 BCDIC(binary-coded decimal interchange Code，二进制编码十进制交换编码)基于 Hollerith 代码，在 20 世纪 60 年代逐步扩展为 8 位 EBCDIC，并一直是 IBM 大型主机的标准，但没有在其他地方使用。

美国信息交换标准码(American Standard Code for Information Interchange，ASCII)起始于 20 世纪 50 年代后期，最后完成于 1967 年。开发 ASCII 的过程中，在字符长度是 6 位、7 位、还是 8 位的问题上产生了很大的争议。从可靠性的观点来看，不应使用替换字符，因此 ASCII 不能是 6 位编码。由于费用的原因也排除了 8 位版本的方案(当时每位的储存空间成本仍很昂贵)。这样，最终的字符码就有 26 个小写字母、26 个大写字母、10 个数字、32 个符号、33 个句柄和一个空格，总共 128 个字符集。ASCII 现在记录在 ANSI X3.4—1986 字符集——用于信息交换的 7 位美国国家标准码(7-bit ASCII: 7-bit American National Standard Code for Information Interchange)，由美国国家标准协会(American National Standards Institute)发布。

ASCII 有许多优点。例如，26 个字母代码是连续的(在 EBCDIC 代码中就不是这样的)；大写字母和小写字母可通过改变一位数据而相互转化；10 个数字的代码可从数值本身方便地得到。最好的是，ASCII 是一个可靠的标准。在我们的键盘上、视频播放器、系统硬盘、打印机、字体文件、操作系统及 Internet 中，没有什么标准比 ASCII 更适用、更根深蒂固了。

ASCII 的最大问题就是该缩写的第一个字母。ASCII 是一个真正的美国标准，所以它不能很好地满足其他英语国家的需要。例如，英国的英镑符号(£)在哪里？

英语使用拉丁(或罗马)语字母表。在使用拉丁语字母表的书写语言中，英语中的单词通常很少需要重音符号(或读音符号)。即使那些传统惯例加上读音符号也无不当的英语单词，如 cooperate 或者 résumé，即使拼写中没有读音符号也会被完全接受。

但在美国以南、以北，以及大西洋地区的许多国家，在语言中使用重音符号很普遍。这些重音符号最初是为使拉丁字母表适合这些语言读音不同的需要。在远东或西欧的南部旅游，你会遇到根本不使用拉丁字母的语言，如希腊语、希伯来语、阿拉伯语和俄语(使用斯拉夫字母表)。如果你向东走得更远，就会发现中国的表意汉字，日本和朝鲜也采用汉字系统。

在小型计算机开发的初期，就已经严格地建立了 8 位字节。因此，如果使用一个字节来保存字符，则需要 128 个附加的字符来补充 ASCII。1981 年，当最初的 IBM PC 推出时，视频卡的 ROM 中有一个提供 256 个字符的字符集，这也成为 IBM 标准的一个重要组成部分。

对 C 语言程序员来说，16 位字符的想法的确让人扫兴。一个 char 和一个字节同宽是最不能确定的事情之一。没几个程序员清楚 ANSI/ISO 9899—1990，这是"美国国家标准程序设计语言——C"(也称作"ANSI C")通过一个称为"宽字符"的概念支持用多个字节代表一个字符的字符集。这些宽字符与常用的字符完美地共存。

ANSI C 也支持多字节字符集，如中文、日文和韩文版本 Windows 支持的字符集。然而，这些多字节字符集被当成单字节构成的字符串看待，只不过其中一些字符改变了后续字符的含义而已。多字节字符集主要影响 C 语言程序执行时链接库函数。相比之下，宽字符比正常字符宽，而且会引起一些编译问题。

宽字符不一定是 Unicode。Unicode 是一种可能的宽字符集。然而，因为焦点是 Windows 而不是 C 语言程序执行的理论，所以将把宽字符和 Unicode 作为同义语。

假定我们都非常熟悉在 C 程序中使用 char 数据类型来定义和储存字符和字符串。但为了便于理解 C 语言程序如何处理宽字符，让我们先回顾一下可能在 Win32 程序中出现的标准字符定义。下面的语句定义并初始化了一个只包含一个字符的变量：

    char c ='A' ;

变量 c 需要 1 字节来保存，并将用十六进制数 0x41 初始化，这是字母 A 的 ASCII 码。

你可以像这样定义一个指向字符串的指针：

    char * p ;

因为 Windows 是一个 32 位操作系统，所以指针变量 p 需要用 4 字节保存。你还可初始化一个指向字符串的指针：

    char * p = "Hello!" ;

像前面一样，变量 p 也需要用 4 字节保存。该字符串保存在静态内存中并占用 7 字节，其中 6 字节保存字符串，另外 1 字节保存终止符号 0。

你还可以像这样定义字符数组：

    char a[10];

在这种情况下，编译器为该数组保留了 10 字节的储存空间。表达式 sizeof(a)将返回 10。如果数组是整体变量(即在所有函数外定义)，你可使用像下面的语句来初始化一个字符数组：

    char a[] = "Hello!" ;

如果你将该数组定义为一个函数的局部变量，则必须将它定义为一个 static 变量，如下：

    static char a[] = "Hello!" ;

无论哪种情况，字符串都储存在静态程序内存中，并在末尾添加 0，这样就需要 7 字节的储存空间。

Section C　窗口和消息

建立窗口很简单，只需调用 CreateWindow 函数即可。

虽然建立窗口的函数的确名为 CreateWindow，而且你也能在/Platform SDK/User Interface Services/Windowing/Windows/Window Reference/Window Functions 找到此文件，但你将发现 CreateWindow 的第一个参数就是所谓的"窗口类名称"，并且该窗口类连接所谓的"窗口处理程序"。在我们调用 CreateWindow 之前，一些背景知识可能会对你大有帮助。

进行 Windows 程序设计，实际上是在进行一种面向对象的程序设计。这一点在 Windows 中使用得最多的对象上表现最为明显。这种对象正是 Windows 之所以命名为"Windows"的原因，它具有人性化的特征，甚至可能会在你的梦中出现，这就是"窗口"。

桌面上最明显的窗口就是应用程序窗口。这些窗口含有显示程序名称的标题栏、菜单栏，甚至可能还有工具栏和滚动条。另一类窗口是对话框，它可以有标题栏也可以没有标题栏。

装饰对话框表面的还有一些不太明显的各式各样的按钮、单选按钮、复选框、列表框、滚动条和文本框。其中每一个小的可视对象都是一个窗口。更确切地说，这些都称为"子窗口"或"控件窗口"或"子窗口控件"。

作为对象，使用者会在屏幕上看到这些窗口，并通过键盘和鼠标直接与它们进行交互操作。更有趣的是，程序员的观点与使用者的观点极其类似。窗口以"消息"的形式接收用户输入的信息，窗口也用消息与其他窗口通信。对消息的理解将是学习如何编写 Windows 程序非常重要的一步。

这有一个 Windows 的消息范例。我们知道，大多数的 Windows 程序都有大小合适的应用程序窗口。也就是说，你能够通过鼠标拖动窗口的边框来改变窗口的大小。通常，程序将通过改变窗口中的内容来响应这种大小的变化。你可能会猜测(并且你也是正确的)，是 Windows 本身而不是应用程序在处理与使用者重新调整窗口大小相关的全部复杂程序。由于应用程序能改变其显示的外观,所以它也"知道"窗口大小改变了。

应用程序是如何知道使用者改变了窗口的大小的呢?由于程序员习惯了往常的文字模式程序,操作系统没有设置将此类消息通知给使用者的机制。问题的关键在于理解 Windows 所使用的架构。当使用者改变窗口的大小时,Window 给程序发送一个消息指出新窗口的大小。然后程序就可以调整窗口中的内容,以响应大小的变化。

"Windows 给程序发送消息",我们希望读者不要对这句话视而不见。它到底表达了什么意思呢?我们在这里讨论的是程序代码,而不是一个电子邮件系统。操作系统怎么给程序发送消息呢?

当我说"Windows 给程序发送消息"是指 Windows 调用了程序中的一个函数,该函数是由你所编写,并构成了你的程序代码的重要部分。该函数的参数描述了这个特定消息(由 Windows 发出,由你的程序接收)。这种位于 Windows 程序中的函数称为"窗口处理程序"。

无疑,读者对程序调用操作系统的做法是很熟悉的。例如,程序在打开磁盘文件时就要使用有关的系统调用。读者所不习惯的可能是操作系统调用程序,而这正是 Windows 面向对象架构的基础。

程序建立的每一个窗口都有相关的窗口处理程序。这个窗口处理程序是一个函数,既可以在程序中,也可以在动态链接库中。Windows 通过调用窗口处理程序来给窗口发送消息。窗口处理程序根据此消息进行处理,然后将控制传回给 Windows。

更确切地说,窗口通常是在"窗口类"的基础上建立的。窗口类标示了处理窗口消息的窗口处理程序。使用窗口类使得多个窗口能够属于同一个窗口类,并使用同一个窗口处理程序。例如,所有 Windows 程序中的所有按钮均依据同一个窗口类。这个窗口类与一个处理所有按钮消息的窗口处理程序(位于 Windows 的动态链接库中)联结。

在面向对象的程序设计中,对象是程序与数据的组合。窗口是一种对象,其代码是窗口处理程序。数据是窗口处理程序保存的信息和 Windows 为每个窗口以及系统中那个窗口类保存的信息。

窗口处理程序处理发给窗口发送的消息。这些消息经常是告知窗口,使用者正使用键盘或者鼠标进行输入。这正是按钮窗口知道它被"单击"的奥妙所在。在窗口大小改变,或者窗口表面需要重画时,由其他消息通知窗口。

Windows 程序开始执行后,Windows 为该程序建立一个"消息队列"。这个消息队列用来存放该程序可能建立的各种不同窗口的消息。程序中有一小段程序代码,叫做"消息循环",用来从队列中取出消息,并且将它们发送给相应的窗口处理程序。有些消息直接发送给窗口处理程序,不用放入消息队列中。

如果你对这段 Windows 架构过于简略的描述将信将疑,就去看看在实际的程序中,窗口、窗口类、窗口处理程序、消息队列、消息循环和窗口消息是如何相互配合的,这或许会对你有些帮助。

Chapter 6 Software Engineering
(软件工程)

Section A The Tar Pit

No scene from prehistory is quite so vivid as that of the mortal struggles of great beasts in the **tar pits**. In the mind's eye one sees dinosaurs, mammoths, and saber-toothed tigers struggling against the grip of the tar. The fiercer the struggle, the more **entangling** the tar, and no beast is so strong or so skillful but that he **ultimately** sinks.

Large-system programming has over the past decade been such a tar pit, and many great and powerful beasts have thrashed violently in it. Most have emerged with running systems——few have met goals, schedules, and **budgets**. Large and small, massive or wiry, team after team has become entangled in the tar. No one thing seems to cause the difficulty——any particular paw can be pulled away. But the accumulation of **simultaneous** and interacting factors brings slower and slower motion. Everyone seems to have been surprised by the stickiness of the problem, and it is hard to **discern** the nature of it. But we must try to understand it if we are to solve it.

Therefore let us begin by identifying the craft of system programming and the joys and woes **inherent** in it.

The Programming Systems Product

One occasionally reads newspaper accounts of how two programmers in a remodeled garage have built an important program that **surpasses** the best efforts of large teams. And every programmer is prepared to believe such tales, for he knows that he could build any program much faster than the 1000 **statements**/year reported for industrial teams.

Why then have not all industrial programming teams been replaced by dedicated garage duos? One must look at what is being produced.

In the upper left of Fig. 6.1 is a program. It is complete in itself, ready to be run by the author on the system on which it was developed. That is the thing commonly produced in garages, and that is the object the individual programmer uses in estimating productivity.

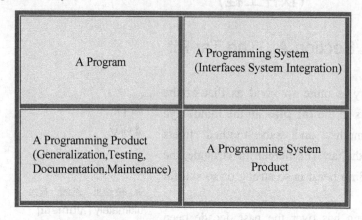

Fig. 6.1 **Evolution** of the programming systems product

There are two ways a program can be converted into a more useful, but more costly, object. These two ways are represented by the boundaries in the diagram.

Moving down across the **horizontal** boundary, a program becomes a programming product. This is a program that can be run, tested, repaired, and extended by anybody. It is usable in many operating environments, for many sets of data. To become a generally usable programming product, a program must be written in a generalized fashion. In particular, the range and form of inputs must be generalized as much as the basic **algorithm** will reasonably allow. Then the program must be thoroughly tested, so that it can be depended upon. This means that a **substantial** bank of test cases, exploring the input range and probing its boundaries, must be prepared, run, and recorded. Finally, promotion of a program to a programming product requires its thorough documentation, so that anyone may use it, fix it, and extend it. As a **rule of thumb**, I **estimate** that a programming product costs at least three times as much as a **debugged** program with the same function.

Moving across the **vertical** boundary, a program becomes a **component** in a programming system. This is a collection of interacting programs, coordinated in function and disciplined in format, so that the assemblage constitutes an entire facility for

evolution [,i:vəˈluːʃən, ,evə-]
n. 发展，演变

horizontal [,hɔriˈzɔntl]
adj. 水平的

algorithm [ˈælɡəriðəm]
n. 算法
substantial [səbˈstænʃəl]
adj. 真实的

rule of thumb
n. 单凭经验的方法
estimate [ˈestimeit]
v. 估计
debug [diːˈbʌɡ]
vt. 调试
vertical [ˈvəːtikəl]
adj. 垂直的
component [kəmˈpəunənt]
n. 组件

large tasks. To become a programming system component, a program must be written so that every input and output conforms in **syntax** and **semantics** with precisely defined interfaces. The program must also be designed so that it uses only a prescribed budget of resources——memory space, input——output devices, computer time. Finally, the program must be tested with other system components, in all expected combinations. This testing must be extensive, for the number of cases grows combinatorial. It is time-consuming, for subtle **bugs** arise from unexpected interactions of debugged components. A programming system component costs at least three times as much as a stand-alone program of the same function. The cost may be greater if the system has many components.

In the lower right-hand corner of Fig. 6.1 stands for the programming systems product. This differs from the simple program in all of the above ways. It costs nine times as much. But it is the truly useful object, the intended product of most system programming efforts.

The Joys of the Craft

Why is programming fun? What delights may its **practitioner** expect as his reward?

First, it is the sheer joy of making things. As the child delights in his mud pie, so the adult enjoys building things, especially things of his own design. I think this delight must be an image of God's delight in making things, a delight shown in the distinctness and newness of each leaf and each snowflake.

Second, it is the pleasure of making things that are useful to other people. Deep within, we want others to use our work and to find it helpful. In this respect, the programming system is not **essentially** different from the child's first **clay** pencil holder "for Daddy's office".

Third, it is the **fascination** of fashioning complex puzzle—— like objects of interlocking moving parts and watching them work in subtle cycles, playing out the consequences of principles built in from the beginning. The programmed computer has all the fascination of the pinball machine or the **jukebox** mechanism, carried to the ultimate.

Fourth, it is the joy of always learning, which springs from

syntax ['sintæks]
n. 语法, 句法
semantics [si'mæntiks]
n. 语义学

bug [bʌg]
n. 程序缺陷

craft [krɑ:ft]
n. 工艺, 手艺, 飞行器
practitioner [præk'tiʃənə]
n. 从业者, 开业者

essentially [ɪ'senʃəlɪ]
adv. 本质上, 本来
clay [kleɪ]
n. 黏土
fascination [fæsɪ'neɪʃ(ə)n]
n. 魔力, 入迷
jukebox ['dʒu:kbɔks]
n. 自动唱片点唱机

the non-repeating nature of the task. In one way or another, the problem is ever new, and its solver learns something: sometimes practical, sometimes theoretical, and sometimes both.

Finally, there is the delight of working in such a **tractable** medium. The programmer, like the poet, works only slightly removed from pure thought-stuff. He builds his castles in the air, from air, creating by exertion of the imagination. Few media of creation are so flexible, so easy to **polish** and rework, so readily capable of realizing grand conceptual structures. (As we shall see later, this very tractability has its own problems.)

Yet the program construct, unlike the poet's words, is real in the sense that it moves and works, producing **visible outputs** separate from the construct itself. It prints results, draws pictures, produces sounds, moves arms. The magic of myth and legend has come true in our time. One types the correct **incantation** on a keyboard, and a display screen comes to life, showing things that never were nor could be.

Programming then is fun because it **gratifies** creative longings built deep within us and delights sensibilities we have in common with all men.

The Woes of the Craft

Not all is delight, however, and knowing the inherent woes makes it easier to bear them when they appear.

First, one must perform perfectly. The computer **resembles** the magic of legend in this respect, too. If one character, one pause, of the incantation is not strictly in proper form, the magic doesn't work. Human beings are not accustomed to being perfect, and few areas of human activity demand it. Adjusting to the requirement for perfection is, I think, the most difficult part of learning to program.

Next, other people set one's objectives, provide one's resources, and furnish one's information. One rarely controls the **circumstances** of his work, or even its goal. In management terms, one's authority is not sufficient for his responsibility. It seems that in all fields, however, the jobs where things get done never have formal authority **commensurate** with responsibility. In practice, actual (as opposed to formal) authority is acquired from the very **momentum** of accomplishment.

tractable ['træktəbl]
adj. 易处理的

polish ['pɔliʃ]
vt. 推敲

visible output
可见光输出(信号)

incantation [,inkæn'teiʃən]
n. 咒语

gratify ['grætifai]
vt. 使满足

resemble [ri'zembl]
vt. 像, 类似

circumstance ['sə:kəmstəns]
n. 环境, 详情, 境况

commensurate [kə'menʃərit]
adj. 相称的, 相当的

momentum [məu'mentəm]
n. 动力, 要素

Chapter 6 Software Engineering

The dependence upon others has a particular case that is especially painful for the system programmer. He depends upon other people's programs. These are often **mal**-designed, poorly implemented, incompletely delivered (no source code or test cases), and poorly documented. So he must spend hours studying and fixing things that in an ideal world would be complete, available, and usable.

The next woe is that designing grand concepts is fun; finding nitty little bugs is just work. With any creative activity come dreary hours of tedious, **painstaking** labor, and programming is no exception.

Next, one finds that debugging has a **linear convergence**, or worse, where one somehow expects a **quadratic** sort of approach to the end. So testing drags on and on, the last difficult bugs taking more time to find than the first.

The last woe, and sometimes the last straw, is that the product over which one has labored so long appears to be obsolete upon (or before) completion. Already colleagues and competitors are in hot pursuit of new and better ideas. Already the displacement of one's thought-child is not only conceived, but scheduled.

This always seems worse than it really is. The new and better product is generally not available when one completes his own; it is only talked about. It, too, will require months of development. The real tiger is never a match for the paper one, unless actual use is wanted. Then the **virtues of** reality have a satisfaction all their own.

Of course the technological base on which one builds is always advancing. As soon as one freezes a design, it becomes obsolete in terms of its concepts. But implementation of real products demands phasing and **quantizing**. The obsolescence of an implementation must be measured against other existing implementations, not against unrealized concepts. The challenge and the mission are to find real solutions to real problems on actual schedules with available resources.

This then is programming, both a tar pit in which many efforts have **floundered** and a creative activity with joys and woes all its own.

---

mal- [mæl]
表示"坏，错误"之义

painstaking ['peinsteikiŋ]
adj. 辛苦的，辛勤的，艰苦的
linear convergence
线性收敛
quadratic [kwə'drætik]
adj. 二次的

virtue of
有……优点

quantize ['kwɔntaiz]
v. 使量子化

flounder ['flaundə]
vi. (在水中)挣扎，困难地往前走

Exercises

I. Fill in the blanks with the information given in the text.

1. Large-system programming has over the past decade been such a _____, and many great and powerful beasts have thrashed violently in it. Most have emerged with running systems——few have met _____, schedules, and budgets.

2. To become a programming system component, a program must be written so that every input and output conforms in syntax and semantics with precisely defined _____. The program must also be designed so that it uses only a prescribed _____ of resources——memory space, input-output devices, computer time.

3. To become a _____ usable programming product, a program must be written in a generalized fashion. In particular the range and form of inputs must be generalized as much as the basic _____ will reasonably allow.

4. _____ then is fun because it gratifies creative longings built deep within us and delights sensibilities we have in common with all men.

5. The _____ upon others has a particular case that is especially painful for the system programmer. He depends upon other people's programs. These are often maldesigned, poorly implemented, incompletely delivered (no source code or test cases), and poorly _____.

II. Translate the following passages from English into Chinese.

What is software engineering? Nobody seems to know. Everyone has an opinion, and everyone agrees that it is of the utmost importance, but there is little consensus as to what it is. But before addressing the above question, let us first answer the question: Why is it called "engineering"?

It is called "engineering" because early practitioners wanted to call it "software physics", but that term was already in use. They wanted to call it software physics because they believed that the process of producing software could be formalized with such rigor that it would be on all fours with physics. Indeed, texts from the 1980s are populated with theories, derivations, tables, graphs, equations and formulae, apparently in an attempt to appear mathematical and scientific in nature. Within a few years however, the inadequacy of those books became clear, and the situation changed rapidly, and today's texts contain virtually no formulae or equations.

Section B   The Software Life Cycle

The most fundamental concept in software engineering is the **software life cycle**.

software life cycle
软件生命周期

The Cycle as a Whole

The software life cycle is shown in Fig.6.2. This figure represents the fact that once software is developed, it enters a cycle of being used and modified that continues for the rest of the software's life. Such a **pattern** is common for many manufactured products as well. The difference is that, in the case of other products, the modification **phase** is more accurately called a repair or maintenance phase because other products tend to move from being used to being modified as their parts become worn.

pattern ['pætən]
n. 模范，模式
phase [feiz]
n. 阶段

Chapter 6 Software Engineering

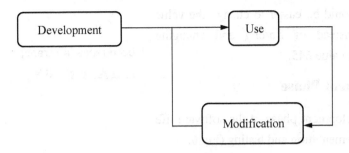

Fig.6.2 Software life cycle

Software, on the other hand, does not wear out. Instead, software moves into the modification phase because errors are discovered, because changes in the software's application occur that require corresponding changes in the software, or because changes made during a previous modification are found to **induce** problems elsewhere in the software. For example, changes in tax laws may require modifications to payroll programs that calculate **withholding taxes**, and all too often these changes may have **adverse effects** in other areas of the program that may not be discovered until sometime later.

Regardless of why software enters the modification phase, the process requires that a person (often not the original author) study the underlying program and its documentation until the program, or at least the **pertinent** part of the program, is understood. Otherwise, any modification could introduce more problems than it solves. Acquiring this understanding can be a difficult task even when the software is well-designed and documented. In fact, it is often within this phase that a piece of software is finally discarded under the **pretense** (too often true) that it is easier to develop a new system from scratch than to modify the existing package successfully.

Experience has shown that a little effort during the development of software can make a **tremendous** difference when modifications in the software are required.

In turn, most of the research in software engineering focuses on the development stage of the software life cycle, with the goal being to take advantage of this effort-versus-benefit **leverage**.

For example, in our discussion of data description statement we saw how the name AirportAlt might be used in **lieu** of the non-descriptive value 645 in a program and reasoned that if a

induce [in'dju:s]
vt. 引起
withholding tax
[wɪð'həʊldɪŋ]
扣交
adverse effect
反作用

pertinent ['pə:tinənt]
adj. 有关的

pretense [pri'tens]
n. 借口

tremendous [tri'mendəs]
adj. 极大的，巨大的

leverage ['li:vəridʒ]
n. 杠杆作用
lieu ['lju:]
n. 场所

change became necessary, it would be easier to change the value associated with the name instead of finding and changing numerous **occurrences** of the value 645.

The Traditional Development Phase

The stages within the development phase of the software life cycle are analysis, design, implementation and testing (Fig.6.3).

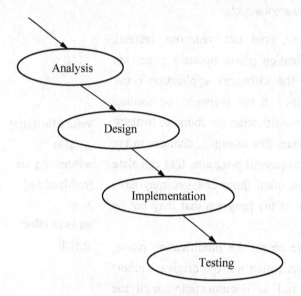

Fig.6.3 Development Phases

Analysis

The development phase of the software life cycle begins with analysis——a major goal being to identify the needs of the user of the **proposed** system. If the system is to be a **generic** product sold in a competitive market, this analysis would involve a **broad-based** investigation to identify the needs of potential customers. If, however, the system is to be designed for a specific user, then the process would be a more narrow investigation.

As the needs of the potential user are identified, they are compiled to form a set of requirements that the new system must satisfy. These requirements are stated in terms of the application rather than in the **technical terminology** of the data processing community. One requirement might be that access to data must be **restricted** to authorized personnel. Another might be that the data must reflect the current state of the **inventory** as of the end of the last business day or that the arrangement of the data as displayed on the computer screen must adhere to the format of the paper forms currently in use.

After the system requirements are identified, they are converted into more **technical** system **specifications**. For example, the requirement that data be restricted to authorized personnel might become the specification that the system will not respond until an approved eight-digit password has been typed at the keyboard or that data will be displayed in **encrypted** form unless preprocessed by a routine known only to authorized personnel.

Design

Whereas analysis concentrates on what the proposed system should do, design concentrates on how the system will accomplish those goals. It is here that the structure of the software system is established.

It is a well-established principle that the best structure for a large software system is a modular one. Indeed, it is by means of this modular **decomposition** that the implementation of large systems becomes a possibility. Without such a breakdown, the technical details required in the implementation of a large system would exceed a human's comprehensive powers.

With a modular design, however, only the details **pertaining to** the module under consideration need be mastered. This same modular design is also conducive to future maintenance because it allows changes to be made on a modular basis. (If a change is to be made to the way each employee's health benefits are calculated, then only modules dealing with health benefits need be considered.)

There are, however, distinctions regarding the concept of a module. If one approaches the design task in terms of the traditional **imperative paradigm**, modules consist of **procedures** and the development of a modular design takes the form of identifying the various tasks that the proposed system must perform. In contrast, if one approaches the design task from the object-oriented **perspective**, modules are seen as objects and the design process becomes that of identifying the entities (objects) in the proposed system as well as how these entities should behave.

---

technical specification
技术规范[说明]

encrypt [in'kript]
v. 加密, 将……译成密码

decomposition
[ˌdiːkɔmpə'ziʃən]
n. 分解, 腐烂

pertain to
v. 属于, 关于, 附属, 相称

imperative [im'perətiv]
adj. 强制的
paradigm ['pærədaim, -dim]
n. 范例
procedure [prə'siːdʒə]
n. 程序
perspective [pə'spektiv]
n. 观点, 看法

Implementation

Implementation involves the actual writing of programs, creation of data files, and development of databases.

Testing

Testing is closely associated with implementation, because each module of the system is normally tested as it is implemented. Indeed, each module in a well-designed system can be tested independently of the other modules by using simplified versions of the other modules, called **stubs**, to simulate the interaction between the target module and the rest of the system. Of course, this testing of components gives way to overall system testing as the various modules are completed and combined.

Unfortunately, the testing and debugging of a system is extremely difficult to perform successfully. Experience has shown that large software systems can contain numerous errors, even after significant testing. Many of these errors may go undetected for the life of the system, but others may cause major **malfunctions**. The **elimination of** such **errors** is one of the goals of software engineering. The fact that they are still prevalent means that a lot of research remains to be done.

Recent Trends

Early approaches to software engineering insisted on performing analysis, design, implementation, and testing in a strictly sequential manner. The feeling was that too much was at risk during the development of a large software system to allow for **trial-and-error** techniques.

As a result, software engineers insisted that the entire analysis of the system be completed before beginning the design and, likewise, that the design be completed before beginning implementation. The result was a development process now referred to as the waterfall model, an analogy to the fact that the development process was allowed to flow in only one direction.

You will notice a similarity between the four problem-solving phases identified by Polya and the analysis, design, implementation, and testing phases of software development. After all, to develop a large software system is to solve a problem.

Chapter 6 Software Engineering

On the other hand, the traditional waterfall approach to software development is in **stark** contrast to the "free-wheeling", trial-and-creative problem solving. Whereas the waterfall approach seeks to establish a highly structured environment in which development progresses in a sequential fashion, creative problem solving seeks a non-structured environment in which one can drop previous plans of attack to pursue sparks of intuition without explaining why.

In recent years, software engineering techniques have begun to reflect this underlying **contradiction** as illustrated by the emergence of the incremental model for software development. Following this model, the desired software system is constructed in increments——the first being a simplified version of the final product with limited functionality.

Once this version has been tested and perhaps evaluated by the future user, more features are added and tested in an incremental manner until the system is complete. For example, if the system being developed is a student records system for a university register, the first increment may **incorporate** only the ability to view student records. Once that version is operational, additional features, such as the ability to add and update records, would be added in a **stepwise** manner.

The incremental model is the evidence of the trend in software development toward prototyping in which incomplete versions of the proposed system, called prototypes, are built and evaluated. In the case of the incremental model these prototypes evolve into the complete, final system——a process known as evolutionary prototyping. In other cases, the prototypes may be discarded in favor of a fresh implementation of the final design. This approach is known as throwaway prototyping.

An example that normally falls within this **throwaway category** is rapid prototyping in which a simple example of the proposed system is quickly constructed in the early stages of development. Such a prototype may consist of only a few screen images that give an indication of how the system will interact with the user and what capabilities it will have.

The goal is not to produce a working version of the product but to obtain a **demonstration** tool that can be used to clarify communication between the parties involved. For example, rapid

stark [stɑːk]
adv. 完全地

contradiction [ˌkɔntrəˈdikʃən]
n. 反驳, 矛盾

incorporate [inˈkɔːpəreit]
vi. 合并, 混合
stepwise
adj. 逐步的

throwaway [ˈθrəuəˌwei]
n. 广告传单, 散单
category [ˈkætiɡəri]
n. 种类

demonstration [ˌdemənsˈtreiʃən]
n. 示范, 实证

prototypes have proved advantageous in **ironing out** system requirements during the analysis stage or as aids during sales presentations to potential clients.

Another development in software engineering has been the application of computer technology to the software development process itself, resulting in what is called computer-aided software engineering (CASE).

These computerized systems are known as CASE tools and include project planning tools (that assist in cost **estimation**, project scheduling, and personnel allocation), project management tools (that assist in monitoring the progress of the development project), documentation tools (that artist in writing and organizing documentation), prototyping and simulation tools (that assist in the development of prototypes), interface design tools (that assist in the development of GUIs), and programming tools (that assist in writing and debugging programs).

Some of these tools are little more than the word processors, spreadsheet systems, and e-mail communication systems used in other applications. However, others are quite **sophisticated** packages designed primarily for the software engineering environment. For example, some CASE tools include code generators that, when given specifications for a part of a system, produce high-level language programs that implement that part of the system.

iron out
v. 熨平, 消除

estimation [esti'meiʃən]
n. 估计, 预算

sophisticated [sə'fistikeitid]
adj. 诡辩的, 久经世故的

Exercises

Ⅰ. Fill in the blanks with the information given in the text.

1. This figure represents the fact that once software is developed, it enters a _____ of being used and modified that continues for the rest of the software's _____. Such a pattern is common for many manufactured products as well.

2. In turn, most of the research in software engineering _____ on the development stage of the software _____, with the goal being to take advantage of this effort-versus-benefit leverage.

3. The development phase of the software life cycle begins with _____ ——a major goal being to identify the needs of the user of the proposed system. If the system is to be a generic product sold in a competitive market, this analysis would involve a broad-based _____ to identify the needs of potential customers.

4. These _____ are stated in terms of the application rather than in the technical terminology of the data processing community. One requirement might be that access to data must be restricted to _____ personnel. Another might be that the data must reflect the current state of the inventory as of the end of the last business day or that the arrangement of the _____ as displayed on the computer screen must adhere to the format of the

paper forms currently in use.

5. It is a well-established principle that the best structure for a large software system is a _____ one. Indeed, it is by means of this modular decomposition that the _____ of large systems becomes a possibility. Without such a breakdown, the technical details required in the implementation of a _____ would exceed a human's comprehensive powers.

Ⅱ. Translate the following passages from English into Chinese.

The Waterfall Model Is Wrong!

The basic fallacy of the waterfall model is that it assumes a project goes through the process once, that the architecture is excellent and easy to use, the implementation design is sound, and the realization is fixable as testing proceeds. Another way of saying it is that the waterfall model assumes the mistakes will all be in the realization, and thus that their repair can be smoothly interspersed with component and system testing.

The second fallacy of the waterfall model is that it assumes one builds a whole system at once, combining the pieces for an end-to-end system test after all of the implementation design, most of the coding, and much of the component testing has been done.

The waterfall model, which was the way most people thought about software projects in 1975, unfortunately got enshrined into DOD-STD-2167, the Department of Defense specification for all military software. This ensured its survival well past the time when most thoughtful practitioners had recognized its inadequacy and abandoned it. Fortunately, the DoD has since begun to see the light.

Ⅲ. Translate the following terms or phrases from English into Chinese and vice versa.

1. modular design   2. prototype
3. specification   4. object-oriented
5. manufactured products
6. 软件生命周期   7. 预处理
8. 维护   9. 瀑布模型
10. 增量式模型

Section C   Design Methodologies

The development of **methodologies** for designing software systems is a major quest within software engineering. In this section we will discuss a variety of the techniques that have been developed as well as directions of current research.

methodology [meθə'dɔlədʒɪ]
n. 方法学，方法论

Top-Down Versus Bottom-Up

Perhaps the most well-known **strategy** associated with system design is the top-down methodology. The point of this methodology is that one should not try to solve a complex problem in a single step. Instead, one's first stop should be to break the problem into smaller, more manageable sub problems. Then, one should proceed by breaking these sub problems into still smaller problems. In this manner, a complex problem

strategy ['strætɪdʒɪ]
n. 策略

becomes a collection of simpler problems whose solutions collectively solve the original problem.

The result of top down design tends to be a **hierarchical** system of **refinements** that often can be translated directly into a modular structure that is compatible with the imperative programming paradigm. The solutions to the smallest problems in the hierarchy become procedural modules that perform simple tasks and are used as abstract tools by more superior modules to solve the more complex problems in the system.

In contrast to the top-down design methodology is the bottom-up approach; in which one starts the design of a system by identifying individual tasks within the system and then considers how solutions to these tasks can be used as abstract tools in the solution to more complex problems. For many years, this approach was considered **inferior** to the top down design paradigm.

Today, however, the bottom-up methodology has gained support. One reason for this shift is that the top-down methodology seeks a solution in which a **dominant** module uses sub modules, each of which relies on sub modules, and so on.

However, the best design for many systems is not of a hierarchical nature. Indeed, a design consisting of two or more modules interacting as equals, as exemplified by the client-server model as well as general parallel processing applications, may be a better solution than a design consisting of a superior module that relies on subordinates to perform its task.

Another reason for increased interest in bottom-up design is that it is more consistent with the goal of building complex software systems from pre-constructed, **off-the-shelf** components——an approach that is a current trend in software engineering.

In an effort to find ways by which software can be constructed from off-the-shelf components, software engineers have turned to the field of architecture for inspiration. Of particular interest is the book *A **Pattern** Language* by Christopher Alexander et al., which describes a set of patterns for designing communities.

hierarchical [,haiə'rɑːkikəl]
adj. 分等级的
refinement [ri'fainmənt]
n. 精致，文雅，精巧

inferior [in'fiəriə]
adj. 下级的

dominant ['dɔminənt]
adj. 有统治权的，占优势的，支配的

off the shelf
现货供应，不用定制的

pattern ['pætən]
n. 模范，式样，模式，样品

Design Patterns

Each pattern consists of the statement of a problem followed by a proposed solution. The problems are intended to be universal, and the proposed solutions are generic in the sense that they address the universal nature of the problem rather than proposing a solution for a particular case.

For example, one pattern, called Quiet Backs, addresses the need to escape the **commotion** of a business center for short periods of refreshment. The proposed solution is to design "quiet backs" into business districts. In some cases, the district could be designed around a main street to which all buildings face——thus, providing for quiet side streets behind the buildings. In other cases, "quiet backs" can be obtained by means of parks, rivers, or **cathedrals**.

The important point for our discussion is that Alexander's work attempted to identify universal problems and provide templates for solving them. Today, many software engineers are attempting to apply this same approach to the design of large software systems. In particular, researchers are applying design patterns as a means of providing generic building blocks with which software systems can be constructed.

An example of such a pattern is the publisher-**subscriber** pattern, consisting of a module (the publisher) that must send copies of its "publications" to other modules (the subscribers). As a specific example, consider a collection of data that is being displayed on a computer screen in more than one format——perhaps as a pie graph as well as a bar graph——simultaneously. In this setting, any change in the data should be reflected in both graphs. Thus the software modules in charge of drawing the graphs should be notified when changes in the data occur. In this case, then, the software module maintaining the data plays the role of the publisher that must send update messages to the subscribers, which are the modules charged with drawing the graphs.

Another example of software design pattern is the **container**-component pattern. It captures the generic concept of a container that contains components that are themselves containers. Such a pattern is exemplified by the directories or

commotion [kəˈməuʃənç]
n. 骚动, 暴乱

cathedral [kəˈθiːdrəl]
n. 大教堂

subscriber [sʌbsˈkraibə]
n. 订户, 签署者

container [kənˈteinə]
n. 容器

folders used by an operating system's file manager. Each of these directories typically contains other directories, which may contain still other directories. In short, the container-component pattern is meant to capture the **recursive** concept of containers that contain containers.

Once a pattern such as publisher-subscriber or container-component has been identified, software engineers propose the development of **skeletal** program units, called frameworks, which implement the **pertinent** features of the pattern's solution while leaving features specific to particular applications as slots to be filled in later. To accompany frameworks, software engineers propose documentation that describes how the framework can be filled in to obtain a complete implementation of the underlying pattern in a particular setting. Such documentation is called a **recipe**. Collections of frameworks along with their recipes are fondly known as cookbooks.

Researchers hope that by means of cookbooks, software engineers will finally be able to construct large, complex software systems from off-the-shelf components——the components being frameworks. Early results have indicated that such an approach can significantly reduce the amount of programming required in the development of a new system.

With all the excitement that has been generated in the software engineering community over design patterns, it is interesting to note that Alexander was not pleased with the results of his patterns in architecture. In short, he found that the systems designed from his patterns were lacking in character, and his work since the early 1980s has focused on ways to capture this **evasive** quality. However, software engineers argue that the goal in software development does not involve such qualities as beauty and character, but instead accuracy and efficiency. Thus, they continue, design patterns will prove to be more successful in the field of software engineering than in architecture.

recursive [rɪˋkɜːsɪv]
adj. 递归的

skeletal [ˈskelɪtl]
adj. 骨骼的，骸骨的
pertinent [ˈpɜːtɪnənt]
adj. 有关的，相关的

recipe [ˈresɪpi]
n. 处方

evasive [ɪˈveɪsɪv]
adj. 逃避的，推托的

Chapter 6 Software Engineering

Exercises

Ⅰ. Fill in the blanks with the information given in the text.

1. Perhaps the most well-known strategy associated with system design is the _____ methodology. The point of this methodology is that one should not try to solve a complex problem in a single step. Instead, one's first stop should be to break the problem into smaller, more manageable _____.

2. Another reason for increased interest in bottom-up design is that it is more consistent with the goal of building complex software systems from preconstructed, _____ components——an approach that is a current trend in software engineering.

3. Another example of software design _____ is the container-component pattern. It captures the generic concept of a _____ that contains components that are themselves containers.

4. Researchers hope that by means of cookbooks, software engineers will finally be able to construct large, complex software systems from off-the-shelf _____ ——the components being _____. Early results have indicated that such an approach can significantly _____ the amount of programming required in the development of a new system.

5. With all the excitement that has been generated in the software engineering _____ over design patterns, it is interesting to note that Alexander was not pleased with the results of his patterns in architecture.

Ⅱ. Translate the following passages from English into Chinese.

The purpose of a programming system is to make a computer easy to use. To do this, it furnishes languages and various facilities that are in fact programs invoked and controlled by language features. But these facilities are bought at a price: the external description of a programming system is ten to twenty times as large as the external description of the computer system itself. The user finds it far easier to specify any particular function, but there are far more to choose from, and far more options and formats to remember.

Ease of use is enhanced only if the time gained in functional specification exceeds the time lost in learning, remembering, and searching manuals. With modern programming systems this gain does exceed the cost, but in recent years the ratio of gain to cost seems to have fallen as more and more complex functions have been added.

Grammar 6 科技英语翻译方法与技巧(Ⅰ)

科技英语文章的主要特点就是客观地阐述科学理论，记录科学事实，报道各种科技新成果。因此，科技英语文章的作者在表达过程中都是语言结构严谨，条理清晰，且在文章中常常附带有公式、数据或者专业词汇等。所以根据这些，我们在翻译过程中，务必要领略好原文的意思，不能违背作者的思想，也要参照中文的语言习惯，避免洋腔洋调。

根据英汉两种语言不同的思维方式、语言习惯和表达方式，可以在翻译时增添一些词、短句或句子，以便更准确地表达出原文所包含的意义。这种方式多半用在汉译英的情况下。

1) 汉语无主语的句子较多，而英语句子一般都要有主语，所以在翻译汉语无主语的句子时，除了少数可用英语无主语的句子、被动语态或"There be…"结构来翻译以外，一般都要根据语境补出主语，使句子完整。

2) 英汉两种语言在名词、代词、连词、介词和冠词的使用方法上也存在很大差别。英语中代词使用频率较高，凡说到人的器官和归某人所有的，或与某人有关的事物时，必须在前面加上物主代词。因此，在汉译英时需要增补物主代词，而在英译汉时又需要根据情况适当地删减。

3) 英语词与词、词组与词组以及句子与句子的逻辑关系一般用连词来表示，而汉语则往往通过上下文和语序来表示这种关系。因此，在汉译英时常常需要增补连词。英语句子离不开介词和冠词。

4) 在汉译英时还要注意增补一些原文中暗含而没有明言的词语和一些概括性、注释性的词语，以确保译文意思的完整。

大多数的情况下，我们面对的主要问题是英译汉的问题，下面主要谈谈翻译的过程及步骤。

● 翻译的步骤

翻译时必须确切理解英语原文的内容，绝对不能凭借主观的意愿凭空想象。翻译前应注意以下几点。

1. 通读全文，理解大意

在这里我们提倡使用略读法和细读法结合使用的原则，对于一篇原文，我们首先建议使用略读方法将全文统览一遍，知道作者要讲叙的大致意思，做到心中有数；然后逐字逐句地仔细体会每句的意思，并且一定要注意文中确切信息的描述，为初步的翻译做基础。

2. 明辨语法，初步表达

在读完文章后，我们可以尝试着初步翻译，此次翻译的重点仍然是用中文表达作者的大致思想，为下一步的逐步加深做基础。

例如：

The development of IC made it possible for electronic devices to become smaller and smaller.

集成电路的发展使电子器件可以做得越来越小。

3. 通读校核，透彻理解

在初步翻译的基础上，进行更深一步的翻译，主要是针对文章中晦涩难懂的地方。这个时候也是对初次翻译的审核过程，并应用一定地翻译技巧。

例如：

Packet switching is a method of slicing digital messages into parcels called "packets," sending the packets along different communication paths as they become available, and then reassembling the packets once they arrive at their destination.

分组交换是传输数据的一种方法，它先将数据信息分割成许多称为"分组"的数据信息包；当路径可用时，经过不同的通信路径发送；当到达目的地后，再将它们组装起来。

(将长定语从句拆成几个并列的分句)。

 参考译文

Section A 焦油坑

在史前史中，没有比巨兽在焦油坑中垂死挣扎更令人震撼的场面。上帝见证了恐龙、猛犸象、剑齿虎

Chapter 6　Software Engineering

在焦油中挣扎的景象。它们挣扎得越猛烈，焦油纠缠得越紧，没有任何猛兽足够强壮或具有足够的技巧能够挣脱束缚，最后它们都沉到了坑底。

过去几十年的大型系统开发就犹如这样一个焦油坑，很多庞大强壮的团队在其中剧烈地挣扎。他们中大多数开发出了可运行的系统——不过，其中只有非常少数的项目满足了目标、时间进度和预算的要求。各种团队，大型的和小型的，庞杂的和精干的，一个接一个淹没在焦油坑中。表面上看起来好像没有任何一个单独的问题会导致困难，每个都能被解决，但是当它们相互纠缠和累积在一起的时候，团队的行动就会变得越来越慢。对问题的麻烦程度，每个人似乎都会感到惊讶，并且很难看清问题的本质。不过，如果我们想解决问题，就必须试图先去理解它。

因此，首先让我们来认识一下软件开发这个职业，以及充满在这个职业中的乐趣和苦恼。

编程系统产品

报纸上经常会出现这样的新闻，讲述两个程序员如何在经改造的简陋车库中，编出了超过大型团队工作量的重要程序。接着，每个编程人员准备相信这样的神话，因为他知道自己能以超过产业化团队的 1000 代码行/年的生产率来开发任何程序。

为什么不是所有的产业化队伍都会被这种专注的二人组合所替代？我们必须看一下产出的是什么。

在图 6.1 的左上部分是程序。它本身是完整的，可以由作者在所开发的系统平台上运行。它通常是产出的产品，也是作为单个程序员生产率的评估标准。

有两种途径可以使程序转变成更有用的，但是成本更高的东西，它们可以用图 6.1 中的边界表示。

水平边界以下，程序变成编程产品。这是可以被任何人运行、测试、修复和扩展的程序。它可以运行在多种操作系统平台上，供多套数据使用。要成为通用的编程产品，程序必须按照普遍认可的风格来编写，特别是输入的范围和形式必须可扩展，以适用于所有可以合理使用的基本算法。然后，对程序进行彻底测试，确保它的稳定性和可靠性，使其值得信赖。这就意味着必须准备、运行和记录详尽的测试用例库，用来检查输入的边界和范围。此外，要将程序提升为程序产品，还需要有完备的文档，每个人都可以加以使用、修复和扩展。经验数据表明，我估计相同功能的编程产品的成本至少是已经过测试的程序的 3 倍。

穿过垂直边界，程序变成编程系统中的一个构件单元。它是在功能上能相互协作的程序集合，调节函数，具有规范的格式，可以进行交互，并可以用来组装和搭建大型任务的整个系统。要成为系统构件，程序必须按照一定的要求编制，使输入和输出在语法和语义上与精确定义的接口一致。同时程序还要符合预先定义的资源限制——内存空间、输入/输出设备、计算机时间。最后，程序必须同其他系统构件单元一起，以任何可能想象到的组合进行测试。由于测试用例会随着组合不断增加，所以测试的范围非常广。因为一些意想不到的交互会产生许多不易察觉的缺陷，测试工作将会非常耗时，因此相同功能的编程系统构件的成本至少是独立程序的 3 倍。如果系统有大量的组成单元，成本还会更高。

图 6.1 的右下部分代表编程系统产品。和以上的所有的情况都不同的是，它的成本高达 9 倍。然而，只有它才是真正有用的产品，是大多数系统开发的目标。

职业的乐趣

编程为什么有趣？作为回报，它的从业者期望得到什么样的快乐？

第一，编程是一种创建事物的纯粹快乐。如同小孩在玩泥巴时感到愉快一样，成年人喜欢创造事物，特别是自己进行设计的。我想这种快乐是上帝创造世界的折射，一种呈现在每片独特、崭新的树叶和雪花上的喜悦。

第二，快乐来自于开发对其他人有用的东西。内心深处，我们期望其他人使用我们的劳动成果，并能对他们有所帮助。从这个方面，这同小孩用黏土为"爸爸办公室"捏制铅笔盒没有本质的区别。

第三，整个过程体现出魔术般的力量——将相互啮合的零部件组装在一起，看到它们精妙地运行，得到预先所希望的结果。比起弹珠游戏或点唱机所具有的迷人魅力,程序化的计算机毫不逊色。

第四,学习的乐趣来自于这项工作的非重复特性。人们所面临的问题在某个或其他方面总有些不同。因而,解决问题的人可以从中学习新的事物:有时是实践上的,有时是理论上的,或者兼而有之。

最后,乐趣还来自于工作在如此易于驾驭的介质上。程序员,就像诗人一样,几乎仅仅工作在单纯的思考中。程序员凭空地运用自己的想象,来建造自己的"城堡"。很少有这样的介质——创造的方式如此的灵活,如此地易于精炼和重建,如此地容易实现概念上的设想(不过我们将会看到,容易驾驭的特性也有它自己的问题)。

然而程序毕竟同诗歌不同,它是实实在在的东西;可以移动和运行,能独立产生可见的输出;能打印结果,绘制图形,发出声音,移动支架。神话和传说中的魔术在我们的时代已变成了现实。从键盘上输入正确的"咒语",屏幕会活动、变幻,显示出前所未有的或是已经存在的事物。

编程非常有趣,因为它不仅满足了我们内心深处进行创造的渴望,而且还愉悦了每个人内在的情感。

职业的苦恼

然而这个过程并不全都是喜悦。我们只有事先了解一些编程固有的烦恼,这样,当它们真的出现时,才能更加坦然地面对。

首先,必须追求完美。因为计算机也是以这样的方式来变戏法:如果"咒语"中的一个字符、一个停顿,没有与正确的形式一致,魔法就不会实现。在现实中,很少人习惯要求完美,也很少有活动领域需要完美。实际上,我认为学习编程的最困难部分,是将做事的方式往追求完美的方向调整。

其次,该工作是由他人来设定目标,供给资源,提供信息。编程人员很少能控制工作环境和工作目标。用管理的术语来说,个人的权威和他所承担的责任是不相配的。不过,似乎在所有的领域中,对要完成的工作,很少能提供与责任相一致的正式权威。而在现实情况中,实际(相对于正式)的权威来自于每次任务的完成。

对于系统编程人员而言,对其他人的依赖是一件非常痛苦的事情。他依靠其他人的程序,而往往这些程序设计得并不合理,实现拙劣,发布不完整(没有源代码或测试用例),或者文档记录得很糟。所以,系统编程人员不得不花费时间去研究和修改,而它们在理想情况下本应该是可靠完整的。

下一个烦恼——概念性设计是有趣的,但寻找琐碎的缺陷却只是一项重复性的活动。伴随着创造性活动的,往往是枯燥沉闷的时间和艰苦的劳动。程序编制工作也不例外。

另外,人们发现调试和查错往往是线性收敛的,或者更糟糕的是,具有二次方的复杂度。结果,测试一拖再拖,寻找最后一个错误比第一个错误将花费更多的时间。

最后一个苦恼,有时也是一种无奈——当投入了大量辛苦的劳动,产品在即将完成或者终于完成的时候,却已显得陈旧过时。可能是同事和竞争对手已在追逐新的、更好的构思;也许替代方案不仅仅是在构思,而且已经在安排了。

现实情况比上面所说的通常还要糟糕。当产品开发完成时,更优秀的新产品通常还不能投入使用,而仅仅是被大家谈论而已。另外,它同样需要月月的开发时间。事实上,只有实际需要时,才会用到最新的设想,因为所实现的系统已经能满足要求,体现了回报。

诚然,产品开发所基于的技术在不断地进步。一旦设计被冻结,在概念上就已经开始陈旧了。不过,实际产品需要一步一步按阶段实现。实现落后与否的判断应根据其他已有的系统,而不是未实现的概念。因此,我们所面临的挑战和任务是在现有的时间和有效的资源范围内,寻找解决实际问题的切实可行方案。

这就是编程,一个许多人痛苦挣扎的焦油坑以及一种乐趣和苦恼共存的创造性活动。对于许多人而言,其中的乐趣远大于苦恼。

Section B 软件生命周期

一个整体软件工程中的最基本概念就是软件生命周期。

在图 6.2 中展示了软件的生命周期。这个图说明了一个事实：一旦软件开发完成，它就进入了使用和修改的循环，并且这个循环将在软件生命周期的剩余时间中不断进行。这样的模式对机器制造的产品而言也是很普通的。不同之处在于，对于其他产品，软件工程中的修改阶段要被更精确地称为修理或者维护阶段，因为其他产品由于部件的磨损会有从使用到修改的过程。

另一方面，软件不存在磨损的问题。但是，软件进入修改阶段或者是因为错误被发现，或者是因为要在软件的应用程序中进行修改从而修改了软件，或者是因为先前的改变又引起了软件其他地方出现了新的问题。例如，税务法案的改变导致对计算扣税的工资程序进行修改，而太频繁的修改则会在软件的其他地方引起反面的作用，而这些是不会被立即发现的。

不管因为什么原因软件进入了修改阶段，这个过程需要人们(通常不是原始的作者)研究程序及其文档，直到程序或者至少是相关部分的程序能够被理解。否则，任何的修改将导致比原本所要解决的还要多的问题出现。即使软件有优秀的设计和齐备的文档，理解也是一个很困难的工作。事实上，常常是在这个阶段，一个有用的软件片段最终就被放弃了(常常是这样)，原因是开发一个新的系统比成功地修改现有软件更容易。

经验告诉我们，软件开发过程中的一丁点付出，会在软件需要修改的时候带来巨大的不同。

反过来，大多数软件工程的研究都集中于软件生命周期的开发阶段，它们的目标是要利用这个付出与收益的杠杆作用。

例如，在讨论数据描述语句中，我们看到名字 AirportAlt 是如何用于程序中的非描述值 645 的情形，并且推导出，如果有一个必要的修改，修改与值有关的名字要比寻找并修改每一个 645 要简单得多。

一般开发步骤

软件生命周期的开发阶段包括分析、设计、实现、测试等步骤(如图 6.3 所示)。

分析

软件生命周期的开发阶段以分析开始——主要目标是确定用户对所提出系统的需求。如果系统是一个在竞争的市场上销售的通用产品，这个分析将会包括一个广泛的调查来发现潜在用户的需要。但是，如果系统是为特殊用户设计的，那么这个过程就是一个更专业的调查。

当潜在用户的要求被确定之后，要将这些要求汇编成使新系统必须能满足的需求。这些需求是从应用的角度来表述，而不是用数据处理领域的技术术语来表达。一种需求可能是对数据的存取必须限制在有权限的人员，另一种可能是当一个工作日结束时，数据必须反映目前的清单状态，或者可能是在计算机屏幕上的数据必须按照用户目前使用的格式来显示。

系统的需求被确定以后，它们就转化为更具技术性的说明书。例如，关于数据须限制在某些有权限的人的需求，就可能转化为以下规范——直到从键盘输入一个被认可的 8 位密码，系统才开始响应，或者除非经过只有授权的人才知道的例程预处理，否则数据将以加密的形式显示在屏幕上。

设计

分析关注这个系统应该做什么，而设计关注这个系统应该怎样来实现目标。正是通过设计建立了软件系统的结构。

大型软件系统最好的结构是模块化系统，这是一条被充分证实的原则。确实，正是借助模块化的分解方法，大型系统的实现才成为可能。没有这样的分解，在大型系统实现过程中所需要的技术细节可能会超过一个人的理解能力。

然而，有了这种模块化设计，仅仅需要熟悉与在考虑中的模块相关的细节。同样，模块化设计对未来的维护是有益的，因为它允许对基本的模块进行修改(如果要对每个雇员的医疗福利计算方法进行修改，那么仅仅需要考虑处理医疗福利模块)。

但是，有关模块的概念也是有差别的。如果一个人以传统的命令式语言范式的方法来进行设计工作，模块由不同程序组成，而模块化设计则以确定有待实现系统的不同任务的方式进行。相反地，如果一个人从面向对象的角度来完成设计工作，模块就被看成了对象，而设计过程变成了确定有待实现系统中的实体(对象)以及确定这些实体是如何工作的。

实现

实现包括程序的实际编写、数据文件的建立以及数据库的开发等过程。

测试

测试与实现紧密联系，因为系统中的每一个模块都要在实现的过程中进行正常测试。确实，通过使用其他模块的简化版本——有时称为桩模块，来模拟目标模块和系统其他部分的交互，从而使设计良好的系统中的每一个模块都可以被独立地测试。当然，在各种模块都开发完成并且整合在一起之后，这个组件的测试将让路给整个系统的测试。

不幸的是，成功地进行系统的测试和调试是极其困难的。经验表明，大型的软件系统可能包含众多的错误，甚至是经过关键测试之后。许多这样的错误在软件的生命期中一直潜伏着，但是也有一些会导致关键性的错误。减少这样的错误是软件工程的一个目标。这些错误的普遍存在说明了在这方面还有许多的研究工作要做。

近期动向

软件工程的早期方法坚持严格地遵守分析、设计、实现以及测试的顺序。在大型软件系统的开发过程中，给人的感觉是采用试错法是在冒着很大的风险进行开发的。

因此，软件工程师应当坚持在设计之前进行完整的系统分析，同样，设计应该在实现之前完成。这就形成了一个现在称为瀑布模型的开发过程，这是对开发过程只允许以一个方向进行的事实的模拟。

你将注意到由Polya提出的解决问题的4个阶段与软件开发的分析、设计、实现和测试阶段的类似性。毕竟，开发一个大型的软件系统的目的是去解决一个问题。

另一方面，传统软件开发的瀑布模型法与随心所欲的反复试验并创造性地解决问题的方法是完全相反的。瀑布模型法寻求建立一个高度结构化的环境，希望在这个环境中的开发可以顺利地进行，而创造性的问题解决要寻找一个非结构化的环境，希望在这个环境中可以抛弃先前的计划，以追逐思维的火花，而不用解释原因。

近年来，软件工程技术已经开始反映这种本质的对立了，这可以由软件开发中出现的增量式模型来说明。根据这个模型，所需的软件系统是通过增量模式来构造的——首先开发最终产品的简化版本，它只有有限的功能。

一旦这个版本经过测试，并且也许经过了未来用户的评估，更多的特性就可以添加进去并且进行测试，这样就以一种增量的方式进行，直到完成系统。例如，如果正在开发的系统是为大学登记员设计的学生记录系统，第一次迭代版本仅仅包括浏览学生记录的功能。一旦这个版本可以运行了，其他特性，如增加和更新记录的功能，就可以分阶段地添加到系统中。

这种增量式模型是软件开发向原型法发展趋势的一个证据——在这种方法中，建立并测试的是不完善系统，它也被称为原型。在增量式模型中，这些原型进化为一个完整的最终系统——被称为演化式原型的过程。对于其他情况，原型的抛弃有利于新的最终设计的实现，这种方法就是抛弃原型。

一个抛弃原型的例子就是快速原型法，在这个方法中，系统的简单版本在开发的早期就被很快搭建起来。这样的原型也许仅仅包含少量界面图片来展示系统怎样与用户交互以及它将具有的功能。

我们的目标不是制作产品的有效版本,而是获得一个示范工具,以便阐明有关方面之间的沟通。例如,在分析阶段解决系统的需求问题,或在销售阶段作为向潜在客户演示的辅助,快速原型具有很大的优势。

软件工程领域中另一个发展是计算机技术在软件开发过程本身的应用,这导致了称为计算机辅助软件工程(CASE)的出现。

这些计算机化系统就是知名的 CASE 工具,且包括项目计划工具(帮助成本估计、项目调度,以及人力资源分配)、项目管理工具(帮助管理开发项目的进程)、 文档工具(帮助撰写和组织文档)、原型和仿真工具(帮助原型开发)、界面设计工具(帮助开发 GUI),以及程序设计工具(帮助编写和调试程序)。

这些工具也许仅仅就是在其他的应用程序中的文字处理软件、表格处理软件,或者是电子邮件通信系统。一些则是相当复杂的软件,它们主要是为了软件工程环境而设计的。例如,一些 CASE 工具包括了代码生成器,当给出一个系统局部的说明书时,它可用来生成实现这个系统局部的高级语言程序。

Section C 设计方法学

设计软件系统的方法学是软件工程领域主要探索的方向之一。本节将讨论一些已经形成的方法以及当前的研究方向。

自顶向下和自底向上设计方法的比较

也许最著名的系统设计策略就是自顶向下的方法学了。这个方法学的要点就是人们不要试图一下子就将一个复杂问题解决,而是应当将问题分解成更小的、可以管理的子问题。然后,将这些子问题分解成更小的问题。以这种方式,一个复杂的问题变成了相对小的问题的集合,而所有小问题的解决就是原问题的解决。

自顶向下设计的结果是一个逐步求精的层次系统,这个结构通常可以被直接翻译成与命令式语言兼容的模块结构。对层次结构中最小问题的解决变成了执行简单任务的程序模块,这个模块被较高层用做抽象工具来解决系统中更为复杂的问题。

相对于自顶向下的设计方法学,自底向上的方法通过确定系统中的每一个具体任务来开始系统的设计。然后,它考虑如何将这些任务的解决用做解决更复杂问题的抽象工具。多年来,这个方法被认为不如自顶向下的设计范式。

但是,今天,自底向上的方法学又获得了支持。这种转变的一个原因就是自顶向下的方法寻求一个支配模块使用子模块,而每一个支配模块依赖于子模块的解决,等等。

但是,对于许多系统来说,最好的设计不是一个层次的结构。确实,一个设计包括两个或更多模块——它们平等交互,这也是被包含通用并行处理应用程序的客户/服务器模型或者系统所例证了的,比起依赖于从属模块来执行任务的较高级模块构成的设计,它也许是一个更好的解决方案。

对自底向上设计产生更多兴趣的另一个原因,就是它与从预先构建的现成组件中构建复杂软件系统的目标更加一致——这体现了软件工程当前的趋势。

为了寻求新的方法(通过这种方法软件可以由非定制组件构建),软件工程师转向体系结构领域寻求灵感。特别有趣的是一本由 Christopher Alexander 等人编著的《模式语言》,书中为设计团体描述了一整套模式。

设计模式

每种模式都包括了一个问题描述以及建议性的解决方案。这些问题是很普遍的,而这个建议性的解决方案也是一般性的——旨在强调他们阐述的是问题的一般本质而不是仅仅为一个特殊的例子提出一个解决方案。

例如,一个称为"安静的后面"的模式,阐述了躲避商业中心的喧嚣而寻求短暂的精力恢复的需求。

其建议性的解决方案就是在商业区中设计一个"安静的后面"。在某些情况下，这个商业区要设计在所有建筑都要朝向的主要街道周围——因此可以将安静的辅路铺在建筑的后面。在其他的情况下，"安静的后面"可以采用公园、河流或者是教堂的形式。

我们所讨论的重点就是 Alexander 在著作中试图确定的一般性问题并且提供解决它们的模板。今天，许多软件工程师也试图应用同样的方法来设计大型的软件系统。特别地，研究人员正在应用设计模式作为提供软件构建所需通用单元的方法。

这种模式的一个例子就是出版商和订户的模式：一个模块(出版商)将其出版物发送给其他模块(订户)。作为一个特殊的例子，考虑在计算机屏幕上同时显示多种格式的数据集，如饼图和条形图。这样，任何对数据的修改都将会被反映在两张图上。因此，当数据发生更改的时候，这个负责画图的软件模块将会被告知。在这种情况下，维护数据的软件模块就会扮演出版商的角色——它必须要给订户发送更新的消息，而这些订户也是模块，它们负责画图。

软件设计模式的另一个例子是容器组件模式。它阐述了容器包括一些组件，而组件本身又是容器的一般性概念。这种模式的例子就是操作系统的文件管理器使用的目录或者文件夹。每个这样的目录都包括了其他目录，而这个被包含的目录可能又包含了其他目录。简而言之，容器组件模式可以描述容器包含容器的递归概念。

一旦像出版商与订户或者是容器和组件这样的模式被确定，软件工程师就会计划开发一组程序单元作为骨架，这称为框架，它实现模式方法所要解决的主要特征，而将特殊应用程序的特性作为缺口，留待以后填入。为了补充框架，软件工程师提出了如何填充框架的描述文档。这种文档被称为处方，与处方在一起的框架集被昵称为菜谱。

研究人员希望，借助菜谱，软件工程师最终可以从现成的组件(组件就是框架)构建大型的复杂软件系统。早期的结果表明，这种方法可以大大减少开发新系统所需的编程工作量。

设计模式在软件工程领域中引起了极大的热情，而对于 Alexander 而言，他对自己应用于建筑学的模式却不是很满意，这是十分有趣的事。他发现根据自己的模式所设计的系统缺乏个性，并且他从 20 世纪 80 年代初期开始主要致力于捕获这个遗漏性质的方法。但是，软件工程师认为软件开发的目标不是去追求诸如美观和个性的特性，而是追求准确和高效。因此，他们将这种方法发扬光大，设计模式在软件工程领域中将比在建筑领域中更加成功。

Chapter 7 Get Your Arms around Microsoft SQL Server
(拥抱 SQL Server)

Section A Introduction to SQL Server 2005

SQL Server 2005 was the **most-awaited release** of Microsoft's SQL Server product line. After millions of e-mails, hundreds of specifications, and dozens of builds, SQL Server 2005 promises to be the most **dramatic** new **database** platform for Windows-based database applications. This section is a guided tour of the essential new features of the entire SQL Server 2005 product. SQL Server 2005 covers the **Online Transaction Processing (OLTP)** technologies as well as the **Online Analytical Processing (OLAP)** technologies, and almost everything in between. Microsoft left no part of its flagship database product untouched. More than five years in the making, SQL Server 2005 is a completely different technology than its predecessors. This section covers the major features across the entire product. It'll try to **distill** the best and most interesting features while providing some insight into how the feature or technology was intended to be used. Topics include a bit of history about the evolution of the SQL Server Engine, the various editions of SQL Server 2005, **scalability**, availability, maintaining large databases, and business intelligence (BI). SQL Server 2005 provides the following:

- Database engine enhancements. SQL Server 2005 introduces many improvements and new features to the database engine. These improvements and features include integrating with the Microsoft. NET **Framework**, new XML technologies, Transact-SQL enhancements, new data types, and improvements to the scalability and availability of the relational database.
- Management tools. SQL Server 2005 introduces an integrated suite of management tools and management

---

most-awaited
最值得等待的
release [ri'li:s]
n. 释放, 让渡, 豁免, 发行的书, 释放证书
dramatic [drə'mætik]
adj. 戏剧性的, 生动的
database ['deitəbeis]
n. [计] 数据库, 资料库
Online Processing (OLTP)
在线事务处理
Online Analytical Processing (OLAP)
在线分析处理
distill [dɪ'stɪl]
vt. 蒸馏, 提取

scalability [ˌskeɪlə'bɪlɪti]
n. 可伸缩性

framework ['freimwə:k]
n. 构架, 框架, 结构

APIs to provide ease of use, manageability, and support for operations of large-scale SQL Server deployments.

- Data Transformation Services (**DTS**) enhancements. DTS for SQL Server 2005 introduces a complete redesign, providing a **comprehensive** enterprise extraction, transformation, and loading (ETL) platform. It's even been renamed SQL Server Integration Services.
- **Replication** enhancements. SQL Server 2005 introduces several improvements and enhancements to replication services that **simplify** the setup, configuration, and monitoring of replication **topologies**.
- Data access interfaces. Improvements to ADO.NET have been made. A new SQL Native client is introduced.
- Analysis Services enhancements. SQL Server 2005 Analysis Services introduces extensions to the scalability, manageability, **reliability**, availability, and programmability of data warehousing, business intelligence, and line of business solutions.
- Reporting Services. SQL Sever 2005 Reporting Services is a new report server and tool set for building, managing, and deploying enterprise reports. Reporting Services allows businesses to easily integrate business data from **heterogeneous** data sources and data warehouses into rich, interactive, managed reports that can be browsed and navigated over Intranet, Extranet, and Internet.
- Notification Services. SQL Server Notification Services is a platform that helps you develop centralized **notification** applications and deploy these applications on a large scale. Notification Services let businesses build rich notification applications that deliver personalized and timely information, such as stock market alerts, news **subscriptions**, package-delivery alerts, and airline ticket prices, to any device and to millions of subscribers.

SQL Server 2005 ships with significant enhancements to the core database engine architecture. These changes reflect increased needs by customers for greater performance scalability as well as support for decision support systems in both relational and data **warehousing** Models. One topic that is always brought up at database application architecture meetings is scale-up **versus**

DTS: 数据传输服务

comprehensive [ˌkɔmpriˈhensiv]
adj. 全面的，广泛的，能充分理解的，包容的
replication [ˌrepliˈkeiʃən]
n. 复制
simplify [ˈsimplifai]
vt. 单一化，简单化
topology [təˈpɔlədʒi]
n. 拓扑，布局，拓扑学布局技术

reliability [riˌlaiəˈbiliti]
n. 可靠性

heterogeneous [ˌhetərəuˈdʒi:niəs]
adj. 不同种类的，异类的

notification [ˌnəutifiˈkeiʃən]
n. 通知，布告，告示

subscription [sʌbˈskripʃən]
n. 捐献，订金，订阅，签署，同意，下标处方
warehousing [ˈwɛəhauziŋ]
n. 仓库费，入仓库，仓库储存
versus [ˈvə:səs]
prep. 对(指诉讼，比赛等中)，与……相对

Chapter 7 Get Your Arms around Microsoft SQL Server

scale-out. Scale-up is defined as a single computer with its maximum capacity for hardware: RAM, hard drives, processors, and more. Scale-out is defined as breaking a large database into smaller, more manageable pieces and dividing the workload between multiple servers. In practice, most Microsoft customers prefer scale-up. It makes it easier to add CPUs to servers and requires less operator intervention and fewer physical resources to manage. From a **theoretical standpoint**, scale-up should deliver appropriate performance for applications, depending on the quality of code in the application.

SQL Server 2005 comes in several **flavors**. Microsoft has pushed most of the new high-availability features into **Enterprise Edition** (EE) while keeping the price of Standard Edition competitive. The **Microsoft Desktop Engine** (MSDE) engine has been replaced with SQL Server Express. Express is designed to be competitive with other free databases, such as MySQL. Microsoft has introduced a low-end pay-for-database edition called Workgroup. Designed for small businesses, it removes Express Edition's limitation on database size and adds some better administration technologies. All the various versions use the same database and query formats so that **upgrading** from Express to Workgroup to Standard to Enterprise Edition happens seamlessly.

One of the most basic questions is which version of SQL Server you need. This section answers this question. The issue comes down to **Standard Edition** versus Enterprise Edition. In previous versions of SQL Server, Standard Edition was different from Enterprise Edition only in the level of high-availability features. Some would say that you paid a "high-availability" tax. Well, that has changed. SQL Server Standard Edition includes all the key high-availability features, and some new features such as database **mirroring** with some exceptions. Microsoft draws the line between Standard and Enterprise in the completeness of **coverage** around specific highly sought-after features. For instance, only Enterprise Edition's database mirroring includes the automatic **redirect** technology. Good programmers should be able to work around that issue. The real difference between Standard and Enterprise Edition is visible in scalability. Standard Edition supports only four CPUs. Although Enterprise Edition

---

theoretical [θiəˈretikəl]
adj. 理论的
standpoint [ˈstændpɔɪnt]
n. 立场, 观点
flavor [ˈfleivə]
n. 情味, 风味, 滋味, 香料
vt. 加味于
Enterprise Edition
企业版
Microsoft Desktop Engine
微软桌面引擎

upgrade [ˈʌpgreid]
vt. 使升级, 提升

Standard Edition
标准版

mirror [ˈmirə]
n. DOS 命令: 在磁盘安全区域存储根目录和文件分配表
coverage [ˈkʌvəridʒ]
n. 覆盖
redirect [ˈriːdiˈrekt]
vt. (信件)重寄, 使改道, 使改变方向

isn't limited per se, Windows Server 2003 Datacenter Edition and later support 64 processors. Thus, SQL Server 2005 is **constrained** to 64 processors. Of course, the reality of finances means that the selection of core CPU technology is limited to **budget**. Microsoft has always been good about one thing: the **migration** path from the entry-level products to Enterprise Edition is a straight one. The same on-disk formats and programming features are available across the product editions.

How to explain SQL Server Workgroup Edition? It fits somewhere between standard Edition and Express Edition. It has more CPU capability. It supports two CPUs and up to 3GB of RAM. Workgroup Edition also has no database size limit. But who are the customers for Workgroup Edition? If your company is big enough that it can afford a database, but it can't afford Standard Edition, Workgroup Edition is for you. From a feature point of view, Workgroup **aligns** more closely with Standard Edition. If you're a **hobbyist** or a beginning database programmer, SQL Server Express may be your choice.

Microsoft has introduced a replacement for MSDE called SQL Server Express. SQL Server Express has all the best features of a free database. It's small, easy to install, and has **decent** management tools. It is throttled in capacity and concurrent workload scalability. SQL Server Express uses the same reliable and **high-performance** database engine as the other versions of SQL Server 2005. It also uses the same data-access **APIs**, such as ADO.NET, SQL Native Client, and **Transact**-SQL.

constrain [kən'streɪn]
vt. 强迫，抑制，拘束
budget ['bʌdʒɪt]
vi. 做预算，编入预算
migration [maɪ'greɪʃən]
n. 移植，移往，移动

align [ə'laɪn]
vi. 排列
hobbyist ['hɒbɪɪst]
n. 沉溺于某种癖好者，嗜某爱好成癖的人

decent ['diːsnt]
adj. 正派的，端庄的，有分寸的
high-performance
高效的
API
abbr. Application Program Interface
应用程序接口
transact [træn'zækt, -'sækt]
v. 办理，交易，谈判，处理

Exercises

Ⅰ. **Fill in the blanks with the information given in the text.**

1. Microsoft left no part of its _____ product untouched. More than five years in the making, SQL Server 2005 is a completely different technology than its predecessors.

2. Microsoft has introduced a replacement for MSDE called _____.

3. Microsoft has always been good about one thing: the _____ path from the entry-level products to Enterprise Edition is a straight one.

4. In previous versions of SQL Server, _____ was different from Enterprise Edition only in the level of high-availability features.

5. From a feature point of view, _____ aligns more closely with Standard Edition.

Ⅱ. **Translate the following passages from English into Chinese.**

SQL Server 2000 shipped a 64-bit Enterprise Edition in 2003. This release was in response to pressure derived from customer workloads. In simpler terms, customers were clamoring for scalability increases for memory-intensive workloads. Because scale-out wasn't possible, Microsoft needed a scale-up capability that was less restricted than current 32-bit Microsoft operating systems (OSs). From an architectural point of view, SQL Server 2000 64-bit is the same as SQL Server 2000 32-bit. The 64-bit version was mostly a core engine upgrade that worked seamlessly, because the original algorithms were designed for 64-bit. The release of the 64-bit version created an opportunity to prove SQL Server's performance capability. There are some caveats. Only the core engine technology was supported in the 64-bit edition. This meant that Data Transformation Services, Notification Services, and Analysis Services were not 64-bit operating system—— or database——capable. Although you could manage the 64-bit database from the Enterprise Manager, the tools themselves needed a 32-bit operating system host.

Section B Database Scalability Revisited

Scalability is one of the main decision factors for choosing an enterprise database system. It refers to the **capability** to process higher volumes of **transactions**, larger volumes of data, more complex queries, and more complex application **requirements**. Scalability is factored into hardware and software components, with each being dependent on the other. A truly scalable system is balanced in its interaction between hardware and software. In the world of transaction processing (**OLTP**), scalability primarily describes a system's capability to handle higher volumes of transactions. Secondarily, it describes the capability to handle more complex applications. In the world of data warehousing (**OLAP**), the term is typically used to describe a system's capability to handle larger volumes of data (**VLDB**) and more complex queries against that data.

As an industry, **manufacturers** of database and application software spend much of their time either trying to figure out how to **exploit** new developments in hardware or trying to figure out how to deliver capabilities that go beyond those available from the hardware. In the area of scalability, this has resulted in two basic approaches scale-up and scale-out. With scale-up, hardware designers provide bigger and faster computer systems, and software designers have to figure out how to take advantage of those systems. With scale-out, software designers connect **multiple** computer systems to create a larger network of systems that can handle transaction volumes far in excess of a single computer system. Scale-up and scale-out each have advantages and disadvantages, and each basic approach has several variations.

capability [ˌkeipəˈbiliti]
n. (实际)能力, 性能, 容量
transaction [trænˈzækʃən]
n. 办理, 处理, 会报, 学报, 交易, 事务, 处理事务
requirement [riˈkwaiəmənt]
n. 需求, 要求, 必要条件, 需要的东西, 要求必备的条件
OLTP(abbr.)
联机事务处理
OLAP(abbr.)
联机分析技术
VLDB
abbr. Very Large Data Base
超大型数据库
manufacturer [ˌmænjuˈfæktʃərə]
n. 制造业者, 厂商
exploit [iksˈplɔit]
vt. 开拓, 开发, 开采

multiple [ˈmʌltipl]
adj. 多样的, 多重的

hybrid [ˈhaibrid]

In reality, customers like yourself tend to do a **hybrid** of both approaches. So what did Microsoft ever do with scale-out?

First, Microsoft renamed scale-out **federated** databases and used Distributed Partition View (**DPV**) to link the database and data. This was done for SQL Server 2000. This solution for Microsoft customers at the time was unwieldy. Microsoft didn't have significant success with DPVs. SQL Server 2005 **reflects** this, with changes made to DPVs. **Frankly**, scale-up is looking better than ever, with the new 64-bit editions. With the capability to process more than one million transactions per minute, scale-up has plenty of headroom. The original idea of scale-out was to weave together smaller tables across several servers to provide less of a single point of workload for processing systems.

SQL Server was borne from "shared nothing" parallel processing on "**commodity** hardware". The original design calls for automatic parallelism in processing of requests, and the relational database model and SQL query language are suited to parallel processing. At the same time, **parallelism** can be increased by partitioning data.

By partitioning the data inline with processor and RAM resources, increased parallelism provides greater performance. Scale-up, shared nothing unfortunately, doesn't provide unlimited scalability, and the challenge of federating servers increases the **administrative** workload. Although in theory scale out can provide unlimited performance, in reality the performance of these systems has always been questionable. And, as usual, it's cumbersome to manage these systems, because it's difficult to vet problems and keep the systems working **harmoniously**.

In terms of physically partitioning data, Microsoft SQL Server 2005 does introduce a new partition **scheme** for the horizontal partitioning of data in a table. Table partitions provide a means for dividing very large tables across file groups, which are the basic file structures for storing table data.

The last five years have seen a 20-fold increase in the peak volume of transactions a database system can support. This improvement, from **approximately** 50,000 transactions per minute to one million transactions per minute, is the result of hardware, operating system, and database management system improvements. For example, if we look at the non clustered results

n. 混合物
federate ['fedərit]
adj. 同盟的，联合的，联邦制度下的
DPV
abbr. Distributed Partition View 分布式分区视图
reflect [ri'flekt]
v. 反射，反映，表现，反省，
vt. 带给，招致
frankly ['fræŋkli]
adv. 坦白地，真诚地

commodity [kə'mɔditi]
n. 日用品
parallelism ['pærəlelizəm]
n. [数]平行，对应，类似

administrative [əd'ministrətiv]
adj. 管理的，行政的
harmoniously [hɑː'məunjəsli]
adj. 和谐的，协调的，和睦的，悦耳的
in terms of
根据，按照，用……的话，在……方面
scheme [skiːm]
n. 安排，配置，计划，阴谋，方案，图解，摘要
approximately [əprɔksɪ'mətlɪ]
adv. 近似地，大约

for Microsoft SQL Server 2000 from 2001 to 2005, you'll see that SQL Server 2000 using 64-bit technology crossed the one million transactions per minute **benchmark.** At the same time, looking into the benchmark results, you'll see that SQL Server 2000 was used to generate **terabytes** (TB) of data. This is a **watershed** event for SQL Server, because that is 60 million transactions per hour! At the same time, modern application coding practices followed and guided by the realities of **commerce**, these practices evolved how applications are written. Consider a simple e-commerce application. It has a **catalog** database that is largely static, except for product changes. It has an order-placing **functionality** that is placed behind Secure Socket Layer (**SSL**). It also has back-end processing capabilities such as real-time credit card **authorization** and shipping/inventory management. Ideally, all these processes would happen sequentially and with only one database. The reality, though, is that for many applications, maybe only credit card authorization and order capture are done in real time, and the rest are done in batches. In this new architecture where the database and software provide a service to a customer the **e-commerce** application is the salesperson. Database applications today look much different than they did only 10 years ago.

Over the last decade, the **proliferation** of web-enabled applications has brought up the issue of inter application communication. The loosely connected application model has created a means for applications and servers to act as service providers. This section shows you why applications live in the database. By loosely coupling one part of an application with another, greater scalability is achieved by creating **specialist** database applications that respond to only certain requests. Modern database systems are becoming containers for more and more business logic. The self-service nature of modern applications has driven the business logic and data closer together. **In reality**, the smallest unit of parallel processing one request and one response from one responder is **essentially** handled by the database. At the heart of this communication model is the reality that complex application systems are hard to manage. It's a good idea to place all the pieces in one container, especially when you want the basic transactional qualities defined by ACID.

- **Atomicity** states that database **modifications** must

benchmark
[计] 基准
terabyte
$1024(2^{10})$吉[千兆]字节[GB];
watershed ['wɔːtəʃed]
n. 分水岭
commerce ['kɔme(ː)s]
n. 商业
catalog ['kætəlɔg]
n. 目录, 目录册
functionality
[ˌfʌŋkəʃə'næliti]
n. 功能性, 泛函性
SSL
abbr. Secure Socket Layer
加密套接字协议层
authorization
[ˌɔːθəraiˈzeiʃən]
n. 授权, 认可
e-commerce
电子商务
proliferation
[prəuˌlifə'reiʃən]
n. 增殖, 分芽繁殖

specialist ['speʃəlist]
n. 专门医师, 专家

in reality
实际上, 事实上
essentially [i'senʃəli]
adv. 本质上, 本来
atomicity [ˌætə'misiti]
n. 原子数
modification [ˌmɔdifi'keiʃən]
n. 更改, 修改, 修正

follow an "all or nothing" rule. Each transaction is said to be "atomic". If one part of the transaction fails, the entire transaction fails.

- **Consistency** states that only valid data is written to the database. If a transaction is executed that **violates** the database's consistency rules, the entire transaction is rolled back, and the database is restored to a state consistent with those rules. On the other hand, if a transaction executes successfully, it takes the database from one state that is consistent with the rules to another state that is also consistent with the rules.
- **Isolation** requires that multiple transactions occurring at the same time not affect each other's execution.
- **Durability** ensures that any transaction committed to the database is not lost. Durability is ensured through the use of database backups and transaction logs that facilitate the **restoration** of committed transactions in spite of any subsequent software or hardware failure.

consistency [kən'sɪstənsɪ]
n. 连接，结合，坚固性
violate ['vaɪəleɪt]
vt. 违犯，冒犯，干扰，违反，妨碍，侵犯

isolation [ˌaɪsəʊ'leɪʃən]
n. 隔绝，孤立，隔离
durability [ˌdjʊərə'bɪlɪtɪ]
n. 经久，耐久力

restoration ['restə'reɪʃən]
n. 恢复，归还，赔偿，修补

Exercises

Ⅰ. **Read the following passage and talk about the application characteristics of the SQL Server 2005.**

SQL Server 2005 comes with no less than three application server-type technologies: Notification Services (NS), Replication, and the newest, SQL Service Broker (SSB). There are also native Web Services and the capability to host the .NET Framework. Originally, the purpose of the application server was to provide a middle-tier bridge between the database tier and customer presentation tier. The middle tier contained the business logic. The application server hid the data tier from the presentation layer. The idea was that business logic could be encapsulated in the middle tier. This meant that each tier was a specialist, and scalability and the other "abilities" would come along for the ride. In reality, three-tier applications are difficult to do. Moreover, the advances in hardware meant that more value could be derived from a single server by putting more code on it meaning more applications. As business logic was being moved to the database, captured in stored procedures, queries, and database views, the need for the middle tier dissolved. Thanks to the e-commerce revolution, databases are exposed to the presentation layer on a scale never before seen.

The way e-commerce applications are designed, reflecting the integration of business processes with databases, brings us to the architectural model called Service-Oriented Architecture (SOA). SOA can loosely be defined as a collection of services that communicate with each other. The database logic is directly tied to business logic. Moreover, the database objects have expectations about what data will be passed to them and what data they should send back. For example, many credit card processing services expose a web service for submitting a credit card authorization request. The replying database application knows what valid data is and how to process it. Any data that is passed to the credit card authorization service that is not in the correct form is rejected. The Microsoft version of the SOA movement has its origins in the Distributed Component Object Model (DCOM). DCOM is a foundational technology of the Microsoft Windows operating system and is complementary to the current object framework:. NET. DCOM and the .NET Framework represent the modern system approach to computer science that sprang from the object-oriented programming (OOP) model. In OOP, the idea of creating objects and applying methods to them is very similar to the SOA. At the core of OOP is the idea that code serves a function. This means that the very essence of OOP is a service. The SOA at its deepest level is what makes the operating system useful. In business applications, the service approach lets you do things like place an order, ship a box, and capture credit card authorization. Under the service model is a communication model that is not unlike the human communication model. In SQL Server 2005, a new framework called SQL Service Broker allows message and data transport to happen while encapsulating business processes and logic in a parallel fashion.

Section C Features for Database Development

This section discusses the feature sets with which database application developers are typically familiar. Database administrators might **be inclined to** skip this section, but I wouldn't. What has happened in this release of SQL Server can simply be described as a re-architecture of the frameworks for developing new classes of applications. In SQL Server 2005, the **extensibility** of the overall database platform has been greatly increased. Don't be distracted by SQL Server's capability to "host" the Common Language Runtime (**CLR**). It's much more than that. The introduction of **managed code** into SQL Server means greater integration **opportunities** for packaged and custom application development. Basically, SQL Server has three layers:

- The first layer is core functionality, such as the SQL Server Engine SQLServer.exe.
- The second layer is the **framework** from which all the interfaces into the components are accessed. This layer is private to Microsoft.
- In the third layer, you find the program **assemblies** Microsoft provides to hook up application forms to the objects found in SQL Server. SQL Server 2005 ships with a new range of functionality that includes Analysis Services and **Replication**, as well as cope functionality found in SQL Server.

As a developer, you can work with the third layer without **coupling** to a user interface. This means that you can use functionality such as SQL Server Integration Service to move data around programmatically. You can create a service that

be inclined to
倾向于
extensibility [iks,tensə'biliti]
n. 可扩展性, 展开性
CLR
abbr. Common Language Runtime
通用语言运行环境
managed code
托管代码
opportunity [,ɔpə'tju:niti]
n. 机会, 时机

framework ['freimwə:k]
n. 构架, 框架, 结构
assembly [ə'sembli]
n. 集合, 装配, 汇编
replication [,repli'keiʃən]
n. 复制

couple ['kʌpl]
vt. 连合, 连接, 结合

manages the backup of an entire database server without actually using SQL Management Studio. In fact, one of the best ways to develop SQL applications is to use the user interfaces to build the basic skeleton and then script the entire thing.

Visual Studio Integration

If you're a database administrator or database developer, Visual Studio .NET 2005 represents a **monumental** leap forward in working with databases. Microsoft has always supported "its" database, SQL Server, better than, say, IBM DB2. With the **simultaneous** release of SQL Server 2005, .NET Framework 2.0, ASP.NET 2.0, and the development tools, Microsoft has effectively **synchronized** the product line. Because different versions of the .NET Framework can **reside** side by side on the same operating system, the **implementation** of the new products should be seamless and should not require you to uninstall previous versions.

In previous versions of SQL Server, you had to develop Data Transformation Services packages, Analysis Services cubes, and Transact-SQL modules in specific tools oriented to that technology. With SQL Server 2005, you can use Visual Studio to develop everything and deploy it with a click. Having Visual Studio as a one-stop shop for development offers numerous benefits:

- Team development. Using the project system and source control, the entire application, from database modules to user interfaces, can be controlled and versioned.
- Debugging and deploying. Visual Studio now supports direct debugging of stored procedures and managed code in the same debug process. You can **deploy** a new application via the one-click deployment feature.
- User experience. The new SQL Server Management Studio and Business **Intelligence** Development Studio are designed from the Visual Studio user interfaces. Help **functionality** is **integrated** such that a developer can access both the SQL Server and Visual Studio Books Online from one application.

If you are a straight database user, SQL Server gives you all the tools you need via the SQL Server Management Studio. If

monumental [ˌmɔnjuˈmentl]
adj. 纪念碑的，纪念物的，不朽的，非常的
simultaneous [ˌsiməlˈteinjəs]
adj. 同时的，同时发生的
synchronize [ˈsɪŋkrənaɪz]
v. 同步
reside [riˈzaid]
vi. 居住
implementation [ˌimplimenˈteiʃən]
n. 执行

deploy [diˈplɔi]
v. 展开，配置
intelligence [inˈtelidʒəns]
n. 智力，聪明，智能
functionality [ˌfʌŋkʃəˈnæliti]
n. 功能性，泛函性
integrate [ˈintigreit]
vt. 使成整体，使一体化，求……的积分
v. 结合

you are a straight business intelligence developer, you can do **server-level** work for Analysis Services, data mining, SQL Server Integration Services, and Reporting Services from the Business Intelligence Development Studio. What if you do SQL Server database development, business intelligence development, and ASP.NET development and have Visual Studio 2005? If all the SQL Server components are installed on a machine with Visual Studio 2005, you get all the tools, but Visual Studio is **enhanced** with new **project** types for the SQL Server components. The reverse isn't true; you can't create a C# application from within the Business Intelligence Development Studio. Now let's look at one of the most commonly discussed features of SQL Server 2005: the .NET Framework.

.NET Framework Integration

When it comes to developing applications, Microsoft customers are some of the most enterprising and creative people there are. When Microsoft program managers and product managers talk to customers about their applications, it's always interesting to find how they have used the technologies. Customers are **clamoring** for new features to develop applications with their favorite product or language. With the implementation of SQL Server as a runtime host, we are entering a new era of **creativity**.

Using CLR integration, you can code your stored **procedures** and functions in the .NET Framework language of your choice. Microsoft Visual Basic .NET and the C# programming language both offer **object-oriented** constructs, **structured exception** handling, arrays, namespaces, and classes. In addition, the .NET Framework provides thousands of classes and methods that have extensive built-in capabilities that you can easily use on the server side. Many tasks that were **awkward** or difficult to perform in Transact-SQL can be accomplished by using managed code. Additionally, two new types of database objects are available **aggregates** and user-defined types. You can now better use the knowledge and skills that you have already acquired to write in-process code. In short, SQL Server 2005 lets you extend the database server to more easily perform appropriate computations and operations on the back end.

---

server-level
服务层

enhanced [in'hɑːnst]
adj. 增强的，提高的，放大的
project ['prɔdʒekt]
n. 计划，方案，事业，企业，工程

clamor ['klæmə]
v. 喧嚷，大声地要求
creativity [ˌkriːeɪ'tɪvətɪ]
n. 创造力，创造
procedure [prə'siːdʒə]
n. 程序，手续
object-oriented
面向对象的
structured
结构化的
exception [ik'sepʃən]
n. 除外，例外，反对
awkward ['ɔːkwəd]
adj. 难使用的，笨拙的
aggregate ['ægrigeit]
n. 合计，总计，集合体

You can capitalize on the CLR integration to write code that has more complex logic and is more suited for computation tasks by using languages such as Visual Basic .NET and C#. In addition, Visual Basic .NET and C# offer object-oriented capabilities, such as encapsulation, inheritance, and polymorphism. You can now easily organize related code into classes and namespaces. This means that you can more easily organize and maintain your code **investments** when you are working with large amounts of code. This ability to logically and physically organize code into assemblies and namespaces is a huge benefit. It allows you to better find and relate different pieces of code in a large database implementation.

.NET code uses code access security. This uses a security policy that is based on the **principal** running the code. Remember that a principal typically is a user account. The principal's user privileges affect the code itself, the location from where the code was loaded. When an assembly is loaded into memory, it is automatically limited to the execution or process of the memory and system environment that loaded it. In a sense, the assembly is forced to play in only one **sandbox**. In SQL Server 2005, this concept is **morphed** into something called the **AppDomain**. The AppDomain isolates all the resources that the .NET code uses from the resources that SQL Server uses. This is true even when the SQL Server and .NET code are in the same process space. The AppDomain protects SQL Server from misuse or **malicious** use, which is something extended stored procedures can't do.

When you install SQL Server 2005, you'll notice that the new security architecture keeps installed features turned off by default. Moreover, the database administrator or system administrator must explicitly grant a user permission to create an assembly in SQL Server 2005. Creating an assembly is really loading a precompiled **Data Definition Language** (**DDL**) into the database. The assembly itself is stored in a row in the database. You can find out which assemblies are loaded by running the catalog view sys.assemblies. When an assembly is loaded, the DDL used for setting the assembly's security state.

investment [in'vestmənt]
n. 投资，可获利的东西

principal ['prinsəp(ə)l, -sip-]
adj. 主要的，首要的

sandbox ['sændbɔks]
n. 沙箱，沙盒
morph [mɔf]
n. 变种，变体，语子，语素形式，形素
AppDomain
应用程序域
malicious [mə'liʃəs]
adj. 怀恶意的，恶毒的

DDL
addr. Data Definition Language
数据定义语言

Exercises

Ⅰ. Fill in the blanks with the information given in the text.

1. The introduction of _____ into SQL Server means greater integration opportunities for packaged and custom application development.

2. In fact, one of the best ways to develop SQL applications is to use the _____ to build the basic skeleton and then script the entire thing.

3. If you are a straight database user, SQL Server gives you all the tools you need via the _____.

4. .NET code uses code access security. This uses a security policy that is based on the _____.

5. Using _____, you can code your stored procedures and functions in the .NET Framework language of your choice.

Ⅱ. Translate the following sentences into Chinese.

SQL Server 2005 gives you a couple of choices: you can store the XML data as the Varchar(max) data type or the XML data type. Varchar(max) may be a good solution if you need only a low-level storage locale. For anything beyond just storage outside the file system, the XML data type is recommended. The XML data type is a native SQL Server type with all the characteristics of other SQL native types. In general, you may need to use a combination of these approaches. For example, you may want to store your XML data in an XML data type column and promote properties from it into relational columns. Alternatively, you may want to use mapping technology and store non recursive parts in non-XML columns and only the recursive parts in XML data type columns.

Grammar 7　科技英语翻译方法与技巧(Ⅱ)

英语中词的翻译

1. 词义的选择

我们知道，在科技英语中，有许多词汇是借用的日常英语，但是词汇的意义发生了很大的转变。在翻译中，我们十分重视词汇意义的选择，在某种意义上，词汇意义的选择是否正确直接决定了翻译的成败。

例如：

bus: 在普通英语中译为"公共汽车"，在计算机英语中译为"总线"。

character: 在普通英语中译为"性格，特性"，在计算机英语中译为"字符"。

character packing density: 字符存储或记录密度。

character sensing equipment: 字符读出装置。

character string expression: 字符串表达式。

flag: 在普通英语中译为"旗，旗帜"，在计算机英语中译为"标记，特征位"。

Conductor: 在普通英语中译为"售票员和乐队指挥"，在计算机英语中则翻译为"导体"。

2. 合成词类和转化词类

在科技英语中，常常有许多的合成词类，有时候为了翻译的需要，对于不了解的合成词，可以大胆地猜测其意思是两个词的叠加。合成指由两个相互独立的词合成一个新词。

例如：

    work + shop (workshop)　　　　feed + back (feedback)
    in + put (input)　　　　　　　　large + scale (large-scale)
    some + one (someone)

转化指通过只改变单词的词性和读音，不改变词形而得到新词的方法。

    use (名词)用途，效用　——　to use (动词) 使用，利用
    water (名词)水　　　　——　to water(动词) 浇水

所以在翻译过程中，可以针对其名词的意思，翻译成其动词的意思。

3. 派生类词

对于派生类的词汇，在翻译过程中，可以根据其前缀和后缀来翻译，固定的前缀或者后缀常常有固定的翻译方法。而大多数的派生类词都是在加上前、后缀后，只改变了词义，没有改变词类。

(1) 一些名词前缀和后缀及其固定翻译方法如下。

    inter - (between, among)　　international, interface
    counter- (against)　　　　　　counteract, counterpart
    sub   - (beneath, less than)　subway, submarine

(2) 一些形容词前缀及其固定翻译方法如下。

    im - (not)　　　　　　impossible, impolite
    in - (not)　　　　　　informal, nconvenient
    un - (not)　　　　　　untrue, unhappy
    -able, - ible　　　　　　acceptable, responsible

(3) 一些动词词缀及其固定翻译方法如下。

    de - (cause not to be)　　demagnetize, defrost
    dis - (the opposite)　　　　disconnect, discharge
    ex - (out)　　　　　　　　exit
    over - (too much)　　　　　overdo, overestimate
    re - (again)　　　　　　　rewrite, retell

(4) 加后缀构成新词可能改变也可能不改变词义，但一定会改变词类。

    reality　　　　n.————　　　real　(a.) + ity
    discussion　　n.————　　　discuss (v.) + ion
    sailor　　　　n.————　　　sail　(v.) + or

 参考译文

Section A　SQL Server 2005 简介

    SQL Server 2005 是微软 SQL 生产线上最值得期待的产品。在经过了上百万个邮件，成千上万的规范说明，以及数十次修订后，微软承诺 SQL Server 2005 是最新的基于 Windows 数据库应用的数据库开发平台。本节内容将指出 SQL Server 2005 产品的一些新的重要的特征。SQL Server 2005 几乎覆盖 OLTP

及 OLAP 技术的所有内容。微软公司的这个旗舰数据库产品几乎覆盖了所有的东西。这个软件在经过5年多的制作后，SQL Server 2005 成为一个与它任何一个前辈产品都完全不同的产品。本节涵盖了该产品的主要特征。当人们去寻求其想要的一些功能和技术时，它就会从中提取出最重要的和最感兴趣的功能，这些包括 SQL Server Engine 的一些蜕变的历史，以及各种各样的 SQL Server 2005 的版本、可伸缩性、有效性、大型数据库的维护以及商业智能等。SQL Server 2005 提供了下面的内容：

- 数据库引擎增强技术。SQL Server 2005 对数据库引擎进行了许多改进，并引入新的功能。这些改进和功能包括与微软的.NET 框架的结合、新的 XML 技术、Transact-SQL 增强技术、新的数据类型，以及对关系数据库的可伸缩性及有效性的改进等。
- 管理工具。SQL Server 2005 引入了一套集成的管理工具和 APIS 管理技术，提供更轻松的使用、管理以及对大型 SQL 数据库配置操作的支持。
- DTS 增强技术。对 SQL Server 2005 中的 DTS 技术进行了全新的设计，提供了广泛的企业扩展、传送、装载平台。它甚至将 SQL Server 改名为综合化服务。
- 复制增强技术。SQL Server 2005 对复制服务进行了许多的改进和提高，能够简化复制技术的安装、配置和监控。
- 数据访问接口。对于 ADO.NET 已经进行了改进。一个全新的 SQL 本地客户端被引入了。
- 分析服务增强技术。SQL Server 2005 分析服务对可伸缩性、易管理性、可靠性、有效性及数据仓库的可编程性、商业智能以及商务解决方案等技术进行了扩展。
- 报表服务。SQL Sever 2005 报表服务是一个全新的报表服务系统和工具，它能够构造、管理、配置企业的报表。报表服务允许企业很容易地从异种数据源或数据仓库的商业数据进行集成，从而形成丰富的、交互的及可管理的报表，这些报表能够通过 Intranets、Extranets 或 Internet 的浏览器浏览及导航。
- 通告服务。SQL Server 的通告服务是一个能够帮助你开发集中式通告应用以及如何大范围地布置这些通告的开发平台。通告服务让企业可以构建丰富的通告服务，用来发送个性化和及时的信息，如股票市场预警、新闻订阅、包裹单通知、飞机票价格预报以及成千上万的其他的预定信息。

SQL Server 2005 对于数据库核心的体系结构进行了重要的改进。这些变化折射了消费者巨大的性能伸缩性的需求，以及在关系和数据仓库模型中的决策支持系统的需求。在数据库体系结构中一直有一个困扰的话题："向上扩展"还是"向外扩展"。向上扩展被定义为：一台单独的计算机，它拥有最大的硬件容量，如 RAM、硬盘、处理器以及更多。而向外扩展被定义为：将一个大的数据库分成更小的、更加容易管理的部分，并且将工作量分到多个服务器上。实际上，大多数微软的消费者喜欢向上扩展，它使得人们容易地在服务器上增加 CPU,且很少需要操作员的干预以及很少的物理资源管理。从一个技术观点上看，向上扩展依赖于应用程序的代码质量来实现合适的应用功能。

SQL Server 2005 形成了许多的风格。微软已经在企业版中增加了绝大多数的新的、高效的、可利用的功能，并且保持标准版的竞争价格。微软的 SQL Server Express 已经替代 MSDE 引擎。快递版设计的目的是为了和其他的免费数据库产品，如 MySQL 进行竞争。微软已经引入了一个低端数据库版本，即 Workgroup，主要为小型企业而设计的。它解除了 Express 版在数据库大小上的限制，增加了一些好的管理技术。所有这些版本均用同样的数据库以及查询格式，使得从 Express 到 Workgroup、Standard 以及 Enterprise 版都能实现无缝升级。

最基本的问题之一就是，你到底需要什么版本的 SQL Server，本将会回答这个问题。该问题可归结为对标准版和企业版的选择。在 SQL Server 以前的版本中，标准版仅仅是在高性能上同企业版有所不同。一些人可能要说了，那是你支付"高性能"的税了。很好，这点已经改变了。现在标准版囊括了所有的高性能的特点，而且包括一些新的特征，如数据库异常镜像等。微软公司在标准版和企业版之间关于覆盖面的完整性以及高性能特征方面几乎是平等的。例如，企业版仅仅是在数据库镜像中包括了自动重定位技术。

优秀的程序员应该有能力处理这个。标准版与企业版真正的不同在于可视的伸缩性。标准版仅支持 4 个 CPU。尽管企业版本身没有限制，但是 Windows Server 2003 Datacenter 版以及后来的版本支持 64 微处理器。这样，SQL Server 2005 被限制在 64 个处理器范围内。当然，经济能力让 CPU 核心技术只能被限制在预算当中。微软一直很擅长一件事，即从入门级产品到企业版的通路是平坦的。同样在磁盘数据格式以及编程特点上也都是有效的。

怎样描述 SQL Server 工作组版呢？它介于标准版和快递版之间，具有更多 CPU 处理能力。它支持 2 个 CPU，并升级至 3GB 的内存管理。工作组版也没有数据库大小的限制。但是到底什么样的用户要使用工作组版的呢？如果你的公司足够大而且能负担一个数据库，但是支付不起企业版的时候，工作组版就是你的选择。从特征上看，工作组版与标准版更加接近。如果你是数据库的初级编程人员或业余爱好者，那么快递版就是你的选择。

微软公司已经用快递版替代了 MSDE。快递版具有一个免费数据库的所有最好的特征。它体积小，容易安装，而且具有适合的管理工具。它在容量上和一致工作负载上进行了限制。快递版具有其他版本如 SQL Server 2005 相同的可靠性和高效的数据引擎。它也拥有同样的数据访问 API 技术，如 ADO.NET、SQL 本地客户端及 Transact-SQL 等。

Section B 再谈数据库可伸缩性

可伸缩性的主要决定因素之一就是选择一个企业数据库系统。它涉及的性能包括处理更大的交易、更大的数据量、更复杂的查询、更复杂的应用需求。可伸缩性可分解成硬件和软件的组件，以及可依赖的其他的每一种东西。一个真实的可伸缩系统在它的硬件和软件系统间得到平衡。在一个在线交易处理系统中，可伸缩性主要指一个系统能否处理更多的交易量；其次，它指的是能否处理更复杂的应用。而在在线数据仓库系统中，它指的是系统能否对大量的数据进行处理以及能否处理更为复杂的数据查询。

作为一种产业，数据和应用软件的制造商总是花费时间在构造如何利用新开发的硬件，或者试图去构建如何有效地利用硬件使其发挥更大的能力。在可伸缩性的领域中，这将导致两个方法的产生：向上扩展及向外扩展。对于向上扩展，硬件设计者提供更大的和更快的计算机系统，而软件设计者必须勾勒出怎么利用这些硬件。对于向外扩展，软件设计者将多重系统连接以制造一个更大的网络系统，它能够完成单机系统无法完成的巨大的事务处理。向上扩展和向外扩展都有自己的优缺点，每种基本的方法也都有许多的变化。实际上，消费者倾向于两种方法的融合。那么微软公司对向外扩展都做了些什么呢？

首先，微软公司将向外扩展重新命名为联合数据库，并用分布式分区视图来连接数据库与数据，这是 SQL Server 2000 的做法。这个解决方案对于微软的消费者来说是笨拙的。微软在 DPV 上没有获得很大的成功。SQL Server 2005 的 DPV 的变化就反映了这一点。坦白地说，向上扩展看上去比以往的要好，拥有全新的 64 位版本的，具有每分钟处理超百万的事务的能力，具有很大的向上空间。而向外扩展的最初想法是分解成横跨几台服务器的更小的表，从而为处理系统提供无足轻重的单点工作量。

SQL Server 诞生在商业硬件的"无共享"的并行处理的时期。最初的设计要求能在处理请求过程中实现自动并行机制，并且关系数据库和 SQL 查询语言与并行处理匹配。同时，能够通过划分数据来增加并行性。

通过划分数据给处理器和内存资源，增强并行机制以提供更高的性能。不幸的是，向上扩展不能提供无限的可伸缩性，且对增加了管理工作负荷的联合服务器来说是个挑战。尽管向外扩展在理论上能够提供无限的性能，但实际上这些系统的性能一直是有疑问的。而且，和往常一样，管理这些系统是费劲的，因为修复问题和使系统协调工作很困难。

就物理上划分数据而言，微软的 SQL Server 2005 针对一个表中的数据的水平划分引入了一个新的划分模式。表划分为跨文件组的超大数据表的划分提供一种手段，它是存储数据表的基本文件结构。

在过去的 5 年中，我们可以看到 20 个在数据库系统能支持交易时高峰容量的增量。大约每分钟 5 万个交易量到每分钟一百万个交易量的进步是硬件、操作系统及数据库管理系统进步的结果。例如，如果我们查看微软 SQL Server 2000 从 2001 到 2005 的非聚类的查询结果的话，你会发现 SQL Server 2000 使用的 64 位技术每分钟可处理一百万的基准数据。同时，观察这个基准结果，你会看到它产生的是太字节(百万兆字节)的数据。这对 SQL Server 是一个重大的事情，因为那是每小时 6 亿的交易量。同时，现代的应用程序的编码常常被商业化，这些实践包括怎么编写应用程序。以一个简单的电子商务应用为例。它有一个目录数据库，它是静态的除非产品发生了变化。它拥有被安排在加密套接字协议层的排序功能。它也具有后台处理能力，如实时信用卡授权或配货管理。理论上，所有这些处理应该顺序发生，但实际上，尽管对于许多的应用，可能仅仅是信用卡授权及命令捕获工作被实时处理，而其余的则批处理完成。在这个新的体系结构中，由数据库和软件提供给消费者电子商务应用的服务，被称做推销员。今天，数据库的应用与十年前的数据库相比就有很大的不同。

在过去的十年中，Web 应用的传播提出了相互通信应用的问题。松散的应用连接模型已经为应用和服务扮演服务提供者提供了一种手段。本节将告诉你为什么应用存在于数据库中。通过一个应用和另一个应用的松散连接，更大的伸缩性可通过构建专家库来获得，这个专家库仅对某一种请求回应。现代的数据库系统已经成为越来越多的业务逻辑的容器。现代应用的自服务本质上已经驱使业务逻辑和数据更紧密。实际上，作为并行处理的最小单元，一个请求和一个来自回应者的回应是必须由数据库来处理的。这个连接模型的核心问题是，事实上复杂的应用系统是很难管理的。把所有的小片段放到一个容器里是一个很好的主意，尤其是当你要求达到所谓的 ACID 的交易质量时，这点显得非常重要。

- 原子性表示数据库的修改必须遵循"要么都做，要么都不做"的原则。每笔数据交易都被称为"原子"，如果一个交易的部分失败了，那么整个交易将失败。
- 一致性表示只能将有效的数据写到数据库中。如果一笔交易的执行违反了数据库一致性的规则，整个交易回滚，数据库被恢复到遵循同规则的一致的状态。另一方面，如果一笔交易成功了，那么它将让数据库从一个一致性状态到另一个也是一致性的状态转变。
- 独立性要求当多重交易同时发生时，彼此互不影响执行。
- 持久性确保通过数据库备份和那些用于方便恢复已确认交易的日志，不管以后软件或硬件是否发生错误，它都能使被数据库确认的交易数据不丢失。

Section C 数据库开发的特点

本节主要讨论数据库应用开发者熟悉的典型特征。数据库管理员可能想要跳过本节的内容，但我想不应该那样做。SQL Server 的发行可以被描述成是为应用开发的新类库重新定义体系结构的框架。在 SQL Server 2005 中，整个数据库平台的可扩展性已经得到很大的提高。不要单纯地看到 SQL Server 的主机的通用语言运行环境，还有比这更多的功能。将托管代码引入到 SQL Server 意味着对包应用和定制应用开发能提供更多的集成机会。基本上，SQL Server 有 3 层：

- 第一层是核心功能，如 SQL Server 引擎及 SQL Server.exe。
- 第二层是所有的能访问的组件的接口框架。这一层知识是微软私有的。
- 在第三层，你会发现程序在 SQL Server 2005 对象集成了微软提供的应用表单。SQL Server 2005 装备有包分析服务和复制功能的一个全新的领域以及在 SQL 服务器能完成的功能。

作为一名开发者，你可以不用连接一个用户的接口就可以在第三层工作，这意味着你能使用一些功能，如 SQL Server 集成服务以及通过编程移动数据。你能构建一个服务，用来管理在没有实际使用 SQL Management Studio 的情况下完成对整个数据库的备份。实际上，开发一个 SQL 应用的最好方式就是使用用户接口区创建一个基本的框架，然后通过脚本方式解决所有的事情。

Visual Studio 集成

如果你是一个数据库管理员或者数据库的开发者，Visual Studio.NET 2005 代表了一个巨大的数据库应用的飞跃。微软一直都在支持其数据库 SQL Server，这点要比 IBM DB2 要好。.NET Framework 2.0 及 ASP.NET 2.0 以及开发工具，微软有着有效的同步生产线。因为不同的.NET 框架版本可能与同样的操作系统并存，因此新产品的执行应该是不需要你卸载先前的版本的，即无缝执行。

在 SQL Server 先前的版本中，你必须在面向该技术的工具中开发数据传送服务包、分析服务立方体、交互式 SQL 模块。而对于 SQL Server 2005，你可以用 Visual Studio(可视化集成环境)来开发每件工作，并通过鼠标的单击操作就可以完成。让 Visual Studio 作为开发的一站式服务有无数的好处：

- 组开发。使用项目系统和控制技术，整个应用从数据库模块到用户接口都能被控制和可视化。
- 调试和配置。Visual Studio 现在支持直接对存储过程及托管代码以相同的调试过程进行直接的调试。你可以通过单击配置功能就可以配置一个新的应用。
- 用户帮助。新的 SQL Server 管理集成环境和商业智能开发集成环境设计了用户接口的可视化集成。帮助功能被集成以至于一个开发者能够既访问 SQL Server 又可以查阅一个应用的 Visual Studio 在线帮助书籍。

如果你是一个数据库的直接用户，SQL Server 将通过 SQL Server Management 集成环境提供给你所有需要的工具。如果你是直接的商业智能软件开发者，你可以在商业智能集成开发环境中做一些服务级的工作，如分析服务、数据挖掘、SQL Server 集成服务以及报表服务。如果你既是一个 SQL Server 数据库开发人员，又想进行商业智能和 ASP.NET 开发，Visual Studio 2005 能提供什么呢？如果所有的 SQL Server 组件都被安装到一台机器上，那么你能获得所有的开发工具，但 Visual Studio 通过提供新的 SQL Server 组件的项目类型得到了增强。相反，你不可能在商业智能集成开发环境下创建一个 C#应用程序。现在我们来看 SQL Server 2005 被谈论得最多的特点之一：.NET 框架。

.NET 框架集成

当谈到开发应用，微软的消费者是最有进取心，并且最赋有创造力的。当微软的程序领导者和产品的开发者讨论消费者关于应用问题时，他们对消费者如果使用技术感兴趣。消费者呼唤利用更符合他们口味的产品或语言去开发应用程序的新功能。随着 SQL Server 能作为一个运行时的主机的实现，我们就进入了一个创造性的新纪元。

使用通用语言运行集成环境，你就能通过编码将你的存储过程和功能放到你选择的.NET 框架语言中。微软的 VB.NET 和 C#.NET 编程语言都能提供面向对象的结构，以及结构异常处理、数组、名空间和类。此外，.NET 框架还提供成千上万的类与方法，它们能够使你在服务器端的开发更简单。许多在交互式 SQL 看似困难或棘手的问题通过托管代码都能完成。另外，还有两种新类型的数据库对象：用户定义的类型及可用的聚合类型。你现在能够很好地使用你在编写过程码时获得的知识和技术。简单地说，SQL Server 2005 让你的数据库在后台更容易执行合适的计算和操作。

你可以利用通用语言运行集成环境编写代码，使其具有更复杂的逻辑，并通过像 VB.NET 及 C#.NET 语言来完成计算机任务。VB.NET 及 C#.NET 提供处理面向对象的能力，如封装、继承及多态。你现在可以更加容易地将相关的代码组织到类和名空间中。这意味着当你需要大量的代码时，你能更容易地组织和维护你的代码。这种能够将代码在逻辑上和物理上组织成汇编和名空间的能力是能够获得巨大利益的。它允许你更好地发现和关联不同的、在大型数据库中执行的代码片断。

.NET 代码使用代码保证安全性。这是使用了一个基于运行原理的代码的安全策略。一个典型的原理就是用户的账户。用户的优先权原理影响代码本身以及代码装载的位置。当一个程序集被装载到内存时，它被自动限制到其装载的内存和系统环境中。实际上，程序集就像被装到一个沙盒中执行。在 SQL Server 2005 中，这个概念被变种成了应用程序域。这个应用程序域将.NET 代码同 SQL Server 所使用的所有资源进行了隔离。即使当 SQL Server 和.NET 代码处在同一处理空间，这也能实现。应用程序域保护 SQL 服务器免受误用或恶意使用，这是扩展存储过程所不能做的。

当你安装 SQL Server 2005 时，你将注意到默认情况下新的安全结构安装的功能被关闭。而且，数据库管理员或者系统管理员必须明确地确认用户关于在 SQL Server 2005 中是否同意创建一个程序集。创建一个程序集就真正地将预编译的数据定义语言装载到了数据库中。这个程序集本身被存储数据库的一行中。你可以通过运行目录查看 sys.assemblies 了解哪些程序集被装载。当一个程序集被装载后，数据定义语言就会设置程序集的安全状态。

Chapter 8 Computer Networking and Networking Security
(计算机网络和网络安全)

Section A Computer Networking

Introduction

Most of us use computer-based networks every day. They are woven into the **fabric** of our everyday lives——at home, at school, and at work-making it is almost impossible to function without them. Almost all of us grew up with a telephone network, and we use it automatically, without any special training. Networks of computers-data networks have now moved into the same position in our society. In a **remarkably** short time, our lives have become virtually dependent upon them. The global Internet is **ubiquitous**, with the exception of some third world countries. Young people have grown up using the Internet, just as the previous two generations grew up using the telephone network. They sit down and use it without the assistance of manuals, help screens, or classes. They simply access the network through the computer and tap into a wealth of information, games, and other resources that were **unavailable** to their parents and grandparents when they were growing up.

As you can see, networks have become so much a part of daily living that we are almost unaware that they exist. That is the way it ought to be. We should not need to worry about the details of their operation or whether they will function properly when we need them，just as we don't worry about whether water will flow when we turn on a **spigot** or whether lights will come on when we **flip** a switch. Water and electricity "networks" are elements of the utility infrastructure in most countries, but we don't even think about what it takes to deliver those services to our homes or offices. Data and computer networks are a much newer technology. Their communications capabilities are generally quite

fabric ['fæbrik]
n. 织品 结构

remarkably [rɪˈmɑːkəb(ə)li]
adv. 非常地, 显著地
ubiquitous [juːˈbɪkwɪtəs]
adj. 普遍存在的

unavailable [ˌʌnəˈveɪləbl]
adj. 难以获得的

spigot ['spɪɡət]
n. 栓, 龙头, 套管
flip [flɪp]
vt. 弹, 轻击

reliable, although they do not yet measure up to the fail-safe services of the older utilities, computer networks, however, are as essential to our lifestyles today as the older networks.

Why study networks?

As a network user, why might you want to study networks, and the way they work, in greater detail than the average person? Probably the most common reason is that you hope to work in a communications field. You may have heard that there are good, high paying jobs in communications, and you want a part of the "action". It is true. **Telecommunications** and networking fields are expanding rapidly, and companies that provide the services, as well as organizations that use network services, need many skilled employees. Furthermore, it is an exciting field because it changes very rapidly. Networking technology advances continually, and the **regulatory** environment changes as governments gain new perspective on the potential uses and abuses of networking capabilities.

You might, however, have more of an academic interest in networking. Because you use net works every day, you may simply want to understand more about the way they work and you may not have any intention of working in the communications industry. You may want to learn more about some of the newer communications technologies, such as **broadband** or wireless communications. Studying networking will broaden your general knowledge, expand your vocabulary, and open your eyes to uses of communications that you may not have been aware of; which may be useful to you, regardless of which career you choose.

Networks Classified by Geography

One Common way of classifying networks is by the geographic area they cover. The most common designations are the local area network(LAN) and the wide area network(WAN). A third category, which is less well defined, is the **metropolitan** area network(MAN).

1. Local Area Networks(LANs)

Perhaps the network you are most familiar with is the network that connects your personal computer at school to other

---

reliable [rɪ'laɪəbl]
adj. 可靠的, 可信赖的

telecommunication
['telɪkəmjuːnɪ'keɪʃən]
n. 电信, 电信学

regulatory ['regjulətəri]
adj. 调整的, 管理

broadband ['brɔːdbænd]
n. 宽带

metropolitan
[metrə'pɒlɪt(ə)n]
adj. 主要都市的, 大城市

personal computers in the building or around the campus. Because university campuses normally cover a rather small geographic area, the networks on them are considered to be local, and are called local area networks(LANs). We will define LANs more precisely later, but you can easily understand the difference between the locality of a campus network and the geographic **diversity** of the public telephone network that covers the entire world. There are also data networks that cover a wide geographical area, such as all of the U.S. or even the world, and these are called wide area networks(WANs). A WAN that you have undoubtedly used is the Internet, although the Internet is technically a **collection** of LANs and WANs that are connected together.

diversity [dai'və:siti]
n. 差异，多样性

collection [kə'lekʃən]
n. [计]集合，聚集

Coming back to the network on your campus, it probably has hundreds or even thousands of workstations and servers attached to it. Each of these devices is a node on the network. The key attribute of a LAN is its limited geographic scope, not the number of nodes that are attached to the network. Some LANs, such as one you may have established in your home, are very small and may have only a few nodes. A LAN is a geographically localized network consisting of both hardware and software that links personal computers, workstations, printers, servers, and other **peripherals**. Devices on the LAN typically communicate within buildings or between buildings located near each other.

peripheral [pə'rifərəl]
n. 外围设备

LANs are almost certainly the most common type of network in existence today. Because of the capabilities they offer, they are widely installed in organizations of all sizes. The discussion of LANs is extensive and deals with many topics.

2. Wide Area Networks(WANs)

WANs may be made up of a combination of switched and **leased**, terrestrial and satellite, and private microwave circuits. Because communication carrier **facilities** are used, almost any circuit speed can be found in WANs.

lease [li:s]
vt. 出租，租出，租得
facility [fə'siliti]
n. 设备，工具

The WAN for a large multinational company may be global, whereas the WAN for a small company may cover only several cities or counties. One large bank has built a private WAN to link its offices in **Massachusetts**, Hong Kong, London, Munich, and Sydney. It reports that international circuits operating at speeds of

massachusetts [ˌmæsə'tʃu:sits]
n. 马萨诸塞州

Chapter 8 Computer Networking and Networking Security

256 Kbs or 1Mb/s provide a three-second response time to users at workstations anywhere in the world. Most international financial organizations have similar networks, because they must have them if they are to compete. Manufacturing companies that operate on a national or international scale have similar networks that link their offices and plants. Information about sales orders, sales forecasts, production, **inventory**, **revenue**, and expenses is routinely exchanged on a daily or more frequent basis. Every industry has numerous examples of WANs used to make organizations more productive.

3. Metropolitan Area Networks(MANs)

By way of contrast, there are networks that cover a geographical **territory** larger than a building or campus, but smaller than a state or country. Networks that are between a WAN and LAN in size are sometimes referred to as metropolitan area networks(MANs).

Suppose your school has a primary campus but also conducts classes at other locations around the city. LANs would be used on the primary campus, and perhaps within other classroom buildings throughout the city. A MAN should be used to connect all of the LANs and tie all of the school's facilities into a single network. Students would have the same communication and computing capability regardless of where they attend class.

In the past few years, a number of communications companies have begun business by installing optical **fiber** cable in metropolitan areas and then selling it to other companies that use it to establish MANs by interconnecting their locations within the city. Rights-of-way are obtained in many ways, such as on telephone poles, in subway tunnels, and under city streets. These companies primarily sell high-speed digital **bandwidths** and typically offer no value-added or other services. If the media used is optical fiber cable, the term frequently applied is dark fiber, because the fiber cable itself is supplied without the accompanying electronics and light source, such as an LED or a **laser** that puts light into the fiber to make it usable. When a customer leases dark fiber, he or she is responsible for providing all the equipment required to drive and operate the circuit.

The primary market for this service is the customer who

inventory ['invəntri]
n. 存货, 财产清册, 总量
revenue ['revinju:]
n. 收入, 国家的收入, 税……收

territory ['teritəri]
n. 领土, 版图, 地域

fiber ['faibə]
n. 光纤

bandwidth ['bændwidθ]
n. 带宽

laser ['leizə]
n. 激光

needs a lot of high-speed communication service within a relatively small, often metropolitan, geographic area. These customers are often large companies with multiple offices or other locations within a city. The MAN providers typically offer lower prices than other communications carriers and diverse routing that provides backup in emergencies. They also claim to offer quicker installation and better service than the other carriers.

MAN technology has been **standardized** by a committee of the Institute of Electrical and Electronics Engineers, Inc.(IEEE), which developed the MAN standard known as IEEE 802.6. The work was produced by the committees that defined LANs and was a result of their unresolved concerns about how LANs could be connected across distances of a few kilometers or greater.

standardize ['stændədaɪz]
vt. 使符合标准，使标准化

Exercises

Ⅰ. Fill in the blanks with the information given in the text.

1. Because university campuses normally cover a rather small geographic area, the networks on them are considered to be local, and are called _____.

2. There are also data networks that cover a wide geographical area, such as all of the U.S. or even the world, and these are called _____.

3. Networks that are between a WAN and LAN in size are sometimes referred to as _____.

4. MAN technology has been standardized by _____, which developed the MAN standard known as _____.

Ⅱ. Translate the following sentences from Chinese into English.

同样，工作用户通过计算机或工作站可以连接到任何办公室或校园网(局域网或 LAN)，或对一个大型企业/公司而言，连接到企业专用网。它们是由通过一个跨站点的骨干网互联的多个局域网组成的。

Section B History and Present Situation of the Internet

A Brief History of the Internet

The Internet **evolved** from the Arpanet, which was developed in 1969 by the Advanced Research Projects Agency (ARPA) of the U.S. Department of Defense. It was the first operational packet-switching network. Arpanet began operations in four locations: University of California, Los Angeless (UCLA), University of Santa Barbara, the University of Utah, and Stanford Research Institute(SRI). Today the number of **hosts** is in the tens

evolve [i'vɔlv]
v. (使)发展，(使)进展

host [həust]
n. 主机

Chapter 8 Computer Networking and Networking Security

of millions, the number of users in the hundreds of millions, and the number of countries participating nearing 200. The number of connections to the Internet continues to grow exponentially.

Arpanet made use of the new technology of **packet switching**, which offered advantages over circuit switching, as discussed in the following paragraphs.

When **circuit switching** is used for data transmission, it is essential that the data rates of the transmitting device and the receiving device be the same. With packet switching this is not necessary. A packet can be sent at the **data rate** of the transmitting device into the network, travel through the network at a variety of different data rates, usually higher than the **transmitter**'s rate, and then be metered out at the data rate that the receiver was expecting. The packet-switching network and its interfaces can buffer backed-up data to make speed conversion from a higher rate to a lower one possible. It was not just differing data rates that made interconnections difficult at the time of Arpanet's **invention**; the complete lack of open communication standards made it virtually impossible for a computer made by one manufacturer to communicate electronically with a computer made by another. Of particular interest to its **military** sponsors, Arpanet also offered adaptive routing. Each packet, individually, was routed to its destination by whatever route seemed fastest at the time of its transmission. Thus, if parts of the network got congested or failed, packets would automatically be routed around the **obstacles**.

Some of the early applications developed for the Arpanet also offered new functionality. The first two important applications were Telnet and FTP. Telnet provided a lingua franca for remote **computer terminals**. When the Arpanet was introduced, each different computer system needed a different terminal. The Telnet application provided a common denominator terminal. If software was written for each type of computer to support the "Telnet terminal", then one terminal could interact with all computer types. The File Transport **Protocol**(FTP) offered a similar open functionality. FTP allowed the transparent transfer of files from one computer to the other over the network. This is not as trivial as it may sound because various computers had different word sizes, stored their bits in different orders, and used different word

---

packet switching
包交换，又称"报文分组交换"

circuit switching
电路交换

data rate
数据传输率

transmitter [trænz'mitə]
n. 转送者，发报机，话筒

invention [in'venʃən]
n. 发明，创造

military ['militəri]
adj. 军事的，军用的

obstacle ['ɔbstəkl]
n. 障碍，妨害物

computer terminals
计算机终端机，计算机终端设备

protocol ['prəutəkɔl]
n. 草案，协议

formats. However, the first "killer app" for the Arpanet was electronic mail. Before Arpanet there were electronic mail systems, but they were all single computer systems. In 1972, Ray Tomlinson of Bolt Beranek and Newman(BBN) wrote the first system to provide **distributed** mail service across a computer network using multiple computers. By 1973, an ARPA study had found that three quarters of all Arpanet traffic was E-mail.

distributed [dis'tribju:tid]
adj. 分布式的

The technology was so successful that ARPA applied the same packet-switching technology to **tactical** radio communication (packet radio) and to satellite communication (SATNET). Because the three networks appropriate values for certain parameters, such as maximum packet size, were different in each case. Faced with the **dilemma** of integrating these networks, Vint Cerf and Bob Kahn of ARPA started to develop methods and protocols for internetting; that is, communicating across arbitrary, multiple, packet-switched networks. They published a very influential paper in May of 1974 outlining their approach to a Transmission Control Protocol. The proposal was refined and details filled in by the Arpanet community, with major contributions from participants from European Networks, such as Cyclades(France), and EIN, eventually leading to the TCP and IP protocols, which, in turn, formed the basis for what eventually became the TCP/IP protocol suite. This provided the foundation for the Internet. In 1982-1983, Arpanet convered from the original NCP protocol to TCP/IP. Many network then were connected using this technology through the world. Nevertheless, use of the Arpanet was generally restricted to ARPA contractors.

tactical ['tæktikəl]
adj. 战术的

dilemma [di'lemə, dai-]
n. 进退两难的局面

The World Wide Web

In the spring of 1989, at the European Laboratory for Particle Physics(CERN), Tim Berners-Lee proposed the idea of a distributed **hypermedia** technology to facilitate the international exchange of research findings using the Internet. Two years later, a prototype World Wide Web(WWW of the Web for short) was developed at CERN using the NeXT computer as a platform. By the end of 1991, CERN **released** a line-oriented browser or reader to a limited population. The explosive growth of the technology came with the development at the first graphically oriented browser, Mosaic, developed at the NCSA Center at the

hypermedia ['haɪpəmi:dɪə]
n. 超媒体

release [ri'li:s]
vt. 释放, 发表

University of Illinois by Mark Andreasson and others in 1993. Two million copies of Mosaic were delivered over the Internet. Today, the characteristic Wed addresses, the URLs (**universal** resource locators), are ubiquitous. One cannot read a newspaper or watch TV without seeing the addresses everywhere.

The Web is a system consisting of an internationally distributed collection of multimedia files supported by **clients** (users) and servers (information providers). Each file is addressed in a consistent manner using its URL. The files from the providers are viewed by the clients using browsers such as Netscape Navigator or Microsoft's Internet Explore(IE). Most browsers have graphical display and support multimedia ——text, **audio**, image, video. The user can move from file to file by clicking with a mouse or other pointing device on specially highlighted text or image elements on the browser display; the transfer from one file to the next is called a **hyperlink**. The layout of the browser display is controlled by the Hypertext Markup Language (HTML) standard, which defines embedded commands in text files that specify features of the browser display, such as the **fonts**, colors, images and their placement on the display, and the location of the locations where the user can invoke the hyperlinks and their targets. The last important feature of the Web is the Hypertext Transfer Protocol (HTTP), which is a communications protocol for use in TCP/IP networks for fetching the files from the appropriate servers as specified by the hyperlinks.

What the internet looks like today?

Users now ordinarily connect to the Internet through an Internet service provider(ISP). For home users the provider is often one of the major online services such as America Online. Today most **residential** users connect to the ISPs over voice –grade lines using modems at data rates of 56.6 kb/s. This is perfectly adequate for e-mail and related services but **marginal** for graphics——intensive Web surfing. New alternatives have become available in many areas, including ISDN, ADSL, and cable modem.

Users who connect to the Internet through their work often use workstations or PCs connected to their employer——owned LANs, which in turn connect through shared organizational trucks

universal [,juːniˈvəːsəl]
adj. 普遍的，全体的，通用的

client [ˈklaiənt]
n. 客户机，客户程序

audio [ˈɔːdiəu]
adj. 音频的，声音的

hyperlink
n. [计]超链接

font [fɔnt]
n. 字体，字形

residential [,reziˈdenʃəl]
adj. 住宅的，与居住有关的

marginal [ˈmɑːdʒinəl]
adj. 边缘的，边际的

to an ISP. In these cases the shared circuit is T-1 connection, while for very large organizations T-3 connections are sometimes found. Smaller organizations may use 56 kb/s or ISDN connections.

The ISPs are connected by "**wholesalers**", which we can call network service providers. They, in turn, interconnect using Internet connection points, such as CIX, MAE East and West, and the network access point. The network service providers use transmission at T-3 rates, with some moving to ATM connections at rates 155 Mb/s.

The **commercial** uses of the Internet came in stages. In the early days limited by the access rules of the Arpanet and, later, by the Acceptable Use Policy, commercial use was limited to R&D or other technical units using the Net for research and educational uses, although some informational activities that could be considered marketing were carried on under the name of research and education. The Internet was privatized in 1995. The first new applications were mainly informational ones for sales and marketing information and public relations. Electronic data interchange (EDI) transactions for intercompany **invoices**, **billing**, and the like, which were originally designed for use on dedicated wide area net works and commercial public networks began to be carried on the Internet. Commercial networks, especially America Online, have long played a customer service role by providing bulletin board type services dealing with technical and usage problems. These activities were gradually extended to the Internet as well. However, the most tempting activity is direct sales to the tens of millions of Internet users throughout the world. The initial **infrastructure** of the Internet did not support online transactions well. There were three limitations: lack of an easy to use graphical user interface, lack of security, and lack of effective payment systems. The most popular and easy to use interface, the World Wide Web and its browsers, did not become commonly available until 1993 at the earliest. In its early **incarnations**, there was very little support to allow the client browser to submit information (forms) to the server. Moreover, there were not many options for payment for online ordering, and all the options were insecure. One obvious payment method is to use credit card accounts. However, most people are uncomfortable about sending credit card numbers over the

wholesaler ['həulseilə]
n. 批发商

commercial [kə'mə:ʃəl]
adj. 商业的, 贸易的

invoice ['invɔis]
n. 发票, 发货单, 货物
billing ['biliŋ]
n. 记账(法), 票据

infrastructure
['infrə'strʌktʃə]
n. 基础下部组织, 基础设施

incarnation [,inka:'neiʃən]
n. 赋予肉体, 具人形, 化身

Internet, with good reason, because of the lack of security. For example, if the credit card information is not encrypted it is very easy to "listen in" on Internet communications. Moreover, several files of customer's **credit card** numbers on merchant's computers have been compromised. The ease of collecting and integrating information on customer transactions when they are in electronic form also raises privacy concerns for customers. One of the hottest application areas in financial information systems is "**data mining**", which often involves collection large amounts of customer transaction information to improve the targeting of marketing efforts. These limitations are beginning to be **ameliorated**. The latest browsers support communication with the server by the user filling in forms.

credit card
n. 信用卡, 签账卡

data mining
数据采掘, 又称"数据挖掘"

ameliorate [əˈmiːljəreit]
v. 改善, 改进

Exercises

I. Fill in the blanks with the information given in the text.

1. The Internet evolved from the _____, which was developed in 1969 by the Advanced Research Projects Agency (ARPA) of the U.S. Department of Defense. It was the first operational _____ network.

2. Some of the early applications developed for the ARPANET also offered new functionality. The first two important applications were _____ and _____.

3. Most browsers have graphical display and support multimedia _____, _____, _____, _____. The user can move from file to file by clicking with a mouse or other pointing device on specially highlighted text or image elements on the browser display; the transfer from one file to the next is called a _____.

4. Users now ordinarily connect to the Internet through a (an) _____. For home users, the provider is often one of the major online services such as _____.

5. One of the hottest application areas in financial information systems is _____, which often involves collection large amounts of customer transaction information to improve the targeting of marketing efforts.

II. Translate the following passages from English into Chinese.

In general, within a small business/site, the basic communications requirement——in addition to telephony——is to enable a number of users, each with a desktop PC/workstation, to access a server computer that is used as, say, a print server and an e-mail server for the site. To achieve the latter function, the server is connected to the Internet through an Internet service provider that also provides access to the Web.

III. Translate the following terms or phrases from English into Chinese and vice versa.

1. URL
2. HTML
3. HTTP
4. SSL
5. data mining
6. 标准通用标识语言
7. 互联网服务提供商
8. 电子数据交换
9. 文件传输协议
10. 万维网

Section C Networking Security

Why network security is needed?

In just the last few years, the world has become a more dangerous place. When **terrorist** attacks, which have occurred all over the world, recently struck the U.S., our own level of awareness and concern about the threat of such events jumped several notches. Almost daily, we read about computer and network **viruses**——either about new attacks or the dangers of more potent viruses that are difficult to track and stop. We are strongly encouraged to install antivirus software if we own a computer. You may have experienced an attack on the Internet, during which you weren't able to access your favorite websites for several hours. Most corporations have experienced one or more **outages** because of viruses or denial of service attacks, although they are often **loathe** to report the attacks, sometimes out of embarrassment.

This increase in terrorist attacks on the general population, as well as on special segments of our society's infrastructure, comes at a time when large and small organizations of all types are becoming increasingly dependent on networks to carry on their activities. Networks have become **assets** like computers, data, and information. Without these assets, most organizations find it impossible to conduct business. Communications with customers, suppliers, employees, and other organizations are handled primarily through networks. The loss of the network communications channel could effectively **cripple** an organization. No longer can a business be operated without having access to information and a reliable communication system. The network asset must be protected like other assets and surrounded with proper controls and the appropriate security. No wonder there is such a strong interest in the subjects of network and computer security. Organizational leaders and employees in all segments want to know what they can do to safeguard networks, their computers, and their **livelihoods**.

In the past, networks, when they existed, were mainly private. Therefore, they were fairly easy to control. With the rise

terrorist ['terərɪst]
n. 恐怖分子

virus ['vaɪərəs]
n. [微]病毒 毒害

outage ['autɪdʒ]
n. 储运损耗；停止，运转中断
loathe [ləuð]
vt. 厌恶，憎恶

asset ['æset]
n. 资产，有用的东西

cripple ['krɪpl]
v. 削弱

livelihood ['laɪvlɪhud]
n. 生计, 谋生

of the Internet and its use for conducting business, parts of most organizations' networks are more open and vulnerable to **unauthorized** access, computer viruses, and attacks that are more aggressive than ever. The potential disruptions of application systems running on computer networks or the corruption of the underlying data are good reasons for organizations to take network security very seriously and to take action. Usually, the value of the data stored on networked computers far exceeds the cost of the networks themselves.

Notice that we did not say, "the chances of a network security problem are **eliminated**". It is virtually impossible to eliminate all network security problems. Solutions that work well today may not provide adequate protection tomorrow because technology continues to advance. Determined, creative, and **unscrupulous** people find ways to bypass or work around even the most stringent network security measures. We can minimize the risk of a major network security incident, however, by making it extremely difficult, expensive, or both to break through an organization's security defenses.

Management's Responsibility

In addition to the traditional responsibilities of designing and operating networks, the network management staff has a very important security responsibility, but **senior** management must lead the way by understanding the security issues and indicating to all employees that network security is important to the organization's well being. Without senior management **sponsorship** of security initiatives, the network management staff may not get the cooperation and support it requires from employees at all levels in the organization.

The fact that the information and tools needed to penetrate corporate networks are widely available has provided further impetus for a **heightened** concern about network security by companies throughout the world. For a company to adequately manage information security on the network, it must have the following:
- a net work security policy that clearly defines the reasons why security is important to the company;
- clearly defined roles and responsibilities to ensure that

unauthorized [ˌʌnˈɔːθəraizd]
adj. 未被授权的，未经认可的

eliminate [iˈlimineit]
vt. 排除，消除

unscrupulous [ʌnˈskruːpjuləs]
adj. 无道德的，不谨慎的

senior [ˈsiːnjə]
adj. 年长的，资格较老的，地位较高的，高级的

sponsorship [ˈspɔnsəʃip]
n. 赞助者的地位、任务等

heighten [ˈhaitn]
v. 提高，升高

- all aspects of security are performed;
- a security implementation plan that describes the steps needed to implement the policy;
- an effective implementation of appropriate security hardware and software;
- a plan to deal with any security **breaches** that do occur;
- a management review process to periodically ensure that the security policies and standards are adequate, effective, and the being enforced.

Each of these elements must be present. The network security policy is management's statement of the importance of and their commitment to network security. The policy needs to describe in general terms what will be done, but does not deal with the way the protection is to be achieved. Writing the policy is complex because, in reality, it is normally a part of a broader document: the organization's information security policy. The network security policy needs to clearly state management's position about the importance of network security and the items that are to be protected. Management must understand that there is no such thing as a perfectly secure network. Furthermore, network security is a constantly moving target because of advances in technology and the **creativity** of people who would like to break in to a network or its attached computers. Measures put in place to minimize security risks today will need to be upgraded in the future, and upgrades usually have a price attached, for which management will have to pay.

Simply writing the policy does not put the practices, **procedures**, or software in place to improve the security situation. That requires follow through and communication with all employees so that they understand the emphasis and importance senior management is placing on security. Management, at all levels, needs to support the policy and periodically reinforce it with employees in various ways. IT and network staff may need to install additional hardware, software, and procedures to perform automated security checking.

Sometimes management appoints a network security officer who is responsible for seeing that the security policy and practices and **carried out**. The security officer also investigates

breach [briːtʃ]
n. 违背, 破坏, 破裂, 裂口

creativity [ˌkriːeiˈtivəti]
n. 创造力, 创造

procedure [prəˈsiːdʒə]
n. 程序, 手续

carry out
v. 完成, 实现, 贯彻, 执行

violations of the security policy and makes recommendations about additions to the security plan or changes that should be made. Most often, the security officer role is a part-time job for a member of the networking staff. However, it is important to ensure that the security responsibilities aren't short-changed by the press of other day-to-day work.

The management review process is a periodic check that the security program is operating properly. The initial step in the review process may be a security audit performed by the company's inside or outside **auditors**. The audit report serves as the basis for the management review.

Types of Threats

Security threats to a network can be divided into those that involve some sort of unauthorized access and all others. Once someone gains unauthorized access to the network, the range of things they can do is large. At the **innocuous** end of the scale, they may do nothing. Some people are just interested in the challenge of breaking through the security and have no interest in doing anything further. They may, however, choose to monitor network traffic, called **eavesdropping**, for the purpose of learning something specific and perhaps disclosing it to others, or for the purpose of analyzing traffic patterns, traffic analysis could lead to the observation. They are difficult to detect because the **perpetrator** does nothing overt but simply listens on the network.

The types of unauthorized access we usually think of, however, are the active security attacks whereby, after someone gains unauthorized access to the network, they take some overt action. Active attacks include **altering** message contents, masquerading as someone else, denial of service, and planting viruses.

Altering message contents means changing the contents of a message, causing the message recipient to be misinformed or deceived. Examples include changing the value in a financial transaction, the name of a person authorized to conduct certain business, or a flight number.

Masquerading is pretending to be someone else on the network, typically someone who had more privileges. A person

auditor ['ɔːditə]
n. 计员, 核算师

innocuous [i'nɔkjuəs]
adj. 无害的, 无毒的

eavesdrop ['iːvzdrɔp]
v. 偷听

perpetrator ['pəːpitreitə]
n. 犯罪者, 作恶者

alter ['ɔːltə]
v. 改变

masquerade [ˌmæskə'reid, mɑːs-]
v. 化装, 冒充

might masquerade as a legitimate business on the Internet in order to obtain an unsuspecting purchaser's credit card number.

Denial of service occurs when someone floods a site with messages faster than they can be handled, thereby degrading network performance. Other forms of denial of service include anything that prevents the normal use of communication facilities. For example, simply passing on email chain letters can clog a network with unnecessary traffic and effectively deny service to **legitimate** users.

legitimate [l i'dʒitimit]
adj. 合法的, 合理的, 正统的

Planting viruses can occur in many ways, but the most common are through an attachment to an e-mail or by downloading software containing a virus when a user logs on to an Internet website. Viruses range widely in their sophistication, destructiveness, and ease of **eradication**, but they are almost all troublesome.

eradication [i,rædi'keiʃən]
n. 连根拔除, 根除

Physical damage to the network control center or any network facilities, such as circuits, switches, modems, servers, or data files.

Nonmalicious disruptions caused by routine occurrences such as circuit failures, server failures, software bugs, and mistakes made by service or operations personal. These kinds of disruptions need to be planned for as a part of normal network operation, and **contingency** plans should be put in place for the times these disruptions occur. These kinds of problems are usually not too serious unless they continue for long periods of time.

contingency [kən'tindʒənsi]
n. 偶然, 可能性, 意外事故, 可能发生的附带事件

Disasters caused by "acts of God" or acts of man, such as floods, fires, **tornadoes**, earthquakes, and bombings. These outages are severe and are usually of long duration. If contingency plans are not in place, disasters can literally put companies out of business.

tornado [tɔː'neidəu]
n. 旋风, 龙卷风, 大雷雨, 具有巨大破坏性的人(或事物)

Exercises

Ⅰ. **Fill in the blanks with the information given in the text.**

1. Most corporations have experienced one or more outages because of _____ or _____, although they are often loathe to report the attacks, sometimes out of embarrassment.

2. The _____ is management's statement of the importance of and their commitment to network security.

3. The management review process is a _____ that the security program is operating properly. The initial step in the _____ may be a security audit performed by the company's inside or outside auditors.

4. Active attacks include _____, _____ as someone else, _____, and _____.

5. _____ caused by routine occurrences such as circuit failures, server failures, software bugs, and mistakes made by service or operations personal.

Ⅱ. **Translate the following passages from English into Chinese.**

As the knowledge of computer networking and protocols has become more widespread, so the threat of intercepting and decoding message data during its transfer across a net work has increased. For example, the end systems (stations/hosts) associated with most applications are now attached to a LAN. The application may involve a single LAN or in an inter networking environment, the Internet.

Grammar 8　科技英语翻译方法与技巧(Ⅲ)

英语中句型的翻译

被动语态是科技语体特点之一。在科技英语文献中，被动语态是频繁出现的现象。下面简要说明一下如何正确地理解和翻译这种句子。

1. 将原有的被动句译成汉语的被动句

在采用此方法时，英语中的许多被动句可以翻译成汉语的被动句，常用"被"、"给"、"遭"、"挨"、"为……所"、"使"、"由……"、"受到"等表示。

例如：

These signals are produced by colliding stars or nuclear reactions in outer space.

这些信号是由外层空间的星球碰撞或者核反应所造成的。

Over the years, tools and technology themselves as a source of fundamental innovation have largely been ignored by historians and philosophers of science.

工具和技术本身作为根本性创新的源泉多年来在很大程度上被科学史学家和科学思想家们忽视了。

2. 将被动句译成汉语的主动句

汉语的被动句没有英语被动句运用得广泛。在翻译英语被动句时，我们往往在译文中使用"加以"、"经过"、"用……来"等词来体现原文中的被动含义。若当英语被动句在语义上着重谓语动词本身的意义，可直接用汉语被动结构来翻译。

例如：

In other words mineral substances which are found on earth must be extracted by digging, boring holes, artificial explosions, or similar operations which make them available to us.

换言之，矿物就是存在于地球上，但须经过挖掘、钻孔、人工爆破或类似作业才能获得的物质。

And it is imagined by many that the operations of the common mind can be by no means compared with these processes, and that they have to be acquired by a sort of special training.

许多人认为，普通人的思维活动根本无法与科学家的思维过程相比，而且认为这些思维过程必须经过某种专门的训练才能掌握。

3. 将被动句译成汉语的无主语句子

当遇到不带 by 的短语，并含有情态动词的英语被动句时，我们可以转译成汉语的无主语句子。

例如：

Therefore logic must be used when making decisions, or when calculating or processing data.

因此，在做判定或者计算或处理数据时，必须采用逻辑。

Life can't be understood without much charity.

没有爱心，就无法了解生活。

Many strange new means of transport have been developed in our century, the strangest of them being perhaps the hovercraft.

在我们这个世纪内研制了许多新奇的交通工具，其中最奇特的也许就是气垫船了。

4. 固定译法

科技英语中有不少常用的被动结构已经有了习惯译法。

例如：

It is hoped that … 希望……

It is reported that … 据报道……

It is said that … 据说……

It is supposed that … 据推测……

It may be said without fear of exaggeration that … 可以毫不夸张地说……

It must be admitted that … 必须承认……

It must be pointed out that … 必须指出……

It will be seen from this that … 由此可见……

参考译文

Section A 计算机网络

简介

我们大多数人每天都在使用计算机网络。它已经融入了我们的生活，无论在家，在学校，还是在工作中，离开了它，我们几乎做不了任何事。我们几乎所有人都伴随着电话网长大，我们不需要任何训练就可以很自如地使用它。现在，计算机数据网在我们的社会中也进入了相同的角色。事实上，在非常短的时间里，我们的生活就已经开始依靠它了。除了一些第三世界的国家，全球 Internet 几乎无处不在。正如前两代人使用电话网长大一样，现在的年轻人都使用着 Internet 长大。他们无需借助手册、帮助屏幕或者辅导班就可以坐下来使用它。他们通过计算机很轻易地接入网络，跳转到一个信息、游戏和其他资源都很丰富的地方。这是他们的父辈和祖父辈在成长中都不曾用过的。

正如你所见到的，与其说计算机网络已经成为我们日常生活中的一部分，还不如说我们几乎感觉不到它的存在。这也是它所要达到的目的。正如我们不必担心打开水龙头水是否会流出来，或者按了开关灯是否会亮一样，我们也不必担心网络运转的细节，或者担心我们需要它们时，它们是否会完全适用。在大多数国家，水和电的网络是公共基础设施的基本要素，但我们根本不会去想这些服务是如何提供到我们的家

Chapter 8 Computer Networking and Networking Security

中或者办公室的。数据和计算机网络是一个更新的技术。它们的通信能力,一般都是相当可靠的,虽然他们尚未达到水、电等老基础设施的故障安全服务,但是,和那些老基础设施的网络一样,计算机网络对我们的生活方式也是至关重要的。

为什么要学习计算机网络?

和一般人相比,你作为一个网络用户,为什么可能要学习网络和网络工作方式更多的细节呢?大概最常见的理由就是,你希望能在通信领域工作。你可能已经听说在通信领域,有好的、高薪的职位,而你想参与这个"行动"。这是事实。电信及网络领域的迅速扩张,提供这种服务的公司和组织都利用网络服务,他们需要大量技术熟练的员工。此外,这是一个令人兴奋的领域,因为它的变化非常迅速。而且,因为政府站在了计算机网络的使用潜能与滥用的新角度,这使得管理环境产生变化。

然而,在计算机网络中,你可能更感兴趣学术。因为你每天利用计算机工作,你可能并没有任何想在通信产业工作的念头,而是仅仅想了解它们工作的方式。你可能想更多地了解一些较新的通信技术,如宽带或无线通信。学习网络将扩展你的知识,扩大词汇量,而且你可能察觉不到,使用通信技术会开阔你的视野;无论你选择什么职业,它都可能对你有用。

计算机网络的地理位置分类

计算机网络的一个常用的分类方式是通过其所覆盖的地理区域进行分类。最常见的命名为局域网(LAN)和广域网(WAN)。第三类不太好界定,这就是城域网(MAN)。

1. 局域网

也许,你最熟悉的网络是在学校里能将你的个人计算机连接到校园中或附近其他楼宇中的个人计算机上的网络。因为大学校园通常只包括一个相当小的地理区域,在这个区域内建立的网络被视为是本地的,因此称为局域网。我们稍后会更准确地定义局域网,但现在你可以很容易理解一个校园网的局域性和覆盖整个世界的公用电话网的地理多样性的不同。还有一些数据网络,覆盖广阔的地理区域,如美国全境,甚至是整个世界,这些都是所谓的广域网。毋庸置疑,你使用过的一个广域网就是 Internet,尽管从技术上来说,Internet 是互联的局域网和广域网的集合。

我们继续说校园网,它可能有上百个甚至上千个工作站和服务器连接在上面。每个这样的设备都是网络上的一个结点。局域网的一个关键特征是它受限的地理范围,而不是结点的数量。一些局域网非常小,而且可能只有几个结点,如在家建立的局域网。局域网是由连接个人计算机、工作站、打印机、服务器和其他外部设备的硬件和软件组成的地理范围是局部性的网络。局域网上的设备通常在楼宇内部或相邻楼宇之间互联。

几乎可以肯定,局域网是当今最常见的网络存在类型。因为局域网提供的性能,它们被广泛地用于各种规模的机构。关于局域网的讨论非常广泛,涉及许多话题。

2. 广域网

广域网可以由可交换的和租用的、地面的和卫星的、专用微波线路组成。由于通信载波设备的使用,在广域网中几乎可以找到任何线路速度。

一个跨国公司的广域网可能是全球性的,而一些小型公司的广域网可能只涉及几个市或县。一个大型银行已经建立了一个专业的广域网,连接了其设在马萨诸塞州、香港、伦敦、慕尼黑、悉尼的办事处。它报告说,其国际线路运营速度在 256 Kb/s 或 1 Mb/s,无论用户在世界上任何地方的工作站上,它都可以在 3 秒内响应。大多数国际金融组织也有类似的网络,因为如果他们要面对竞争,他们就必须有网络。在一国国内或国际范围内经营的制作业公司也有类似的网络来连接它们的办事处和工厂。涉及销售订单、销售预测、生产、库存、收入、费用等信息每日或更频繁地定期交换。每个行业都有使用广域网来使公司更富有成效的很多例子。

3. 城域网

与此对比的是，有一种网络的覆盖地域大于一个楼宇或校园，但小于一个市或县。这样在规模上介于广域网和局域网之间的网络有时被称为城域网。

如果你的学校设有一个主校园，但在这个城市周围的其他地方还有教室。局域网将用于主校园，也许还用于遍及这个城市的其他教学楼。城域网则用于连接所有的这些局域网，并将所有学校的设备连接到一个单一的网络中。这样，无论学生在哪里上课，他们都将具有相同的通信和信息处理能力。

在过去几年中，一些通信公司已经开始该业务了，他们先在城市范围内安装光缆，然后将其售给使用其服务的其他公司，这些公司将他们在市内的各个地点互联起来以建立城域网。可行的方法有很多途径，如通过电线杆、地铁隧道或将其埋在城市的街道下面。这些公司主要是销售高速数字宽带，而且一般来说，不提供增值或其他服务。如果媒介用的是光纤电缆，这个词通常是指暗光纤，因为光纤自身不提供附带电子和光源，用一个发光二极管或一个激光器将光送入光纤都可以使之使用。当客户租用暗光纤，他(或她)就有责任提供所有需要的设备来驱动和操作线路。

这项服务的主要市场是那些需要大量高速通信服务用于相对较小的，往往是大城市、地理区域的客户。这些客户通常是在一个城市里有着很多办公地点的大公司。城域网供给者通常提供比其他通信运营商和紧急情况提供备份的多样路由给予更低的价格。他们还声称能比其他运营商提供更快的安装和更好的服务。

城域网技术已经得到电子电气和电子工程师协会(IEEE)的进一步规范，并由其开发了我们熟知的城域网标准 IEEE 802.6。这项工作是由定义局域网的协会进行的，并解决了关于局域网怎样连接横跨几千米或更大距离的悬而未决的问题。

Section B 互联网的历史和现状

互联网发展简史

互联网是由阿帕网发展而来，它在 1969 年由美国国防部的高级研究计划局(ARPA)建立。这是第一个运行的分组交换网络。阿帕网首先在 4 个地点运行：加利福尼亚大学洛杉矶分校、圣巴巴拉大学、犹他大学、美国斯坦福研究所(SRI)。今天，主机数以千万计，用户数以亿计，而参与的国家接近 200 个。连接到互联网的数目继续成倍增长。

阿帕网使用了分组交换的新技术，正如在以下几段中讨论的，它比电路交换具有更多的优点。

当电路交换用于数据传输时，发送装置和接收装置的数据传输率必须是一样的。而这不需要数据包转换。一个数据包能以发送端的传输速率传入网络，而以多种不同速率在网络中传输，通常高于发送端的速率，然后转换成接收端所需要的数据传输速率。数据包交换网络及其接口可以缓冲备份数据，使其从高速率到低速率的速率变换成为可能。在阿帕网发明的时候，不是仅仅为了改变数据传输速率来使得互联更困难；完全缺乏开放的通信标准使得一个厂商制造的计算机和其他厂商制造的计算机事实上完全不可能实现电子通信。对军事赞助商的特殊利益而言，阿帕网还提供自动适应路由。每个数据包单独经由任何在传输时看上去最快的路径到它的目的地。因此，如果得知部分网络拥挤或失效，数据包将自动绕过障碍。

一些早期为阿帕网开发的应用程序也提供了新的功能。最重要的两项应用就是 Telnet 和 FTP 。Telnet 为计算机远程终端提供了通用语言。当阿帕网提出时，每一个不同的计算机系统都需要一个不同的终端。Telnet 程序提供了一个不同的终端。如果为每一类型的计算机都编写软件来支持"远程终端"，那么一个终端可以与所有类型计算机连接。文件传输协议(FTP)提供了类似的开放功能。FTP 允许一台计算机向网络上的其他计算机进行文件透明传输。这没有听起来那么烦琐，因为各种计算机都有不同的字大小，用不同的顺序存储它们的位，并使用了不同的字格式。然而，第一个"杀手铜应用"是电子信箱。在阿帕网前，也有电子邮箱系统，但他们都是单一计算机系统。1972 年，Bolt Beranek and Newman(BBN) 公司的 Ray

Tomlinson 编写了第一个系统来提供分布式邮件服务,这项服务可以覆盖使用多个计算机的计算机网络。到了 1973 年,一项阿帕网的研究发现,阿帕网 3/4 的流量是 E-mail。

这项技术是如此的成功,它使得阿帕网将相同的分组交换技术应用于战术无线通信(分组无线)和卫星通信(SATNET)。因为这 3 种网络对特定参数的适当值,如最大数据包大小是各不相同的。面对整合这些网络两难的情况,阿帕网的 Vint Cerf 和 Bob Kahn 开始为互联研究方法和协议,就是说能跨越任意的、多样的、包交换网络进行的通信。在 1974 年 5 月,他们发表了一篇很有影响力的论文,概述了其传输控制协议的方法。这个建议由阿帕网团队简化并填补了细节,主要贡献来自于欧洲网络的参与者,如 Cyclades(法国)和 EIN,最终产生了 TCP 和 IP 协议,事实上,这两者又依次构成了 TCP/IP 协议套件的基础。这些都为互联网奠定了基础,在 1982 年和 1983 年,阿帕网从原来的 NCP 的协议换为 TCP/IP 协议。接着,就有许多网络使用这些技术连接到整个世界。但是,阿帕网的使用却通常限定于阿帕网的合约商。

万维网

1989 年春,在欧洲粒子物理研究中心(CERN), Tim Berners-Lee 提出了分布式超媒体技术以利用互联网来促进研究成果的国际交流的构想。两年后,在 CERN,用 NeXT 计算机作为平台开发出了原型万维网(简称 WWW)。到 1991 年年底,CERN 对有限的人发布了命令行的浏览器或阅读器。1993 年由 Mark Andreasson 等人在伊利诺伊大学的 NCSA 中心开发了第一个面向图形的浏览器 Mosaic,它带来了技术爆炸式的增长。两百万份 Mosic 的副本通过互联网传输出去。今天,专门的 Web 地址,即 URL(统一资源定位器)无处不在。无论是看报纸还是看电视,我们都不可避免地看到到处都是这些地址。

万维网是一个由客户机(用户)和服务器(信息提供商)支持的媒体文件的国际分式集合组成的系统。每一个文件都可以用它的 URL 作为统一的方式找到。用户可以使用例如网景公司的 Navigator 或微软的 Internet Explore(IE)这样的浏览器来浏览供应商提供的文件。大多数浏览器都有图形显示功能,并支持多媒体——文本、音频、图片、视频。用户只需要用鼠标或其他指示设备单击浏览器上的特定高亮文本或图形元素,就可以在文件间切换。这种在文件间的切换称为超链接。浏览器显示的布局是由超文本标记语言(HTML)的标准控制的,这个标准在文本文件中定义了内嵌指令,而这些指令规定了浏览器显示的面貌,如字体、颜色、图像和它们在显示器上的位置。万维网最后一个重要特征是超文本传输协议(HTTP),这是一个通信协议,用户可以用来在 TCP/IP 网络中从适合的服务器中取得由超链接指向的文件。

互联网现状如何?

现在用户通常通过互联网服务提供商(ISP)来连接互联网。对许多家庭用户来说,这些提供商往往是在线服务商,如美国在线公司。今天大部分住宅用户通过音频线路调制解调器连接到互联网服务供应商,数据率为 56.6 Kb/s。这对电子邮件和相关服务是完全够用的,但对于图像密集的网上冲浪就不够用了。新的替代品已经在许多领域得到使用了,包括 ISDN、ADSL 和电缆调制解调器。

那些用互联网工作的用户经常使用工作站或个人计算机连接到他们的雇主所有的局域网,它们会依次通过共享组织交换连接到 ISP。在这些情况中,共享电路是 T-1 连接,而对一些非常大的机构,有时会发现 T-3 连接。一些小的机构可能用 56kb/s 或 ISDN 连接。

互联网服务供应商通过"批发商"相连接,我们称其为网络服务供应商。他们使用互联网连接点依次互联,如 CIX、MAE East、MAE West 和 NAP。这些网络服务提供商使用 T-3 速率进行数据传输,有些转向 ATM 的连接可以达到 155Mb/s 的速率。

互联网的商业使用分阶段到来。在早期受制于阿帕网的准入规则,稍后政策允许,商业化又受限于将网络用于科学和教育的研发或其他技术单位,尽管一些可以认为是营销的宣传活动在研究和教育的名义下开展。在 1995 年,互联网被私有化。最早的新应用主要是为销售和商业信息以及公共关系的宣传活动。电子数据交换(EDI)对公司间的发票、账单等进行处理,它原本设计用在专门的广域网的和商业公用网,但现在开始在互联网上使用了。商业网络，特别是美国在线公司，通过提供电子公告类型的服务来处理技术和使用上的问题，从而长期发挥着客户服务的作用。这些活动也逐步扩展到互联网。不过，最诱人的活动是将产品直接销售给在世界各地数以千计的互联网用户。早期的互联网设备并不能很好地支持在线交易，存在3个限制：缺乏一个易于使用的图形用户界面，缺乏安全保障，以及缺乏有效的支付系统。最流行和易于使用的用户界面、万维网以及其浏览器，直到1993年初期才得到普遍使用。在其早期的版本，只有非常少的程序允许客户端浏览器提交资料(表格)到服务器上，而且所有可供的选择都是不安全的。其中一个显而易见的付款方式是使用信用卡账户。然而，大多数人对在互联网上发送信用卡账号感到不舒服，这有很充分的理由：缺乏安全感。例如，如果信用卡资料是不加密的，它是很容易在互联网通信中被"监听"。此外，已经有商家计算机上的几个客户信用卡号码文件泄密。当客户交易时，信息以电子表格形式存储，收集和整合信息的便利也增加了客户对保密的担忧。在财务信息系统中，一个最热门的应用领域是"数据挖掘"，其往往含有收集了的大量客户交易资料，以提高营销活动的有效性。这些限制都已开始有所改善。最新的浏览器支持由用户填写表格来进行与服务器的通信。

Section C 网络安全

在刚刚过去几年中，世界已经成为一个更加危险的地方。恐怖袭击遍布世界各地，最近袭击了美国，我们对这类活动的认识水平和造成的威胁都留下了深刻的印记。几乎每天，我们都可以读到关于计算机和网络病毒的信息，或者是新的攻击或是危险性更强大的病毒，而且很难对它们进行追踪和阻止。如果我们拥有属于自己的计算机，我们强烈鼓励安装防病毒软件。你可能在互联网上已经经历了一次袭击，在此期间，长达数小时你不能访问你喜爱的网站。由于病毒或拒绝服务的攻击，大部分公司都经历了一次或多次的运转中断，但有时出于避免尴尬，他们往往不愿报道这些攻击。

当各类大小组织都越来越依赖网络来进行它们的活动时，对一般民众，以及社会的基础设施的特定部分的恐怖袭击事件也增加了。像计算机、数据和信息一样，网络也已成为资产。如果没有这些资产，大多数组织就会发现他们生意不可能运转。与顾客、供应商、员工及其他组织的通信都主要通过网络来处理，网络通信渠道的缺失会大大地削弱一个组织。失去了信息的获取和一个可靠的通信系统，生意就不再能运转下去。网络必须像其他资产一样受到保护，并伴有适当的管理和适当的安全性。那么，对网络和计算机安全这个科目有强烈的兴趣也不足为奇了。在各阶层的组织领导和员工都想知道他们怎样做才能保障网络、计算机和他们的安全。

网络在过去存在之初就主要是专用的，因此比较容易控制。随着互联网的兴起，以及它的商业管理用途的增加，大多数组织的部分网络更加开放，也更容易受到未授权访问、计算机病毒和比以往更具侵略性的攻击。运行在计算机网络上的应用系统的潜在破坏或基本数据的讹误是组织重视网络安全并采取行动的很好的理由。通常情况下，存储在互联网计算机上的数据的价值已远远超过网络本身的花费。

注意我们并没有说"网络安全问题是可以消除的"。事实上，消除所有网络安全问题是不可能的。今天能很好运行的解决方案，明天可能就不能提供足够的保护，因为技术在不断进步。有决心、有创意但没有道德的人可以在即使最严格的网络安全保密措施下工作或另觅"新"径。我们可以最大限度地减少可能发生的重大网络安全事件，使得突破该机构的安全防护变得极为困难，代价昂贵，或者二者兼有。

管理者的责任

除了设计和运行网络的传统责任，网络的管理人员还有一个很重要的安全责任，但是，为了该组织的福祉，高级管理层必须通过了解安全问题，并对所有雇员指出网络安全是很重要的带头示范。如果没有高级管理层发起的可靠倡议，网络管理人员就不可能获得他所需要来自该组织各层面员工的合作与支持。

用于渗透企业网络需要的信息和工具被广泛提供这一事实为世界各地的公司对网络安全的高度关注提供了进一步的动力。对于一个公司，它要在网络上充分地管理信息安全，必须具备以下几点：

Chapter 8 Computer Networking and Networking Security

- 有一个能明确说明安全性对公司如此重要的原因的网络安全政策;
- 有明确规定的角色和职责,以确保安全的所有方面都能执行;
- 有一个描述实施政策所需要必要步骤的可靠执行计划;
- 有一个合适的安全硬件和软件的有效实施;
- 有一个可以应付任何可能发生的安全破坏的预案;
- 有一个管理审查程序能定期确保安全正常和标准是足够用,有效并正在执行。

上述每个要素都必须具有。网络安全政策是管理部门对网络安全的重要性的声明,也是他们对网络安全所承担的义务。该政策需要用一般条款来描述应该怎样做,但并不涉及达到保护目的的方法。编写这个政策是非常复杂的,因为在现实中,它通常是一个更宽泛文件,即该组织的信息安全政策的组成部分。网络安全政策需要明确声明管理层对网络安全和需要保护内容非常重要的立场。管理层必须明白一个绝对安全的网络是绝不可能存在的。此外,由于科技的进步和那些想入侵网络和计算机的人的创造性,网络安全是一个不断变化的目标。今天,为最大限度地减少安全风险而落实的措施在将来还需要升级,通常升级需要附加资金,管理层需要为之支付。

简单写写政策并不能改善安全状况。这需要后续通过与所有员工的沟通,使他们认识到高层管理人员在安全上布置的重点和重要性。在各个层面,管理层都需要去支持这项政策,并定期与员工用各种方式强化它。IT和网络的工作人员可能需要安装额外的硬件、软件和程序来自动进行安全检查工作。

有时管理层委任一个网络安全人员负责看管安全政策执行和实现。这个安全人员同时也对违反安全政策的违规行为进行调查,并提出建议以增补安全计划或做适当变更。在多数情况下,安全人员的任务是其中一名网络工作人员的兼职工作。不过,重要的是要确保安全责任不能因为其他日常工作的压力而总在频繁变化。

管理审查过程是对该安全计划正常运作的一个定期检查。审查过程的第一步可能是由单位的内部或外部的审查员进行的安全审查。审查报告作为管理审查的依据。

威胁的类型

对一个网络的安全威胁可分为含有某种形式的未经授权访问和所有其他情况。一旦有人得到了对网络的未经授权的访问,那么他们可以做事的范围就很大了。在这个尺度的无害底线,他们可能做不了什么。一些人只是对突破安全的挑战很感兴趣,而没有采取进一步行动的兴趣。他们可能选择监控网络流量,即所谓的窃听,其目的是为了了解一些特别的事情或者将其泄露给其他人,或者为了分析通信量曲线,通信量分析可以得到观测数据。这些都难以发现,因为作恶者并没有明显做什么,而只是监听网络。

我们能经常想起的这类未授权访问都是主动安全攻击,在一些人得到了对网络的未授权访问后,他们就采取一些明显动作了。主动攻击包括修改消息内容、冒充他人、拒绝服务攻击和种植病毒。

修改消息内容意思是改写一个消息的内容,造成消息接收人被误导或欺骗。例如,改变在金融交易中的数额,改变一个管理某些业务的授权人的名字或航班号。

冒充就是伪装成在网络上的其他人,特别是那些有更多特权的人。一个人可能在互联网上伪装成一个合法商人以获取某个不知情购买者的信用卡账号。

拒绝服务攻击的发生是指有人能用比网站处理信息速度更快的速度向其发送洪水般的信息,致使其网络性能降低。其他形式的拒绝服务攻击包括任何妨碍通信设施的正常使用的攻击。例如,仅仅传输链式电子邮件就可以阻塞一个网络,那些无用的流量可以有效地阻滞对合法用户的服务。

种植病毒可能发生的方式很多,但最常见的是通过电子邮件附件或者用户登录到一个互联网站点下载了含有病毒的软件。病毒因其完善度、破坏性,以及易于消除而范围很广,但这些是几乎所有的麻烦。

对网络控制中心或任何网络设施的物理损害,如集成电路、交换机、调制解调器、服务器或数据文件。

由常规事件造成的恶意破坏,如电缆故障、服务器故障、软件错误和由人为服务或操作造成的错误。这些类型的破坏需要事先预案,作为日常网络运转的一部分,而且应急预案应该落实到位以备这些破坏发生时用。这类问题通常并不严重,除非它们持续很长时间。

由天灾或人祸造成的事故,如洪水、火灾、龙卷风、地震和爆炸事件,这样的事故造成运行中断是严重的,而且通常要持续很长时间。如果应急计划不到位,灾难几乎会让公司因此倒闭。

Chapter 9 .NET Framework
(.NET 框架)

Section A What is .NET?

Why network programming in .NET?

One of the first technical decisions to be made whenever a new project is **undertaken** is what language to use. .NET is a capable platform on which to develop almost any solution, and it offers **substantial** support for network programming. In fact, .NET has more **intrinsic** support for networking than any other platform developed by Microsoft.

We assume that you have already decided to develop with .NET, and languages outside the .NET platform will not be discussed in any great detail, except for **comparative** purposes. This is not to say that .NET is the be-all and end-all of network-programming applications. If your application runs over a UNIX-only **infrastructure** communicating via Java remote method invocation (**RMI**), then .NET is not the way to go. In most circumstances, however, you will find that .NET is more than capable of handling whatever you throw at it.

What can a network program do?

A network program is any application that uses a computer network to transfer information to and from other applications. Examples range from the ubiquitous Web browser such as Internet Explorer, or the program you use to receive your email, to the software that controls **spacecraft** at NASA.

All of these pieces of software share the ability to communicate with other computers, and in so doing, become more useful to the end-user. In the case of a browser, every Web site you visit is actually files stored on a computer somewhere else on the Internet. With your email program, you are communicating with a computer at your Internet service provider (ISP) or company email exchange, which is holding your email for you.

---

undertake [,ʌndə'teik]
vt. 承担, 担任, 保证
substantial [səb'stænʃəl]
adj. 坚固的, 实质的
intrinsic [in'trinsik]
adj. 固有的, 本质的

comparative [kəm'pærətiv]
adj. 比较的, 相当的
infrastructure ['infrə'strʌktʃə]
n. 基本结构
RMI
远程方法调用,是用 Java 在 JDK 1.1 中实现的, 它大大增强了 Java 开发分布式应用的能力。

spacecraft ['speiskrɑːft]
n. 太空船

This chapter is largely concerned with creating network programs, not Web sites. Although the capabilities of Web sites and network programs are quickly **converging**, it is important to understand the arguments for and against each system. A service accessed via a Web site is instantly accessible to users across many different platforms, and the whole networking architecture is ready-built for you; however, there is a point at which features are simply **unfeasible** to implement using Web sites and at which you have to turn to network applications.

Users generally trust network applications; therefore, these programs have much greater control over the computers on which they are running than a Web site has over the computers viewing it. This makes it possible for a network application to manage files on the local computer, whereas a Web site, for all practical purposes, cannot do this. More importantly, from a networking **perspective**, an application has much greater control over how it can communicate with other computers on the Internet.

To give a simple example, a Web site cannot make the computer that is viewing it open a **persistent** network connection to another computer (except the computer from which the Web site was served). This applies even when the Web site contains embedded content such as a Java applet or Flash movie. There is one exception to this rule, when **executable** content (such as an ActiveX control) is included in a page. In this case, the page is capable of everything a network program could do, but most browsers and antivirus software will warn against or deny such executable content. Therefore, this **scenario** is commonly accepted as being unfeasible because of public distrust.

What is .NET?

.NET is not a programming language. It is a development framework that **incorporates** four official programming languages: C#, VB.NET, Managed C++, and J# .NET. Where there are overlaps in object types in the four languages, the framework defines the framework class library (**FCL**).

All four languages in the framework share the FCL and the common language runtime (**CLR**), which is an object-oriented platform that provides a runtime environment for .NET applications. The CLR is **analogous** to the virtual machine (VM)

---

converging [kən'və:dʒiŋ]
adj. 收敛［缩］的

unfeasible ['ʌn'fi:zəbl]
adj. 不能实行的,难实施的

perspective [pə'spektiv]
n. 透视图，远景，观点

persistent [pə'sistənt]
adj. 持久稳固的

executable ['eksikju:təbl]
adj. 实行的，执行的
scenario [si'nɑ:riəu]
n. 游戏的关,或是某一特定情节
incorporate [in'kɔ:pəreit]
adj. 合并的，一体化的
FCL
框架类库
CLR
.NET 提供了一个运行环境，叫做公共语言运行时。CLR 管理代码的执行，并使开发过程变得更加简单。CLR 是一种受控的执行环境,其功能通过编译器与其他工具共同展现。
analogous [ə'næləgəs]
adj. 类似的，相似的

in Java, except it is designed for Windows, not cross-platform, use; however, a stripped-down version of the .NET framework, known as the .NET compact framework, is capable of running on Windows CE devices, such as **palmtops** and certain cell phones.

In this chapter, the two most popular .NET programming languages, C# and VB.NET, are used. Both languages differ **syntactically**, but are equally capable and offer identical performance characteristics. Languages in the .NET framework are highly **interoperable**, so there is no need to be confined to a single language. A class compiled from VB.NET can be called from a C# application and vice versa. Similarly, a class written in VB.NET can derive from a compiled class written in C#. Exceptions and **polymorphism** are also supported across languages.

When an application written in a .NET language is compiled, it becomes the Microsoft intermediate language (**MSIL**) byte code, which is then executed by the CLR. MSIL code generated from compiling C# is generally identical to MSIL code generated from compiling VB.NET code. Exceptions to this lie with a few language-specific features, such as how C# can use classic C-style pointers within unsafe code and how VB.NET can use VB6-style Windows API definitions.

One of the failings of interpreted, or semicompiled, languages is a performance loss. .NET avoids this problem by using a just-in-time (**JIT**) compiler, which is generally transparent to the user. JIT acts on demand, whenever MSIL code is first executed. JIT compiles MSIL code to machine code, which is optimized for the processor of the computer that is executing the code.

.NET languages are object-oriented rather than procedurally based. This provides a natural mechanism to encapsulate interrelated data and methods to modify this data within the same logical construct. An object is a programmatic construct that has properties or can perform actions. A core concept of object orientation is the ability of one class to **inherit** the properties and methods of another.

You can make your own classes, which could form a base class from which other classes inherit. A typical example would be a class representing a car that could inherit from the vehicle class. .NET does not support multiple inheritance, so the car class cannot inherit from a vehicle class and a Windows form. Interestingly, every class within .NET derives from a root called System.Object.

The code examples are designed to be **stand-alone** Windows applications, rather than portable, self-contained classes. This approach is used to ensure that examples are kept as concise as possible. In real-world applications, networking code is generally kept separate from other **facets** of the application (e.g., user interface (UI), database access). Therefore, it is commonplace to keep classes associated with networking in a separate assembly.

An assembly is generally a **DLL** file that contains precompiled (MSIL) code for a collection of .NET classes. Unlike standard Win32 DLLs in which developers had to rely on documentation, such as header files, to use any given dll, .NET assemblies contain **metadata**, which provides enough information for any .NET application to use the methods contained within the assembly correctly. Metadata is also used to describe other features of the assembly, such as its version number, the **originator** of the code, and any custom attributes that were added to the classes.

.NET provides a unique solution to the issue of sharing assemblies between multiple applications. Generally, where an assembly is designed for use with only one application, it is contained within the same folder (or bin **subfolder**) as the application. This is known as a private assembly. A public assembly is copied into a location where all .NET applications on the local system have access too. Furthermore, this public assembly is designed to be versioned, unique, and **tamperproof**, thanks to a clever security model. This location into which public assemblies are copied is called the global assembly cache (**GAC**).

stand-alone [ˈstændəˌləun]
n. 单机，卓越
facet [ˈfæsit]
n. 小平面，方面
DLL
Abbr.Dynamic Linkable Library
一种磁盘文件，以.dll、.drv、.fon、.sys 和许多以.exe 为扩展名的系统文件都可以是DLL。Windows 系统平台上提供了一种完全不同的较有效的编程和运行环境，可以将独立的程序模块创建为较小的DLL 文件，并可对它们单独编译和测试。
metadata
n. [计]元数据
originator [əˈridʒəneitə(r)]
n. 创作者,发明人
subfolder [ˈsʌbfɔːm]
n. [计]子文件夹
tamperproof [ˈtæmpəpruːf]
adj.可防止乱摆弄的
GAC
全局程序集缓存,计算机范围内的代码缓存,用于存储专门安装的程序集,这些程序集由计算机上的许多应用程序共享。在全局程序集缓存中部署的应用程序必须具有强名称。

Exercises

Fill in the blanks with the information given in the text.

1. In fact, .NET has more intrinsic support for _____ than any other platform developed by Microsoft.

2. A network program is any application that uses a computer network to _____ to and from other applications.

3. Users generally trust _____; therefore, these programs have much greater control over the computers on which they are running than a Web site has over the computers viewing it.

4. .NET is not a _____. It is a development _____ that incorporates four official programming

languages: C#, VB.NET, Managed C++, and J# .NET.

5. However, a stripped-down version of the .NET framework, known as the .NET compact framework, is capable of running on _____ devices, such as palmtops and certain cell phones.

6. When an application written in a .NET language is compiled, it becomes the _____ byte code, which is then executed by the _____.

7. _____ compiles MSIL code to machine code, which is optimized for the processor of the computer that is executing the code.

8. An assembly is generally a _____ file that contains precompiled (MSIL) code for a collection of .NET classes.

9. .NET assemblies contain _____, which provides enough information for any .NET application to use the methods contained within the assembly correctly.

10. Generally, where an assembly is designed for use with only one application, it is contained within the same folder (or bin subfolder) as the application. This is known as a _____ assembly.

Section B Using Visual Studio.NET

The examples in this section require you to have access to Microsoft Visual Studio .NET. To program in Microsoft .NET, you need to have the Microsoft .NET SDK or Microsoft Visual Studio .NET. The SDK can be used to create .NET applications, but it is **awkward** to create graphical user interfaces (GUIs) and use command-line-based compilers.

awkward ['ɔːkwəd]
adj. 难使用的，笨拙的

Visual Studio .NET is not free, but no serious .NET developer should attempt to write .NET applications without it.

All examples are given in the two most popular .NET languages: C# and Visual Basic .NET. Both languages have exactly the same capabilities, and there is **absolutely** no difference in performance between the two languages. If you are familiar with C or C++, you should choose to develop in C#. If you are familiar with Visual Basic, you should choose to develop in Visual Basic .NET. When developing an application, you should not swap between languages.

absolutely ['æbsəluːtli]
adv. 完全地，绝对地

The first example **demonstrates** how to display a Web page within a .NET application.

demonstrate ['demənstreit]
vt. 示范，证明

Open Visual Studio .NET, and click New Project. Then type in a name and location for your project (Fig. 9.1).

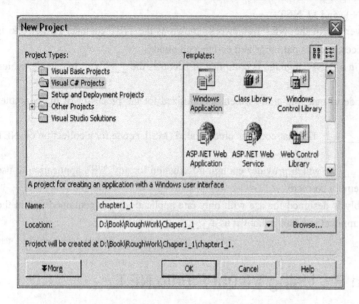

Fig. 9.1   Visual Studio .NET, New Project dialog

Select the Visual Basic Windows application or Visual C# Windows application, depending on which language you wish to develop in.

When the form appears, right-click on the toolbox and select **Customize** Toolbox or Add/Remove Items. Then select Microsoft Web Browser from the **dialog box** (as shown in Fig. 9.2), and click OK.

customize [kʌstəmaiz]
v. [计] 定制, 用户化
dialog box
对话框

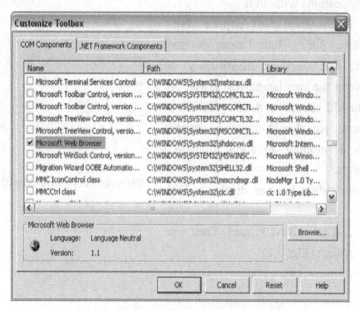

Fig. 9.2   Visual Studio .NET, Customize Toolbox dialog

Drag the Explorer icon onto the form, and then drag a button and textbox onto the form. The finished form should look like Fig. 9.3.

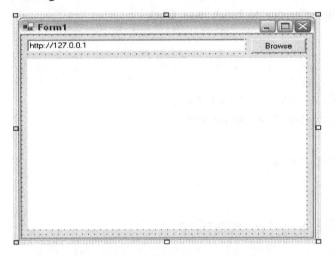

Fig. 9.3 Visual Studio .NET, form design view

The next step is to set the properties of all the user interface elements. Right-click on the button and select the Properties option. You will see the Properties window appearing. Scroll up to the top of this window, and click on the property labeled (Name). Enter in the new name, btnBrowse, as shown in Fig. 9.4.

Fig. 9.4 Visual Studio .NET, Properties tool window

Similarly, name the textbox tbURL and the Microsoft Web Browser control webBrowser.

If you double-click on the button, you will see a page of code already written for you. Find the reference to btnBrowse_Click and insert the following code:

VB.NET

```
Private Sub btnBrowse_Click(ByVal sender As _
System.Object,ByVal e As System.EventArgs) Handles _
btnBrowse.Click
webBrowser.Navigate(tbURL.Text)
End Sub
```

C#

```
private void btnBrowse_Click(object sender, System.EventArgse)
{
   object notUsed = null;
   webBrowser.Navigate(tbURL.Text,ref  notUsed,ref notUsed, ref notUsed, ref notUsed);
}
```

The code consists simply of a single method call, navigate. This **invokes** the standard process that Internet Explorer goes through as it navigates the Web. The reason for the extra parameters to the method in the C# version is that C# does not support **optional** parameters. The navigate method has four optional parameters: Flags, targetFrameName, postData, and Headers. None of these is needed for this simple example.

In the application, click Debug Start, type in the name of a Web page in the space provided, and click the Browse button. You will see that Web page appearing in the Web Browser control on the page, such as that shown in Fig. 9.5.

invoke [in'vəuk]
v. 调用

optional ['ɔpʃənəl]
adj. 可选择的，随意的

Chapter 9 .NET Framework

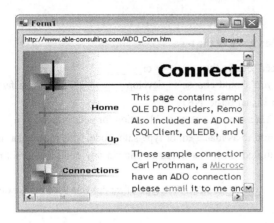

Fig. 9.5 Visual Studio .NET, form at runtime

You will quickly notice that the Web browser window behaves **identically** to Internet Explorer. This is because the component that was added to the toolbox is the main processing engine behind Internet Explorer.

Applications written in .NET are referred to as managed or type-safe code. This means that the code is compiled to an **intermediate** language (IL) that is strictly controlled, such that it cannot contain any code that could potentially cause a computer to crash. Applications written in native code have the ability to modify **arbitrary** addresses of computer memory, some of which could cause crashes, or general protection faults.

Components designed before the **advent** of .NET are written in native code and are therefore unmanaged and deemed unsafe. There is no technical difficulty in combining unsafe code with a .NET application, as shown previously; however, if an underlying component has the potential to bring down a computer, the whole application is also deemed unsafe. Unsafe applications may be subject to restrictions; for instance, when they are executed from a network share, they could be prevented from operating.

The Internet Explorer component is a Common Object Model (**COM**) control. This type of model was used most **extensively** in Visual Studio 6.0. When a COM object is imported into a .NET application, a Runtime callable wrapper (RCW) class is created. This class then exposes all the properties and methods of the COM object to .NET code.

identically [ai'dentikəli]
adj. 同一的, 同样的

intermediate [ˌintə'mi:djət]
adj. 中间的

arbitrary ['ɑ:bitrəri]
adj. 任意的

advent ['ædvənt]
n. 出现, 到来

COM
公共对象模型
extensively [iks'tensivli]
adv. 广大地, 广泛地

Exercises

Ⅰ. Fill in the blanks with the information given in the text.

1. To program in Microsoft .NET, you need to have the _____ or _____.
2. If you are familiar with C or C++, you should choose to develop _____. If you are familiar with Visual Basic, you should choose to develop in Visual Basic .NET.
3. Open Visual Studio .NET, and click. Then type in a name and location for your project.
4. Applications written in .NET are referred to as managed, or type-safe, code. This means that the code is compiled to an _____ that is strictly controlled, such that it cannot contain any code that could potentially cause a computer to crash.
5. The Internet Explorer component is a _____ control. This type of model was used most extensively in Visual Studio 6.0.

Ⅱ. Translate the following passages from English into Chinese.

Learn .NET Framework 3.0

Microsoft's .NET Framework 3.0 (formerly codenamed "WinFX"), is the new managed code programming model for Windows. It combines the power of the .NET Framework 2.0 with four new technologies: Windows Presentation Foundation (WPF), Windows Communication Foundation (WCF), Windows Workflow Foundation (WF), and Windows CardSpace™. Use the .NET Framework 3.0 to build applications that have visually compelling user experiences, seamless communication across technology boundaries, the ability to support a wide range of business processes, and an easier way to manage your personal information online.

Section C Using the .NET SDK

Using the .NET SDK to develop .NET applications makes a lot more work for a developer. This section shows you how to write and compile a .NET application from the command line.

The command line may be adequate for development of **console** applications, ASP.NET, and components, but it is not feasible to develop large Windows forms applications from the command line. The previous example, although easy to implement in Visual Studio .NET, would require a large and complex program. Nevertheless, it should be **informative** to Visual Studio .NET developers to be aware of the code that is **autogenerated** by Visual Studio .NET.

In the true programming tradition, we shall start with a program that simply displays "Hello World". To make this different, the program will be written as a Windows form. After all, DOS console applications are very much past their sell-by date, and there seems little point in using them at all.

The code for this application may seem **daunting** at first, but this should illustrate how much extra work is required to

console [kən'səul]
n. [计] 控制台

informative [in'fɔ:mətiv]
adj. 情报的，见闻广博的
autogenerate
自动产生

daunt [dɔ:nt]
v. 沮丧

implement applications without Visual Studio .NET.

First, decide which language you want to develop in, either C# or Visual Basic .NET. Open a text editor, such as Notepad, and type in the following code:

C#
```
using System;
using System.Windows.Forms;
namespace helloWorld
{
  public class Form1 : System.Windows.Forms.Form
  {
    public Form1( )
    {
      this.Text = "Hello World";
    }
    [STAThread]
    static void Main( )
    {
      Application.Run(new Form1( ));
    }
  }
}
```

VB.NET
```
Imports System
Imports System.Windows.Forms
Public Class Form1
  Inherits System.Windows.Forms.Form
Public Sub New ( )
  InitializeComponent( )
End Sub
 Private Sub InitializeComponent( )
  Me.Text = "Hello World";
End sub
End Class
Module Module1
  Sub Main ( )
    Application.Run ( new Form1 ( ) )
  End sub
End Module
```

All this code does is open a window with the caption "Hello World", which is somewhat **underwhelming** for the amount of code entered. Looking closely at the code, you can see the process of events that make up a Windows application in .NET.

An application in .NET is made up of namespaces, some of which are system defined and others are coded in. This application contains three namespaces: System, System.Windows.Forms, and helloWorld. The latter is the only namespace of the three that is actually supplied by the programmer. The helloWorld namespace contains a class, named Form1. This class inherits from System.Windows.Forms.Form. This means that the class will have a visible presence on screen.

Whenever a class is created, a function known as the **constructor** is called. This function can be recognized in C# when the name of the function is the same as that of the class. In VB.NET, the constructor is a **subroutine** named New. In the case of the previous example and in most Windows applications, this constructor is used to place user interface elements (sometimes referred to as widgets) on the form. In the previous example, the constructor calls InitializeComponent, which then sets the window name of the current form (this) to "Hello World".

Every application must have a starting point. It is tradition in virtually every programming language that the stating point should be called Main. In C#, the STAThread attribute indicates the function which acts as the entry point for this single threaded apartment (**STA**) application. Every application must have one, and only one, entry point.

```
[STAThread] static void Main( )
```

In VB.NET, the main function is coded in a different way but operates identically. The main function must appear in a separate module and be coded as follows. A module is a **programmatic** element that contains code that is global to the entire application.

```
Module Module1: Sub Main ( )
```

Once a Windows application starts, at least one form (a class inheriting from System.Windows.Forms.Form) must be created in order for there to be a visual interface. To create a new form, we call Application.Run, passing an instance of the form.

---

underwhelming [ˌʌndə'waind]
vt. 未留下深刻印象

constructor [kən'strʌktə]
[计] 构造器
subroutine [ˌsʌbruː'tiːn]
n. [计] 子程序

STA
单线程单元模式

programmatic
[ˌprəʊɡrə'mætik]
adj. 标题音乐的，节目的

Chapter 9 .NET Framework

Compiling with Visual Basic.NET

Save the file to D:\temp\helloworld.vb. Open the command prompt by pressing Start → Run and then typing cmd for Windows NT, 2000, or XP or command for Windows 95, 98, or ME.

Type the following:

DOS

```
D:\temp> path %path%;C:\WINDOWS\Microsoft.NET\Framework\v1.0.3705
D:\temp> Vbc /t:winexe /r:system.dll /r:system.windows.forms.dll helloworld.vb
D:\temp> helloworld
```

Compiling with C#

Save the file to D:\temp\helloworld.cs. Open the command prompt by pressing Start → Run and then typing cmd for Windows NT, 2000, or XP or command for Windows 95, 98, or ME.

DOS

```
D:\temp> path %path%;C:\WINDOWS\Microsoft.NET\Framework\v1.0.3705
D:\temp> csc /t:exe helloworld.cs
D:\temp> helloworld
```

Testing the Application

To run the application, you need to compile it first. Depending on what language you used to program the application, skip to the relevant section. Once it has compiled, you can run the application by clicking on the executable (.exe) file generated from the **compilation**.

compilation [ˌkɔmpiˈleiʃən]
n. 编辑

Exercises

Ⅰ. **Fill in the blanks with the information given in the text.**

1. The command line may be adequate for development of console applications, ASP.NET, and components, but it is not feasible to develop large _____ from the command line.

2. An application in .NET is made up of _____, some of which are system defined and others are coded in.

3. Whenever a class is created, a function known as the _____ is called. This function can be recognized in C# when the name of the function is the same as that of the class.

4. Every application must have a starting point. It is tradition in virtually every programming language that the stating point should be called _____.

5. A _____ is a programmatic element that contains code that is global to the entire application.

Ⅱ. **Type the following the C# codes into your computer and execute it.**

```
FileStream fs;
byte[] fileContents;
AsyncCallback callback;
private void btnReadAsync_Click(object sender,
System.EventArgs e)
{
  openFileDialog.ShowDialog();

callback = new AsyncCallback(fs_StateChanged);
  fs = new FileStream(openFileDialog.FileName, FileMode.Open,
  FileAccess.Read, FileShare.Read, 4096, true);
  fileContents = new Byte[fs.Length];
  fs.BeginRead(fileContents, 0, (int)fs.Length, callback,
null);
}
```

Grammar 9 谈科技翻译中的长句的翻译

前面提到，科技英语有一个特点就是复杂的长句多。在翻译的过程中，我们务必根据每个长句的特点进行翻译。具体来说，为什么在科技英语中句子都比较长？首先，我们知道有时候为了将事物说明得更确切和具体，在句子中会使用很多的修饰语。其次，我们在实际翻译中也发现一个问题，那就是在科技英语中并列成分很多，这样也容易让句子很长。最后，语言结构层次多也是导致科技英语中长句多的原因。

在翻译过程中，我们可以采用以下方法去应对长句。

1. 找出全句的主语、谓语和宾语，从整体上把握句子的结构

例如：

For a family of four, for example, it is more convenient as well as cheaper to sit comfortably at home, with almost unlimited entertainment available, than to go out in search of amusement elsewhere.

分析：

(1) 该句的主干结构为 it is more … to do sth than to do sth else.是一个比较结构，而且是在两个不定式之间进行比较。

(2) 该句中共有三个谓语结构，它们之间的关系如下：it is more convenient as well as cheaper to … 为主体结构，但 it 是形式主语，真正的主语为第二个谓语结构 to sit comfortably at home, 并与第三个谓语结构 to go out in search of amusement elsewhere 进行比较。

(3) 句首的 for a family of four 作为状语，表示条件。另外，还有两个介词短语作为插入语：for example, with almost unlimited entertainment available,其中第二个介词短语作为伴随状语，修饰 to sit comfortably at home。

[译文]譬如，对于一个四口之家来说，舒舒服服地在家中看电视，就能看到几乎数不清的娱乐节目，这比到外面别的地方去消遣又便宜又方便。

2. 找出句中所有的谓语结构、非谓语动词、介词短语和从句的引导词

例如：

Summary must be a condensed version of body of the report, written in language understandable by those members of mine management who may not be specialists I the field of rock testing, but who are nonetheless responsible for the work.

原译：摘要必须是报告的编写本，要以矿山管理部门人员能够理解的语言编写，这些人虽不是岩石试验方面的专家，但他们对这方面的工作负责。

分析：我们先来看一下原文的语言：两个"who-"定语从句，第一个可以看作表示原因的状语从句，第二个是非限制性定语从句，对先行词进行补充说明，but 不是单纯的转折，而是和第一个从句中的 not 呼应，意思是"而是"或"只是"。由此，本句的意思已经比较明朗了：所以要以非专家的语言编写，是因为这些管理人员不是专家，而不是因为他们对这方面的工作负责。

现译：摘要必须是报告的编写本，要以矿山管理部门人员能够理解的语言编写；他们虽然负责岩石试验工作，但不是这方面的专家。

3. 分析从句和短语的功能

主要分析句子是否为主语从句、宾语从句、表语从句等,若是状语,它是表示时间、原因、结果，还是表示条件等。

例如：

Even when we turn off the beside lamp and are fast asleep, electricity is working for us, driving our refrigerators, heating our water, or keeping our rooms air-conditioned.

分析：该句子由一个主句、三个做伴随状语的现在分词以及位于句首的时间状语从句组成，共有五层意思：①即使在我们关掉了床头灯深深地进入梦乡时；②电仍在为我们工作；③帮我们开动电冰箱；④加热水；⑤或是室内空调机继续运转。上述五层意思的逻辑关系以及表达的顺序与汉语完全一致。

[译文]即使在我们关掉了床头灯深深地进入梦乡时，电仍在为我们工作：帮我们开动电冰箱，把水加热，或使室内空调器继续运转。

4. 分析从句和短语的功能

例如，句子是否为主语从句、宾语从句、表语从句等,若是状语,它是表示时间、原因、结果，还是表示条件等。

5. 注意插入语等其他成分

注意分析句子中是否有固定词组或固定搭配。

 参考译文

Section A .NET 是什么？

为什么网络编程要用.NET？

无论什么时候，一个新的项目被承担下来时，要做的第一个技术决定就是要使用什么语言。.NET 是一个几乎可以解决任何开发问题，并对网络编程提供大量支持的可以胜任的开发平台。事实上，.NET 比微软发展的其他平台在本质上更支持网络应用。

我们假设，您已经决定用.NET 进行开发，并且在.NET 平台之外的语言的任何细节都不会讨论，当然除非用于比较目的。但这并不是说.NET 是网络编程应用最重要的部分。如果您的应用程序是运行在 UNIX 基础之上，而且底层通过 Java 远程方法调用来实现的，则.NET 并不适合。然而在大多数情况下，您能发现，无论你想处理什么，.NET 都能绰绰有余地胜任。

一个网络程序能够做什么？

一个网络程序是使用计算机网络从其他应用传送信息时的所有应用。例如，普遍存在的浏览器，如 Internet Explorer 或者是您使用接受您的电子邮件的程序，以及控制美国航空航天局太空船的软件。

所有这些软件模块均具有与其他计算机通信的能力，并且这样做能够对终端用户更加有用。在浏览器模式下，您浏览的每个网站实际上是存放在互联网其他地方的计算机上的文件。利用电子邮件程序，您可以同保留有您的电子邮件的网络服务提供商或公司的计算机进行收发电子邮件。

本章主要介绍的是网络编程，而不是建立网站。尽管网站和网络程序是有交叉的，但是理解每个系统的正反论据是非常重要的。被访问的一个网站上的服务对于跨越许多不同的平台的用户来说是很容易进入的，且整个网络体系结构已经为您构建好了，然而，这里存在一些使用网站不能简单实现的功能，这时，您必须求助于网络应用了。

用户通常信任网络应用，因此，这些程序对于运行它们的计算机来说，拥有比网站更大的控制权。这使得一个网络应用可以管理本地计算机的文件，而一个网站实际上是不能做这个工作的。更重要的是，从网络的角度看，一个应用程序拥有更大的权限去控制它怎样与互联网上的其他计算机通信。

举一个简单的例子，一个网站不能使正在浏览它的计算机和另一台计算机（除非是提供网站服务的计算机）之间建立永久的连接，即使网站包含嵌入内容，如 Java 小程序或 Flash 电影。但这个规则有一个例外，即一个网页中含有可执行的内容（如一个 ActiveX 控件）。在这种情况下，一个网页能够胜任一个网络程序能够完成的任何事情，但大多数浏览器和杀毒软件将警告和拒绝那样的可执行内容。因此，这个特定的情形通常因为公开的不信任而被认为是不能实现的。

.NET 是什么？

.NET 不是编程语言，它融合了4种官方编程语言：C#、VB.NET、Managed C++与 J#.NET 的开发框架。4种语言的对象类型是有交叉的，.NET 框架定义了框架类库。

框架中的4种语言均共享框架类库和一个提供.NET 应用运行环境的面向对象的开发平台，即公共语言运行系统（CLR）。这个 CLR 同 Java 语言的虚拟机（VM）类似，但它是为 Windows 设计的，而不像 VM 可跨平台使用。然而，.NET 框架的一个拆开版本，即.NET 精简架版，能够运行在基于 Windows CE 的设备上，如掌上型计算机和手机。

在本章，将使用两种最为流行的.NET 编程语言 C#和 VB.NET。两种语言在语法上是不同的，但具备同样的能力和性能特征。在 .NET 框架中的语言是能够共同操作的，因此不需要限制成一种单一的语言。一个来自 VB.NET 的类被编译后能够被一个 C#应用程序调用；反之亦然。类似地，一个用 VB.NET 编写

的类能够从一个编译的 C#.异常类中获得，并且多态在跨语言时也是支持的。

当一个用.NET 语言编写的应用程序被编译时，它变成微软中间语言的字节码，这个字节码随后通过 CLR 执行。不管是 C# 还是 VB.NET 产生的 MSIL 码都是一样的。当一个新的具体语言特性出现时，这个也有例外，如 C#如何在不安全代码范围内使用传统的 C 风格的指针以及 VB.NET 如何使用 Windows API 定义的 VB6 风格。

一旦程序解释失败或者半编译，就会有性能损失。.NET 为了避免这个问题，使用一个及时制（JIT）的编译器，它通常对用户是透明的。JIT 按要求执行，但无论什么时候，MSIL 代码都是首先被执行的。JIT 将 MSIL 代码编译成机器代码，这个机器代码已经被执行它的计算机的处理器进行了优化处理。

.NET 语言不是面向过程的，而是面向对象的语言。这就在同样的逻辑结构中提供了一个自然而然的机制去封装相互联系的数据以及修改这些数据的方法。一个对象是一个程序化的具有某些特征或者能够执行操作的结构。面向对象的核心概念是一个类继承另一个类的特征和方法的能力。

你能够创建你自己的类，这对于其他的类形成一个可以继承的基类。一个典型的例子就是一个表征汽车的类，它可以继承一个交通工具类。.NET 不能支持多重继承，因此汽车类不能同时继承一个交通工具类和一个窗体类。有趣的是，在.NET 中的每个类都来源于一个被称为 System.Object 的类。

设计的示例代码主要针对单机版的 Windows 应用，而不是可移植的、自包含的类。该方法用于保证例子尽可能地简练。在现实应用中，网络代码通常同其他应用（用户界面（UI），数据库访问）分开保存。因此，用一个分开的程序集保留与网络相关的类是常见的。

程序集通常是一个包含.NET 类集的预编译代码的.dll 文件。不像标准 Win32 动态链接库那样，开发者需要必须依赖于文档，如头文件等。利用给定的 DLL，.NET 汇集了一定的元数据，它利用在程序集中恰当地包含一些方法来提供任何网络应用足够的信息。元数据也用来描述程序集的其他特征，如它的版本号、代码的创始人，以及被加到类中的任何自定义属性。

.NET 在多重应用之间的共享程序集问题上能够提供一个唯一的解决方案。通常，当一个程序集被指定仅为一个应用程序使用时，则它将被包含在和应用程序相同的文件夹（或子文件夹）中，这就是所谓的私有程序集。一个共享程序集被复制到一个本地系统所有的.NET 应用也能访问的地方。而且，这个共享程序集被设计成为版本化的、唯一的且防作弊的。这要感谢一个优秀的安全模型。共享程序集存放的地方被称为全局程序集缓冲器（GAC）。

Section B 使用 Visual Studio .NET

本节的例子要求你能够使用 Microsoft Visual Studio .NET 集成开发环境。为了进行.NET 编程，你需要安装 Microsoft .NET SDK 或 Microsoft Visual Studio .NET。 利用 SDK 能够创建.NET 应用程序，但是当创建图形用户接口（GUI）是难使用的，它使用命令行进行编译。

Visual Studio .NET 不是免费的，但严格的.NET 开发人员不应该企图在没有它的情况下编写.NET 应用程序。

所有的例子均采用两种最为流行的.NET 语言，即 C#和 VB.NET 来描述。两种语言均具有相同的处理能力，而且两种语言在性能上也没有绝对的不同。如果你熟悉 C 或者 C++，你应该选择 C#语言来开发。如果你熟悉 VB，你应该选择 VB.NET 来开发。在开发应用程序过程中，你就不应该在两种语言之间交换了。

第一例子展示的是在一个.NET 应用中如何显示一个网页。

打开 Visual Studio .NET, 然后单击 New Project. 然后输入名字和你的项目存放位置（如图 10.1 所示）。究竟选择 Visual Basic Windows 应用还是 Visual C# Windows 应用，取决于你要用哪种语言进行开发。

当窗体出现后，右击工具箱，并选择 Customize 工具箱或者 Add/Remove 选项。然后从选择对话框中（如图 10.2 所示）选择 Microsoft Web Browser 选项，然后单击 OK 按钮即可。

拖动 Explorer 图标到窗体上，然后拖动一个按钮和文本框到窗体上。制作完成的窗体如图 10.3 所示。

接下来的步骤是设置所有的用户界面元素的属性。右击按钮然后选择 Properties 选项，你将看到属性窗口，将鼠标指针移动到窗口的顶部，单击 property labeled (Name)。输入新的名字：btnBrowse，如图 10.4 所示。

类似地，将 textbox 命名为 tbURL，Microsoft Web Browser control 命名为 webBrowser。

如果你双击按钮，你会看到已经为你写好的代码页，找到 btnBrowse_Click 的 reference，然后插入如下代码：（代码略）。

这些代码只是由简单的单一方法调用和导航组成。当它导航网页时，调用了 Internet Explorer 的标准过程。原因是额外参数对于 C#版本中的方法来说，是不支持可选择参数的。导航方法有 4 个可选择的参数：Flags、targetFrameName、postData 及 Headers。在此例中没有一个是必需的。

在此应用程序中，单击 Debug Start，并输入网页的名称，然后单击 Browse 按钮。你将会看到网页出现在 Web 浏览器控制页面中，如图 10.5 所示。

你将很快注意到 Web 浏览器窗口同 Internet Explorer 是一样的。这是因为被添加到工具箱中的组件是 Internet Explorer 的主要处理引擎。

在.NET 中编写的应用程序的代码是指托管的、类型安全的代码。这意味着代码被编译成被严格控制的中间语言，这样它就不能包含那些可能潜在地导致计算机崩溃的代码了。但以原生代码编写的应用程序能够任意修改计算机内存的地址，其中一些有可能导致系统崩溃，或者常规的保护错误。

在.NET 出现之前，组件的设计是通过原生代码编写的，因此是非托管的、被认为是不安全的。在.NET 中结合不安全的代码没有技术上的困难，正如前面所述的。然而，如果一个基本组件能够使一台计算机瘫痪，那么整个应用也被认为是不安全的。不安全的应用可能要受到限制。例如，当他们从网络共享上执行时，他们可能会被阻止操作。

IE 组件是一个公共对象模型（COM）控制，这种类型的模型在 Visual Studio 6.0 用的最为广泛。当一个 COM 对象被引入到.NET 应用程序中时，一个运行时调用包装类被创建。然后这个类使 COM 对象的所有特征和方法对.NET 代码均可见。

Section C 使用.NET 的 SDK

利用.NET SDK 来开发.NET 应用程序对于开发者来说会有更多工作要做。本节将要告诉你通过命令行如何编写和编译一个.NET 应用程序。

命令行方式对于控制台应用、ASP.NET 及组件开发是足够胜任的，但是要开发窗体应用程序则是不行的。在先前的例子中，尽管在 Visual Studio .NET 容易实现，但它需要大量而又复杂的程序。不过，对于 Visual Studio .NET 的开发人员来说，他们想要的代码是通过 Visual Studio .NET 自动生成的。

在实际的编程过程中，我们都要从一个简单的显示"Hello World."的程序开始。为了使其不同，这个程序将要被写成窗体的形式。毕竟，DOS 控制台应用程序是非常过时了，而且看起来我们很少使用它。

这个应用程序的代码起初看起来非常令人沮丧，但是我们必须展示一下在没有 Visual Studio .NET 的情况下，我们执行应用程序需要完成多少额外的工作。

首先，要决定你使用哪种语言来开发，C#或者是 VB.NET。打开一个文本编辑器，如记事本，输入如下的代码：（代码略）。

这代码所做的工作就是要打开一个带有标题"Hello World"的窗体，它看起来似乎没有什么大量的代码的输入。但仔细看这些代码，你能看到在.NET 中组成一个 Window 应用程序的事件的过程。

一个.NET 应用程序是由名空间组成，其中一些是由系统定义的，而其他是输入的。这个应用程序包括 3 个名空间：System、System.Windows.Forms 及 helloWorld。后者是 3 个名空间中唯一的被编程者提供的。这个 helloWorld 名空间包含一个类，叫 Form1。这个类继承了 System.Windows.Forms.Form。这意味着这个类将要在屏幕上有所显示。

Chapter 9 .NET Framework

一个类无论什么时候被创建,一个叫做构造器的函数都会被调用。当其名字与类的名字相同时,这个函数在 C#中就会被识别。 在 VB.NET 中,这个构造器就是叫 New 的子例程。在先前的例子中以及在大多数 Windows 应用程序中,这个构造器被用于将用户的界面元素(有时指 widgets)放到窗体上。在先前的例子中,构造器调用 InitializeComponent,然后将当前窗体的名字设置为 "Hello World"。

每个应用程序必须有一个开始点。实际上在每种编程语言中传统上这个开始点应该被称为 Main. 在 C#中,STAThread 属性表明这个单线程单元模式的应用程序的入口点函数。每个应用程序有且仅有一个入口点。

```
[STAThread] static void Main( )
```

在 VB.NET 中,这个主函数代码是不同的,但操作是一致的。主函数必须在一个独立的模块中出现,其代码如下所示。一个模块是一个程序化的元素,它包含的代码对于整个应用程序来说是全局性的。

```
Module Module1: Sub Main ( )
```

一旦开始执行一个 Windows 应用程序,为了显示一个可视化的界面,至少要创建一个窗体(一个从 System.Windows.Forms.Form 窗体类继承的类)。为了要创建一个新的窗体,我们通过窗体的实例来调用 Application.Run 。

编译 VB.NET

将文件存储到 D:\temp\helloworld.vb。单击 Start→Run,打开命令行窗口,然后输入 Windows NT、2000,或者 XP 的命令,或者 Windows 95、98,或 ME 支持的命令。

然后输入下面的命令:

```
D:\temp> path %path%;C:\WINDOWS\Microsoft.NET\
Framework\v1.0.3705
D:\temp> Vbc /t:winexe /r:system.dll /r:system.
windows.forms.dll
helloworld.vb
D:\temp> helloworld
```

编译 C#

将文件存储到 D:\temp\helloworld.cs。单击 Start→Run,打开命令行窗口,然后输入 Windows NT、2000,或者 XP 的命令,或者 Windows 95、98,或 ME 支持的命令。

然后输入下面的命令:

```
D:\temp> path %path%;C:\WINDOWS\Microsoft.NET\
Framework\v1.0.3705
D:\temp> csc /t:exe helloworld.cs
D:\temp> helloworld
```

测试应用程序

为了运行应用程序,你首先要编译它。根据你使用语言的不同,你可以跳到相关的章节。一旦它被编译,你就可以通过单击由编译产生的可执行文件来执行应用程序了。

Chapter 10 Distributed Systems
(分布式系统)

Section A Characterization of Distributed Systems

Introduction

Networks of computers are everywhere. The Internet is one, as are the many networks of which it is composed. Mobile phone networks, **corporate** networks, factory networks, campus networks, home networks, in-car networks, all of these, both separately and in combination, share the essential **characteristics** that make them relevant subjects for study under the heading distributed systems. In this section we aim to explain the characteristics of networked computers that impact system designers and implementers and to present the main concepts and techniques that have been developed to help in the tasks of designing and implementing systems that are based on them.

We define a distributed system as one in which hardware or software components located at networked computers communicate and **coordinate** their actions only by passing messages. This simple definition covers the entire range of systems in which networked computers can usefully be deployed.

Computers that are connected by a network may be **spatially** separated by any distance. They may be on separate continents, in the same building or the same room. Our definition of distributed systems has the following **significant** consequences:

- **Concurrency**: In a network of computers, concurrent program execution is the norm. I can do my work on my computer while you do your work on yours. Sharing resources such as Web pages or files when necessary. The capacity of the system to handle shared resources can be increased by adding more resources (for example computers)to the network. We will describe ways in which this extra capacity can be usefully deployed at

corporate ['kɔ:pərit]
adj. 共同的，全体的
characteristics
[ˌkærɪktəraɪ'zeɪʃən]
n. 描述，人物之创造

coordinate [kəu'ɔ:dinit]
vt. 调整，整理

spatially ['speiʃəli]
adj. 空间的
significant [sig'nifikənt]
adj. 有意义的，重大的，重要的
concurrency [kən'kʌrənsi]
n. 同时(或同地)发生，同时存在，合作

Chapter 10 Distributed Systems

many points in this chapter. The coordination of concurrently executing program that share resources is also an important and **recurring** topic.

- No global clock: When programs need to cooperate, they coordinate their actions by exchanging messages. Close coordination often depends on a shared idea of the time at which the programs' actions occur. But it turns out that there are limits to the accuracy with which the computers in a network can **synchronize** their clocks——there is no single global notion of the correct time. This is a direct consequence of the fact that the only communication is by sending messages through a network.

- Independent failures: All computer systems can fail and it is the responsibility of system designers to plan for the consequences of possible failures. Distributed systems can fail in new ways. Faults in the network result in the **isolation** of the fact programs on them may not be able to detect whether the network has failed or has become unusually slow. Similarly, the failure of a computer, or the unexpected termination of program somewhere in the system (a crash) is not immediately made known to the other components with which it communicates. Each component of the system can fail **independently**, leaving the others still running.

The motivation for **constructing** and using distributed system from a desire to share resources. The term "resources" is a rather abstract one, but it best characterizes the range of things that can usefully be shared in networked computer system. It extends from hardware components such as disks and printers to software-defined **entities** such as files, databases and data objects of all kinds. It includes the stream of video frames that **emerges** from a digital video camera and the audio connection that a mobile phone call represents.

Examples of Distributed Systems

Our examples are based on familiar and widely used computer networks: the Internet, **intranets** and the emerging technology of networks based on mobile devices. They are designed to exemplify the wide range of services and applications that are supported by computer networks and to begin the discussion of the technical issues that **underlie** the implementation.

The Internet is also a very large distributed system. It enables users, wherever they are, to make use of services such as the World Wide Web, email and file transfer.(Indeed, the Web is sometimes incorrectly equated with the Internet.)The set of services is **open-ended**, it can be extended by the addition of server computers and new types of service. Internet Service Providers (**ISPs**) are companies that provide modern links and other types of connection to individual users and small organizations, enabling them to access anywhere in the Internet as well as providing local services such as E-mail and Web hosting. The Intranets are linked together by **backbones**. A backbone is network link with a high transmission capacity, employing satellite connections, **fibre optic cables** and other high-**bandwidth** circuits.

An Intranet is a portion of the Internet that is separately administered and has a boundary that can be **configured** to enforce local security policies. It is composed of several local area networks (LANs) linked by backbones connections. The network configuration of a particular Intranet is the **responsibility** of the organization that administers it and may vary widely-ranging from a LAN on a single site to a connected set of LANs belonging to branches of a company or other organization in different countries.

An Intranet is connected to the Internet via a **router**, which allows the users inside the Intranet to make use of services elsewhere such as the Web or email. It also allows the users in other Intranets to access the services it provides. Many organizations need to protect their own services from **unauthorized** use by possibly malicious users elsewhere. For example, a company will not want secure information to be accessible to users in competing organizations, and a hospital will not want **sensitive** patient data to be revealed. Companies also want to protect themselves from harmful programs such as viruses entering and attacking the computers in the intranet and possibly destroying valuable data.

The role of a **firewall** is to protect an Intranet by messages leaving or entering. A firewall is implemented by filtering

---

underlie [ˌʌndəˈlai]
vt. 位于……之下，成为……的基础

open-ended
adj. 可修整的，末端开口的

ISP
[计] Internet 服务提供者

Backbone [ˈbækbəun]
n. 脊椎，中枢，[计]广域网中的一种高速链路

fibre optic cables
[计]光缆

bandwidth [ˈbændwidθ]
[计]带宽

configure [kənˈfigə]
vt. 使成形，使具一定形式

responsibility [risˌpɔnsəˈbiliti]
n. 责任，职责

router [ˈrautə]
[计] 路由器(读取每一个数据包中的地址，然后决定如何传送的专用,智能性的网络设备)

unauthorized [ˈʌnˈɔːθəraizd]
adj. 未被授权的

sensitive [ˈsensitiv]
adj. 敏感的,感光的

firewall
[计]Internet 防火墙

Chapter 10 Distributed Systems

incoming and **outgoing** messages, for example according to their source or destination. A firewall might for example allow only those messages related to email and web access to pass into or out of the intranet that it protects.

Some organizations do not wish to connect their internal network to the Internet at all. For example, police and other security and law **enforcement** agencies are likely to have at least some internal networks that are isolated from the outside world, and the UK National Health Service has chosen to take the view that sensitive patient-related medical data can only be adequately protected by **maintaining** a physically separate internat network. Some military organizations disconnect their internal network from the Internet at times of war. But even those organizations will wish to benefit from the huge range of application and system software that employs Internet communication **protocols**. The solution that is usually adopted by such organizations is to operate an Intranet as described above, but without the connections to the Internet .Such an Intranet can dispense with the firewall; or, to put it another way, it has the most effective firewall possible——the absence of any physical connections to the Internet.

The main issues arising in the design of components for use in intranets are:
- File services are needed to enable users to share data.
- Firewalls tend to **impede legitimate** access to services ——when resource sharing between internal and external users is required, firewalls must be complemented by the use of **fine-grained** Security **mechanisms**.
- The cost of software installation and support is an important issue. The costs can be reduced by the use of system architectures, such as network computers and thin clients.

Mobile and Ubiquitous Computing

Technological advances in device **miniaturization** and wireless networking have led increasingly to the **integration** of small and portable computing devices into distributed systems. These devices include:
- laptop computers;
- handheld devices, including personal digital assistants

outgoing ['autgəuiŋ]
adj. 即将离职的，对人友好的

enforcement [in'fɔ:smənt]
n. 执行，强制

maintain [men'tein]
vt. 维持，维修

protocol ['prəutəkɔl]
n. 草案，协议

impede [im'pi:d]
v. 阻止
legitimate [l i'dʒitimit]
adj. 合法的，合理的
fine-grained ['fain`greind]
adj. 有细密纹理的
mechanism ['mekənizəm]
n. 机械装置，机构，机制

miniaturization
['miniətʃəraizeiʃən]
n. 小型化
integration [,inti'greiʃən]
n. 综合

(PDAs), mobile phones, pagers, video cameras and digital cameras;
- wearable devices, such as smart watches with **functionality** similar to a PDA;
- devices embedded in appliances such as washing machines, hi-fi systems, cars and refrigerators.

The portability of many of these devices together with their ability to connect **conveniently** to network in different places, make mobile computing possible. Mobile computing is the performance of computing tasks while the user is on the move, or visiting places other than their usual environment. In mobile computing, users who are away from their "home" Intranet are still provided with access to resources via the devices they carry with them. They can continue to access the Internet; they can continue to access resources in their home Intranet; and there is increasing provision for users to utilize resources such as printers that are conveniently nearby as they move around. The latter is also known as location-aware computing.

Ubiquitous computing is the **harnessing** of many small, cheap computational devices that are present in users' physical environments, including the home, office and elsewhere. The term "ubiquitous" is intended to suggest that small computing devices will eventually become so **pervasive** in everyday objects that they are scarcely noticed. That is, their computational behaviour will be **transparently** and **intimately** tied up with their physical function.

functionality [ˌfʌŋkʃəˈnæliti]
n. 功能性，泛函性

conveniently [kənˈviːnjəntli]
adv. 便利地，方便地

ubiquitous [juːˈbikwitəs]
adj. 到处存在的，(同时)普遍存在的
harness [ˈhɑːnis]
n. (全套)马具，甲胄
transparent [trænsˈpɛərənt]
adj. 透明的，显然的，明晰的
pervasive [pəˈveisiv]
adj. 普遍深入的
intimate [ˈintimit]
adj. 亲密的，隐私的

Exercises

I. Fill in the blanks with the information given in the text.

1. We define a distributed system as one in which hardware or software components located at networked computers _____ and _____ their actions only by passing _____.

2. The motivation for constructing and using distributed system from a desire to _____.

3. The _____ is also a very large distributed system. It enables users, wherever they are, to make use of services such as the World Wide Web, email and file transfer.

4. An intranet is connected to the Internet via a _____, which allows the users inside the intranet to make use of services elsewhere such as the Web or email.

5. The role of a _____ is to protect an intranet by messages leaving or entering.

II. Translate the following passages from English into Chinese.

The term thin client refers to a software layer that supports a window-based user interface on a computer that is local to the user while executing application programs on a remoter computer. This architecture has the same low management and hardware costs as the network computer scheme, but instead of downloading the code of applications into the user's computer, it runs them on a compute server——a powerful computer that has the capacity to run large numbers of applications simultaneously. The computer server will typically be a multiprocessor or cluster computer running a multiprocessor version of an operating system such as UNIX or Windows NT.

The main drawback of the thin client architecture is in highly interactive graphical activities such as CAD and image processing, where the delays experienced by users are increased by the need to transfer image and vector information between the thin client and the application process, incurring both network and operating system latencies.

Section B Challenges of Distributed Systems

The examples in section A are intended to illustrate the scope of distributed system and to suggest the issues that arise in their design. Although distributed systems are to be found everywhere, their design is quite simple and there is still a lot of scope to develop more **ambitious** services and applications. Many of the challenges discussed in this section have already been met, but future designers need to be aware of them and to be careful to take them into account.

ambitious [æm'biʃəs]
adj. 有雄心的，野心勃勃的

Heterogeneity

The Internet enables users to access services and run applications over a **heterogeneous** collection of computers and networks. Heterogeneity (that is, variety and difference) applies to all of the following:
- networks;
- computer hardware;
- operating systems;
- programming languages;
- implementations by different developers.

heterogeneous [ˌhetərəu'dʒi:niəs]
adj. 不同种类的，异类的

Although the Internet consists of many different sorts of network, their differences are masked by the fact that all of the computers attached to them use the Internet protocols to communicate with one another. For example, a computer attached to an **Ethernet** has an implementation of the Internet protocols over the Ethernet, whereas a computer on a different sort of network will need an implementation of the Internet protocols for

Ethernet
n. [计]以太网

that network.

Data types such as integers may be represented in different ways on different sorts of hardware for example, there are two **alternatives** for the byte ordering of integers. These differences in representation must be dealt with if messages are to be exchanged between programs running on different hardware.

Although the operating systems of all computers on the Internet need to include an implementation of the Internet protocols, they do not necessarily all provide the same application programming interface to these protocols. For example the calls for exchanging messages in **UNIX** are different from the calls in Windows NT.

Different programming languages use different **represen -tations** for characters and data structures such as arrays and records. These differences must be addressed if programs written in different languages are to be able to communicate with one another.

Programs written by different developers can not communicate with one another unless they use common standards, for example for network communication and representation of primitive data items and data structures in messages. For this to happen, standards need to be agreed and adopted ——as have the Internet protocols.

Openness

The openness of a computer system is the characteristic that determines whether the system can be extended and re-implemented in various ways. The openness of distributed systems is determined **primarily** by the degree to which new resource-sharing services can be added and be made available for use by a variety of client programs.

Openness can not be achieved unless the **specification** and documentation of the key software interfaces of the components of a system are made available to software developers. In a word, the key interfaces are published. This process is **akin** to the standardization of interfaces, but it often bypasses official standardization procedures, which are usually **cumbersome** and slow-moving.

However, the publication of interfaces is only the starting

---

alternative [ɔːlˈtəːnətiv]
adj. 选择性的，二选一的

UNIX
n. UNIX 操作系统，一种多用户的计算机操作系统
representation
[ˌreprizenˈteiʃən]
n. 表示法，表现，陈述

primarily [ˈpraimərili]
adv. 首先，主要地，根本上

specification
[ˌspesifiˈkeiʃən]
n. 详述，规格，说明书，规范
akin [əˈkin]
adj. 同族的，类似的
cumbersome [ˈkʌmbəsəm]
adj. 讨厌的，麻烦的

Chapter 10 Distributed Systems

point for adding and extending services in a distributed system. The challenge to designers is to tackle the complexity of distributed systems consisting of many components engineered by different people.

Security

Many of the information resources that are made available and maintained in distributed systems have a high **intrinsic** value to their users. Their security is therefore of considerable importance. Security for information resources has three components: **confidentiality** (protection against disclosure to unauthorized individuals); **integrity** (protection against alteration or corruption); and **availability** (protection against **interference** with the means to access the resources).

Although the Internet allows a program in one computer to communicate with a program in another computer **irrespective** of its location, security risks are associated with allowing free access to all of the resources in an intranet. Although a firewall can be used to form a **barrier** around an intranet, restricting the traffic that can enter and leave, this does not deal with ensuring the appropriate use of resources by users within an intranet, or with the appropriate use of resources in the Internet ,that are not protected by firewalls.

Scalability

Distributed systems operate effectively and efficiently at many different scales, ranging from a small intranet to the Internet. A system is described as scalable if will remain effective when there is significant increase in the number of resources and the number of users. The Internet provides an illustration of a distributed system in which the number of computers and services has increased dramatically.

The design of scalable distributed systems presents the following challenges:
- controlling the cost of physical resources;
- controlling the performance loss;
- preventing software resources running out;
- avoiding performance **bottlenecks**.

intrinsic [in'trinsik]
adj. 固有的, 内在的, 本质的
confidentiality [kɔnfi'denʃəliti]
adj. 秘密的, 机密的
integrity [in'tegriti]
n. 正直, 诚实, 完整
availability [ə,veilə'biliti]
n. 可用性, 有效性, 实用性
interference [,intə'fiərəns]
n. 冲突, 干涉
irrespective [,iris'pektiv]
adj. 不顾的, 不考虑的
barrier ['bæriə]
n. 障碍物, 屏障

scalability [,skeilə'biliti]
n. 可伸缩性

bottleneck ['bɔtl,nek]
n. 瓶颈

Failure handling

Computer systems sometimes fail. When faults occur in hardware or software, programs may produce incorrect results or they may stop before they have completed the intended computation.

Failures in a distributed system are partial, that is, some components fail while others continue to function. Therefore the handling of failures is particularly difficult.

The following techniques for dealing with failures are discussed.

- Detecting failures.some failures can be detected. For example, **checksums** can be used to detect **corrupted** data in a message or a file. But this is difficult or even impossible to detect some other failures such as a remote crashed server in the Internet. The challenge is to manage in the presence of failures that can not be detected but may be suspected.

- Masking failures.some failures that have been detected can be hidden or made less severe. Two examples of hiding failures.

    (1)messages can be **retransmitted** when they fail to arrive;

    (2)file data can be written to a pair of disks so that if one is corrupted, the other may still be correct.

- Tolerating failures.Most of the services in the Internet do exhibit failures——it would not be practical for them to attempt to detect and hide all of the failures that might occur in such a large network with so many components. Their clients can be designed to tolerate failures, which generally involves the users tolerating them as well. For example, when a web browser cannot contact a web server, it dose not make the user wait for ever while it keeps on trying-it informs the user about the problem, leaving them free to try again later.

- **Recovery** from failures. Recovery involves the design of software so that the state of **permanent** data can be recovered or "rolled back"after a server has crashed. In general, the computations performed by some programs

Checksum
n. 校验和
corrupt [kəˈrʌpt]
adj. 腐败的,误用的

retransmit [ˌriːtrænzˈmit]
vt. 转播,转发,中继站发送

recovery [riˈkʌvəri]
n. 恢复,痊愈,防御
permanent [ˈpəːmənənt]
adj. 永久的,持久的

Chapter 10 Distributed Systems

will be incomplete when a fault occurs, and the permanent data that they update (files and other material stored in permanent storage) may not be in a consistent state.

Distributed systems provide a high degree of availability in the face of hardware faults. The availability of a system is a measure of the proportion of time that it is available for use. When one of the components in a distributed system fails, only the work that was using the failed component is affected. A user may move to another computer if the one that they were using fails: a server process can be started on another computer.

Concurrency

Both services and applications provide resources that can be shared by clients in a distributed system. There is therefore a possibility that several client will attempt to access a shared resource at the same time. For example, a data structure that records **bids** for an **auction** may be accessed very frequently when it gets close to the **deadline** time.

The process that manages a shared resource could take one client request at a time. But that approach limits throughput. Therefore services and applications generally allow multiple client requests to be processed concurrently. To make this more concrete, suppose that each resource is **encapsulated** as an object and that **invocations** are executed in concurrent threads. In this case it is possible that several threads may be executing concurrently within an object, in which case their operations on the object may conflict with one another and produce inconsistent results. For example, if two concurrent bids at an auction are "Smith:$122" and " Jones:$111",and the corresponding operations are **interleaved** without any control, then they might get stored as "Smith:$111"and "Jones:$122".

The **moral** of this story is that any object that represents a shared resource in a distributed system must be responsible for ensuring that it operates correctly in a concurrent environment. This applies not only to services but also to objects in applications. Therefore any programmer who takes an implementation of an object that was not intended for use in a distributed system must do whatever is necessary to make it safe in a concurrent environment.

concurrency [kən'kʌrənsi]
n. 同时存在, 合作

bid [bid]
vt. 出价, 投标
auction ['ɔːkʃən]
n. 拍卖
deadline ['dedlain]
n. 最终期限
encapsulate [in'kæpsjuleit]
vt. 装入胶囊, 压缩
invocation [,invəu'keiʃən]
n. 祈祷, 符咒

interleave [,intə(ː)'liːv]
vt. 插入纸
moral ['mɔrəl]
n. 道德

Transparency

Transparency is defined as the **concealment** from the user and the application programmer of the separation of components in a distributed system, so that the system is perceived as a whole rather than as a collection of independent components. The implications of transparency are a major influence on the design of the system software.

The ANSA Reference **Manual** [ANSA 1989] and the International Standards Organization's Reference Model for Open Distributed Processing (RM-ODP) [ISO 1992] identify eight forms of transparency. We have **paraphrased** the original ANSA definitions, replacing their migration transparency with our own mobility transparency, whose scope is broader.

- Access transparency enables local and remote resources to be accessed using identical operations.
- Location transparency enables resources to be accessed without knowledge of their location
- Concurrency transparency enables several processes to operate concurrently using shared resources without interference between them.
- **Replication** transparency enables multiple instances of resources to be used to increase reliability and performance without knowledge of the replicas by users or application programmers.
- Failure transparency enables the concealment of faults, allowing users and application programs to complete their tasks despite the failure of hardware or software components.
- **Mobility** transparency allows the movement of resources and clients within a system without affecting the operation of users or programs.
- Performance transparency allows the system to be **reconfigured** to improve performance as loads vary.
- Scaling transparency allows the system and applications to expand in scale without change to the system structure or the application algorithms.

transparency [træns'pεərənsi]
n. 透明，透明度
concealment [kən'si:lmənt]
n. 隐藏，隐蔽，隐蔽处

manual ['mænjuəl]
n. 手册，指南

paraphrase ['pærəfreiz]
v. 解释

replication [,repli'keiʃən]
n. 复制

mobility [məu'biliti]
n. 活动性，灵活性

reconfigure [,ri:kən'figə(r)]
v. 重新装配，改装

Exercises

Ⅰ. Fill in the blanks with the information given in the text.

1. Although the operating systems of all computers on the Internet need to include an implementation of the Internet protocols, they do not necessarily all provide the same _____ to these protocols.

2. The openness of a computer system is the characteristic that determines whether the system can be _____ and _____ in various ways.

3. Many of the information resources that are made _____ and maintained in distributed systems have a high intrinsic value to their users. Their _____ is therefore of considerable importance.

4. Both services and applications provide resources that can be shared by _____ in a distributed system. There is therefore a possibility that several client will attempt to access a _____ at the same time.

5. Transparency is defined as the _____ from the user and the application programmer of the separation of components in a distributed system, so that the system is perceived as a whole rather than as a collection of independent components.

Ⅱ. Translate the following passages from English into Chinese.

Users of interactive applications require a fast and consistent response to interaction, but client programs often need to access shared resources. When a remote services is involved, the speed at which the response is generated is determined not just by the load and performance of the server and the network but also by delays in all the software components involved——the client and server operating systems' communication and middleware services (remote invocation support, for example)as well as the code of the process that implements the service. In addition, the transfer of data between processes and the associated switching of control is relatively slow, even when the processed reside in the same computer. To achieve good interactive response times, systems must be composed of relatively few software layers, and the quantities of data transferred between the client and server must be small.

These issues are demonstrated by the performance of Web-browsing clients. Where the fastest response is achieved when accessing locally cached pages and images because these are held by the client application. Remote text pages are also accessed reasonably quickly because they are small, but graphical images incur longer delays because of the volume of data involved.

Section C Architecture Models of Distributed Systems

Introduction

System that are intended for use in real-world environments should be designed to function correctly in the widest possible range of circumstances and in the face of many possible difficulties and threats suggest that distributed systems of different types share important **underlying** properties and give rise to common design problems. In this section we bring out the common properties and design issues for distributed systems in the form of **descriptive** models. Each model is intended to provide an abstract, simplified but consistent description of a

underlying [ˌʌndəˈlaiiŋ]
adj. 在下面的，根本的
descriptive [disˈkriptiv]
adj. 描述的，叙述的

relevant aspect of distributed system design.

An architectural model defines the way in which the components of systems interact with one another and the way in which they are mapped onto an underlying network of computers.

Difficulties for and Threats to Distributed Systems

Here are some of the problems that the designers of distributed systems face:

- Widely vary models of use. The component parts of systems are subject to wide variations in workload-for example, some Web pages are accessed several million times a day. Some parts of a system may be **disconnected**, or poorly connected some of the time——for example when mobile computers are included in a system. Some applications have special requirements for high communication bandwidth and low **latency**——for example, multimedia applications.
- Wide range of system environments. A distributed system must **accommodate** heterogeneous hardware, operating systems and networks. The networks may differ widely in performance——wireless networks operate at a fraction of the speed of local networks. Systems of widely differing scales——ranging from tens of computers to million of computers-must be supported.
- Internal problems. **Non-synchronized** clocks, conflicting data updates, many models of hardware and software failure involving the individual components of a system.
- External threats. Attacks on data integrity and secrecy, denial of service.

Architectural Models

The architecture of a system is its structure in terms of separately specified components. The overall goal is to ensure that the structure will meet present and likely future demands on it. Major concerns are to make the system reliable, manageable, adaptable and **cost-effective**. The architectural design of a

disconnected [ˌdiskəˈnektid]
adj. 分离的，不连贯的
latency [ˈleitənsi]
n. 潜伏，潜在，潜伏物

accommodate [əˈkɔmədeit]
vt. 供应，供给，使适应

non-synchronized
[计]异步的

cost-effective
adj. 有成本效益的，划算的
gothic [ˈgɔθik]
adj. 哥特式的，野蛮的

building has similar aspects——it determines not only its appearance but also its general structure and architectural style (**gothic**, **neo-classical**, modern) provides a **consistent** frame of reference for the design.

An initial simplification is achieved by classifying **processes** as server processes, client processes and peer processes——the latter being processes that cooperate and communicate in a **symmetrical** manner to perform a task. This classification of processes identifies the responsibilities of each and hence helps us to assess their **workloads** and to determine the impact of failures in each of them. The results of this analysis can then be used to specify the placement of the processes in manner that meets performance and reliability goals for the resulting system.

There are several widely used patterns for the allocation of work in a distributed system that have an important impact on the performance and effectiveness of the resulting system. The actual placement of the processes that make up a distributed system in a network of computers is also influenced by many detailed issues of performance, reliability, security and cost. The architectural models described here can provide only a somewhat simplified view of the more important patterns of distribution.

Software Layers

The term software architecture referred **originally** to the structuring of software as layers or modules in a single computer and more recently in terms of services offered and requested between processes located in the same or different computers. This process and **service-oriented** view can be expressed in terms of service layers. A server is process that accepts requests from other processes. A distributed service can be provided by one or more server processes, interacting with each other and with client processes in order to maintain a consistent system-wide view of the service's resources. For example, a network time service is implemented on the Internet based on the Network Time Protocol (NTP) by server processed running on hosts throughout the Internet that supply the current time to any client that requests it and adjust their version of the current time as a result of **interaction** with each other.

Neo-Darwinism ['niːəuˈdɑːwinizm]
n. 新达尔文主义

consistent [kənˈsistənt]
adj. 一致的, 调和的

Process
[计]进程

symmetrical [siˈmetrikəl]
adj. 对称的, 均匀的

workload [ˈwəːkləud]
n. 工作量

originally [əˈridʒənəli]
adv. 最初, 原先

service-oriented
adj. 面向服务的

interaction [ˌintərˈækʃən]
n. 交互作用, 交感

System Architectures

The division of responsibilities between system components (applications, servers and other processes) and the placement of the components on computers in the network is perhaps the most evident aspect of distributed system design. It has major **implications** for the performance, reliability and security of the resulting system.

Variations on the Client-Server Model

Several **variations** on the client-server model can be derived from the consideration of the following factors:
- the use of mobile code and mobile agents;
- users' need for low-cost computers with limited hardware resources that are simple to manage;
- the requirement to add and remove mobile devices in a convenient manner.

Interfaces and Objects

The set of functions available for invocation in process (whether it is a server or a peer process) is specified by one or more interface definitions. The concept will be familiar to those already conversant with languages such as **Modula**, C++ or Java. In the basic form of client-server architecture, each server process is seen as a single entity with a fixed interface defining the functions that can be **invoked** in it.

In object-oriented languages such as C++ and Java, with appropriate additional support, distributed processes can be constructed in a more objected-oriented manner. Many objects can be encapsulated in server or peer processes, and references to them are passed to other processes so that their methods can be accessed by remote invocation. This is the approach adopted by **CORBA** and by Java with its remote method invocation (**RMI**) mechanism. In this model, the number and the types (in languages that support mobile code such as Java) of objects hosted by each process may vary as system activities require, and in some implementations the locations of objects may also change.

Whether we adopt a static client-server architecture or the

more dynamic object-oriented model outlined in the preceding paragraph, the distribution of responsibilities between processed and between computers remains an important aspect of the design. In the traditional architectural model, the responsibilities are statically allocated(a file server, for example, is responsible only for files, not for Web pages, their **proxies** or other types of object).But in the object-oriented model new services, and in some cases new types of object, can be **instantiated** and immediately be made available for invocation.

Design Requirements for Distributed Architectures

The factors motivating the distribution of objects and processes in a distributed system are numerous and their **significance** is **considerable**. Sharing was first achieved in the timesharing systems of the 1960s with the use of shared files. The benefits of sharing were quickly recognized and exploited in multi-user operating systems such as UNIX and multi-user database systems such as **Oracle** to enable processes to share system resources and devices (file storage capacity, printers, audio and video streams) and application processes to share application objects.

The arrival of cheap computing power in the form of **microprocessor** chips removed the need for the sharing of central processors, and the availability of medium-performance computer networks and continuing need for the sharing of relatively costly hardware resources such as printers and disk storage led to the development of the distributed systems of the 1970s and 1980s.Today, resource sharing is taken for granted. But effective data sharing on a large scale remains a **substantial** challenge——with changing data (and most data changes with time),the possibility of concurrent and **conflicting** updates arises.

proxy
代理服务器, 即 Proxy 服务器, 在 Internet 上的完成传输服务。当在浏览器中设置了某个 Proxy 服务器之后, 由浏览器所发出的任何要求都会被送到 Proxy 服务器上去, 由这台 Proxy 服务器代为处理。
instantiate [in'stænʃieit]
vt. 示例
significance [sig'nifikəns]
n. 意义, 重要性
considerable [kən'sidərəbl]
adj. 相当大(或多)的, 值得考虑的, 相当可观的
Oracle ['ɔrəkl]
[计]美国 Oracle 公司, 主要生产数据库产品, 也是主要的网络计算机的倡导者
microprocessor
[maɪkrəʊ'prəʊsesə(r)]
[计]微处理器

substantial [səb'stænʃəl]
adj. 坚固的, 实质的
conflicting [kən'fliktiŋ]
adj. 相冲突的, 相矛盾的

Exercises

Ⅰ. **Fill in the blanks with the information given in the text.**

1. An architectural model defines the way in which the _____ of systems interact with one another and the way in which they are mapped onto an underlying network of computers.

2. There are several widely used patterns for the allocation of work in a distributed system that have an important impact on the _____ and _____ of the resulting system.

3. The term software architecture referred originally to the structuring of software as _____ or modules in a single computer and more recently in terms of services offered and requested between _____ located in the same or different computers.

4. Many objects can be encapsulated in _____ or _____ processes, and references to them are passed to other processes so that their methods can be accessed by remote invocation.

5. In object-oriented languages such as C++ and Java, with appropriate additional support, _____ can be constructed in a more objected-oriented manner.

Ⅱ. **Translate the following passages from English into Chinese.**

An architectural model of a distributed system is concerned with the placement of its parts and the relationships between them. Examples include the client-server model and the peer process model. The client-server model can be modified by:
- the partition of data or replication at cooperating servers;
- the caching of data by proxy servers and clients;
- the use of mobile code and mobile agents;
- the requirement to add and remove mobile devices in a convenient manner.

Fundamental models are concerned with a more formal description of the properties that are common in all of the architectural models.

There is no global time in a distributed system, so the clocks on different computers do not necessarily give the same time as one another. All communication between processes is achieved by means of messages. Message communication over a computer network can be affected by delays, can suffer from a variety of failures and is vulnerable to security attacks.
- The interaction model deals with performance and with the difficulty of setting time limits in a distributed system, for example for message delivery.
- The failure model attempts to give a precise specification of the faults that can be exhibited by processes and communication channels. It defines reliable communication and correct processes.
- The security model discusses the possible threats to processes and communication channels. It introduces the concept of a secure channel, which is secure against those threats.

Grammar 10 科技文献翻译中的汉语表达

在进行翻译工作的时候，往往最成功的作品就是看不出其是翻译的。诚然，翻译者和作者本身就存在着生活空间和文化的巨大差异，所以翻译最重要的是，在适当尊重原文的基础上，符合本土阅读者的思维习惯和阅读习惯。下面提示几个在翻译过程中经常出现的问题，仅供参考。

1. 避免出现不符合汉语逻辑

汉语的逻辑是符合中文人说话的思维，而英语则和汉语逻辑不同。在翻译过程，可以为了使译文流畅和更符合汉语叙事论理的习惯，在理清英语长句的结构、弄懂英语原意的基础上，彻底摆脱原文语序和句子形式，对句子进行重新组合，这样达到符合汉语逻辑的目的。

(1) Decision must be made very rapidly; physical endurance is tested as much as perception, because an enormous amount of time must be spent making certain that the key figures act on the basis of the same

information and purpose.

必须把大量时间花在确保关键人物均根据同一情报和目的行事,而这一切对身体的耐力和思维能力都是一大考验。因此,一旦考虑成熟,决策者就应迅速做出决策。

(2) Where pooling arrangements are set in place, appropriate management structures are required and voting rules should ensure a high degree of consensus on the operation of the pool.

在已签定电力市场协议的地方,需要适当的管理机构,并且选举制度应能确保电力市场运转的高度一致。

上面两个例子很好地达到了符合汉语逻辑的要求。

2. 不必过于强调"忠实"原文

在进行翻译的过程中,不必过于强调忠诚于原文,有的时候,甚至在改变原文意思的基础上,可以添加一些自己的理解,这样的目的是让语言更流畅。

(1) The development of IC made <u>it</u> possible for electronic devices to become smaller and smaller.

集成电路的发展是电子器件可以做得越来越小。(省译形式主语 it)

(2) You will be staying in this hotel during <u>your</u> visit in Beijing.

你在北京访问期间就住在这家饭店里。(省译物主代词 your)

3. 尽量在翻译中不存在明显的翻译腔

有的时候,翻译后的语句常常反而不如原文简明,为了减少翻译腔,提倡进行适度的更改。

This is yet another common point <u>between</u> the computers of the two generations.

这是这两代计算机之间的又一个共同点。

4. 避免表达啰嗦、不简洁

This consumption of memory is not the result of the queue's size but is a side effect of the queue's access procedure(A small yet active queue can easily require more of a machine's memory resources than a large, inactive one.) One solution to this memory space problem might be to move the entries in a queue forward as the leading ones are removed, in the same manner as people waiting to buy theater tickets step forward each time a person has been served. However, this mass movement of data would be very inefficient. What we need is a way of confining the queue to one area of memory without being forced to perform major rearrangements of data.

存储器的消耗问题并不是因队列的大小而产生的,其真正原因在于队列的实现问题(一个小而动态变化的队列比一个大而保持不变的队列需要更多的机器存储资源)。解决存储器空间问题的一个可能方法是,当最前面的条目被移出时,前移队列中的其他条目,就好像人们在购买戏票时所采用的方法一样,每当一个人买到票后,就前移一人。然而这种方法在计算机中运行的效率很低,因为它将需要对数据进行大量的移动。

参考译文

Section A 分布式系统的特征

简介

计算机网络无处不在。互联网是由许多网络组成的一个网络。移动电话网、公司网络、工厂网络、校园网、家庭网络、车内网络，所有这些(或单独或组合到一起)具有相同的本质特征，都可以放在分布式系统的领域来研究。本节旨在解释影响系统设计者和实现者的网络化计算机的特征，并描述已有的可帮助完成设计和实现分布式系统任务的主要概念和技术。

我们定义分布式系统为一个硬件或软件组件分布在网络计算机上，仅仅通过消息传递进行通信和动作协调的系统。这个简单的定义覆盖了所有有效地部署了网络化计算机的系统。

同一网络中的计算机可能在空间上有距离，可能在不同的洲，也可能在同一个楼或同一个房间。我们关于分布式系统的定义产生下列重要的结论。

- 并发性。在一个计算机网络中，程序并发执行是常见的行为。大家可以在各自的计算机上工作，在必要时共享诸如 Web 页面或文件之类的资源。系统处理共享资源的能力应该随着网络资源(如计算机)的增加而增加。在本节的许多地方将描述如何有效实施这种额外能力。如何协调并发执行的共享资源型程序也是一个重要的并经常被提及的话题。

- 缺乏全局时钟。在程序需要协作时，它们通过交换消息来协调它们的动作。紧密的协调经常依赖于对程序动作发生时间的共识，但是事实证明，网络上计算机同步时钟的准确性会受到限制，即没有一个正确时间的全局概念。这是通过网络发送消息作为唯一的通信方式这一事实带来的直接结果。

- 故障独立性。所有的计算机系统都可能发生故障。一般由系统设计者负责处理可能出现的故障。分布式系统可能以新的方式出现故障。网络故障导致与之互联的计算机的隔离，但这并不意味着它们停止运行。事实上，计算机中的程序不能够检测出网络是出现故障了还是网络运行得比通常慢。同样，计算机的故障或系统中程序的异常终止并不能马上被与之通信的其他组件感知。系统的每个组件会单独地出现故障，而其他组件还在运行。

构造和使用分布式系统的动力来源于对资源共享的愿望。"资源"一词是相当抽象的，但它很好地描述了能在网络化计算机系统中共享的事务的范围。它涉及的范围从硬件组件如硬盘、打印机到软件定义的实体如文件、数据库和所有数据对象，包括来自数字摄像机的视频流和移动电话表示的声频连接。

分布式系统实例

本节选用的实例都是大家熟悉和广泛使用的计算机网络：互联网、企业内部网和正在兴起的基于移动设备的网络技术，这些系统说明计算机网络支持的服务和应用的范围很广。随后我们将从这些系统展开，讨论支撑系统实现的技术问题。

互联网也是一个非常大的分布式系统，它使得世界各地的用户能利用诸如万维网、电子邮件和文件传输等服务。(事实上，万维网有时并不与互联网等同。)服务集是可伸缩的，它能够通过服务器计算机和新的服务类型的增加而扩展。互联网服务提供商(ISP)是为个体用户和小型组织提供调制解调器连接和其他类型连接的公司，通过 ISP 提供的连接，用户能够访问互联网上的服务，同时，ISP 还提供如电子邮件和 Web 接入等本地服务。企业内部网通过主干网连接在一起。主干网是具有高传输性能的网络连接，通常采用卫星线路、光纤和其他宽带线路作为传输介质。

企业内部网是互联网的一部分，实行独立管理，具有边界，通过配置能执行本地安全策略。它由几个通过主干网连接的局域网(LAN)组成。企业内部网的网络配置由管理企业内部网的组织负责。它的变化范围很广，可以仅仅由位于一个场所的 LAN 构成，也可以是由位于不同国家的同一公司的分支机构或公司之外的其他组织的多个 LAN 连接而成。

企业内部网通过路由器连接到互联网，这使得企业内部网内的用户能利用其他地方的服务如 Web 服务或电子邮件服务。它也允许其他企业内部网的用户访问它提供的服务。许多组织需要保护自己的服务，以免外部的恶意用户对其进行未经授权的使用。例如，公司不希望机密信息被竞争对手获取，医院不希望敏感的病人数据被曝光。公司还希望避免病毒等有害程序入侵并攻击企业内部网内的计算机，同时还要防止这些有害程序破坏有用的数据。

防火墙的作用是通过防止未授权消息发出或进入来保护企业内部网。防火墙是通过过滤进出消息实现其功能的，例如，根据消息的源地址或目的地址进行过滤。一个防火墙可能仅允许与电子邮件和 Web 访问存关的消息进出它保护的企业内部网。

一些组织并不希望将自己的内部网连接到互联网。例如，警察机构和其他安全法律执行机构可能有几个内部网与外部世界隔离，英国国家健康服务也选择了这样的观点，它保留了一个物理分离的内部网来保护敏感的病人数据。一些军事组织在战争时会将它们的内部网与互联网断开，但这些组织仍然希望从大量地采用互联网通信协议的应用和系统软件中受益：它们通常采用的方案还是像上面描述的那样构造企业内部网，但不与互联网相连。这样一个企业内部网没有防火墙也行，或者说，它有最有效的防火墙，因为它与互联网没有任何物理连接。

在设计用于企业内部网的组件时，会遇到下列这些主要问题：
- 需要文件服务以便用户能共享数据。
- 防火墙可能阻止对服务的合法访问。当需要在内部和外部之间共享资源时，防火墙必须增加小粒度的安全机制。
- 用于软件安装和支持的开销是一个重要的问题。通过使用如网络计算机和瘦客户机等系统体系结构，能减少这些开销。

移动计算和无处不在的计算

设备小型化和无线网络技术的进步已经逐步使小型和便携式计算设备集成到分布式系统中，这些设备包括：
- 膝上型计算机。
- 手持设备，包括个人数字助理(PDA)、移动电话、摄像机和数字照相机。
- 可穿戴设备，如具有类似 PDA 功能的智能手表。
- 嵌入在家用电器中，如洗衣机、音响系统、汽车和冰箱中的设备。

这些设备大多数具有便携性，再加上它们在不同地方连接网络的能力，使得移动计算成为可能。移动计算是指用户在移动中执行计算任务的能力或访问他们所处的通常环境以外的位置的能力。在移动计算中，即使用户远离常用的企业内部网(指工作环境的企业内部网，或他们住处的企业内部网)、他们仍然能够通过随身携带的设备访问资源。他们能继续访问互联网，继续访问企业内部网上的资源。在移动时，用户可利用的如打印机等能在附近方便地获得资源的供应量正在不断地增加，这种在移动时使用邻近资源的方式也称为位置清楚的计算。

无处不在的计算是指对多种在用户的物理环境(包括家庭、办公室和其他的地方)中存在的小型的、便宜的计算设备的控制。术语"无处不在"意指小型计算设备最终将普及到现在的日常用品中而不被人注意，就是说，它们的计算行为将紧密地、透明地捆绑到它们的物理功能上。

Section B 分布式系统面临的挑战

本章 A 节的例子试图说明分布式系统的范围，提出在设计中出现的问题。虽然分布式系统随处可见，但它们的设计相当简单，还存在很大的空间来开发更富有挑战性的服务和应用。本节讨论的许多要求已经被满足，但将来的设计者还需要了解它们。在设计分布式系统时还应仔细地考虑它们。

异构性

互联网使得用户能够在大量异构计算机和网络上访问服务和运行应用程序系统。异构性(相互有区别)被应用在以下方面：
- 网络；
- 计算机硬件；
- 操作系统；
- 编程语言；
- 由不同开发者完成的实现。

虽然互联网由多种网络组成，但由于所有连接到互联网的计算机都使用互联网协议相互通信，因而屏蔽了它们的区别。例如，以太网中的计算机要在以太网上实现互联网协议，而在另一种网络上的计算机需要在自己的网络上实现互联网协议。

整数之类的数据类型在不同种类的硬件上可以有不同的表示方法。例如，整数的字节顺序有两种方法表示。如果要在不同硬件上运行的两个程序之间进行消息交换，那么就要处理这些在表示上的不同。

虽然互联网上所有计算机的操作系统都要实现互联网协议，但它们没必要提供相同的协议接口。例如，UNIX 中的消息交换的调用方法与 Windows NT 中的调用方法不同。

不同的编程语言对字符和数据结构采用不同的表示方法，如数组和记录。如果要求用不同语言编写的程序能够相互通信，就必须解决这些差异。

除非使用公共标准，否则不同开发者编写的程序不能相互通信，例如，网络通信和消息中原始数据项和数据结构的表示均要求使用公共标准。所以，要制定和采用像互联网协议那样的标准。

开放性

计算机系统的开放性决定系统是否能以各种不同的方式扩展和重构。分布式系统的开放性主要取决于新的资源共享服务能被增加和供多种客户程序使用的程度。

除非软件开发者能够获得系统组件的主要软件接口的规范和文档，否则无法达到开放性，总之要发布主要接口。这个过程类似接口的标准化，出于官方的标准化程序通常麻烦且进度缓慢，因此，它经常绕过官方的标准化程序。

然而，发布接口仅是分布式系统增加和扩展服务的起点。对设计者的挑战是，如何解决由不同人构造的且由多个组件组成的分布式系统的复杂性。

安全性

分布式系统维护的众多信息源对用户具有很高的内在价值，因此它们的安全性相当重要。信息源的安全有 3 个部分：机密性(防止泄漏给未授权的个人)、完整性(防止改变或讹误)、可用性(防止对访问资源的手段的干扰)。

虽然互联网允许一台计算机中的程序与另一台计算机上的程序通信，而不管它们的位置，但安全风险与允许自由访问企业内部网的所有资源相关。虽然防火墙能被用于形成围绕企业内部网的屏障，限制进入和外出的流量，但这不能确保用户恰当地使用企业内部网资源以及互联网的资源。而后一种资源不能被防火墙保护。

可伸缩性

从小型企业内部网到互联网，分布式系统可在不同规模的网络中有效地运转。如果资源数量和用户数量激增，系统仍能保持有效，那么该系统可被描述成可伸缩的。互联网就是一个计算机数量和服务动态增长的分布式系统的例子。

可伸缩的分布式系统将面临下面的挑战：
- 控制物理资源的开销；
- 控制性能的丢失；
- 防止软件资源的耗尽；
- 避免性能瓶颈。

故障处理

计算机系统有时会发生故障。当硬件或软件发生故障时，程序可能产生不正确的结果或者在它们完成应该进行的计算之前就停止了。

分布式系统的故障是部分的，也就是说，有些组件正常运行时，有些组件却会发生故障。因此，故障的处理相当困难。本节将讨论下列处理故障的技术：

- 检测故障。有些故障能被检测。例如，校验和用于检测出错的消息数据或文件数据。但是很难或甚至可能检测不到某些故障，如互联网上一台远程服务器的崩溃。该技术面临的挑战是如何管理不能被检测但可以被怀疑的故障。
- 故障覆盖。有些被检测到的故障能被隐藏或降低危害性。下面是隐藏故障的两个例子:
  (1)在消息不能到达时进行重传。
  (2)将文件数据写入两个磁盘，这样如果一个磁盘坏了，另一个磁盘的数据仍是正确的。
- 容错。互联网上的大多数服务确实会有故障——在这么大的网络上，在这么多组件中试图检测和隐藏所有可能发生的故障是不太现实的。这些服务的客户端能设计成容错的，这通常也涉及让用户参与到容错的动作中。例如，当 Web 浏览器不能与 Web 服务器相连时，它不能让用户一定等待它与服务器建立连接，它会通知用户出现了这个问题，让用户自由选择是否以后再试。
- 故障恢复。恢复涉及软件的设计，以便在服务器崩溃后，永久数据的状态能被恢复或"回滚"。通常，在出现错误时，程序完成的计算是不完整的，被修改的永久数据(文件和其他保存在永久存储中的资料)可能处在一个不一致的状态。

并发

分布式系统中服务和应用两者均提供可被客户共享的资源。因此，可能几个客户同时试图访问一个共享的资源。例如，在接近拍卖最终期限时记录拍卖竞价的数据结构可能被非常频繁地访问。

管理共享资源的进程在一个时刻接受一个客户请求，但这种方法限制了吞吐量。因此服务和应用通常允许并发地处理多个客户的请求。为了详细说明此问题，假设每个资源被封装成一个对象，调用在并发线程中执行。在这种情况下，几个线程可能在一个对象内并发地执行，它们对于对象的操作可能相互冲突，产生不一致的结果。例如，如果拍卖中两个并发的竞标是"Smith: 122 美元"和"Jones: 111 美元"，那么相应的操作在没有任何控制下可能是交叉进行的，它们可能被保存为"Smith: 111 美元"和"Jones: 122 美元"。

这个例子说明在分布式系统中代表共享资源的任何一个对象必须负责确保它在并发环境中操作正确，这不仅适用于服务器也适用于应用中的对象。因此，负责实现那些不用于分布式系统的对象的程序员必须确保对象在并发环境中能安全使用。

透明性

透明性被定义成对用户和应用程序员屏蔽分布式系统的组件的分散性，系统被认为是一个整体，而不是独立组件的集合。透明性的含义对系统软件的设计有重大的影响。

ANSA 参考手册[ANSA 1989]和国际标准化组织的开放分布式处理的参考模型(RM-ODP)[ISO 1992]识别 8 种透明性。下面将解释原始的 ANSA 定义，并用移动透明性替换迁移透明性，前者的范围更广。
- 访问透明性：允许用相同的操作访问本地和远程的资源。
- 位置透明性：不需要知道资源的位置就能够访问它们。
- 并发透明性：几个进程能并发地对共享资源进行操作而互不干扰。
- 复制透明性：使用资源的多个实例增加可靠性和性能，而用户和应用程序员无须了解副本的存在。
- 故障透明性：屏蔽错误，不论是硬件故障还是软件组件故障，允许用户和应用程序完成它们的任务。
- 移动透明性：在不影响用户或程序的操作的前提下允许资源和客户在系统内移动。
- 性能透明性：当负载变化时，允许系统重构以提高性能。
- 伸缩透明性：在不改变系统结构或应用算法的前提下，允许系统和应用扩展。

Section C 分布式系统的体系结构模型

简介

在实际环境中使用的系统无论在何种可能的环境下，无论面对何种可能的困难和威胁，都应该能保证其功能的正确性。前面几节的讨论和举例表明不同类型的分布式系统相互共享重要的基本特性，并且引发公共的设计问题。本节以描述型模型的形式给出分布式系统的公共特性和设计问题，每个模型试图对分布式系统设计的一个相关方面给出一个抽象、简化但是一致的描述。

体系结构模型定义了系统中组件相互交互方式以及它们映射到计算机基础网络的方式。

分布式系统设计的困难和挑战

下面是分布式系统设计者要面对的一些问题：
- 使用模式多样性：系统的组件会承受不同的工作负载，如有些 Web 页面每天会有几百万次的访问量。系统的有些部分可能断连或连接不稳定，如当系统中包括移动计算机时，一些应用对通信带宽和延迟有特殊的需求，如多媒体应用。
- 系统环境的多样性：分布式系统必须适应异构的硬件、操作系统和网络。网络可能在性能上有很大不同——无线网的速度只有局域网的一小部分。系统必须能支持不同的规模——从几十台计算机到上百万台计算机。
- 内部问题：非同步的时钟、冲突的数据修改、多种涉及系统单个组件的软硬件故障模式。
- 外部问题：对数据完整性、私密性的攻击以及拒绝服务。

体系结构模型

一个系统的体系结构是用指定组件表示的结构。其整体目标是确保结构能满足现在和将来可能的需求，主要关心的是如何使系统可靠、可管理、可适应和低成本高效益。这与一个建筑物的体系结构设计有类似的方面——它不仅仅决定了建筑物的外观，而且决定了建筑物的总体结构，体系结构风格(哥特式、新古典式、现代式)为设计提供了一个一致的参考框架。

最初的简化是将进程分成服务器进程、客户进程和对等进程。对等进程是以对称方式进行协作和通信以完成任务的进程。进程分类用于识别每类进程的责任，因此有助于评估它们的负载，并决定每个进程出现故障时可能带来的影响。该分析结果可用于指定进程的放置，使进程的分布能满足目标系统的性能和可靠性目标。

已经有一些广泛使用的模式用于分布式系统的工作分配，它们对目标系统的性能和有效性有重要的影响，在计算机网络中组成分布式系统的进程的实际分配也受到许多具体的性能问题、可靠性问题、安全问

Chapter 10 Distributed Systems

题和成本问题的影响。此处描述的体系结构模型仅提供重要的分布模式的一个简化的观点。

软件层

术语软件体系结构原指在一台计算机中软件的分层或模块结构,近来更多地指同一计算机或不同计算机上进程之间所请求和提供的服务,这个面向进程和面向服务的观点能用服务层表达。服务器是一个接收其他进程请求的进程。一个分布式服务可由一个或多个服务器进程提供,这些进程相互交互,并与客户进程交互,维护该服务在系统范围内关于资源的一致视图。例如,在互联网上基于网络时间协议(NTP)可实现一个网络时间服务,其中运行在主机上的服务器进程将当前的时间提供给任何发出请求的客户,作为与服务器交互的结果,客户调整它们的当前时间。

系统体系结构

系统组件(应用、服务器和其他进程)之间责任的划分和网络上计算机组件的放置可能是分布式系统设计最明显的方面。这些对最终系统的性能、可靠性和安全性有较大的影响。

客户-服务器模型变种

在考虑了下列因素后,客户-服务器模型能派生出几个变种:
- 使用移动代码和移动代理;
- 用户需要硬件资源有限的、便于管理的低价格计算机;
- 能方便地增加和删除移动设备。

接口和对象

在一个进程(不论它是一个服务器进程或一个对等的进程)中可调用的函数集合由一个或多个接口定义指定。该概念与那些熟悉的语言如 Modula、C++或 Java 类似。在客户-服务器体系结构的基本形式中,每个服务器进程可看成是一个具有固定接口的实体,其中的接口定义了能被调用的功能。

用面向对象语言如 C++和 Java,再加适当额外的支持,分布式处理能以更面向对象的方式构造。许多对象能封装在服务器或对等的进程中,对它们的引用能传递到其他进程,这样它们的方法能由远程调用访问,CORBA 和带远程方法调用(RMI)机制的 Java 采用了这种方法。在这个模型中,每个进程具有的对象的数量和类型(在支持移动代码的语言如 Java 中)可能随系统活动要求而变化,在一些实现中对象的位置也可能改变。

不论我们采用静态的是客户-服务器体系结构,还是前一段概述的更动态的面向对象模型,在进程之间和在计算机之间责任的分布仍然是设计的一个重要方面。在传统的体系结构模型中,责任是静态分配的(例如,一个文件服务器只负责文件,不负责 Web 页面或它们的代理或其他对象类型)。但在面向对象模型中新的服务以及在某些情况下新的对象类型,能被实例化并马上可供调用。

分布式体系结构的设计需求

在分布式系统中,催发对象和进程分布的因素有许多,它们的重要性是不可忽视的。20 世纪 60 年代通过使用共享文件,共享第一次在分时系统中出现,大家很快认识到共享的好处,并在多用户操作系统如 UNIX 和多用户数据库系统如 Oracle 中得到了开发。使得进程能共享系统资源和设备(文件存储能力、打印机、音频和视频流),使得应用进程能共享应用对象。

以多处理器芯片形式出现的低廉的计算能力消除了对中央处理器共享的需要,中等性能的计算机网络的可用性和对相对昂贵的硬件资源,如打印机和磁盘存储共享的要求导致了 20 世纪 70 和 80 年代分布式系统的开发。今天,资源共享被认为是想当然的,但大规模的有效的数据共享仍然是巨大的挑战,随着数据变化(大多数数据随时间变化),可能出现并发和有冲突的修改。

Chapter 11 Artificial Intelligence
(人工智能)

Section A Expert Systems

Expert Knowledge

One major insight gained from early work in problem solving was the importance of domain-specific knowledge. A doctor, for example, is not effective at **diagnosing** illness solely because she possesses some **innate** general problem-solving skill; she is effective because she knows a lot about medicine. Similarly, a geologist is effective at discovering **mineral** deposits because he is able to apply a good deal of theoretical and **empirical** knowledge about geology to the problem at hand.

Expert knowledge is a combination of a theoretical understanding of the problem and a collection of **heuristic** problem-solving rules that experience has shown to be effective in the domain. Expert systems are constructed by obtaining this knowledge from a human expert and coding it into a form that a computer may apply to similar problems.

Expert System

This **reliance** on the knowledge of a human domain expert for the system's problem solving strategies is a major feature of expert systems.

Although some programs are written in which the designer is also the source of the domain knowledge, it is far more typical to see such programs growing out of **collaboration** between a domain expert such as a doctor, chemist, geologist, or engineer and a separate artificial intelligence specialist. The domain expert provides the necessary knowledge of the problem domain through a general discussion of her problem-solving methods and by **demonstrating** those skills on a carefully chosen set of sample problems. The AI specialist, or knowledge engineer, as expert systems designers are often known, is responsible for

---

diagnose ['daiəgnəuz]
v. 诊断
innate ['ineit]
adj. 先天的，天生的
mineral ['minərəl]
n. 矿物，矿石
empirical [em'pirikəl]
adj. 经验主义的
heuristic [hjuə'ristik]
adj. 启发式的

reliance [ri'laiəns]
n. 信任，信心，依靠

collaboration [kə,læbə'reiʃən]
n. 协作

demonstrating ['demənstreit]
vt. 示范，证明

implementing this knowledge in a program that is both effective and seemingly intelligent in its behavior. Once such a program has been written, it is necessary to **refine** its expertise through a process of giving it example problems to solve, letting the domain expert **criticize** its behavior, and making any required changes or modifications to the program's knowledge. This process is repeated until the program has achieved the desired level of performance.

Earliest Systems

One of the earliest systems to **exploit** domain-specific knowledge in problem solving was DENDRAL, developed at Stanford in the late 1960s.

DENDRAL was designed to **infer** the structure of **organic** molecules from their chemical **formulas** and mass **spectrographic** information about the chemical bonds present in the molecules. Because organic molecules tend to be very large, the number of possible structures for these molecules tends to be huge. DENDRAL addresses the problem of this large search space by applying the heuristic knowledge of expert chemists to the structure **elucidation** problem.

DENDRAL's methods proved remarkably effective, routinely finding the correct structure out of millions of possibilities after only a few trials. The approach has proved so successful that descendants of the system are used in chemical and **pharmaceutical** laboratories throughout the world.

Features of AI

The reasoning of an expert system should be open to **inspection,** providing information about the state of its problem solving and explanations of the choices and decisions that the program is making. Explanations are important for a human expert, such as a doctor or an engineer, if he or she is to accept the **recommendations** from a computer. Indeed, few human experts will accept advice from another human, let alone a machine, without understanding the **justifications** for it.

The exploratory nature of AI and expert system programming requires that programs be easily **prototyped,** tested, and changed. AI programming languages and environments are designed to support this iterative development **methodology**. In a pure production system, for example, the modification of a single rule has no global **syntactic** side effects. Rules may be added or removed without requiring further changes to the large program. Expert system designers often comment that easy modification of the knowledge base is a major factor in producing a successful program.

A further feature of expert systems is their use of heuristic problem-solving methods. As expert system designers have discovered, informal "**tricks of the trade**" and "**rules of thumb**" are an essential complement to the standard theory presented in textbooks and classes. Sometimes these rules **augment** theoretical knowledge in understandable ways; often they are simply shortcuts that have, **empirically**, been shown to work.

Applications of AI

Expert systems are built to solve a vide range of problems in domains such as medicine, mathematics, engineering, chemistry, geology, computer science, business, law, defense, and education. These programs address a variety of problems; the following list is a useful summary of general expert system problem categories.

- Interpretation: forming high-level conclusions from collections of **raw** data.
- Prediction: projecting probable consequences of given situations.
- Diagnosis: determining the cause of **malfunctions** in complex situations based on observable **symptoms**.
- Design: finding a configuration of system components that meets performance goals while satisfying a set of design constraints.
- Planning: devising a sequence of actions that will achieve a set of goals given certain starting conditions and run-time constraints.
- Monitoring: comparing a system's observed behavior to its expected behavior.
- Instruction: assisting in the education process in technical domains.
- Control: governing the behavior of a complex environment.

methodology [meθəˈdɔlədʒi]
n. 方法学, 方法论
syntactic [sinˈtæktik]
adj. 句法的, 词法的

tricks of the trade
某门生意或职业的诀窍
rule of thumb
单凭经验的方法
augment [ɔːgˈment]
v. 增加, 增大
empirically [emˈpirikəli]
adv. 经验主义地

raw [rɔː]
adj. 原始的, 未处理的

malfunction [mælˈfʌŋkʃən]
n. 故障
symptom [ˈsimptəm]
n. 症状, 征兆

Limitations of AI

It is interesting to note that most expert systems have been written for relatively specialized, expert level domains. These domains are generally well studied and have clearly defined problem-solving strategies. Problems that depend on a more loosely defined **notion** of "common sense" are much more difficult to solve by these means. In spite of the promise of expert systems, it would be a mistake to **overestimate** the ability of this technology. Current **deficiencies** include:

(1) Difficulty in **capturing** "deep" knowledge of the problem domain. MYCIN, for example, lacks any real knowledge of human **physiology**. It does not know what blood does or the function of the **spinal cord. Folklore** has it that once, when selecting a drug for treatment of meningitis, MYCIN asked whether the patient was **pregnant,** even though it had been told that the patient was male. Whether this actually occurred or not, it does illustrate the potential narrowness of knowledge in expert systems.

(2) Lack of robustness and flexibility. If humans are presented with a problem instance that they cannot solve immediately, they can generally return to an examination of first principles and come up with some strategy for attaching the problem. Expert systems generally lack this ability.

(3) Inability to provide deep explanations. Because expert systems lack deep knowledge of their problem domains, their explanations are generally restricted to a description of the steps they took in finding a solution. For example, they often cannot tell "why" a certain approach was taken.

(4) Difficulties in **verification**. Though the correctness of any large computer system is difficult to prove, expert systems are particularly difficult to verify. This is a serious problem, as expert systems technology is being applied to critical applications such as air traffic control, nuclear reactor operations, and weapons systems.

(5) Little learning from experience. Current expert systems are **handcrafted**; once the system is completed, its performance will not improve without further attention from its programmers, leading to doubts about the intelligence of such systems.

---

notion ['nəuʃən]
n. 概念, 观念, 想法
overestimate ['əuvə'estimeit]
vt. 评价过高
deficiency [di'fiʃənsi]
n. 缺乏, 不足
capture ['kæptʃə]
n. 捕获, 战利品
physiology [ˌfizi'ɔlədʒi]
n. 生理学
spinal cord
n. 脊髓, 脊索
folklore ['fəuklɔː(r)]
n. 民间传说
pregnant ['pregnənt]
adj. 怀孕的, 孕育的

verification [ˌverifi'keiʃən]
n. 确认, 查证, 作证

handcraft ['hændkrɑːft]
vt. 手工制作

In spite of these limitations, expert systems have proved their value in a number of important applications. It is hoped that these limitations will only encourage the student to **pursue** this important branch of computer science.

pursue [pə'sju:]
vt. 追赶，追踪，从事

Exercises

I. Fill in the blanks with the information given in the text.

1. Expert systems are constructed by obtaining this_____ from a human expert and coding it into a form that a _____ may apply to similar problems.

2. This reliance on the knowledge of a human domain _____ for the system's problem solving strategies is a major feature of _____.

3. The domain expert provides the necessary knowledge of the _____ through a general discussion of her problem-solving methods and by _____ those skills on a carefully chosen set of _____ problems.

4. Once such a program has been written, it is necessary to _____ its _____.

5. The approach has proved so successful that _____ of the system are used in chemical and pharmaceutical laboratories _____.

II. Translate the following passages from English into Chinese.

1. Rule-based expert systems

Rule-based expert systems represent problem-solving knowledge as if…then…. This approach is one of the oldest techniques for representing domain knowledge in an expert system. It is also one of the most natural, and remains widely used in practical and experimental expert system.

2. Breadth-first search

Breadth-first search is more common in data-driven reasoning. The algorithm for this is simple: compare the working memory with the conditions of each rule in the rule base according to the order of the rules in the rule base. If the data in working memory supports a rule's firing the result is placed in working memory and then control moves on to the next rule. Once all rules have been considered, search starts again at the beginning of the rule set.

3. Reasoning in uncertain situations

An issue for expert system reasoning is how to draw useful results from data with missing, incomplete, or incorrect information. Drawing useful conclusions from incomplete and imprecise data is not an impossible task; we do it very successfully in almost every aspect of our daily life. We comprehend language statements that are often ambiguous or incomplete; we recognize friends from their voices or their gestures; and so on. For expert systems, we may use certainty measures to reflect our belief in the quality of data. Beliefs of imperfect data can be propagated through rules to constrain conclusions. This technique is founded on Bayes' theorem for reasoning about the frequency of events, based on prior information about these events.

Section B Strategies for State Space Search

The Theory of State Space Search

To successfully design and implement search algorithms, a

Chapter 11 Artificial Intelligence

programmer must be able to analyze and predict their behavior. Questions that need to be answered include:

(1) Is the problem solver **guaranteed** to find a solution?

(2) Will the problem solver always **terminate**, or can it become caught in an infinite loop?

(3) When a solution is found, is it guaranteed to be **optimal**?

(4) What is the **complexity** of the search process in terms of time usage? Memory usage?

(5) How can the interpreter most effectively reduce search complexity?

The theory of state space search is our primary tool for answering these questions. By representation a problem as a state space graph, we can use graph theory to analyze the structure and complexity of both the problem and the search procedures that we employ to solve it.

State Space Graph

A graph consists of a set of **nodes** and a set of **arcs** or links connecting pairs of nodes. In the state space model of problem solving, the nodes of a graph are taken to represent **discrete** states in a problem-solving process, such as the results of logical **inferences** or the different configurations of a game board. The arcs of the graph represent transitions between states. These transitions correspond to logical inferences or legal **moves** of a game. In expert system, for example, states describe our knowledge of a problem instance at some stage of a reasoning process. Expert knowledge, in the form of if…then rules, allows us to generate new information; the act of applying a rule is represented as an arc between states.

In the state space representation of a problem, one or more initial states, corresponding to the given information in a problem instance, form the root of the graph. The graph also defines one or more goal conditions, which are solutions to a problem instance. State space search characterizes problem solving as the process of finding a solution path from the start state to a goal.

Arcs of the state space correspond to steps in a solution process and paths through the space represent solutions in various stages of completion. Paths are searched, beginning at the start state and continuing through the graph, until either the goal

---

guarantee [,gærən'ti:]
vt. 保证, 担保
terminate ['tə:mineit]
v. 停止, 结束, 终止
optimal ['ɔptiməl]
adj. 最佳的, 最理想的
complexity [kəm'pleksiti]
n. 复杂度, 复杂性

node [nəud]
n. 结点
arc [ɑ:k]
n. 弧, 弓形, 拱
discrete [dis'kri:t]
adj. 不连续的, 离散的
inference ['infərəns]
n. 推论
move [mu:v]
n. 下一步棋, 动一个棋子

description is satisfied or they are **abandoned**. The actual generation of new states along the path is done by applying **operators**, such as "legal moves" in a game or inference rules in a logic problem or expert system, to existing states on a path.

Strategies for State Space Search

The task of a search algorithm is to find a solution path through such a problem space. Search algorithms must keep track of the paths from a start to a goal node, because these paths contain the series of operations that lead to the problem solution.

A state space may be searched in two directions: from the given data of a problem **instance** toward a goal or from a goal back to the data.

In data-driven search, sometimes called forward chaining, the problem solver begins with the given facts of the problem and a set of legal moves or rules for changing state. Search proceeds by applying rules to facts to produce new facts, which are in turn used by the rules to generate more new facts. This process continues until (we hope!) it generates a path that satisfies the goal condition.

An alternative approach is possible: take the goal that we want to solve. See what rules or legal moves could be used to generate this goal and determine what conditions must be true to use them. These conditions become the new goals, or subgoals, for the search. Search continues, working backward through **successive** subgoals until (we hope!) it works back to the facts of the problem. This finds the chain of moves or rules leading from data to a goal, although it does so in backward order. This approach is called goal-driven **reasoning**, or backward chaining, and it recalls the simple childhood trick of trying to solve a **maze** by working from the finish to the start.

To summarize: data-driven reasoning takes the facts of the problem and applies the rules and legal moves to produce new facts that lead to a goal; goal-driven reasoning focuses on the goal, finds the rules that could produce the goal, and chains backward through successive rules and subgoals to the given facts of the problem.

abandoned [əˈbændənd]
adj. 被抛弃的，没有约束的
operator [ˈɔpəreitə]
n. 算子

instance [ˈinstəns]
n. 实例，情况，场合

successive [səkˈsesiv]
adj. 继承的，连续的
reasoning [ˈriːzəniŋ]
n. 推理，评理，论证
maze [meiz]
n. 曲径，迷宫，迷津

Determination of Search Strategies

In the final analysis, both data-driven and goal-driven problem solvers search the same state space graph; however, the order and actual number of states searched can differ. The preferred strategy is determined by the properties of the problem itself. These include the complexity of the rules, the "shape" of the state space, and the nature and **availability** of the problem data. All of these vary for different problems.

As an example of the effect a search strategy can have on the complexity of search, consider the problem of **confirming** or denying the statement "I am a **descendant** of Thomas Jefferson." A solution is a path of direct **lineage** between the "I" and Thomas Jefferson. This space may be searched in two directions, starting with the "I" and working along **ancestor** lines to Thomas Jefferson or starting with Thomas Jefferson and through his descendants.

Some simple **assumptions** let us estimate the size of the space searched in each direction. Thomas Jefferson was born about 250 years ago; if we assume 25 years per generation, the required path will be length 10. As each person has exactly two parents, a search back from the "I" would examine on the order of 210 ancestors. A search that worked forward from Thomas Jefferson would examine more states, as people tend to have more than two children (particularly in the eighteenth and nineteenth centuries). If we assume an average of only three children per family, the search would examine on the order of 310 nodes of the family tree. Thus, a search back from the "I" would examine fewer nodes. Note, however, that both directions yield **exponential** complexity.

The decision to choose between data- and goal-driven search is based on the structure of the problem to be solved.

Goal-Driven Search

Goal-driven search is suggested if:

(1) A goal or **hypothesis** is given in the problem statement or can easily be **formulated**. In a mathematics theorem proved, for example, the goal is the theorem to be proved. Many diagnostic systems consider potential diagnoses in a **systematic**

availability [ə,veilə'biliti]
n. 可用性, 实用性
confirm [kən'fəːm]
vt. 确定, 使有效
descendant [dɪ'send(ə)nt]
n. 子孙, 后代
lineage ['liniidʒ]
n. 血统, 世系
ancestor ['ænsistə]
n. 祖先, 祖宗
assumption [ə'sʌmpʃən]
n. 假定, 设想

exponential
[,ekspəu'nenʃəl]
adj. 指数的, 幂数的

hypothesis [hai'pɔθisis]
n. 假设, 假说
formulate ['fɔːmjuleit]
vt. 用公式表示
systematic [,sisti'mætik]
adj. 系统的, 体系的

fashion, confirming or elimination them using goal-driven reasoning.

(2) There are a large number of rules that match the facts of the problem and thus produce an increasing number of conclusions or goals. Early selection of a goal can **eliminate** most of these branches, making goal-driven search more effective in **pruning** the space. In a mathematics theorem prover, for example, the total number of rules used to produce a given **theorem** is usually much smaller than the number of rules that may be applied to the entire set of **axioms**.

(3) Problem data are not given but must be acquired by the problem solver. In this case, goal-driven search can help guide data **acquisition**. In a medical diagnosis program, for example, a wide range of diagnostic tests can be applied. Doctors order only those that are necessary to confirm or deny a particular hypothesis.

Goal-driven search thus uses knowledge of the desired goal to guide the search through **relevant** rules and eliminate branches of the space.

Data-Driven Search

Data-driven search is appropriate to problems in which:

(1) All or most of the data are given in the initial problem statement. **Interpretation** problems often fit this **mold** by presenting a collection of data and asking the system to provide a high-level interpretation. Systems that analyze particular data (e.g., the PROSPECTOR or Dipmeter programs, which interpret geological data or attempt to find what minerals are likely to be found at a site) fit the data-driven approach.

(2) There are a large number of potential goals, but there are only a few ways to use the facts and given information of a particular problem instance. The DENDRAL program, an expert system that finds the molecular structure of organic **compounds** based on their formula, mass spectrographic data, and knowledge of chemistry, is an example of this. For any organic compound, there are an **enormous** number of possible structures. However, the mass spectrographic data on a compound allow DENDRAL to eliminate all but a few of these.

(3) It is difficult to form a goal or hypotheses. In using DENDRAL, for example, little may be known initially about the

eliminate [i'limineit]
vt. 排除，消除
pruning ['pru:niŋ]
n. 剪枝，修剪
theorem ['θiərəm]
n. [数]定理，法则
axiom ['æksiəm]
n. [数]公理
acquisition [,ækwi'ziʃən]
n. 获取，搜索

relevant ['relivənt]
adj. 有关的，相应的

interpretation
[in,tə:pri'teiʃən]
n. 解释，阐明
mold [məuld]
n. 模子，铸型

compound ['kɔmpaund]
n. 混合物，[化]化合物

enormous [i'nɔ:məs]
adj. 巨大的，庞大的

Chapter 11 Artificial Intelligence

possible structure of a compound.

Data-driven search uses the knowledge and **constraints** found in the given data of a problem to guide search along lines known to be true.

constraint [kən'streint]
n. 约束，限制

To summarize, there is no **substitute** for careful analysis of the particular problem, considering such issues as the branching factor of rule applications (on average, how many new states are generated by rule applications in both directions?), availability of data, and ease of determining potential goals.

substitute ['sʌbstitjuːt]
n. 代用品，代替者

Exercises

Ⅰ. **Fill in the blanks with the information given in the text.**

1. By representation a problem as a state space graph, we can use _____ to analyze the structure and _____ of both the problem and the search procedures that we employ to solve it.

2. In the state space representation of a problem, one or more _____ states, corresponding to the given information in a problem instance, form the _____ of the graph.

3. Paths are searched, beginning at the start state and continuing through the graph, until either the _____ is satisfied or they are _____.

4. Goal-driven search thus uses knowledge of the _____ to guide the search through relevant rules and eliminate _____ of the space.

5. Data-driven search uses the knowledge and _____ found in the given data of a problem to guide _____ along limes known to be true.

Ⅱ. **Translate the following passages from English into Chinese.**

1. Heuristics

Expert systems research has affirmed the importance of heuristics as an essential component of problem solving. When a human expert solves a problem, he or she examines the available information and makes a decision. The "rules of thumb" that a human expert uses to solve problems efficiently are largely heuristic in nature. These heuristics are extracted and formalized by expert systems designers.

2. The problem of hill-climbing strategies

A major problem of hill-climbing strategies is their tendency to become stuck at local maxima. If they reach a state that has a better evaluation than any of its children, the algorithm halts. If this state is not a goal, but just a local maximum, the algorithm may fail to find the best solution. That is, performance might well improve in a limited setting, but because of the shape of the entire space, it may never reach the overall best. An example of local maxima in games occurs in the 8-puzzle. Often, in order to move a particular tile to its destination, other tiles already in goal position need be moved out. This is necessary to solve the puzzle but temporarily worsens the board state. Because "better" need not be "best" in an absolute sense, search methods without backtracking or some other recovery mechanism are unable to distinguish between local and global maxima.

3. Rooted graphs

A rooted graph has a unique node, called the root, such that there is a path from the root to all nodes within the graph. In drawing a rooted graph, the root is usually drawn at the top of the page, above the other nodes. This is a directed graph with all arcs having a single direction. Note that this graph contains no cycles; players cannot undo a move as much as they might sometimes wish.

Section C Current Challenges and Future Directions

Introduction

Although the use of AI techniques to solve practical problems has demonstrated its utility, the use of these techniques to found a general science of intelligence is a difficult and continuing problem. Is it possible to give a formal, computational account of the processes that enable intelligence?

The computational **characterization** of intelligence begins with the abstract specification of computational devices. Research through the 1930s, 1940s, and 1950s began this task, with Turing, Post, Markov, and Church all contributing **formalisms** that describe computation. The goal of this research was not just to specify what it meant to compute, but rather to specify limits on what could be computed. The Universal Turing Machine is the most commonly studied specification, although Post's rewrite rules, the basis for production system computing, is also an important contribution. Church's model, based on partially **recursive** functions, offers support for modern high-level functional languages, such as Scheme and Standard ML.

Equivalence of computational specifications

Theoreticians have proven that all of these formalisms have equivalent computational power in that any function computable by one is computable by the others. In fact, it is possible to show that the universal Turing machine is **equivalent** to any modern computational device. Based on these results, the Church-Turing hypothesis makes the even stronger argument: that no model of computation can be defined which is more powerful than these known models. Once we establish equivalence of computational specifications, we have freed ourselves from the medium of **mechanizing** these specifications: we can implement our algorithms with vacuum tubes, silicon, protoplasm, or tinker toys. The automated design in one medium can be seen as equivalent to mechanisms in another. This makes the empirical **enquiry** method even more

characterization [ˌkærɪktəraɪˈzeɪʃən]
n. 特性描述
formalism [ˈfɔːməlɪzəm]
n. 形式主义

recursion [rɪˈkəːʃən]
n. 递归(式); 循环

theoretician [ˌθɪərəˈtɪʃən]
n. 精通于理论的人,理论家

equivalent [ɪˈkwɪvələnt]
adj. 相等的, 相当的

mechanize [ˈmekənaɪz]
v. 机械化
enquiry [ɪnˈkwaɪəri]
n. 询问

critical, as we experiment in one medium to test our understanding of mechanisms implemented in another.

Paradoxically, intelligence may require a less powerful computational mechanism with more focused control. Levesque and Brachman have suggested that human intelligence may require more computationally efficient (although less expressive) representations, such as **Horn clauses** for reasoning, the restriction of factual knowledge to **ground literals**, and the use of computationally **tractable** truth maintenance systems. Agent-based and emergent models of intelligence also seem to **espouse** this philosophy.

Another point addressed by the formal equivalence of our models of mechanism is the **duality** issue and the mind-body problem. At least since the days of **Descartes,** philosophers have asked the question of the interaction and integration of mind, **consciousness,** and a physical body. Philosophers have offered every possible response, from total **materialism** to the denial of material existence, even to the supporting intervention of a **benign** god! AI and **cognitive** science research reject Cartesian dualism in favor of a material model of mind based on the physical implementation or **instantiation** of symbols, the formal specification of computational mechanisms for manipulating those symbols, the equivalence of representational **paradigms,** and the mechanization of knowledge and skill in embodied models. The success of this research is an indication of the **validity** of this model.

Questions within the Epistemology

Many consequential questions remain, however, within the **epistemological** foundations for intelligence in a physical system. We summarize again several of these critical issues.

(1) The representation problem. Newell and Simon hypothesized that the physical symbol system and search are necessary and sufficient characterizations of intelligence. Are the successes of the **neural** or sub-symbolic models and of the **genetic** and emergent approaches to intelligence refutation of the physical symbol hypotheses, or are they simply other instances of it?

Even a weak interpretation of this hypothesis——that the

paradoxical [ˌpærəˈdɔksikəl]
adj. 荒谬的；自相矛盾的
Horn clauses
霍恩子句
ground literal
基础文字，没有变量的文字
tractable [ˈtræktəbl]
adj. 易驾驭的，易处理的
espouse [isˈpauz]
vt. 支持，赞成
duality [djuˈæliti]
n. 二元性
Descartes [deiˈkɑːt, dɛkart]
n. 笛卡儿(哲学家、数学家)
consciousness [ˈkɔnʃəsnis]
n. 意识，知觉
materialism [məˈtiəriəlizəm]
n. 唯物主义
benign [biˈnain]
adj. 仁慈的，和蔼的
cognitive [ˈkɔgnitiv]
adj. 认知的，有感知的
instantiation [inˌstænʃiˈeiʃən]
n. 实例化,例示
paradigm [ˈpærədaim, -dim]
n. 范例
validity [vəˈliditi]
n. 有效性，合法性，正确性
epistemological [ˌepistiˌməˈlɔdʒikəl]
adj. 认识论的

neural [ˈnjuərəl]
adj. 神经系统的，神经中枢的
genetic [dʒiˈnetik]
adj. 遗传的，起源的

physical symbol system is a sufficient model for intelligence——has produced many powerful and useful results in the modern field of cognitive science. What this argues is that we can implement physical symbol systems that will demonstrate intelligent behavior. Sufficiency allows creation and testing of symbol-based models for many aspects of human performance. But the strong interpretation——that the physical symbol system and search are necessary for intelligent activity——remains open to question.

(2) The role of embodiment in cognition. One of the main assumptions of the physical symbol system hypothesis is that the particular instantiation of a physical symbol system is **irrelevant** to its performance; all that matters is its formal structure. This has been challenged by a number of thinkers who essentially argue that the requirements of intelligent action in the world require a physical **embodiment** that allows the agent to be fully integrated into that world. The architecture of modern computers does not support this degree of situatedness, requiring that an artificial intelligence interact with its world through the extremely limited window of **contemporary** input/output devices. If this challenge is correct, then, although some form of machine intelligence may be possible, it will require a very different interface than that afforded by contemporary computers.

(3) Culture and intelligence. Traditionally, artificial intelligence has focused on the individual mind as the **sole** source of intelligence; we have acted as if an explanation of the way the brain **encodes** and **manipulates** knowledge would be a complete explanation of the origins of intelligence. However, we could also argue that knowledge is best regarded as a social, rather than as an individual construct. In a **meme** based theory of intelligence, society itself carries essential components of intelligence. It is possible that an understanding of the social context of knowledge and human behavior is just as important to a theory of intelligence as an understanding of the dynamics of the individual mind/brain.

(4) Characterizing the nature of interpretation. Most computational models in the representational tradition work with an already interpreted domain: that is, there is an **implicit** and a

irrelevant [i'relivənt]
adj. 不相关的，不切题的

embodiment [im'bɔdimənt]
n. 体现，具体化，化身

contemporary [kən'tempərəri]
n. 同时代的人
adj. 当代的，同时代的

sole [səul]
adj. 单独的，唯一的，专有的，排他的
encode [in'kəud]
vt. 编码
manipulate [mə'nipjuleit]
vt. (熟练地)操作，操纵，处理
meme
模因，文化信息的传播单位

Implicit [im'plisit]
adj. 暗示的，含蓄的

Chapter 11 Artificial Intelligence

priori commitment of the system's designers to an interpretive **context.** Under this commitment there is little ability to shift contexts, goals, or representations as the problem solving evolves. Currently, there is little effort at **illumination** the process by which humans constructs interpretations.

The Tarskian view of **semantics** as a mapping between symbols and objects in a domain of discourse is certainly too weak and doesn't explain, for example, the fact that one domain may have different interpretations in the light of different practical goals. **Linguists** have tried to **remedy** the limitations of Tarskian semantics by adding a theory of **pragmatics. Discourse analysis**, with its fundamental dependence on symbol use in context, has dealt with these issues in recent years.

The **semiotic** tradition started by C. S. Peirce and continued by Eco, Seboek, and others takes a more **radical** approach to language. It places symbolic expressions within the wider context of signs and sign interpretation. This suggests that the meaning of a symbol can only be understood in the context of its role as **interpretant,** that is, in the context of an interpretation and interaction with the environment.

(5) Representational **indeterminacy.** Anderson's representational indeterminacy conjecture suggests that it may in principle be impossible to determine what representational scheme best **approximates** the human problem solver in the context of a particular act of skilled performance. This conjecture is founded on the fact that every representational scheme is **inextricably** linked to a larger computational architecture, as well as search strategies. In the detailed analysis of human skill, it may be impossible to control the process sufficiently so that we can determine the representation; or establish a representation to the point where a process might be uniquely determined. As with the **uncertainty** principle of physics, where phenomena can be altered by the very process of measuring them, this is an important concern for constructing models of intelligence but need not limit their utility.

But more importantly, the same criticisms can be leveled at the computational model itself where the inductive **biases** of symbol and search in the context of the Church-Turing hypothesis still under constrain a system. The **perceived** need

---

priori
先验的
Context ['kɔntekst]
n. 上下文, 语境
illumination [i,lju:mi'neiʃən]
n. 照明, 阐明, 启发
semantics [si'mæntiks]
n. 语义学, 符号学
linguist ['liŋgwist]
n. 语言学家
remedy ['remidi]
vt. 治疗, 补救, 矫正
pragmatics [præg'mætiks]
n. 语用论
discourse analysis
语篇分析
Semiotic [,semi'ɔtik]
adj. 符号学的, 症状的
radical ['rædikəl]
adj. 根本的, 基本的

interpretant
解释项

indeterminacy [indi'tə:minəsi]
n. 不确定, 不明确
approximate [ə'prɔksimeit]
v. 近似, 接近, 接近
inextricable [in'ekstrikəbl]
adj. 无法解脱的, 逃脱不掉的
uncertainty [ʌn'sə:tnti]
n. 不确定, 不可靠

bias ['baiəs]
n. 偏见, 偏差
perceive [pə'si:v]
vt. 察觉

of some optimal representational scheme may well be the **remnant** of a **rationalist's** dream, while the scientist simply requires modes sufficiently **robust** to constrain empirical questions. The proof of the quality of a model is in its ability to offer an interpretation, to predict, and to be revised.

(6) The necessity of designing computational models those are **falsifiable**. Popper and others have argued that scientific theories must be falsifiable. This means that there must exist **circumstances** under which the model is not a successful approximation of the phenomenon. The obvious reason for this is that any number of confirming experimental instances is not sufficient for confirmation of a model. Furthermore, much new research is done in direct response to the failure of existing theories.

(7) The limitations of the scientific method. A number of researchers claim that the most important aspects of intelligence are not and, in principle, cannot be modeled, and in particular not with any **symbolic** representation. These areas include learning, understanding natural language, and the production of speech acts. These issues have deep roots in our **philosophical** tradition. Winograd and Flores's criticisms, for example, are based on issues raised in **phenomenology.**

Arguments

Most of the assumptions of modern AI can trace their roots back from Carnap, Frege, and Leibnoz through Hobbes, Locke, and Hume to Aristotle. This tradition argues that intelligent processes conform to universal laws and are, in principle, understandable.

Heidegger and his followers represent an alternative approach to understanding intelligence. For Heidegger, reflective awareness is founded in a world of embodied experience (a life-world). This position, shared by Winoggrad and Flores, Dreyfus, and others, argues that a person's understanding of things is rooted in the practical activity of "using" them in coping with the everyday world. This world is essentially a context of socially organized roles and purposes. This context, and human functioning within it, is not something explained by **propositions** and understood by theorems. It is rather a flow that shapes and is itself continuously created. In a fundamental sense, human **expertise** is not knowing that, but rather, within a world of evolving social **norms** and implicit purposes, knowing how. We are **inherently** unable to place our knowledge and most of our intelligent behavior into language, either formal or natural.

Let us consider this point of view. First, as a criticism of the pure rationalist tradition, it is correct. Rationalism **asserts** that all human activity, intelligence, and responsibility can, in principle at least, be represented, formalized, and understood. Most reflective people do not believe this to be the case, reserving important roles for emotion, self-**affirmation** and responsible commitment (at least!). Aristotle himself said, in his Essay on Rational Action, "Why is it that I don't feel compelled to perform that which is entailed?" There are many human activities outside the **realms** of science that play an essential role in responsible human interaction; these cannot be reproduced by or **abrogated** to machines.

This being said, however, the scientific tradition of examining data, construction models, running experiments, and examining results with model refinement for further experiments has brought an important level of understanding, explanation, and ability to predict to the human community. The scientific method is a powerful tool for increasing human understanding.

Caveats

Nonetheless, there remain a number of caveats to this approach that scientists must understand.

Scientists must not confuse the model with the phenomenon being modeled. The model allows us to **progressively** approximate the phenomenon: there will, of necessity, always be a **"residue"** that is not empirically explained. In this sense also representational indeterminacy is not an issue. A model is used to explore, explain, and predict; and if it allows scientists to accomplish this, it is successful. Indeed, different models may successfully explain different aspects of a phenomenon, such as the wave and particle theories of light.

Furthermore, when researchers claim that aspects of intelligent phenomena are outside the scope and methods of the scientific tradition, this statement itself can only be **verified** by using that very tradition. The scientific method is the only tool we have for explaining in what sense issues may still be outside our current understanding. Every viewpoint, even that from the phenomenological tradition, if it is to have any meaning, must relate to our current **notions** of explanation—even to be **coherent** about the extent to which phenomena cannot be explained.

verify ['verifai]
vt. 检验, 校验, 查证

notion ['nəuʃən]
n. 概念, 观念, 想法
coherent [kəu'hiərənt]
adj. 一致的, 连贯的

For Future Explorations

The most exciting aspect of work in artificial intelligence is that to be coherent and contribute to the **endeavor** we must address these issues. To understand problem solving, learning, and language we must comprehend the philosophical level of representations and knowledge. In a **humbling** way we are asked to resolve Aristotle's tension between theoria and **praxis**, to fashion a union of understanding and practice, of the theoretical and practical, to live between science and art.

endeavor [in'devə]
n. 努力, 尽力
humble ['hʌmbl]
adj. 卑下的, 微贱的
praxis ['præksis]
n. 实践, 实习, 现实

AI practitioners are tool makers. Our representations, algorithms, and languages are tools for designing and building mechanisms that exhibit intelligent behavior. Through experiment we test both their computational adequacy for solving problems as well as our own understanding of intelligent phenomena.

Indeed, we have a tradition of this: Descartes, Leibniz, Pascal, Hobbes, Babbage, Turing, and others whose contributions were presented in textbooks of AI. Engineering, science, and philosophy; the nature of ideas, knowledge, and skill; the power and limitations of **formalism** and mechanism; these are the limitations and tensions with which we must live and from which we continue our explorations.

formalism ['fɔːməlizəm]
n. 拘泥形式, 形式主义

Exercises

I. Fill in the blanks with the information given in the text.

1. At least since the days of Descartes, philosophers have asked the question of the interaction and integration of mind, consciousness, and a physical body. This reliance on the knowledge of a human domain _____ for the system's problem solving strategies is a major feature of _____.

2. _____ allows creation and testing of _____ models for many aspects of human performance.

3. A number of researchers claim that the most important aspects of intelligence are not and, in principle,

cannot be _____, and in particular not with any _____.

4. To understand _____, _____, and _____ we must comprehend the philosophical level of representations and knowledge.

5. Our representations, algorithms, and languages are tools for _____ and building mechanisms that exhibit _____.

Ⅱ. **Translate the following passages from English into Chinese.**

1. Probabilistic analysis

Medical diagnosis programs based on probabilistic analysis have been able to perform at the level of an expert physician in several areas of medicine. Heckerman describes a case where a leading expert on lymph-node pathology scoffs at a program's diagnosis of an especially difficult case. The creators of the program suggest he ask the computer for an explanation of the diagnosis. The machine points out the major factors influencing its decision and explains the subtle interaction of several of the symptoms in this case. Eventually, the expert agrees with the program.

2. Agent

Perhaps encouraged by the progress in solving the subproblems of AI, researchers have also started to look at the "whole agent" problem again. The work on SOAR is the best-known example of a complete agent architecture. The so-called situated movement aims to understand the workings of agents embedded in real environments with continuous sensory inputs. One of the most important environments for intelligent agents is the Internet.

3. Association rule mining

Association rule mining finds interesting association or correlation relationships among a large set of data items. With massive amounts of data continuously being collected and stored, many industries are becoming interested in mining association rules from their databases. The discovery of interesting association relationships among huge amounts of business transaction records can help in many business decision making processes, such as selective marketing, decision analysis, and management.

Grammar 11　英语科技文献的阅读技巧(Ⅰ)

当代科学技术发展迅速，每时每刻有大量的英语科技文章、新闻及其他科技资料发表在各类报刊和网络上。实际上，要想把这些所有的英文材料都翻译成中文，这个想法是不切实际的。但是，如果想要把这些最新的资料和信息都在最短的时间内掌握，最好的解决方法就是自己直接去阅读英文材料。我们相信，只要有一定的英语基础，再加上适当的阅读技巧，掌握这些资料不是很难的。下面介绍一下阅读的技巧。实际上，我们可以将阅读这些英文材料的方法分成以下几类。

1. 精读

精读(Intensive Reading Skill)是在所有的阅读技巧中要求最高的。对所阅读的文章，要做到逐字细读，不但要了解文章的主题思想和内容，了解文章的文法结构，而且要掌握每个字词的意义和用法，必要时还需要把文章翻译成中文，但对于只需要查阅英语科技文献和信息的科技工作者而言，在多数情况下不需要使用精读技能。运用精读技能，不是看文章的长短，而在于是否需要对所阅读的英语资料文章进行深度了解和研究，可以说，精读的阅读技能是学习和研究英语的人或从事翻译人员必须掌握的技能。

例如：

In time, higher-level languages evolved, such as BASIC and COBOL. These languages let people work with something appropriating words and sentences. Such as Let I=100. These instructions were translated back into machine language by interpreters and compilers. An interpreter translates a program as it reads it, turning the program instructions, or code, directly into actions. A compiler translates the code into an intermediary form. This step is called compiling, and produces an object file. The compiler then invokes a linker, which turns the object file into an executable program.

随后，又推出了高级语言，如 BASIC 和 COBOL。这些语言使用的是近似于人常用的词句，如 Let I=100。这些指令由解释器或编译器翻译成机器语言。解释器边读边翻译，将程序指令或代码直接实现。编译器把代码翻译成中间代码。这一步骤称为编译，然后生成目标文件。编译程序调用链接程序，链接程序将目标代码转变成可执行程序。

2．泛读

见名知意，泛读(Extensive Reading)的意义就是指广泛、大量地阅读，是从量的检测指标来约束阅读者。但是实际上，泛读不是仅仅为了读而读，在采用这种方法的时候，常常要带着问题去阅读，达到对词汇量的累积和熟悉的程度。

例如：

Computer languages have undergone dramatic evolution since the first electronic computers were built to assist in telemetry calculations during World War Ⅱ. Early on, programmers worked with the most primitive computer instructions——machine language. These instructions were represented by long strings of ones and zeros. Soon, assemblers were invented to map machine instructions to human-readable and manageable mnemonics, such as ADD and MOV.

自从第一代电子计算机在第二次世界大战中用于自动计算以来，计算机语言已发生了巨大的变化。早期编程员使用最原始的计算机指令——机器语言来工作。这些指令由一长串的 0、1 组成。不久，发明了汇编程序，它能将机器指令转换成易读、易管理的助记符，如 ADD、MOV 等。

在阅读过程中，要带着问题去读，如"第一代计算机的最早用途是什么？""汇编程序是怎么出现的？"等。

 参考译文

Section A 专家系统

专家知识

人们从早期的问题求解工作获得的一个主要共识是领域特定知识的重要性。例如，一个医生如果仅有先天的一般解决问题的能力，不可能有效地诊断疾病，除非她掌握大量的医学知识。同样，地质学家可以发现矿藏，是因为他能够把许多地质学的理论和经验知识应用到面临的问题上。

专家知识由对问题的理论上的理解和启发式问题求解规则集合构成，后者主要体现为特定领域的经验知识。构建专家系统就要获取人类专家的这种知识，并对其进行编码，使计算机可以应用于类似问题的求解。

专家系统

依赖人类领域专家的知识作为系统的问题求解策略是专家系统的主要特征。

虽然有些程序是由程序设计者提供领域知识,不过更典型的是由领域专家,如医生、化学家、地质学家或工程师,与一位单独的人工智能专家合作编写程序。领域专家通过问题求解方法的一般性讨论和对精心选定的问题样本的示范性求解,提供专业领域必要的知识;而人工智能专家或知识工程师,作为专家系统的设计者,则负责在程序中实施这些知识,程序应既是有效的,从行为上看又是智能的。程序一旦编写完成,就要训练它解决一些样本问题,请领域专家对其行为进行评判,对程序的专业知识做必需的改变或修正,以完善程序的专业知识。这一过程需要反复重复,直到程序达到期望的性能标准。

最早的专家系统

在问题求解方面运用领域专门知识的最早的系统之一是 DENDRAL,这是斯坦福大学在 20 世纪 60 年代后期开发的软件。

DENDRAL 的设计者希望根据化学分子式和分子中各化学键的完整的质谱信息推断有机分子的结构。因为有机分子一般都很大,这些分子可能的结构数目也很庞大。DENDRAL 处理这个巨大的搜索空间问题的方法是,运用经验丰富的化学家的探索知识解决分子的结构说明问题。

事实证明 DENDRAL 的方法非常有效,在几次试验后,就从数百万的可能中发现了正确的分子结构。这一方法如此成功,以至于由此派生的系统应用于世界各地的化学和药物实验室。

人工智能的特点

专家系统的推理应受到公开检验,提供问题求解状态的相关信息以及程序做出选择和决定的解释。对医生或工程师等人类专家来说,如果要他或她接受计算机的建议,合理的解释很重要。实际上,很少人类专家愿意听取他人的建议,更何况是一台不能说明理由的机器。

人工智能和专家系统设计的探索性本质要求程序便于原型化、测试和修改。人工智能的编程语言和环境应支持这种反复迭代的开发方法。例如,在完全的产生式系统中,单一规则的改动不会影响全局的句法。规则可以添加也可删除,无须过多更改整个程序。专家系统的设计者们通常认为知识库是否便于修改是衡量成功系统的一个主要因素。

专家系统的另一特性是启发式问题求解方法的运用。人工智能系统的设计者发现,非正规的"窍门"和"经验法则"是教科书和课堂正统理论的必要补充。有时,这些规则是以可理解的方式扩充了理论知识,更多的时候仅仅是工作中经验性的捷径而已。

人工智能的应用

构建专家系统是为了广泛解决特定领域内的问题,如医学、数学、工程学、化学、地质学、计算机科学、商业、法律、国防,以及教育等。这些程序用来解决各种各样的问题,下面概括了专家系统求解的一般问题。

- 解释:从原始数据集合形成高级的结论。
- 预测:根据已知情况预测可能的结果。
- 诊断:基于可见症状确定复杂情况下故障的原因。
- 设计:在满足一系列设计约束的前提下找到符合性能目标的系统部件的一种布局。
- 规划:在已知起始条件和运行时间的情况下设计能够达到一系列目标的行动的序列。
- 监控:将系统的观测行为与预期行为进行比较。
- 指导:在专业领域的教学过程中提供辅助。
- 控制:操控复杂环境的行为。

人工智能的局限性

有趣的是大多数专家系统针对的都是相对专业性较强的、专家级的领域。这些领域通常已认真研究过，问题求解策略有明确的定义。而那些依赖于模糊定义的常识性概念的问题则很难用这些方法解决。无论专家系统的前景如何，过高估计这项技术的能力是个错误。其局限性表现在：

(1) 获取问题领域"深层"知识的困难性。以 MYCIN 为例，它缺少人类生理学知识，它不知道血液是做什么的，也不知道脊髓的功能。传说有一次在选择脑膜炎的处方药物时，MYCIN 询问病人是否怀孕，虽然它已被告知病人为男性。无论此事是否属实，它的确说明了专家系统的潜在的知识狭隘性。

(2) 缺乏强健性和灵活性。如果人面临一个无法立即解决的问题实例，他们一般会重新考察基本原理并提出一些适用于该问题的策略。专家系统一般缺少这种能力。

(3) 无法提供深入的解释。由于专家系统缺少问题领域的深奥的知识，其解释一般局限于系统在寻找解决办法的过程中采取各步骤的描述。例如，它们通常无法说明"为什么"采用某种方法。

(4) 验证的困难性。虽然大型计算机系统的正确性很难证明，但专家系统尤其难于验证。这是一个严重的问题，因为专家系统技术被用于一些充满危险的应用，如空中交通控制、核反应操作和武器系统等。

(5) 不能从经历中学习知识。目前的专家系统都是手工开发的，系统一旦完成，其性能如果没有程序设计者的进一步关注将无法提高。这类系统的智能性值得怀疑。

尽管有这些局限性，专家系统仍在大量的应用中证明了它们的价值。希望这些局限将会激励学生们继续研究计算机科学的这一重要分支。

Section B 状态空间搜索策略

状态空间搜索的理论

要成功地设计和实现搜索算法，程序设计者必须对算法的行为进行分析和预测。需要回答的问题包括：

(1) 问题求解程序肯定能够找到解决办法吗？
(2) 问题求解程序总能够结束吗？会不会陷入无限循环？
(3) 能够保证找到的解决办法是最优的吗？
(4) 搜索过程的复杂度如何？时间开销与存储器开销是多少？
(5) 解释程序如何能够最有效地降低搜索的复杂度？
(6) 要最有效地利用某种知识表示语言解释程序应如何设计？

状态空间搜索理论是我们解答这些问题的主要方法。把待求解问题表示为状态空间图，我们就可以用图论分析问题的结构和求解问题的搜索程序的复杂度了。

状态空间图

图由一组结点和一组连接结点对的弧或连线构成。在问题求解的状态空间模型中，图中结点用来表示问题求解过程中离散的状态，如逻辑推理的结果或棋类游戏中不同的棋盘布局。图中的弧表示不同状态间的转换，这些转换符合逻辑推理或游戏的合法走棋。例如，在专家系统中，状态用于描述推理过程中的某个阶段我们掌握的关于问题实例的知识。专家知识是形如 if...then 的规则，我们用这些规则生成新的信息；规则的应用就表示为状态之间的弧。

在问题的状态空间表示中，一个或多个初始状态对应于问题实例的已知信息，初始状态构成了图的根。图中还要定义一个或多个代表问题解答的目标状态。状态空间搜索将问题的求解描述为寻找自起始状态至目标状态的一条解路径。

状态空间的弧相当于求解过程的步骤，穿越状态空间的路径代表各种实现旅程的解。从起始状态开始在图中搜索各个路径，直到目标状态找到，否则放弃该路径。路径上新状态的产生实际上是对路径上当前状态应用操作算子实现的，如游戏中的"合理走棋"或者逻辑问题及专家系统中的推理规则。

状态空间的搜索策略

搜索算法的任务就是在问题空间中找到一条解路径。搜索算法必须记住从起始结点到目标结点的路径，因为这些路径包含着问题求解的一系列操作。

状态空间可以从两个方向搜索：从问题实例的已知数据向目标搜索或者从目标状态反向搜索到已知数据。

数据驱动搜索，有时也称演绎法，问题求解是从已知事实和一组改变状态的合法走棋或规则开始的。通过将规则应用于当前事实来生成新的事实，继而再应用规则产生更多新的事实，搜索不断进行下去，直到(希望如此！)生成一条能够满足目标条件的路径。

另一种方法也是可行的：取来我们要达到的目标状态。检查什么规则或合法走棋能够产生这一目标，然后确定应用它们的条件是什么，这些条件继而成为新的搜索目标，或子目标。搜索继续进行，以归纳的方式寻找一个个子目标，直到(希望如此！)回溯至问题的起始事实。这样就能找到从数据到目标的走棋或规则的链路，不过这是以相反的顺序找到的。这种方法称为目标驱动推理或归纳法，这让人回想起孩提时玩迷宫时从终点走回起点的恶作剧。

概括地说，数据驱动推理是根据问题的已知情况运用规则和合法走棋产生趋向目标的新事实；目标驱动推理着眼于目标，寻找能够产生目标状态的规则，并将到达问题已知事实的规则和子目标向后逐一串起来。

搜索策略的决定因素

无论是数据驱动还是目标驱动，问题求解算法搜索的是相同的状态空间图，不过搜索顺序和实际搜索的状态数目有所差别。优先选择的搜索策略应根据问题本身的特性而定，这包括规则的复杂性、状态空间的"形状"，以及问题中数据的自然形式和可用性。所有这些都随着问题的不同而不同。

通过一个例子，我们看看搜索策略对搜索复杂度的影响。问题是确认或否认命题"我是 Thomas Jefferson 的后代"。办法是寻找"我"与 Thomas Jefferson 之间的直系血统路径。这一空间可以从两个方向搜索：从"我"开始沿着祖先的线路上行到 Thomas Jefferson 或从 Thomas Jefferson 开始遍历他的后代。

我们做些简单的假设来估算一下每个方向上搜索到的状态空间数量。Thomas Jefferson 出生在 250 年前，假设家族的每一代为 25 年，则需要搜索的路径长度为 10。由于每人刚好有一对父母，从"我"开始的后向搜索需检查 2^{10} 数量级的祖先数目。从 Thomas Jefferson 开始向前搜索需要检查更多的状态空间，因为人们往往有两个以上的孩子(尤其在 18、19 世纪)。假设每个家庭平均有 3 个孩子，搜索过程需检查家谱中 3^{10} 数量级的结点数目。因此，从"我"开始向后搜索检查的结点要少一些。不过，需要注意的是，这两个方向搜索的复杂度都是指数级的。

数据或目标驱动方法的选择取决于待求解问题的结构。

目标驱动法

以下情形建议选择目标驱动法：

(1) 目标或假设在问题陈述中给出或可以容易地阐明。如在数学定理证明中，目标就是待证的定理。许多诊断系统在系统结构中先考虑到所有可能的诊断，再用目标驱动推理方法对这些诊断进行确认或排除。

(2) 符合问题情况的有大量规则，这样会产生越来越多的结论或目标。目标的早期选择可以除去大部分分支，使得目标驱动搜索在空间剪枝方法更为有效。如在数学定理证明程序中，用于导出已知定理的规则的数目通常远小于可应用于整个公理集合的规则数目。

(3) 问题数据未给出、但需由问题求解程序获取。在这种情况下，目标驱动搜索有助于数据的获取。例如，在医学诊断程序中可以使用广泛的诊断性检查。医生们只要求做那些必要的可以确认或排除某种假设的检查。

因此，目标驱动搜索利用预期目标的知识指导搜索过程，使用相关的规则并去掉状态空间的无关分支。

数据驱动搜索

数据驱动搜索适用于下列问题：

(1) 全部或大部分数据已在起始的问题陈述中给出。解释类问题一般适合这种模式，给出数据集合，让系统做出一个高级别的解释。分析特定数据的系统(如 PROSPECTOR 或 Dipmeter 程序，它们对地质数据做出解释或试图发现某地可能找到的矿藏)适合采用数据驱动方法。

(2) 有大量的潜在的结果，但使用数据和已知信息的方法不多的特殊问题。DENDRAL 专家系统就是一个这样的例子，它根据化学分子式、质谱数据和化学知识确定有机化合物的分子结构。对于任意有机化合物，都有数量巨大的可能的结构。但化合物的质谱数据使得 DENDRAL 可以排除少数几个之外的几乎所有情形。

(3) 难以形成目标条件或假设。以 DENDRAL 为例，开始时对化合物的可能结构一无所知。

数据驱动搜索利用问题的已知数据所蕴涵的知识和限制条件指导搜索沿着正确的方向进行。

总之，无可取代的是对特定问题的认真分析，要全面考虑应用规则的分支系数(分别在两个方向上使用规则，平均起来会产生多少新状态？)、数据的可用性及潜在目标的可确定性。

Section C 当前的挑战和未来的方向

简介

虽然解决实际问题的人工智能技术已经证明了其有效性，但是，运用这些技术创建智能的一般科学仍然是一个艰巨的问题。是否可能给出开启智能的一个形式化的可计算的过程说明？

智能的计算特性开始于计算设备的抽象说明。自 20 世纪 30、40、50 年代开始这项研究，Turing、Post、Markov、Church 都为描述计算法的形式体系做出了贡献。此项研究的目的不仅是指定需要计算的问题，更要明确可计算问题的范围。通用图灵机是最为熟知的研究规范，而波斯特的重写规则，作为产生式系统计算的基础，也是一项重要贡献。基于部分递归函数的丘奇模型为现代的高级函数式语言提供了支持，如 Scheme 和标准 ML 语言。

计算规范的等价性

理论学家已经证明，所有这些形式体系具有相同的计算能力，一种体系中可计算的功能在另一种体系中也可以实现。实际上，可以向人们展示通用图灵机理论上等价于任何现代计算设备。基于这些结论，丘奇-图灵假说提出了更有力的论ం：不可能定义比现有模型功能更强大的计算模型。一旦确定了计算规范的等价性，我们就能够从这些规范的实现介质中解放出来：我们可以用真空管、硅、原生质，甚至拼接组合玩具实现算法。一种介质下的自动化设计等价于用另一种介质的实现机制。这使经验调查法变得尤为重要，因为我们可以在一种介质下进行实验，检验我们对其他介质下实现机制的理解。

荒谬的是，智能可能需要更多集中控制的不那么强大的计算机制。Levesque 和 Brachman 指出，人类智能可能需要更多计算上的高效表示方法，如用于推理的霍恩子句，对基础文字施以实际知识的约束，以及采用计算上易处理的真值维护系统。基于代理的和新生的智能模型看来似乎也信奉这种哲学。

实现智能机制的模型的形式等价性解决的另外一点是二元性问题和心身问题。至少从 Descartes 时代开始，哲学家们就在思考心智、意识和身体的相互作用与结合问题。哲学家们提供了各种可能的答案，从彻底的唯物主义到否认物质存在，甚至归于仁慈的上帝的干预。人工智能和认知科学研究否定了 Descartes 的二元论、基于符号的物理实现或实例化、用于符号处理的计算机制的形式化规范、表示范例的等价性、知识的机械化和模型具体化技术，以及支持智力的物质模型。这项研究的成功是这一模型正确性的象征。

认识论中的问题

但是，在物质体系中智能的认识论基础尚有许多重要问题未解。我们再概括一下部分关键性问题。

(1) 表示法问题。Newell 和 Simon 假说认为物理符号系统和搜索是智能的充分且必要的表征。那么，神经或子符号模型及智能的遗传和新兴方法的成功是对物理符号假说的驳斥，或者仅仅是假说的其他实例呢？

即使是这一假说——物理符号系统是表示智能的充分模型——的不充分解释，也引出了许多现代认知科学领域中有影响的有用的结果。它表明我们能够实现体现智能行为的物理符号系统。假说的充分性为建立和试验基于符号的模型模仿多方面人类行为提供了可能。但假说——物理符号系统和搜索是智能活动的必要条件——的有力解释，仍有待探讨。

(2) 认知中实现体的功能。物理符号系统假说的主要设想之一是，物理符号系统的特定实现方式与其性能无关，其影响的仅是形式结构而已。这一点受到许多学者质疑，他们主要认为世界上智能行为的先决条件需要一个其智能代理完全与那个世界统一的物理实现体。现代计算机的体系结构不能提供如此程度的支持，人工智能需要通过极其有限的输入/输出设备的窗口与世界交互。如果这一说法正确，那么，虽然可能实现某种形式的机器智能，但它需要一种与现代计算机迥然不同的接口。

(3) 文化与智能。传统上，人工智能集中在个体心智作为智能的唯一来源的研究上，我们的做法好像认为，大脑编码和处理知识的方式的解释似乎就是智能起源的全部解释。但是，我们也有理由认为，知识最应该被视为社会的而不是个人的思想结晶。在智能的模因理论中，社会本身承载着智能的基本成分。对于智能理论而言，可能对知识和人类行为的社会背景的了解与对个体心智/头脑原动力的了解同样重要。

(4) 辨别解释的本质。大部分计算模型有代表性的传统工作是使用经过解释的领域，即系统的设计者对解释情境有固有的先验的约定。在这种约定下，当求解问题变化时，完全没有能力转换背景、目标或表示法。目前，还没有说明人类构建解释过程的研究成果。

Tarskian 关于语义学是文章中符号与某领域的对象间的映射的观点的确太缺乏说服力，如它无法解释一个领域因实际目标的不同可以有不同的解释这一事实。语言学家试图添加语用理论弥补 Tarskian 语义学说的不足。语篇分析，因其基本依赖于上下文使用的符号，近年来一直进行这类问题的研究。

符号学始于 C. S. Peirce，Eco、Seboek 继续这方面工作，而其他人则采取了更极端的语言方法。它将符号表达置于符号和符号解释的广阔背景中。它提出一个符号的意义只能在上下文中作为解释项理解，即在解释和解释与环境相互作用的上下文中理解。

(5) 表征的不确定性。Anderson 的表征不确定性猜想的提出，原则上，对于人在熟练表演的特定动作的处理方面，要确定最接近的表征方案是不可能的。这个猜想依据的事实是，每种表征方案都无可逃避地与更大的计算体系和搜索策略连接。对人类技能进行详细分析可知，完全控制这一过程、继而确定表示法或者建立唯一确定一个过程的关键点的表示法都是不可能的。根据物理学的不确定性原理，现象会被测量它们的过程本身所改变，如何构建智能模型又不限制它们的效用是个重要问题。

但更重要的是，同样的批评是针对计算模型本身的，在丘奇-图灵假说的背景下，符号和搜索的归纳偏差仍无意识地束缚了系统。对于某些最佳表征方案的发现需要也许完全是理性主义者残存的梦想，科学家仅仅需要十分强健的模式，以抑制经验性问题。一个模型的品质就体现在它提供解释、预测和修正的能力。

(6) 设计可证伪的计算模型的必要性。Popper 等人主张科学理论必须是可证伪的。这意味着一定存在着模型不能成功逼近现象的情况。显而易见，验证性的实例无论有多少，都不能充分证明一个模型的正确性。而且，许多新的研究成果直接反映了现存理论的不足。

(7) 科学方法的局限性。许多研究学者主张，智能最重要的方法没有且原则上也不能被模拟，尤其不能用任何符号表示法模拟。这些领域包括学习、自然语言理解和演讲的产生。这些问题在我们的哲学传统里有着深厚的根基。例如，Winograd 和 Flores 的批评论就是建立在现象学相关问题基础上的。

观点

现代人工智能的大多数设想的根源可以从 Carnap、Frege、leibnoz，追溯到 hobbes、Locke、Hume，再一直追溯到 Aristotle。传统认为，智能过程是符合普遍规律的，而且原则上也是可理解的。

Heidegger 及其追随者提出理解智能的另一种方法。Heidegger 认为，体验世界(生活世界)里建立了反射意识。Winoggrad、Flores 和 Dreyfus 等人持相同见解，主张人对事物的理解是在日常生活世界中因实际"使用"事物的行为而确立的。本质上，这个世界的背景就是社会组织的角色和用途。这种背景和人类在其中的机能不是能够用命题和定理解释理解的东西。它比较像流水，因器成形，不断创造着自己。从根本意义上讲，人的专门知识不是了解它，而是在一个发展的社会规范和固有意图的世界中知道如何去做。我们天生就不能把我们的知识和我们大部分的智能行为用语言表示，无论是形式的还是自然的。

我们来思考一下这个观点。首先，作为纯理性主义的批判者，这是正确的。理性主义断言，所有人类的行为、智能和职责都能够被表示、形式化和理解，至少从原理上是如此。大多数善于思考的人不相信这是事实，在一些重要职责上，至少在如情感、自我肯定和承担责任的职责上持保留意见。Aristotle 在关于理性行为的随笔中谈到，"完成天赋的功能时我为什么没感觉到是被强迫的？"在科学之外的领域，有许多人类活动在人类交互方面起着重要作用，这些是无法由机器复制或取代的。

尽管如此，检验数据、构建模型、做实验、通过改进模型来检查结果以继续实验，这一科学传统在理解、解释和对人类社会预测的能力上达到了相当的水平。科学方法是增强人类理解力的有力工具。

告诫

但是，科学家必须了解，这种方法存在许多要注意的问题。

首先，科学家不能把模型和被模拟的现象混淆。模型可以让我们逐步接近现象，这就必然永远存在无法用经验解释的"残余"。基于此，具有代表性的不确定性问题也不是问题了。模型是用于探索、解释和预测的。如果科学家能够实现它，它就是成功的。实际上，不同的模型可以成功地解释一个现象的不同方面，如光的波动理论和粒子理论。

此外，研究学者们声称智能现象的问题是在传统科学的范围和方法之外的，这个声明本身恰恰只能用传统科学来证实。要解释问题在何种意义上是我们目前理解力以外的，科学方法是我们拥有的唯一的工具。每一个观点，即使来自现象学传统，如果它具有某种意义，就一定与我们现在的解释性的概念有关——即使扩展到无法解释的现象。

未来的研究

人工智能研究工作中最激动人心的是，我们必须坚持不懈，共同努力，致力于解决所有这些问题。为了解问题求解、学习和语言，我们必须从哲学层面理解表示法和知识。我们要以一种谦逊的态度化解 Aristotle 的理论与实践的压力，从理论上和实践上构建智力与实践的和谐，生活在科学和艺术之间。

人工智能的开拓者们是工具的制造者。我们的表示法、算法和语言是设计、建造、展示智能行为的机械装置的工具。通过实验，我们既检验解决问题的计算合适性，同时也检验我们自己对智能现象的了解。

的确，我们有这方面的传统：Descartes、Leibniz、Pascal、Hobbes、Babbage、Turing，人工智能课本中列举了他们及其他一些人对这一学科做出的贡献。工程学、科学和哲学，思想的本质、知识和技巧，形式化和机械装置的能量和局限性，这是我们必须经历的限制和压力，从这里开始，我们将继续我们的探索。

Chapter 12　Digital Media Technology
(数字媒体技术)

Section A　Introduction of Digital Media Technology

Media and Digital Media

We may regard media as information of various forms of expression. According to the definition of **International Telecommunication Union** (ITU), the media could be divided into perception medium, representation medium, presentation medium, storage medium and transmission medium.

The digital media is an emerging discipline in the widely-used application fields. It is dominated by information science and digital technology, based on the mass communication theory and guided by the **contemporary** art and applied to such fields as culture, art, business, education and management, which reflects a high degree of integration of science and art. It touches upon such fields as computer hardware and software and application, electronics, communication and broadcast technique, digital media management, copyright of digital media, media arts, cultural and creative industry, consumer electronics, etc. The digital media includes text, graph, image, sound, videos and animation as well as digital technology application in various forms of transmission and its contents, i.e. digital process of collection, storage, processing and distribution of information. In a broad sense, the digital media is a media to store, process and spread information in a digitalization form, such as digitalized text, image, sound and video. Therefore, the subject of digital media should be technology, contents, application and human beings. The definition of digital media in *2005 China Digital Media Technology Development White Paper* (**hereinafter** referred to as White Paper) published by the Ministry of Science and Technology of the People's Republic of China on December 26, 2005 states: the digital media is the digitalized works with modern network as its main transmission carrier and is a whole

International
Telecommunication Union
国际电信联盟

contemporary
[kən'tempərəri]
adj. 当代的，同时代的

hereinafter ['hiərin'ɑːftə]
adv. 以下，在下文中

process to distribute information to the **End-User** by the perfect service system. This definition emphasizes the mode of transmission of digital media is through network and excludes such media as the removable storage devices (CD, **USB flash disk**).

The digital media has the following characteristics:

- **Digitization**. The media that people used to familiar with is almost stored and disseminated its information in a simulative way; however, the digital media is stored, processed and **disseminated** through computer in the form of bit.
- **Interaction**. An important concept of digital media is human-computer interaction which is quite difficult to realize in the simulative fields.
- Interesting Internet, digital games, digital television, mobile streaming media, etc, offer a broad entertainment space, which fully reflects the entertaining of the media.
- **Integration**. The digital media is an application integrated with text, image, video, sound, animation and established on the basis of digitalization. At present, the applied range of digital media is far wider than that of the traditional media, such as CAI, audio books, digital movies and business information consultation.
- **Convergence**. At present, the transmission of digital media needs the convergence of information technology and humanities and art, for example, in the development of multi-media products, the technical expert should be responsible for the technology planning while the arts and the designer should be responsible for all visible contents of the multi-media products and understand the needs of the users.

The digital media can be classified into the static media and the continuous media according to the time attribute. The common text and image belong to the static media; however, the content is changed as the time goes by Such digital media as sound and video, however, belong to the latter. The digital media can be categorized into the natural media and the synthetic media according to the source attribute. The digital media that **obtains** from the scenery, sound, etc in the objective world, digitalizes

End-User
终端用户

USB flash disk
U盘

digitization
数字化

disseminate [di'semineit]
vt. 宣传，传播

Interaction
交互性

integration [,inti'greiʃən]
n. 集成，综合

convergence [kən'və:dʒəns]
n. [数] 收敛，会聚，集合

obtain [əb'tein]
vt. 获得

them through the special device and encodes them belongs to the natural media, such as the pictures shoot by the digital camera and video shoot by the digital video. However, the text, music, sound, image and animation that are processed by the computer belong to the synthetic media. The digital media can be divided into the single media and the multi-media according to the **component** elements. The single media means the media that consist of single information carrier while the multi-media is made up of several information carriers both in the form of expression and the form of transmission.

component [kəm'pəunənt]
adj. 组成的，构成的

Definition of Digital Meida Technology

The digital media technology, by means of computer technology and network communication technology **comprehensively** process the text, sound, image, picture and other media information and realize all **aspects** of the expression, record, process, storage, transmission, display and management of the digital media, making the abstract information into a perceptive, manageable and interactive software and hardware technology. The digital media technology mainly studies the theories, methods, technologies and systems related to the acquisition, processing, storage, transmission, management, security and output of the digital media information. Therefore, the digital media technology is comprehensive application technology including the computer technology, network communication technology and information processing technology. Its main technology includes:

comprehensively [kɔmri'hensivli']
adv. 包括地，包括一切地
aspect ['æspekt]
n. 方面，相位

- Digital sound processing technology. It includes the sound and its traditional technology, digitalized sound technology, digital sound editing technology and sound encoding technology.
- Digital image processing technology. It includes the digital image computer **representation**, digital image acquisition technology and image editing and creative design.
- Digital video processing technology. It includes the digital video and its editing technology and after effect processing technology.
- Digital animation design. It includes the animation fundamental principle, animation design basis, digital two

representation [,reprizen'teiʃən]
n. 代表，表现

dimension animation technology, and the creative design of digital animation.
- Digital games design. It includes the software technology and creative design of games related to the games design.
- Digital media compression technology. It includes the digital media **compression** and its classification, general data compression technology and digital media compression standard.
- Digital media storage
- Digital media management and protection
- Digital media transmission technology. It includes the streaming media transmission technology, **P2P** technology and **IPTV** technology.
- Virtual reality technology. It includes the dynamic virtual environment modeling technology, **real-time** three-dimensional graph generation technology, **stereo** display and **sensor** technology, system integration technology and application system development tool.

Digital Media Technology Application

According to the specific content and application objects related to the digital media, the application of digital media technology can be divided into digital movie and television, digital games, digital broadcasting, digital advertisement, digital publishing, etc. The digital movie and television is a **brand new** field, including digital movie, digital TV, **streaming media**, audio-video technology, and mobile TV. The trend of digitalization in the movie and television field is **irresistible**. From the creative design, production and transmission of the movie and television, the digital technology will be used in more and more links, making people feel convenience in technology, rich in contents and integration in forms, which are brought by the digitalization. The digital games are the games developed by means of digital technology and played on the digital **platforms** of digital device. Using the information platform, they provide audio, light and entertainment to the consumers. They include online games, mobile games, PC **console** games and video games. The digital games are not only a brand new mass media with special charm and **participation**, but also a powerful culture

compression [kəm'preʃən]
n. 压缩，浓缩

P2P
peer-to-peer
点对点技术
IPTV
Internet Protocol Television
网络电视
real-time
实时
stereo ['steriəu]
n. 立体声，立体声系统
sensor ['sensə]
n. 传感器

brand new
全新的，崭新的
streaming media
流媒体
irresistible [ˌiri'zistəbl]
adj. 不可抵抗的，不能压制的

platform ['plætfɔ:m]
n. 月台，站台；讲台，平台
console [kən'səul]
n. [计] 控制台；[电] 操纵台
participation [pɑ:ˌtisi'peiʃən]
n. 参与，分享

transmission tool, which take a critical position in the digital media. The digital broadcasting refers to the processing of encoding, **modulating**, transmitting, decoding and playing of digitalized sound signal and various other digital signals under the digitalization condition. With the digital technology rapidly stepping in the broadcasting business, the digital broadcasting has come to the era of digital multi-media broadcasting. The audience can see and hear the rich and varied digital multi-media programs by computer, mobile phones, **portable** receiving terminals and vehicle's terminal. The digital advertisement aided by the digital media technology and relied on the carrier of digital media, spreads or publishes the business information. It keeps **innovation** in the form of advertisement, and at the same time, gives the advertisement more direction, interaction and real time characteristics which perfectly meet various needs of enterprises and consumers. The common digital advertisement includes online advertising, steaming media advertisement, **wireless** advertisement, virtual advertisement, digital television advertisement and digital games advertisement. With the development of digital media technology, the advertisement production technology and the publishing forms have both been improved and extended. Relying on the traditional publication resources and applying the digital media technology, it gives birth to a brand new mode of information transmission, which has the characteristics of big information capacity, various transmission forms, high efficiency and convenience, **flexibility** and interaction, quick search, mass storage, low cost, easy editing and environmental friendly. This is the digital publication.

In spite of these limitations, expert systems have proved their value in a number of important applications. It is hoped that these limitations will only encourage the student to **pursue** this important branch of computer science.

modulate ['mɔdjuleit]
vt. 调节，调整，（信号）调制

portable ['pɔːtəbl]
adj. 手提的，便携式的

innovation [,inəu'veiʃən]
n. 创新，革新

wireless ['waiəlis]
adj. 无线的，无线电的

flexibility [,fleksi'biliti]
n. 灵活性，弹性，适应性

pursue [pə'sjuː]
vt. 追赶，追踪，追击，继续，从事

Exercises

Ⅰ. **Fill in the blanks with the information given in the text.**

1. Digital media technology is including _____, _____ and information processing technology and other kinds of comprehensive application of information technology.

2. Students in the digital media technology option learn about the latest advances in communicating with a global audience using digital media technology. Subjects studied include _____, audio, photography,

computer graphics and animation.

3. Almost everyone discovers that digital media technology and the virtual environment it creates have brought Thomas changes to economic, cultural and ideological _____ of the society, leading mankind into "digital existence".

4. Due to the boosting of the Digital Media Technology, 3D Graphics Technology has fully developed. It is one of the most active _____ in the computer science.

5. _____ must be stored in an electronic way, so there is a lot of digital content on the internet today, including text content, pictures, audio content, as well as video content.

Ⅱ. Translate the following passages from English into Chinese.

Digital media production is the process in which digital files are created, enhanced, encoded, and distributed using numerous methods of processing via computer hardware and software applications. These files represent assorted media types, including audio, video, graphic, and written content as seen on the Internet. These media types are most often specifically coded to function in a pre-determined environment or platform. Digital media production exists as the primary discipline for the creation of digital music, streaming video, and other content made available to a mass audience. This industry makes it possible for the world to see and hear things differently and with more imagination.

The definition of digital media production is constantly changing as the boundaries of technology expand each day. In many cases, digital media production refers to the production of visual media, as in digitally enhanced animation; or new media creation, including website creation, multimedia authoring, and the creation of computer games. Since digital media files are based on the binary numeral system, which refers to the individual states of zero and one as a representation of data, the types and possibilities of creation are endless as technology progresses. Logically, digital media production encompasses an area responsible for multiple processes, which in turn has the potential to create media of numerous genres and styles.

Section B   Virtual Reality Technology

Remember watching "The **Matrix**" for the first time? Remember the mixed emotions of **awe** and excitement you felt at that time? Virtual reality technology is no more a thing of fiction these days! Let's find out more about this **coming-of-age** technology and find out some fascinating facts about it.

"What is real? How do you define real? If you're talking about what you can hear, what you can smell, taste and feel, then real is simply electrical signals interpreted by your brain."

So, what is all this hype and **hoopla** over the likes of virtual and **augmented** reality technology all about? Is it really possible to experience a Matrix-like phenomenon in the real world? To continue with the Matrix **theme**, is the world, as we know it, the REAL world? Well, that was a **rhetoric** question meant to **tease** the technologically curious nerve inside you! Or was it? Okay, enough playing! It's time to get down to the **brass tacks** now! So

matrix ['meitriks]
n. 矩阵，基质，模型
The Matrix
黑客帝国
awe [ɔː]
n. 敬畏
coming-of-age
n. 成年，成熟
morpheus ['mɔːfjuːs]
n. 梦神，睡神，睡眠
hoopla ['huːplɑː]
n. 投环套物游戏，喧闹
augment [ɔːg'ment]
vt. 增加，增大
theme [θiːm]
n. 主题，主旋律，题目

what is this technology all about? Let's get us some answers!

A Layman's Take on Virtual Reality

A computer **simulated** environment that either resembles or substitutes the physical reality so well that the viewer is left wondering whether what he sees or feels is the real thing or if it's all in his mind is known as virtual reality. The concept of virtual reality technology includes all such computer and IT based technologies that can perfectly simulate and project any place or situation of either the real or imaginary plane to the eyes or any other **sensory organ**. However, presently, the major **chunk** of virtual reality experiences fall under the **category** of visual virtual reality with auditory effects coming from additional appendages like speakers, headphones, etc. Research and product development is being carried out for new varieties of virtual reality techniques and technology which would be capable of extending **stimuli** to other sensory organs like touch, taste, smell, etc. The most common and commercial examples of virtual reality technology can be seen in the forms of virtual reality games (such as Dactyl Nightmare, Hero, Legend Quest, Grid Busters, **Mage**, etc.) and virtual reality glasses, gloves and other gear used for playing such games. You can check out the movie How to Make a Monster by Stan Winston to get an idea about how physical reality and virtual reality can, at times, get **confusingly** inter-tangled!

How Virtual Reality Works

In order to grasp the mechanics of virtual reality, we first need to understand what virtual reality space is. A virtual reality space is created using sensory output generated by a computer that is 3D enabled. Such a virtual space enables the users to carry on interactions with the virtual environment while still being in the physical environment. To create an experience of virtual reality, the effect of **telepresence** must be present. The term telepresence refers to the feeling of the user that he/she is present at a location different from his true, physical location. This different location, other than the actual physical location, is what we call the virtual reality environment. The **essence** of complete telepresence is very important as without telepresence, the virtual reality experience would be **flawed** and **incomplete**.

---

rhetoric ['retərik]
adj. 花言巧语的
tease [ti:z]
vt. 取笑，戏弄
brass tacks
基本事实，事实真相
layman ['leimən]
n. 外行，门外汉
simulate ['simjuleit]
vt. 模仿
sensory organ
感觉器官
chunk [tʃʌŋk]
n. 数据块
category ['kætigəri]
n. 种类，分类
stimuli ['stimulai]
n. 刺激，刺激物

mage [meidʒ]
n. 博学者，魔术师

confusingly [kən'fju:ziŋli]
ad. 难懂地，容易混淆地

telepresence
n. 思科网真，远程呈现
essence ['esəns]
n. 本质，实质
flaw [flɔ:]
vt. 使无效，使破裂，使有缺陷
incomplete [,inkəm'pli:t]
adj. 不完全的，不完备的

There are two technological aspects which sum up the concept of telepresence——**immersion** and interaction. Immersion is the phenomenon by which the user gets the feeling of being one with the virtual environment. He/she feels as if he exists in the virtual world and is **sensorily immersed** in his/her virtual surroundings. Immersion consists of the virtual eyes and ears of the user and employs the mechanics of sight and sound. Interaction is the phenomenon by which the user is able to interact with the virtual world as well as with other users in it. This aspect consists of the communication **parameters** and the **modus operandi** of interaction may be via speech or text.

immersion [i'mə:ʃən]
n. 沉浸，陷入

sensorily [ˌsensərili]
adv. 感觉地；传递感觉地
immerse [i'mə:s]
vt. 沉浸，使陷入

parameter [pə'ræmitə]
n. 参数
modus operandi
做法

Virtual Reality Tools

The tools and technology used to create virtual reality environments include (but may not be limited to) virtual **graphics library**, programming languages that are commonly used for games, **scripting** and web applications (such as Java, C++, Perl, Python, etc.), multi threading technology (for better **cluster** computing and enhanced multi-user interactions), etc. Telepresence can be induced by using standard computer interaction devices such as the mouse, keyboard, etc. or by employing multi interaction devices including wired gloves, motion trackers, digitizers, 3D scanners, eye-trackers, ODT, etc.

graphics library
图形库
script [skript]
vt. 脚本
cluster ['klʌstə]
n. 群，簇

The technology of virtual reality employs all these and many more tools and techniques to impart a virtual environment and interaction that very closely resembles and is as good as physical environment and interactions! Nowadays, besides games and 3D movies, we can see virtual reality technology around us in the form of virtual babies, virtual pets, virtual partners/**spouses** (yes, even that! Check out the site V-girl; it features virtual girlfriends!), virtual makeover, etc. We can only keep our fingers crossed over what other virtual wonders this neo-space-age technology has in store for this and future generations!

spouse [spaus]
n. 配偶

Exercises

Ⅰ. **Fill in the blanks with the information given in the text.**

1. Compared with 3D visualization, virtual reality technology is a process to _____ the real world by computer while _____ reality is an advanced technology, which can improve the integration between the

virtual world and the real world.

2. This paper presents the features of virtual reality technology such as multi-sensory, input nature, autonomy and _____ and so on, and virtual reality technology can be _____ into four types which is desktop type, immersion type, enhanced type, network distributed type, and its applications and development trend in the military field, etc.

3. Virtual Reality is a computer generated artifical _____ or object, allows to interact with operator. So it is a closed system to create the experience of "being there". This technology has _____ the human cognitive medium and bound, changed the traditional simulation way, and attracted close attention on many disciplines.

4. In practice, it is currently very difficult to create a high-fidelity virtual reality _____, due largely to technical limitations on processing power, image resolution and communication_____. However, those limitations are expected to eventually be overcome as processor, imaging and data communication technologies become more powerful and cost-effective over time.

5. Virtual reality generally involves a computer-generated, multidimensional sensory environment that users experience via _____ tools that enable them to _____ themselves in the environment, navigate within it, and interact with objects and characters inhabiting the environment.

II. **Translate the following passages from English into Chinese.**

Applications of the three types of virtual reality technology have been used in a variety of fields. Education, industry, military, medicine and architectural design are just a few. Major examples of the importance of virtual reality include the fields of medicine and aviation. Surgeons make extensive use of virtual reality technology to simulate surgery, and scientists working on new drugs use virtual reality to create molecules to learn how they interact with one another. Building new prototypes to test aircraft and spacecraft once proved an expensive process, but with virtual reality, engineers can build virtual models and test those models in a simulated environment.

Advancements in virtual reality technology evidences are considered exciting for their potential. Constructing a prototype of an aircraft or spacecraft is one thing, but using virtual reality to model the universe and make trips to other planets or even beyond is another. Limitations exist in the form of raw processing power, graphics and even understanding how the brain works, but technology and science have worked together to close the gaps in knowledge. Many people hope that humans might——someday——glimpse the quintessence of virtual reality.

Section C Virtual Reality Modeling Language

Our physical world is defined by **three dimensional** objects that react to different stimulus. In the computer world it is difficult to simulate worlds that are as accurate as our physical world. For example, people that use the Internet can see a graphical/text representation of a two dimensional world. We can move **around the world**, but it does not represent exactly what the world is. The need of a more realistic data representation motivated the creation of a Virtual Reality Modeling Language (VRML). This standard establishes a language that describes and specifies virtual three dimensional worlds. There are two

three dimensional
三维

around the world
世界各地，环游世界

versions of this standard, VRML 1.0 and VRML 2.0.

VRML 1.0 was designed to meet the following requirements: **platform independence**, extensibility and ability to work well over low-**bandwidth** connections. It was based on a format called Open Inventor ASCII File Format, that was created by **Silicon Graphics Inc**. This format supports complete descriptions of 3D scenes with **polygonally** rendered objects, lighting, materials, networking, **ambient** properties and realism effects.

VRML 1.0 defines a way for objects to read and write themselves. Objects are define as nodes. Nodes are divided in three different classes that represent the object's characteristics; which are: form, properties and groups. The form nodes describe the geometric specification of an object. The properties nodes define the following items: the appearance of the matrix's properties or transformations and the camera and light effects. The groups nodes contain a conjunction of objects that form a complete object.Each VRML 1.0 function **implicitly** states a coordinate space for each object defined in the file. It **explicitly** defines and composes a set of 3D objects and multimedia. It also defines specific hyperlinks to other files and applications, and how the objects work.

VRML Architecture Group

The **VRML Architecture Group** (VAG) was organized to centralize the selection of newer VRML standards (VRML 2.0). They requested from the VRML-interested community proposals that would add functionality to the next **revisions** of VRML. The Group received six proposals. A brief description of four of them follows.

One of the proposals was **Holoweb**, submitted by **Sun Microsystems**. It was a binary file format and run time **API** for 3D worlds in **real time animation**. It worked over the Internet and permitted , for the first time, the use of Java as a significant integrated tool for 3D real time animations. It also allowed for the use of compressed 3D geometry to reduce the file sizes and improve performance on large worlds.

Another company that submitted a proposal was IBM Japan. Their proposal was called Reactive Virtual Environment.

---

platform independence
跨平台性，平台独立性
bandwidth
宽带
Open Inventor
SGI 公司开发的基于 OpenGL 的面向对象三维图形软件开发包
Silicon Graphics Inc.
硅谷图像公司，简称 SGI
polygonally ['pɔləgənəli]
n. 多边形
ambient ['æmbiənt]
n. 周围环境
implicitly [im'plisitli]
adv. 含蓄地，暗中地
explicitly [ik'splisitli]
adv. 明确地，明白地

VRML Architecture Group
虚拟现实建模语言体系结构组
revision [ri'viʒən]
n. 修正，修订本
Holoweb
全息网
Sun Microsystems
美国 Sun 微系统公司, 简称 Sun 公司
API
abbr. Application Program Interface
应用程序界面

This proposal permitted the user to interact in real time with time-dependent and **autonomous** virtual worlds. This was achieved with the use of **callbacks** and event models.

The other proposal was the Microsoft Active VRML. It arrived in second place in votes. According to Todd Ferkingstad (of Microsoft): "**As for** Active VRML, Earlier this year we've submitted this technology for customer review and feedback. Since then, we've been evolving the technology based on this feedback, and accordingly we've changed the name to **ActiveX** Animation. ActiveX Animation targets interactive animation **embedded** in Web pages, while VRML 2.0 targets immersive 3D spaces. ActiveX Animation provides support for 2D and 3D graphics, **sprites**, audio, and time modeling, While VRML 2 is focused on 3D. Microsoft will be supporting both in Internet Explorer. There will be **announcements** on ActiveX Animation in the next few months." —— posted by Braden N. McDaniel.

In contrast to IBM and Sun, Microsoft actually marketed its technology. ActiveX technology is currently a standard for other software applications.

Moving Worlds was the proposal selected as the new VRML 2.0 standard. It was created by Silicon Graphics Inc. and **Netscape**. It contained a number of interesting innovations. For example, motion detection features let you generate events when the user moves the pointing device around a surface or if it clicks-and-drags an object. The user can define a sound source in a 3D space. Additionally this proposal defines new nodes that allow you to add ground, sky backdrops and different **topologies** to a scene. A system for **collision detection** was added to ensure that solid objects react like real objects. This provides the ability to create moving objects like birds and different animals, and with the use of Scripting it is possible to give a **semblance** of intelligence to the objects. With these new VRML 2.0 features the addition of realism to the static geometry of worlds can be accomplished.

Distributed Virtual Environment

The creation of networked virtual environments is made easier with VRML. This type environment is called Distributed

animation [ˌæniˈmeiʃən]
n. 动画
autonomous [ɔːˈtɔnəməs]
adj. 自治的，自主的，自发的
callback [ˈkɔːlbæk]
n. 回调
As for
关于，至于
ActiveX [ˈæktivˈeks]
n. 插件；控件
embed [imˈbed]
vt. 栽种，使嵌入，使插入
sprite [sprait]
n. 妖精，精灵；[计]游戏界面
announcement [əˈnaunsmənt]
n. 通告，宣告，公告，发表

Moving Worlds
动态境界
Netscape
美国网景公司

topology [təˈpɔlədʒi]
n. 拓扑学，拓扑结构
collision detection
碰撞检测；[计]冲突检出
semblance [ˈsembləns]
n. 外貌，假装，类似

Virtual Environment (DVE). DVE allows a group of geographically separate users to interact in real time. This **user group** could scale up to thousands of users. The environment in which a DVE is immersed is 3D to the eye and the ear. VRML possesses much of the capabilities necessary for this work, but VRML does not have good support for more than one user. Currently efforts such as the Living Worlds and Open Community Standard proposals are attempting to expand VRML into a standard for DVEs.

user group
用户组，用户协会

The Living Worlds and Open Community Standard need the capability for user interaction because they are planning to elaborate a software capable of social interaction. The software can provide certain rules for the social interaction between the users. Some of the rules of this software are the ones that we use in real life. For example when we have a meeting we have to know where, with and when the meeting will take place.

Examples of VRML Graphics

In this section you can see some simple examples of what VRML can do. Those examples was obtain from VRML 2.0 source book write by Andrea L. Ames, David R. Nadeau and John L. Moreland.

In Fig. 12.1, you can see a VRML representation of a **lightbulb**. It is drawn in a dark gray, the lightbulb socket in brass, and the lightbulb itself glows a pure white. The Material node used for the lighbulb's sphere specifies an emissiveColor field value to cause the bulb to glow bright white. The diffuse Color field value of the same node sets the shading color to black, which turns off shading and gives the shape a more pure glow.

lightbulb
电灯泡

Fig. 12.1 a VRML representation of a lightbulb

Using a Switch node, you can build multiple versions of a shape, include all of them in your VRML world. The Fig. 12.2 shows a version of the switch ability. Setting whichChoice field of the node to 2 you can obtain the border effects. For end the effect you need that sings are always readable. For do that you need to add a **billboard** group. This billboard group are automatically rotated to face the viewer as the viewer moves through your world. The billboard use in the Fig. 12.2 has vertical axis rotation. Three box nodes are added outside the billboard group node, creating a base and ground for the sign. As the viewer moves around the sign, the pole and ground remain **stationary**, but the café sign automatically **pivots** about a **vertical axis** to follow the viewer. If the viewer moves upward and **hovers** looking down at the sign from angle, the sign pivots on the vertical axis, but does no **tilt** upward to face the viewer. The sign can make tilt upward the only change are in the axis of Rotation field value of the Billboard node.

billboard ['bilbɔ:d]
n. 广告牌，布告板
stationary ['steiʃənəri]
adj. 固定的，静止的
pivot ['pivət]
n. 枢轴，中心点
vertical axis
垂直轴；纵轴
hover ['hɔvə]
n. 徘徊，盘旋，犹豫
tilt [tilt]
vt. 使倾斜，使翘起

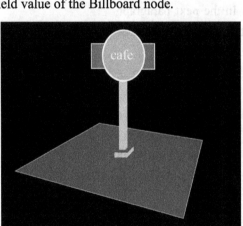

Fig. 12.2 A café sign within a billboard

An existing example of VRML is the model representations of the Star Wars technology. These models do not have good definition, but show the wonderful things that you can do using your imagination. For example in Fig.12.3 shows a representation of the X-Wing Fighter plane that Luke Skywalker used. This representation was done at NASA. In the Fig. 12.4 we can see the famous R2-D2.

Fig. 12.3 Model of the X-Wing   Fig. 12.4 R2-D2

Conclusion

VRML is a powerful tool for three dimensional graphic representations. Its applications vary from art to engineering, being data visualization the main area of development. However, VRML technology has its disadvantages. In the next paragraph we are will discuss what we consider are **the pros and cons** of this technology.

Advantages:
- Ease of drawing 3D objects with movements and collision detection: The **syntax** of the VRML language is relatively simple and flexible. This makes it easy for programmers to learn. Also its easy integration with other languages, i.e. Javascript and Java, contributes to its flexibility and extensibility.
- Accessibility: The low cost and availability of the software (VRML browser or plugins) favor the Internet community's interest in this technology.

Disadvantages:
- Inconsistency of the browser's navigation methods：The way you can **manipulate** a virtual world depends on the navigation tools that your browser provides. For example, with browser X you can rotate an image by clicking on the rotate icon, clicking on the edge of the image that you want to rotate and moving the pointing device until the desired position is reached. In contrast,

the pros and cons
正面和反面的

syntax ['sintæks]
n. 语法，句法

manipulate [mə'nipjuleit]
vt. 操纵，操作

with browser Y you can rotate an image by clicking a rotate icon that will move the icon automatically without the need of selecting the point to rotate. This situation can lead to adaptation problems between the two browsers.
- Browser's refresh **velocity**: In some browsers, navigating through virtual worlds is not smooth and in some cases it is quite slow. **High resolution** drawings imply more updates when moving an object, which slows the drawing update. In addition to this one must consider the issue of the graphic hardware on the machine. Better graphics processors will enhance speed of redrawing.

velocity [vi'lɔsiti]
n.[力] 速率，迅速，周转率
high resolution
高分辨，[光] 高分辨率

The VRML technology is still in its infancy. There are new proposals for the next revision of the standard. We consider that the **user interface** issue should be addressed in a future revision, specially the navigation methods of the browser. Usability of navigation methods on VRML browser can be a topic for future research.

user interface
用户界面

Exercises

I. Fill in the blanks with the information given in the text.

1. VRML is _____ to be used on the Internet, intranets, and local client systems. VRML is also intended to be a universal interchange format for integrated 3D _____ and multimedia.

2. Originally, there was VRML 1.0. This was a very simplistic language, and after a while was revised into _____, which changed the file structure and added a lot of new _____, such as animation, Interactive sensors etc.

3. Discussions continued on the mailing list on how to adapt the Open Inventor format, which SGI had now placed in the public domain, to include _____ and _____ features.

4. Six proposals were received: Active VRML from Microsoft, Dynamic Worlds from GMD and others, _____ from Sun, Moving Worlds from Silicon Graphics and others, Out of this World from Apple, and _____ from IBM Japan.

5. In examine mode, the user can _____ an object or _____ it in relation to the viewpoint. A fly mode simulates moving through the scene, with mouse or keyboard input controlling speed and direction.

II. Translate the following passages from English into Chinese.

The purpose of a programming system is to make a computer easy to use. To do this, it furnishes languages and various facilities that are in fact programs invoked and controlled by language features. But these facilities are bought at a price: the external description of a programming system is ten to twenty times as large as the external description of the computer system itself. The user finds it far easier to specify any particular function, but there are far more to choose from, and far more options and formats to remember.

Ease of use is enhanced only if the time gained in functional specification exceeds the time lost in learning, remembering, and searching manuals. With modern programming systems this gain does exceed the cost, but in recent years the ratio of gain to cost seems to have fallen as more and more complex functions have been added.

Grammar12 英语科技文献的阅读技巧(Ⅱ)

3. 略读(Skimming)

略读(Skimming)是一种很重要的阅读技巧,是指快速地阅读,在查询大量英语文献时非常有用。略读是快速阅读文章,目的是了解文章主题思想。略读时不需要逐字去读,而是寻找文章内关键词语、主题句,从而了解文章的主题思想。在这个基础上,决定是否选取此资料,是否需要进一步精读。这样既节省时间,迅速地为自己得到想要的信息,也可以在短时间内获得大量地信息。

例如:

Ever since computers became available in the 1950s, it has been software that exploited its power to solve application problems. Machine code, capable of driving the raw hardware, was the first language available to programmers. Sequences of code statements were the earliest form of software. It was soon recognized that the communication medium between programmer and computer is a critical factor in the programming productivity and quality of the overall software product.

自从 20 世纪 50 年代计算机开始进入实用阶段以来,软件就在解决应用问题的能力方面崭露头角。控制基本硬件的机器代码是程序员使用的第一种语言。顺序代码语句是软件的最早形式。人们很快就认识到,编程效率和整个软件产品质量的关键因素是程序员和计算机之间的通信手段。

在阅读过程中,要时刻提醒自己这段文字的关键语句是什么,主要描述什么内容,主题思想是什么等。

例如:

Some of the benefits and flexibility of object-oriented programming stem from this separation of function invocation and implementation. The invocation of a functionality is termed "the sending of a message to an object". The execution of its implementation is termed "the receiver of the message executes the corresponding method." The separation of message and method greatly adds to the flexibility possible in an object-oriented program. In our example messages are sent to the plane objects. Each plane object receives a message and executes its desired behavior. In effect, our program "computes" by sending messages to all participating objects. In general, we can observe an object-oriented program as a collection of objects that communicate by sending messages.

面向对象程序设计的一些优点和灵活性源于将功能的引发和实现相互分离这一技术。功能的引发可表达为"把信息送给对象"。实现的过程被称为"信息接收者执行相应的方法"。信息和方法的分离大大地增加了面向对象程序的灵活性。在我们的例子中,信息是送给平面对象的,每一平面对象接收一个信息并执行其所要求的行为。实际上,我们的程序通过向所有在场的对象发送信息而进行"计算"。一般来讲,我们可以把面向对象的程序看成是通过发送信息进行通信的各个对象的集合。

实际上，在日常阅读中，我们常常不自觉就将三种阅读方法(精读、泛读、略读)综合使用。在了解英语三种基本阅读技能和技巧后，就要通过练习，熟练掌握这些阅读技能。掌握了这些阅读技能后，便有了得力助手，就可在浩如烟海的英语文献海洋中随心畅游，迅速查到自己所需要的资料。

参考译文

Section A 数字媒体技术概述

媒体及数字媒体

我们可以把媒体看成是信息的各种表现形式，按照国际电信联盟的定义，媒体可分为感觉媒体、表述媒体、表现媒体、存储媒体和传输媒体五种。

数字媒体是一个应用领域非常广泛的新兴学科，它以信息科学和数字技术为主导，以大众传播理论为依据，以现代艺术为指导，将信息传播技术应用到文化、艺术、商业、教育和管理等领域，是科学与艺术高度融合的综合交叉学科。它涉及计算机软硬件与应用、电子、通信与广播技术，同时涉及数字媒体内容管理、数字媒体的版权、传媒艺术与文化创意产业、消费电子等领域。数字媒体包括文字、图形、图像、音频、视频影像和动画等各种形式以及传播形式和传播内容中采用的数字化技术应用，即信息的采集、存取、加工和分发的数字化过程。一种广义的对数字媒体的定义为，数字媒体就是以数字化形式存储、处理和传播信息的媒体，如数字化的文本、图片、音频和视频等。所以，数字媒体的主体应该是技术、内容、应用和人。由中华人民共和国科技部牵头制定的2005年12月26日发布的《2005中国数字媒体技术发展白皮书》(简称"白皮书")中这样定义了数字媒体：数字媒体是数字化的内容作品，以现代网络为主要传播载体，通过完善的服务体系，分发到终端和用户进行消费的全过程。这个定义强调数字媒体的传播方式是通过网络，而将移动存储设备(光盘、U盘等)媒体内容排除在数字媒体的范畴之外。

数字媒体具有以下特性：

- 数字化。人们过去接触的媒体几乎都是以模拟的方式进行存储和传播的，而数字媒体却是以比特的形式通过计算机进行存储、处理和传播。
- 交互性。数字媒体还有一个很重要的概念就是人机交互作用，这个在模拟领域里面是比较难以实现的。
- 趣味性。互联网、数字游戏、数字电视、移动流媒体等为人们提供了宽广的娱乐空间，媒体的趣味性被彻底地体现出来了。
- 集成性。媒体技术是结合文字、图形、影像、声音、动画等各种媒体的一种应用，并且建立在数字化处理的基础上。现在数字媒体的应用范围也比传统媒体更加广阔，如CAI、有声图书、数字电影、商情咨询等。
- 融合性。现在数字媒体传播需要信息技术与人文艺术的融合。例如，在开发多媒体产品时，技术专家需要负责技术规划，艺术家、设计师需要负责所有可视内容，了解受众的欣赏需求。

如果按照时间属性，数字媒体可以分为静止媒体和连续媒体两类。常见的文本和图片属于静止媒体，而内容随着时间变化的数字媒体，如音频和视频则属于后者。按照来源属性分，数字媒体可以分成自然媒体和合成媒体。客观世界存在的景物、声音等经过特殊的设备进行数字化和编码处理后得到的数字媒体，如数码照相机拍摄的照片、数码摄像机摄录的影像等属于自然媒体，而经过计算机加工后生成(合成)的文本、音乐、语音、图像和动画等则属于合成媒体；按组成元素分，数字媒体又可以分成单一媒体和多媒体。由单一信息载体组成的媒体就是单一媒体，而多媒体在表现形式和传递方式上则体现为多种信息载体的组合。

数字媒体技术定义

数字媒体技术是以通过计算机技术和网络通信技术手段，综合处理文字、声音、图形、图像等媒体信息，实现数字媒体的表示、记录、处理、存储、传输、显示、管理等各个环节，使抽象的信息变成可感知、可管理和可交互的一种软硬件技术。数字媒体技术主要研究与数字媒体信息的获取、处理、存储、传输、管理、安全、输出等环节相关的理论、方法、技术与系统。所以，数字媒体技术是包括计算机技术、网络通信技术和信息处理技术等各类信息技术的综合应用技术，主要技术包括下面几个方面：

- 数字音频处理技术。该技术包括音频及其传统技术、音频的数字化技术、数字音频的编辑技术、话音编码技术。
- 数字图像处理技术。该技术包括数字图像的计算机表示方法、数字图像的获取技术、图像的编辑与创意设计。
- 数字视频处理技术。该技术包括数字视频及其编辑技术、后期特效处理技术等。
- 数字动画设计。该技术包括动画的基本原理、动画设计基础、数字二维动画技术、数字三维动画技术、数字动画的设计与创意等。
- 数字游戏设计。该技术包括游戏设计相关的软件技术、游戏设计与创意等。
- 数字媒体压缩技术。该技术包括数字媒体压缩技术及分类、通用的数据压缩技术、数字媒体压缩标准等。
- 数字媒体存储。
- 数字媒体管理与保护。
- 数字媒体传输技术。该技术包括流媒体传输技术、P2P 技术、IPTV 技术等。
- 虚拟现实技术。该技术包括动态虚拟环境建模技术、实时三维图形生成技术、立体显示和传感器技术、系统集成技术、应用系统开发工具等方面。

数字媒体技术的应用

根据数字媒体涉及的具体内容及应用对象，数字媒体技术的应用可分为数字影视、数字游戏、数字广播、数字广告、数字出版等领域。数字影视是一个全新的领域，包括数字电影、数字电视、流媒体、音视频技术、手机电视等。影视领域的数字化已是大势所趋，从影视创意、制作到传播各个环节都将更多地采用数字技术，使人们越来越多地感受到数字化所带来的技术上的便利性、内容上的丰富性和形式上的融合性。数字游戏是以数字技术为手段设计开发，并以数字化设备为平台实施的各种游戏。它以信息平台提供声光娱乐给一般消费大众，包括网络游戏、手机游戏、单机游戏、电视游戏等。数字游戏是一种全新的具有特别吸引力和参与性的大众媒体，又是具有巨大能量的文化传播的工具，在数字媒体中占据着极其重要的地位。数字广播是指将数字化的音频信号以及各种数据信号，在数字状态下进行各种编码、调制、传递、解码、播放等处理。随着数字技术迅速介入广播业务领域，数字广播已经进入了数字多媒体广播的时代，受众通过计算机、手机、便携式接收终端、车载接收终端等多种接收装置，就可以收听、收看到丰富多彩的数字多媒体节目。数字广告借助数字媒体技术，依托数字媒体这个载体，传播或者发布商业信息，不仅在广告形式上持续创新，同时赋予了广告更多的针对性、交互性和实时性等特点，而这些特点正好满足了企业和消费者的各种需求。常见的数字广告有网络广告、流媒体广告、无线广告、虚拟广告、数字电视广告、数字游戏广告等。随着数字媒体技术的发展，广告的制作技术与发布形式都得到了提高与拓展。依托传统出版的资源和应用数字媒体技术，诞生了一种全新的信息传播方式，它具有信息容量大、形式多样、高效便捷、灵活互动、快速查询、海量存储、成本低廉、编辑方便以及更加环保等特点，这就是数字出版。

Section B 虚拟现实技术

是否记得第一次看《黑客帝国》？是否记得那既敬畏又激动而百感交集时的情景？如今，虚拟现实技术已不再是科幻之物了！让我们更多地了解这一成熟技术和一些惊人的事实。

"什么是真实？你是如何定义它的？如果你在谈论你的所见所闻，那么现实仅仅是你大脑解读的电信号。"

所以，虚拟和增强现实技术的噱头到底是什么？在现实世界中，是否真正可能体验到黑客帝国式的矩阵生活？继续《黑客帝国》的主题，我们所熟知的世界，是否是真实的？这是个设问句，有意取笑你对科技的好奇心！不是吗？ 好了，玩够了！现在是回到基本事实的时候了！那什么是科技呢？让我们获取一些答案！

门外汉从事虚拟现实

在一个与物理现实相似或足以替代物理现实的计算机模拟环境中，观察者不由自主怀疑他所见所感觉之物是否真实或者怀疑在他的脑子里知道的全是虚拟现实。虚拟现实技术的概念包括所有能够完美地模拟和投影任何地点或任何真实或虚平面情景到眼睛或任何其他感觉器官的所有基于计算机和IT技术。然而现在，相当部分的虚拟现实体验都属于视觉虚拟现实一类，它的听觉效果来自像扬声器、耳机等额外附属物。对新的视觉虚拟现实技术和科研产品开发已经展开，这些新技术将刺激器官延伸至触觉、味觉等感觉器官，最常见的虚拟现实技术和商业运用典范在虚拟现实游戏(如手足指趾梦魇、英雄、探索传奇、网格爆破、魔术师等)中可见。此类游戏运用了虚拟现实眼镜、手套和其他装备。你可以看看由Stan Winston主演的《人造怪物》以获取物理现实和虚拟现实时不时地混淆起来的概念。

虚拟现实如何工作？

为掌握虚拟现实工作机制，首先，我们需理解什么是虚拟现实空间。虚拟现实空间是由3D计算机生成通过感官输出而创造出来的。此种虚拟现实空间让用户在虚拟环境中进行互动，就像用户仍然处于物理环境中。为了创造虚拟现实体验，我们必须要达到远程呈现效果。远程呈现一词指用户的处于一个不同于他或她真正的、实际的所在地点的感觉。这种实际地点之外的不同的地点就是我们所称的虚拟现实环境。完整的远程呈现的要素是非常重要的，因为没有远程呈现，虚拟现实体验将是有缺陷的、不完整的。

两个技术层面总结了远程呈现沉浸和交互概念。沉浸是一种现象。通过沉浸，用户获得一种与虚拟环境在一起的感觉。他或她感觉好像她存在于虚拟世界中；在感觉上，沉浸于他或他的虚拟环境中。沉浸由用户虚拟眼睛和耳朵组成并且运用视听机制。交互是另一种用户通过其能与虚拟世界及其虚拟世界中的其他用户互动的现象。这方面由通信参数组成，并且交互可能通过讲话或文字来实现。

虚拟现实工具

用于创造虚拟现实环境的工具和技术包括(但并不局限于)虚拟图形库、通常用于游戏的编程语言、脚本语言、网络运用(如Java、C++、Perl、Python等)、多线程技术(为了更好的簇计算和提高多用户交互)等。使用像鼠标、键盘等标准计算机交互设备能感应远程呈现或运用有线手套、运动跟踪器、3D扫描仪、眼动仪、OTD等多模式交互设备也能感应远程呈现。

虚拟现实技术运用这些甚至更多的工具和技术去创造虚拟交互环境，这种交互环境与现实环境非常相似，并与现实交互无异！当今，除了游戏和3D电影，我们发现虚拟现实技术就在我们身边，它以虚拟宝贝、虚拟宠物、虚拟伙伴、虚拟伴侣(是的！查看虚拟女孩网站，它以虚拟女朋友为特色！)、虚拟化妆等形式出现。我们只能交叉十指祈祷：这个新空间时代的技术将为我们这代和后代人们带来的虚拟奇观！

Section C 虚拟现实建模语言

我们的物质世界被定义为对不同刺激做出反应的三维物体。在计算机世界中,很难模拟与我们物质世界一样精确的世界。例如,使用网络的人们可以看到一个用图形或文本诠释的二维世界。我们可以移居到世界各地,但这并不能彻底诠释世界的意义。一种更为实际的数据表示法的需求激发了虚拟现实建模语言的产生(VRML)。该标准规定了一种用于描述和说明虚拟三维世界的语言。该标准有两个版本:VRML 1.0 和 VRML 2.0。

VRML 1.0 设计符合下列要求:平台无关性、可扩展性、低带宽链接下可工作良好。这是基于一种由 SGI 公司研发的被称为 OIV 的 ASCII 码文件格式。该格式支持通过多调渲染对象、照明、材料、网络、环境属性和现实的影响,对三维场景进行完整描述。

VRML 1.0 规定了一种对象自行读写数据的方法。对象被定义为结点。结点被分为三个不同层次,分别代表对象的形状结点、属性结点和群组结点。形状结点用于描述对象的几何形状。属性结点规定以下项目:描述几何形状物体外观属性的矩阵或转换结点、照相机和灯光效果结点。群组结点包含将结点结合使其形成一个完整对象。每个 VRML 1.0 函数必定为该文件中每一个定义对象制定一个坐标空间,明确规定并制作一套三维模型和多媒体。不仅如此,它还规定一个特定的超链接,链接到其他文件和应用程序,以及如何运作对象。

VRML 语言体系结构组

VRML 语言体系结构组(VAG)的创办是为了对新 VRML(VRML 2.0)标准进行集中选择。他们要求以 VRML 的利益群体为出发点,建议为新版本的 VRML 添加功能。该组收到 6 项建议。以下简要介绍其中 4 项。

其中一项建议是由 Sun 公司提出的全息网。该建议是采取二进制文件格式和 API 接口以实现 3D 实时动画世界。该软件通过联网,首次使 Java 成为 3D 实时动画的一个重要集成工具,并允许将大型世界的 3D 几何图形压缩,以减少文件大小和改进性能。

另一家提交建议的公司是 IBM 日本分公司。他们的建议称为动能的虚拟环境。这项建议允许用户能够在依赖时间和自主的虚拟世界中进行实时互动。该互动通过使用回叫信号和事件模型来完成。

另一项建议是微软的动能 VRML。该项建议在选票中排名第二。据(微软的)Todd •Ferkingstad 称:"关于动能 VRML,今年早些时候,我们已经提交这项技术,以便获取顾客的评论和反馈。从那时起,我们一直根据反馈不断改进技术,因此,我们更名为动画插件。动画插件针对的是将交互式动画嵌入到 Web 网页,而 VRML 2.0 针对的是设计浸入式的三维空间。动画插件为二维和三维的图形、游戏界面、音频和时间建模提供支持,而 VRML 2.0 强调三维。微软将在 IE 浏览器中,同时提供对二者的支持。在未来几个月里,动画插件将被发布"。——Branden N. McDaniel

与 IBM 和 Sun 公司相反,实际上微软是在推销其技术。ActiveX 技术是当前其他应用软件的一项技术标准。

动态境界的建议被选定作为 VRML 2.0 新版本的标准。该建议是由 SGI 公司和 Netscape 公司提出,其中包含了一些有趣的创新。例如,运动检测功能允许用户在移动表面定点设备或点击和拖动对象时,即可生成事件。用户可以定义一个三维空间中的声源。此外,该项建议规定新的结点,让您能够添加地面、天空背景和不同的拓扑结构到一个场景。添加碰撞检测系统确保固体物像实物一样坚实。该系统提供了创建移动物体的能力,如鸟类和不同的动物。脚本的运用使为对象创造一个智能外观成为可能。有了 VRML 2.0 的这些新功能,为世界静态几何添加现实主义将可以实现。

分布式虚拟环境

通过 VRML 使创造网络虚拟环境变得更为简单。这种类型的环境被称为分布式虚拟环境(DVE)。DVE

Chapter 12 Digital Media Technology

允许地域分离的用户进行实时互动。此用户组可以扩展到成千上万。DVE 使眼睛和耳朵都沉浸在三维环境中。VRML 拥有实现这项功能所必需的大部分能力,但 VRML 不具备对多个用户的良好支持。目前,居住世界以及开放社区的标准建议正在试图将 VRML 扩大为 DVE 的标准。

居住世界以及开放社区的标准需要用户的互动能力,因为他们正计划开发具备社交能力的软件。该软件可为用户间的社会互动提供一些特定规则。该软件的一些规则正是我们在现实生活中所使用的。例如,当我们参加一个会议时,我们必须知道会议举行的时间和地址。

VRML 图形的例子

在本节中,你可以通过一些简单的例子来了解 VRML 的功能。那些例子是摘自 Andrea L.Ames、David R. Nadeau 和 John L. Moreland 编写的 VRML 2.0 源书。

在图 12.1 中,你可以看到一个 VRML 代表一个灯泡。它被画成暗灰色,带黄铜灯泡插座的灯泡,其本身发出纯白色的光。用于灯罩的材质结点指定一个发射色场值,导致灯泡发出明亮的白色。一些结点的漫反射色场值将阴影颜色设置为黑色,这去掉了阴影使灯泡发出更纯净的光芒。

使用转换结点,你可以建立一个形状的多个版本,所有版本都在您的 VRML 中。图 12.2 显示了其中一个版本的转换能力。设置选择领域,可以产生你所要的边界效应。你可以设置唱歌时的效果。对此,你需要添加一个广告牌组。当观众移动时,该广告牌组会自动旋转,面对观众。图 12.2 中的广告牌使用垂直轴旋转。三个框结点添加在广告牌组结点的外部,建立一个地基和地面用于放置标志牌。当观众再次移动时,周围的标志牌和地面保持平稳,但咖啡厅标志牌会自动关于轴支点垂直,跟随观众移动。如果观众向上移动,徘徊于某个角度向下看标志牌,在纵轴上的标志牌不会倾斜向上面对观众。不过,也可以使该标志牌倾斜向上,唯一的变化是在广告牌结点字段值旋转轴。

一个 VRML 现成的例子是星球大战技术模型描写。这些模型不具有良好的清晰度,但可以发挥你的想象力表现出精彩纷呈的事物。例如,图 12.3 表示一架卢克天行者使用的 X 翼战机,该表象是在国家航空和航天局采集的。在图 12.4 中,我们可以看到著名的 R2-D2。

结论

VRML 是一种用于三维图形表示的强大工具。它的应用程序范围从艺术到工程,正在将数据可视化作为主要发展区域。然而,VRML 技术也有其缺点。下一段的内容是,依我们之见,对这项技术的优缺点进行讨论。

优点

- 易于绘制三维物体的运动和碰撞检测:VRML 语言的语法是相对简单和灵活的,这使程序员很容易学习,而且它很容易与其他语言集成,如 JavaScript 和 Java,这有利于提高它的灵活性和可扩展性。
- 可扩展性:低成本和软件的可用性(VRML 浏览器或插件),这项技术有利于网络群体的利益。

缺点

- 浏览器的导航方法不一致:操作虚拟世界的方式取决于浏览器提供的导航工具。例如,在浏览器 X 中,你可以通过单击旋转图标旋转图像,单击要旋转和移动指针设备的图像边缘,直到达到所需的位置。相反,在浏览器 Y 中,你可以通过单击旋转图标,不需要选择旋转的图标,就可以自动旋转图像。这种情况可能会导致这两个浏览器之间的适应问题。

- 浏览器刷新速度：在某些浏览器中，遨游于虚拟世界并不是那么顺利，在某些情况下，它是相当缓慢的。高分辨率图纸意味着当移动对象时，需要更多的更新，这会降低绘图更新的速度。除此之外，必须考虑机器上的图形硬件的问题。更好的图形处理器将提高重绘速度。

VRML 技术尚处于起步阶段。对于新标准的修订，还有许多的新的建议。我们认为，应在未来的修订中，解决用户界面的问题，特别是浏览器的导航方法的问题。VRML 浏览器上的导航方法的可用性可能会成为今后的研究主题。

Chapter 13　Embedded System
(嵌入式系统)

Section A　Introduction of Embedded System

Mars probe successfully landed on **Mars**, high-tech precision guided attack on a global scale during the war, the **implanted** electronic **pacemaker** has saved countless lives, and all of these can't be realized without embedded systems. So what is embedded system?

Definition of Embedded System

According to IEEE, embedded system is the devices used to control, **monitor**, or **assist** the operation of equipment, **machinery** or **plant**s. You can see embedded system is a complex of software and hardware also covers machinery and other **auxiliary** equipment.

This definition is a little abstract, currently a widely accepted definition in China is: embedded system is a special-purpose application-**oriented** computer system, based on computer technology, software and hardware can be cropped, adapting application system's **functionality**, **reliability**, cost, size, power consumption and strict requirements. So it's easier to understand. First of all, it is a computer system, including software and hardware resources. Besides it is some kind of application-oriented system, faced with some application in function, **reliability**, cost, size, power consumption, it has strict requirements.

The hardware in embedded systems includes processor/microprocessor, memory, and **peripheral** devices, graphics controller and I/O **ports**, and so on. Software includes operating system software (requires real-time and **multitasking**) and application programming, sometimes designers combined with both these. Application programming controls the system's function, and operating system controls the **interaction** between hardware and application programming. Whether embedded

---

mars [mɑːz]
n. 火星
implant [imˈplʌnt]
v. 深植，嵌入，移植
pacemaker [ˈpeismeikə]
n. [医]心脏起搏器，

monitor [ˈmɒnitə]
v. 监视，监督，监听
assist [əˈsist]
vt. 帮助，协助
machinery [məˈʃiːnəri]
n. 机械，(总称)机器
plant [plɑːnt]
n. 设备
auxiliary [ɔːgˈziljəri]
n. 辅助物
orient [ˈɔːriənt]
vt. 面向
functionality [ˌfʌŋkʃəˈnæliti]
n. 功能(尤指软件、硬件、机械或设备的功能)，功能性
reliability [riˌlaiəˈbiliti]
n. 可靠性
peripheral [pəˈrifərəl]
adj. 外围的，不重要的
ports [pɔːt]
n. [计] 端口
multitasking [ˈmʌltiˌtæskiŋ]
n. 多任务处理
interaction [ˌintəˈrækʃən]
n. 相互作用，相互影响

system is PC or not? No, embedded system is a special-purpose computer system, while PC is a common computer system. This is the most **fundamental** difference between them.

Embedded microprocessor is the **core** of embedded system hardware. The biggest difference between embedded microprocessor and common CPU is that embedded microprocessor mostly works for some special designed systems to some special users. It integrates different functions done by different boards in common CPU in a single chip, so it will **facilitate** embedded system to be smaller, and also has a high level of efficiency and reliability. Processor with embedded features in the world currently has more than 1000 species, popular **architecture** more than 30 series, for example, Power PC, 68000, MIPS, ARM series, 8051, P51XA, MCS-251, and so on.

Embedded operating system is an operating system that support embedded system application software, generally including hardware related low-level driver, kernel, device driver interface, standardization of communication protocols, GUI, browser, etc. Embedded operating systems have some common basic features of the common operating system, such as manage their increasingly complex system resources efficiently; **virtualizes** hardware in order to free developers from the busiest drivers' **porting** and maintenance; provide libraries, drivers, tools, and applications, etc. Compared with General purpose operating system, embedded operating systems have more **prominent** feature in real time system **efficiency**, dependency related to hardware, software **solidifying**, and specific application areas. Common embedded operating systems include VxWorks, Palm OS, Windows CE and Linux etc.

Characteristics of Embedded Systems

Embedded systems have the following characteristics.

(1) Special-purpose computer system. Embedded system is very **individualized**, its software systems and hardware systems are very closely combined. In general, to **transplant** for hardware systems, even within the same **brand** or a series of products also need to modify and change constantly depending on system hardware's change. At the same time different tasks often

fundamental [ˌfʌndəˈmentl]
adj. 基本的，根本的
core [kɔː]
n. 核心，果心，要点

facilitate [fəˈsiliteit]
vt. 促进，帮助，使……容易
architecture [ˈɑːkitektʃə]
n. 结构

virtualize [ˈvɜːtjuəlɪ]
vt. 虚拟化
porting [ˈpɔːtiŋ]
n. 移植(软件)
prominent [ˈprɔminənt]
adj. 显著的，杰出的，突出的
efficiency [iˈfiʃənsi]
n. 效率，功率
solidifying [səˈlidifaiŋ]
n. 凝固，固化

individualize [ˌindiˈvidjuəlaiz]
vt. 使具有个性，个别对待，具体化
transplant [trænsˈplɑːnt]
v. 移栽(植物)，移植(器官)
brand [brænd]
n. 烙印，商标，牌子，标记

require major changes to the system. To **compile** and download the program should be combined with its system, and this change and common software "upgrade" are two completely different concepts.

(2) Small system **kernel**. Since the embedded system is generally used in small electronic devices, system resources are relatively limited, so the kernel is much smaller than the **traditional** operating systems. For example, Enea's OSE **distributed** system's kernel is only 5KB and what about the Windows kernel? Simply not comparable.

(3) Simplified system. Embedded systems generally do not have the clear distinction between system software and application software, not overly complex requirements on the functional design and implementation, which facilitate cost control on the one hand, but also are **conducive** to the realization of system security.

(4) Highly real-time system software (OS) is the basic requirement for embedded software. And the software requires **solid** state storage to improve the speed. Software codes require high quality and high **reliability**. Embedded system application program can be run directly on the chip without the operating system. But to reasonably use system resources, system functions and expert library function interfaces, users must use RTOS (Real-Time Operating System) development platform, so as to **guarantee** the real-time and reliability of the program execution, and reduce development time and guarantee the quality of the software.

(5) In order to move towards **standardization** for embedded software development, **multi-tasking** operating system must be used.

(6) Embedded system development needs development tools and environments. Because it does not have the independent development ability on its own, even if the design had been completed, the users usually can't modify the functionality of the program, there must be a development tool and environment for development. The tools and the environment are usually based on a general-purpose computer hardware and software equipment, mixed signal **oscilloscope** and logic **analyzer**.

---

compile [kəm'pail]
vt. 编译，编制，编纂

kernel ['kə:nl]
n. 核心，仁，中心，精髓

traditional [trə'diʃən(ə)l]
adj. 传统的

distributed [dis'tribju:tid]
adj. 分布的，分散式的

conducive [kən'dju:siv]
adj. 有助的，有益的

solid ['sɔlid]
adj. 固体的，实心的，

reliability [ri,laiə'biliti]
n. 可靠性

guarantee [,gærən'ti:]
vt. 保证，担保

standardization [,stændədai'zeiʃən]
n. 标准化，用标准校验

multi-tasking
n. 多任务

oscilloscope [ɔ'siləskəup]
n. 示波器

analyzer ['ænəlaizə]
分析机

Exercises

I. Fill in the blanks with the information given in the text.

1. The hardware in embedded systems includes processor or _____, memory, and _____ devices, graphics controller and I/O ports, and so on.
2. In General, embedded operating system has two characteristics, one is a _____, another is a _____.
3. The main difference between embedded system and PC is that embedded system is _____ computer system, but PC is _____ computer system.
4. Since the embedded system is generally used in small electronic devices, system resources are relatively limited, so the _____ is much smaller than the traditional operating systems.
5. Embedded operating system generally include hardware related low-level, kernel, device _____ interface, standardization of communication _____, GUI, browser, etc.

II. Translate the following passages from English into Chinese.

An embedded operating system is an operating system for embedded computer systems. These operating systems are designed to be compact, efficient, and reliable, forsaking many functions that non-embedded computer operating systems provide. They are frequently also real-time operating systems, and the term RTOS is often used as a synonym for embedded operating system.

An important difference between most embedded operating systems and desktop operating systems is that the application, including the operating system, is usually statically linked together into a single executable image. Unlike a desktop operating system, the embedded operating system does not load and execute applications. It means that the system is only able to run a single application.

Section B History and Future

Like all things, embedded systems are not appeared suddenly. It also has its development process.

History

One of the first recognizably modern embedded systems was the **Apollo Guidance Computer**, developed by Charles Stark Draper at the MIT Instrumentation Laboratory. At the project's **inception**, the Apollo guidance computer was considered the riskiest item in the Apollo project as it employed the newly developed **monolithic** integrated circuits at that time to reduce the size and weight.

An early mass-produced embedded system was the Automatic D-17 guidance computer for the **Minuteman missile**, released in 1961. It was built from **transistor** logic circuit and had a hard disk for main memory. When the Minuteman II went into production in 1966, the D-17 was replaced with a new computer that was the first high-volume use of integrated circuits.

Apollo Guidance Computer
阿波罗导航计算机
MIT Instrumentation Laboratory
麻省理工学院仪器研究室
inception [in'sepʃən]
n. 开始，起初
monolithic [,mɔnə'liθik]
adj. 单体的，整体的

Minuteman missile
[minitmn misail]
民兵系列导弹
transistor [træn'zistə]
n. 晶体管

This program alone reduced prices on **nand gate ICs** from $1000/each to $3/each, permitting their use in **commercial** products.

Since these early applications in the 1960s, embedded systems have come down in price and there has been a dramatic rise in processing power and functionality. The first microprocessor for example, the Intel 4004, was designed in 1971 for calculators and other small systems but still required many external memory and support chips. In 1978 National Engineering Manufacturers Association released a "standard" for programmable microcontrollers, including almost any computer-based controllers, such as single board computers, numerical, and event-based controllers.

As the cost of microprocessors and microcontrollers fell it became feasible to replace expensive **knob**-based **analog** components such as **potentiometers** and **variable capacitors** with up/down buttons or **knobs** read out by a microprocessor even in some consumer products. By the mid-1980s, most of the common previously external system components had been integrated into the same chip as the processor and this modern form of the microcontroller allowed an even more widespread use, which by the end of the decade were the **norm** rather than the **exception** for almost all electronics devices.

The integration of microcontrollers has further increased the applications for which embedded systems are used into areas where traditionally a computer would not have been considered. A general purpose and comparatively low-cost microcontroller may often be programmed to fulfill the same role as a large number of separate components. Although in this **context** an embedded system is usually more complex than a traditional solution, most of the complexity is contained within the microcontroller itself. Very few additional components may be needed and most of the design effort is in the software. The **intangible** nature of software makes it much easier to **prototype** and test new **revisions** compared with the design and construction of a new circuit not using an embedded processor.

Future

There are several development **trends** for future embedded systems.

(1) Embedded development is a systematic project, and therefore calls for the embedded system **manufacturers** to provide embedded hardware and software systems themselves, while also offering powerful hardware development tools and software packages support. Many manufacturers have to take full account of this point. While pushing system they also focus on promoting the development environment. While Samsung promoted Arm 7, Arm 9 chip they also provided development board and Board-level support package (BSP).

(2) With the **mature** internet and widen bandwidth continuously, previous single function devices such as telephones, cell phones, refrigerators, microwave ovens etc, their function will no longer be single and the structure will be more complex. And this requires the chip design manufacturers integrate more functions on the chip to meet application functionality upgrades. Designers use more powerful embedded processors in 32-bit and 64-bit RISC chip or signal processing DSP to enhance the processing power, and add functional interfaces, such as USB, expand bus types, such as CAN BUS, enhance multimedia, graphics processing to gradually implement system on chip (SOC) concept. Software use real-time programming techniques and cross development tool technology to control complexity and simplify application programming, ensure software quality and shorten development cycles.

(3) In order to meet the needs of network development, the future embedded devices necessarily require that the hardware provide a variety of network communication interface. Traditional **single-chip** didn't support the network well, but new generation of embedded processors have embedded network interface, in addition to supporting TCP/IP Protocol, also supported IEEE1394, USB, CAN, Bluetooth or IrDA communication interface in one or more. But they also need to provide the communication network protocol software and appropriate physical layer driver software. In software system kernel support network module and can even embed a Web browser on the device to use a variety of devices to connect with Internet anywhere and anytime.

(4) Streamlining the system kernel and algorithm to reduce power consumption and the cost of hardware and software.

manufacturer
[,mænju'fæktʃərə]
n. 制造商

mature [mə'tjuə]
adj. 成熟的，(保单)到期的，考虑周到的

single-chip
n. 单片机

Chapter 13 Embedded System

Embedded products in the future are the combination of hardware and software equipment. In order to reduce power consumption and cost the embedded products need designers try to streamline the system kernel, only reserve the hardware and software related to the system function. Using a minimum of resources to achieve the most appropriate function, this requires the designer to use the best programming model and improve the algorithm continuously to optimize compiler performance.

(5) Providing multimedia friendly human-machine interface. The most important factor that Embedded device can contact with the user closely is that it can provide a very friendly user interface. This requires the designer of embedded software to work hard in graphics interface and multimedia technology. Handwriting text input, voice **dial-up** Internet access, send and receive E-mail messages, color graphics and images will make the consumer feel free. Some advanced PDA had achieved the Chinese characters written on the display screen, SMS voice announcement, but there is still a long way to go to the general embedded devices.

dial-up ['daɪəlʌp]
adj. [计]拨号(上网)的

Exercises

I. Fill in the blanks with the information given in the text.

1. An early mass-produced embedded system was the Automatic D-17 guidance computer for the Minuteman missile, released in 1961. It was built from _____ logic circuit and had a hard disk for _____.

2. The intangible nature of software makes it much easier to _____ and test new compared with the design and construction of a new circuit not using an embedded processor.

3. Embedded development is a _____ project, and therefore calls for the embedded system to provide embedded hardware and software systems themselves, while also offering powerful hardware development tools and _____ support.

4. New generation of embedded processors support many communication interfaces, so they also need to provide the _____ protocol software and appropriate _____ driver software.

5. Friendly human-machine interface requires the designer of embedded software to work hard in interface and _____ technology.

II. Translate the following passages from English into Chinese.

Embedded systems often reside in machines that are expected to run continuously for years without errors, and in some cases recover by themselves if an error occurs. Therefore the software is usually developed and tested more carefully than that for personal computers, and unreliable mechanical moving parts such as disk drives, switches or buttons are avoided. Specific reliability issues may include:

(1) The system cannot safely be shut down for repair, or it is too inaccessible to repair. Examples include space systems, undersea cables, and navigational beacons.

(2) The system must be kept running for safety reasons. Examples include aircraft navigation, reactor control systems, safety-critical chemical factory controls, train signals.

(3) The system will lose large amounts of money when shut down: telephone switches, factory controls, bridge and elevator controls, funds transfer and market making, automated sales and service.

Section C   Application Area

Embedded systems have a very broad application prospects and their applications include space exploration, industrial control, traffic management, information technology, environmental engineering, **Mechatronic** Engineering, home automation, intelligence medical, public safety, **military** areas, service areas, robot, and so on.

Application Instance

In the field of industrial control, all kinds of intelligent measurement instrument, **CNC** equipment, programmable logic controllers, distributed control systems, **field bus** instrument and control systems, industrial robots, electromechanical equipment widely used microprocessor/controller chips and embedded computer systems.

In terms of auto **vehicle navigation**, information monitoring and services, embedded systems technologies has access to a wide range of applications. Built-in GPS module, GSM module mobile positioning Terminal has been successful used in a variety of transport industry. Current GPS devices from **leading-edge** products to enter the home of ordinary people, only need thousands of Yuan, you can find your location anytime, anywhere.

In many severe conditions and complicated situation areas, embedded system can be used to achieve unmanned monitoring, such as soil and water quality monitoring, **dam** safety and flood control system, water and air pollution monitoring, **seismic** monitoring network etc.

In the field of information technology, with the development of **triple play** and **the net of things** technologies, application of embedded products are rich more and more. Such as traditional mobile phones gradually developed into **Smart phones** with the combination of PDA, **e-commerce** and entertainment, application of embedded hardware and software

Mechatronic [ˌmekəˈtrɒnik]
adj. 机电的
military [ˈmilitəri]
adj. 军事的

CNC
abbr. Computerized Numerical Control
计算机数控
field bus
现场总线
vehicle [ˈviːikl]
n. 车辆，交通工具
navigation [ˌnæviˈgeiʃən]
n. 导航，航行，航海
leading-edge [ˈliːdiŋ.edʒ]
adj. 领先优势的，尖端的，前沿的
dam [dæm]
n. 水坝，堤，障碍物
seismic [ˈsaizmik]
adj. 地震的
triple play
三网融合
the net of things
物联网
Smart phones
智能手机
e-commerce
电子商务

have a very broad prospect.

In the field of intelligent home, various information household appliances, such as digital televisions, **set-top boxes**, digital cameras, DVD, audio equipment, video telephones, home networking devices, washing machines, refrigerators and smart toys had widely used microprocessor/microcontroller and embedded software.

set-top boxes
机顶盒

In the service areas of life, water, electricity and gas **meters** remote automatic meter reading, fire alarm and **burglar** alarm systems, these special integrated embedded circuits in them will replace traditional human review, and for better, more accurate and safer performance.

meter
n. 计量器，计时器
vt. (用仪表)测量
burglar ['bəːglə]
n. 窃贼

In the field of military, arms control (gun control, missile control, smart bombs' guided **explosion** device), **bombers**, tanks, ships, and other land, sea and air military electronic equipment, radar, electronic **warfare** and military communications equipment, field command operations are indispensable to embedded systems.

explosion [iks'pləuʒən]
n. 爆炸
bomber ['bɔmə]
n. 轰炸机
warfare ['wɔːfɛə]
n. 战争，冲突

In robotics, for programming you can't use regular Java, VB, and must use Embedded C. Robot action, vision, hearing, and other functions are related to the specific program control. **Toys** such as robot "AIBO" play with the people together to bring you great pleasure and lessons learned.

toy [tɔi]
n. 玩具

All in all, as technology continues to progress, applications of embedded systems are more and more widely, will have more space in the future.

Exercises

I. Fill in the blanks with the information given in the text.

1. In the field of industrial control, all kinds of intelligent measurement instrument, _____ equipment, _____ logic controllers, _____ control systems, field bus instrument and control systems, industrial robots, electromechanical equipment widely used microprocessor/controller chips and embedded computer systems.

2. In the field of _____, with the development of _____ and _____ technologies, application of embedded products are rich more and more.

3. In robotics, for programming you can't use regular Java, VB, and must use _____. Robot action, vision, hearing, and other functions are related to the specific _____.

II. Translate the following passages from English into Chinese.

An embedded system is some combination of computer hardware and software, either fixed in capability or programmable, that is specifically designed for a particular function. Industrial machines, automobiles, medical equipment, cameras, household appliances, airplanes, vending machines and toys (as well as the more obvious cellular phone and PDA) are among the myriad possible hosts of an embedded system. Embedded systems that are programmable are provided with programming interfaces, and embedded systems programming is a specialized occupation.

Certain operating systems or language platforms are tailored for the embedded market, such as Embedded Java and Windows XP Embedded. However, some low-end consumer products use very inexpensive microprocessors and limited storage, with the application and operating system both part of a single program. The program is written permanently into the system's memory in this case, rather than being loaded into RAM (random access memory) like programs on a personal computer.

Grammar 13 谈谈科技英语听力的学习方法

在浩如烟海的科技英语材料中,我们也可以通过听广播或者到现场听报告的方式获取我们想要的信息,在这个时候,听力的技巧就显得很重要。下面介绍几种常见的听力技巧。

1. 注意听短文的首句和首段

文章的开首和开首段,往往是对短文内容的概括,如讲话目的、主要内容、作者、论点、故事发生的时间、地点及事由等。有些文章,特别是科技英语文章,大部分的主题句都在第一句,所以一定要集中注意力在前面几句上。

2. 速记是能否听懂的一个关键环节

众所周知,科技英语是专业性特别强的资料,有的时候一个关键的专业词汇往往是整个文章的侧重点。所以,特别是在听大段的报告的时候,要在适当的时候,采用速记的方式,记下主要内容,这样理解其他的内容,就方便多了。

例如:

The use of computer graphics pervades many diverse fields. Applications range from the production of charts and graphs, to the generation of realistic images for television and motion pictures to the interactive design of mechanical parts .To encompass all these uses, we can adopt a simple definition.

计算机图形学的应用扩展到了许多不同领域,应用的范围从表和图形的产生,到用于电视和动画片的真实图像的生成,到机械零件的交互式设计。我们采用一个简单的定义来概括所有这些应用。

在听这段文章的时候,"计算机图形学"就是你应该速记的内容,且是全文的关键点。

3. 注意力一定要集中在整体内容的理解上

练习听力时,千万不能只停留在个别单词或单句上,听不清时马上放弃,不要强迫听清每一个词,要把重点放在听关键词即实词上。有的倾听者往往是一个单词听不懂,就把思绪放在这个单词上,不停地琢磨和回想,这样听力的效果很不理想。

例如:

Professions such as engineering and architecture are concerned with design. Although their applications vary, most designers face similar difficulties and use similar methodologies. One of the principal characteristics of most design problems is the lack of a unique solution. Hence, the designer will examine a potential design and then will modify it, possibly many times, in an attempt to achieve a better solution. Computer graphics has become an indispensable element in this iterative process.

工程和建筑的专业人员关心设计，尽管他们的应用不同，但大多数设计者面对相似的困难，采用了类似的方法。大多数设计问题的基本特点之一是缺少唯一的解决方案，因此，设计者可能需要多次检查原来的设计，修改它，以获得一个更好的解决方案。在这个重复的过程中，计算机图形学已变成一个不可缺少的部分。

4. 注意读音变化，提高听力水平

在平时的英语朗读、说话过程中，应注意连读、失去爆破、弱读、同化等语音变化情况。我们发现，在听科技英语的内容中，对于某些重点的内容，读者的语调和声音是有变化的，这些细节因素需要我们在平时锻炼中，掌握技巧。

参考译文

Section A 嵌入式系统概述

火星探测器在火星的成功登陆，高科技战争中在全球范围内的精确制导攻击，植入人体内挽救了无数人生命的电子起搏器，所有这一切的实现都离不开嵌入式系统。那么，什么是嵌入式系统呢？

嵌入式系统定义

根据 IEEE(电气与电子工程师协会)的定义，嵌入式系统是用于控制、监视或者辅助操作机器和设备的装置。从中可以看出嵌入式系统是软件和硬件的综合体，还可以涵盖机械等附属装置。

这个定义比较抽象，目前国内一个普遍被认同的定义是，以应用为中心，以计算机技术为基础，软件和硬件可裁剪，适应应用系统对功能、可靠性、成本、体积、功耗严格要求的专用计算机系统。这样理解起来就比较容易。首先，它是一个计算机系统，包括软件和硬件资源；另外它是面向某种应用的系统，这种应用在功能、可靠性、成本、体积、功耗等方面都有严格的要求。

嵌入式系统的硬件包括处理器/微处理器、存储器、外设器件、图形控制器和 I/O 端口等。软件部分包括操作系统软件(要求实时和多任务操作)和应用程序编程，有时设计人员把这两种软件结合在一起。应用程序编程控制着系统的功能，而操作系统控制着应用程序编程与硬件的交互作用。那么嵌入式系统是否就是个人计算机呢？不是的，嵌入式系统是专用计算机系统，而个人计算机是通用计算机系统，这是他们之间最根本的区别。

嵌入式微处理器是嵌入式系统硬件层的核心。嵌入式微处理器与通用 CPU 最大的不同在于嵌入式微处理器大多工作在为特定用户群所特定设计的系统中，它将通用 CPU 中由不同板卡完成的任务集成在一块芯片当中，从而有利于嵌入式系统在设计时趋于小型化，同时还具有很高的效率和可靠性。目前世界上具有嵌入式功能特点的处理器已经超过 1000 种，流行的体系结构超过 30 个系列，如 Power PC、68000、MIPS、ARM 系列、8051、P51XA、MCS-251 等。

嵌入式操作系统是一种支持嵌入式系统应用的操作系统软件，通常包括与硬件相关的底层驱动软件、系统内核、设备驱动接口、通信协议、图形界面、标准化浏览器等。嵌入式操作系统具有通用操作系统的基本特点，如能够有效管理越来越复杂的系统资源；能够把硬件虚拟化，使得开发人员从繁忙的驱动程序移植和维护中解脱出来；能够提供库函数、驱动程序、工具集以及应用程序。与通用操作系统相比较，嵌入式操作系统在系统实时高效性、硬件的相关依赖性、软件固态化以及应用的专用性等方面具有较为突出的特点。常用的嵌入式操作系统有 VxWorks、Palm OS、Windows CE、Linux 等。

嵌入式系统的特征

嵌入式系统具有以下几个方面的特征。

(1) 专用性强。嵌入式系统的个性化很强,其中的软件系统和硬件的结合非常紧密。一般要针对硬件进行系统的移植,即使在同一品牌、同一系列的产品中也需要根据系统硬件的变化和增减不断进行修改。同时针对不同的任务,往往需要对系统进行较大更改,程序的编译下载要和系统相结合,这种修改和通用软件的"升级"是两个完全不同的概念。

(2) 系统内核小。由于嵌入式系统一般是应用于小型电子装置的,系统资源相对有限,所以内核较之传统的操作系统要小得多。例如,Enea公司的OSE分布式系统,内核只有5KB,而Windows的内核呢?简直没有可比性。

(3) 系统精简。嵌入式系统一般没有系统软件和应用软件的明显区分,不要求其功能设计及实现上过于复杂,这样一方面利于控制系统成本,同时也利于实现系统安全。

(4) 高实时性的系统软件(OS)是嵌入式软件的基本要求,而且软件要求固态存储,以提高速度,软件代码要求高质量和高可靠性。嵌入式系统的应用程序可以没有操作系统直接在芯片上运行,但是为了合理地利用系统资源、系统函数和专家库函数接口,用户必须使用RTOS(实时操作系统)开发平台,这样才能保证程序执行的实时性、可靠性,并减少开发时间,保障软件质量。

(5) 嵌入式软件开发要想走向标准化,就必须使用多任务的操作系统。

(6) 嵌入式系统开发需要开发工具和环境。由于其本身不具备自主开发能力,即使设计完成以后用户通常也不能对其中的程序功能进行修改,必须有一套开发工具和环境才能进行开发,这些工具和环境一般是基于通用计算机上的软硬件设备以及各种逻辑分析仪、混合信号示波器等。开发时往往有主机和目标机的概念,主机用于程序的开发,目标机作为最后的执行机,开发时需要两者交替结合进行。

Section B 嵌入式系统的历史和未来发展趋势

像所有事物一样,嵌入式系统也不是突然出现的,它也有自己的发展过程。

历史

第一个被大家认可的现代嵌入式系统是麻省理工学院仪器研究室的Charles Stark Draper开发的阿波罗导航计算机。在计划刚开始的时候,阿波罗导航计算机被认为是阿波罗计划风险最大的部分。为了减小尺寸和重量而使用的当时最新的单片集成电路加大了阿波罗计划的风险。

早期大批量生产的嵌入式系统是1961年发布的民兵I导弹上的D-17自动导航控制计算机。它是由独立的晶体管逻辑电路建造的,它带有一个作为主存的硬盘。当民兵II导弹在1966年开始生产的时候,D-17由一部第一次使用大量集成电路的计算机替代了。仅仅这个项目就将与非门集成电路模块的价格从每个1000美元下降到了每个3美元,使集成电路的商用成为可能。

这些20世纪60年代的早期应用,使嵌入式系统得到长足发展,它的价格开始下降,同时处理能力和功能获得了巨大的提高。例如,1971年出品的Intel 4004是第一款微处理器,它在计算器和其他小型系统中找到了用武之地。但是,它仍然需要外部存储设备和外部支持芯片。1978年,国家工程制造商协会发布了可编程微控制器的"标准",包括几乎所有以计算机为基础的控制器,如单片机、数控设备以及基于事件的控制器。

随着微控制器和微处理器价格的下降,一些消费性产品使用微控制器的上下按钮或者旋钮来读出数据,并使得以此取代像分压计和可变电容这样的基于旋钮的昂贵模拟元件成为可能。到了20世纪80年代中期,许多以前是外部系统的元件被集成到了处理器芯片中,这种结构的微处理器得到了更广泛的应用。到了80年代末期,微处理器已经在几乎所有的电子设备中成为了标准而不是例外。

集成化的微处理器使得嵌入式系统的应用扩展到传统计算机无法涉足的领域。对多用途和相对低成本的微控制器进行编程，常常可以做到由很多分离的部件所完成的功能。尽管在这种情况下嵌入式系统比传统的解决方案要复杂得多，但是多数复杂的工作都被包含在微控制器本身里了。但是嵌入式系统很少有额外的元件，大部分设计工作是软件部分。而非物质性的软件不管是建立原型还是测试新修改相对于设计和建造一个不使用嵌入式处理器的新电路来说，都要容易得多。

未来

未来嵌入式系统的发展有以下几个趋势。

(1) 嵌入式开发是一项系统工程，因此要求嵌入式系统厂商不仅要提供嵌入式软硬件系统本身，同时还需要提供强大的硬件开发工具和软件包支持。目前很多厂商已经充分考虑到这一点，在主推系统的同时，将开发环境也作为重点推广。例如，三星在推广 Arm 7、Arm 9 芯片的同时还提供开发板和板级支持包(BSP)。

(2) 随着互联网技术的成熟和带宽的不断提高，以往单一功能的设备如电话、手机、冰箱、微波炉等功能将不再单一，结构也将更加复杂。这就要求芯片设计厂商在芯片上集成更多的功能以满足应用功能的升级。设计师们一方面采用更强大的嵌入式处理器如 32 位、64 位 RISC 芯片或信号处理器 DSP 来增强处理能力，同时增加功能接口，如 USB，扩展总线类型，如 CAN BUS，再加强对多媒体、图形等的处理，以逐步实施芯片上系统(SOC)的概念。软件方面采用实时多任务编程技术和交叉开发工具技术来控制功能复杂性，简化应用程序设计，保障软件质量并缩短开发周期。

(3) 未来的嵌入式设备为了适应网络发展的要求，必然要求在硬件上提供各种网络通信接口。传统的单片机对网络支持不足，而新一代的嵌入式处理器已经开始内嵌网络接口，除了支持 TCP/IP 协议，还有的支持 IEEE 1394、USB、CAN、Bluetooth 或 IrDA 通信接口中的一种或者几种，同时也需要提供相应的通信组网协议软件和物理层驱动软件。系统内核在软件方面支持网络模块，甚至可以在设备上嵌入 Web 浏览器，真正实现随时随地用各种设备上网。

(4) 精简系统内核、算法，降低功耗和软硬件成本。未来的嵌入式产品是软硬件紧密结合的设备。为了降低功耗和成本，设计者需要尽量精简系统内核，只保留和系统功能紧密相关的软硬件，利用最低的资源实现最适当的功能，这就要求设计者选用最佳的编程模型并不断改进算法来优化编译器性能。

(5) 提供友好的多媒体人机界面。嵌入式设备能与用户亲密接触，最重要的因素就是它能提供非常友好的用户界面。这就要求嵌入式软件设计者要在图形界面和多媒体技术上下功夫。手写文字输入、语音拨号上网、收发电子邮件以及彩色图形、图像都会让使用者获得自由的感受。目前一些先进的 PDA 在显示屏幕上已实现汉字写入、短消息语音发布，但一般的嵌入式设备距离这个要求还有很长的路要走。

Section C 嵌入式系统的应用

嵌入式系统具有非常广阔的应用前景，其应用领域包括宇宙探索、工业控制、交通管理、环境工程、信息技术、机械电子、智能家居、智能医疗、公共安全、军事领域、服务领域、机器人等。

应用实例

在工业控制领域，各种智能测量仪表、数控装置、可编程控制器、分布式控制系统、现场总线仪表及控制系统、工业机器人、机电一体化机械设备广泛采用微处理器/控制器芯片及嵌入式计算机系统。

在车辆导航、信息监测与汽车服务方面，嵌入式系统技术已经获得了广泛的应用。内嵌 GPS 模块、GSM 模块的移动定位终端已经在各种运输行业获得了成功的使用。目前 GPS 设备已经从尖端产品进入了普通百姓的家庭，只需要几千元，就可以随时随地找到你的位置。

在很多环境恶劣、地况复杂的地区，嵌入式系统能够实现无人监测，如水土质量监测、堤坝安全、防洪体系、水源和空气污染监测、地震监测等。

在信息技术领域，随着三网融合和物联网技术的不断发展，嵌入式产品的应用也越来越丰富。例如，传统手机逐渐发展成为融合了 PDA、电子商务和娱乐等特性的智能手机，嵌入式软硬件的应用前景非常广阔。

在智能家居领域，我国各种信息家电产品，如数字电视机、机顶盒、数码照相机、DVD、音响设备、可视电话、家庭网络设备、洗衣机、电冰箱、智能玩具等，都广泛采用了微处理器/微控制器及嵌入式软件。

在生活服务领域，水、电、煤气表的远程自动抄表，安全防火、防盗系统，其中嵌有的专用控制芯片将代替传统的人工检查，并实现更高、更准确和更安全的性能。

在军事领域，各种武器控制(火炮控制、导弹控制、智能炸弹制导引爆装置)、轰炸机、坦克、舰艇等陆海空各种军用电子装备，雷达、电子对抗军事通信装备，野战指挥作战用各种专用设备等都离不开嵌入系统。

在机器人领域中，编程不能用普通的 Java、VB，而必须用嵌入式 C。机器人行动、视觉、听觉等功能都涉及具体的编程控制。例如，机器人玩具"爱博"可以与人们共同玩耍，给大家带来极大的愉悦和教益。

总之，随着科技的不断进步，嵌入式系统的应用也越来越广泛，将来还会有更大的应用空间。

Chapter 14　Internet of Things
(物联网)

Section A　The Development History

Every **crisis**, new technologies will be spawned, and the new technology is the great driving force out of crisis to the economy, especially industry. 2008, the global financial crisis also **spawned** the birth of a new economic driving force, the most respected power to people is Internet of Things.

In the past few years, the Internet has been **pervasive** everywhere in the world. A stimulating idea is fast emerging with the **ubiquity** of mobile devices and **proliferation** of wireless networks: the pervasive presence around us of a variety of "things" or "objects", such as RFID, sensors, **actuators**, mobile phones, through unique addressing schemes, are able to interact with each other and cooperate with their neighboring "smart" components to reach common goals. This novel **paradigm**, named "The Internet of Things" (IoT) continues on the concept of smart environments, make these "things" or "objects" access to the Internet anytime and anywhere. Internet of Things is **envisioned** to be the third wave in the global information industry after computer, Internet and mobile communication network.

The Application Scenario

We are standing on the **brink** of a new **ubiquitous** computing and communication era, It will radically our **corporation**, **community**, and our theirselves. Nowadays, the "Internet of Things" is a hot topic, but what is "Internet of Things"? what do it? We described by several scenes which are closely related that people's lives.

Scenario 1: It is 7:00a.m. in a winter morning. When you are still sleeping in bed your sensor detected that you are about to wake up through your **metabolism** activities. Your bed notifies your kitchen management center, car, PDA, alarm clock and etc.

---

crisis ['kraisis]
n. 危机，危急关头
spawn [spɔːn]
vt. 大量生产，引发

pervasive [pə'veisiv]
adj. 无处不在的，遍布的
ubiquity [juː'bɪkwətɪ]
n. 到处存在，普遍存在
proliferation [prəuˌlifə'reiʃən]
n. 增殖，分芽繁殖
actuator ['æktjueitə]
n. 激励者，执行器
paradigm ['pærədaim, -dim]
n. 范例，样式，模范
envision [in'viʒən]
vt. 想象，展望
scenario [si'nɑːriəu]
n. 剧情，脚本，场景
brink [briŋk]
n. 边沿，边缘
ubiquitous [juː'bikwitəs]
adj. 普遍存在的
corporation [ˌkɔːpə'reiʃn]
adj. 社团的，整体的，公司的
community [kə'mjuːniti]
n. 社区，团体，大众
sphere [sfiə]
n. 范围，领域
metabolism [me'tæbəlizəm]
n. 新陈代谢

Then your kitchen started to heat the milk for you, your car starts the engine and pre-heat, your PDA downloads your personal schedule for today from your Google **calendar** account, so your alarm clock starts the beep to wake you up.

Scenario 2: The Internet fridge is one of the most **oft-quoted** example of what the Internet of Things will enable. We can imagine that a refrigerator monitors the food inside it and notifies you something missing when you go to the supermarket. It also perhaps keeps track of the best food websites, gathering **recipes** for your dinners and adding the **ingredients** automatically to your shopping list. This fridge knows what kinds of foods you like to eat, according to the ratings you have given to your dinners. Indeed the fridge helps you take care of your health, because it knows which foods are good for you.

Scenario 3: When you want to drive the car on **vacation**, the RFID sensor system (required by law) of your car has alerted to possible tyre failures, thus you need to check. As you pass through the entrance to your **favourite garage**, a **diagnostic** tool using sensors and radio technology conducts a **comprehensive** check of your car and asks you to proceed to a **specialized maintenance** terminal. The terminal is equipped with fully automated robotic arm. You confidently leave your beloved car behind in order to get some coffee. The "Orange Wall" **beverage** machine knows all about your's love of iced coffee and pours it for you after you waves your internet watch for secure payment. When you get back, a brand new pair of rear tyre has already been installed with **integrated** RFID tags for monitoring pressure, temperature and deformation.

The above scenarios described are a **peek** at the future life in the Internet of Things era. Today, we are on the brink of opening a new chapter of information technology: the ubiquitous computing and communication era. Our personal life, business, and society will be radically transformed.

Touch of a button on the computer or cell phone, even thousands of miles away, you can learn the status of an item, a person's activities. Send a text message, you can turn on the fan; if the **illegal invasion** of your home, you will receive automatic

calendar ['kælində]
n. 日历，日程表

oft [ɔːft, ɔft]
adv. 常常，再三
quote [kwəut]
vt. & vi. 引用，援引
recipe ['resipi]
n. 食谱，诀窍，处方，配方
ingredient [in'griːdiənt]
n. 组成部分，原料
vacation [və'keiʃən;vei'keiʃən]
n. 假期
favourite ['feivərit]
adj. 特别受喜爱的
garage ['gærɑː(d)ʒ]
n. 车库，汽车修理站，加油站
diagnostic [,daiəg'nɔstik]
adj. 诊断的，判断的
comprehensive [,kɔmpri'hensiv]
adj. 广泛的，综合的，全面的
specialized ['speʃiəlaizd]
adj. 专门的，专业的
maintenance ['meintinəns]
n. 维持，维护，保养，维修
beverage ['bevəridʒ]
n. (除水以外的)饮料
integrated ['intigreitid]
adj. 整体的，综合的，集成的
peek [piːk]
n. 偷看，窥视
illegal [i'liːgəl]
adj. 不合法的，违法的
invasion [in'veiʒən]
n. 侵略，侵犯，侵入

Chapter 14 Internet of Things

telephone alarm. This intelligent scene is not only the Hollywood **sci-fi blockbusters** situation, and IoT is gradually approaching our lives.

Some experts predicted that IoT may be a large-scale popularity to become a **trillion**-scale high-tech market after 10 years. Then, at the personal health, traffic control, environmental protection, public safety, peace at home, smart fire, industrial monitoring, elderly care in almost all areas, IoT will play a role. Some experts said that only three to five years, IoT would be full access to people's lives, change people's way of life.

sci-fi ['saiˈfai]
n. science fiction 科幻小说
blockbuster [ˈblɔkˈbʌstə]
n. 重磅炸弹，大片
trillion [ˈtriljən]
n. 万亿，兆

Historical Evolution

As an emerging thing, Internet of Things is not young, it has an evolution history for more than 15 years, as shown in Fig.14.1

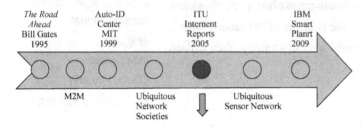

Fig. 14.1 Historical Evolution of IoT

In 1995, communication between machines was mentioned by Bill Gates in his book *The Road Ahead* published.

In 1999, the concept of IoT was attributed to the original Auto-ID Center, founded and based at the time in MIT. The original meaning of IoT refers to connect all articles with Internet by means of information sensing devices, such as the radio frequency **identification** and so on, and realize intelligent **recognition** and management.

In 2005, ITU (International Telecommunication Union) officially **released** a report of "The Internet of Things" on the World Summit held in Tunis. The report extended the concept of IoT. A new **dimension** had been added to the world of information and communication technologies (ICTs): from anytime, and place connectivity for anyone, we will now have **connectivity** for anything (Fig 14.2). Connections will multiply and create an entirely new dynamic network of networks —— an

identification
[ai,dentifiˈkeiʃən]
n. 鉴定，验明，认出，辨认
recognition [,rekəgˈniʃən]
n. 认识，认出，识别
release [riˈliːs]
vt. 释放，放开，发布，发行
dimension [diˈmenʃən]
n. 度量，程度，维度
connectivity [kənekˈtiviti]
n. 连通性

Internet of Things.

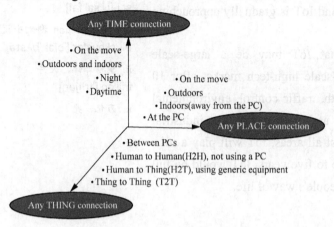

Fig. 14.2 A new dimension

In 2009, IBM **launched** its **Smarter Planet** plan, the Internet of things is one of the **indispensable** part. President Obama made positive response to the concept of "Smarter Planet", and promoted it to the national development strategy, thus caused the wide attention of the whole world.

Smarter Planet

On Nov. 6, 2008, IBM Chairman and CEO Sam Palmisano issued the remark of "*A Smarter Planet: the Next* **Leadership** *Agenda*" at the **Council** on New York Foreign Relations. He officially proposed the concept of "smarter planet", and thought that the realization of smarter planet needed to instrumented, interconnected and intelligent Fig, as shown in 14.3.

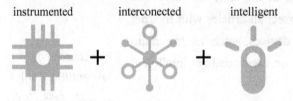

Fig. 14.3 The realization of smarter planet

At IBM, they want intelligence to be infused into the systems and processes that make the world work into things no one would recognize as computers: cars, appliances, roadways, power grids, clothes, even natural systems such as agriculture and waterways. Its application field has been shown in Fig. 14.4. These **unprecedented** "smarter" **infrastructure** provides endless space for innovation.

launch [lɔːntʃ, lɑːntʃ]
n. 发起，发动，发行
Smarter Planet
智慧地球
indispensable
[ˌindisˈpensəbl]
adj. 必不可少的，必需的

Leadership [ˈliːdəʃip]
n. 领导，领导权
council [ˈkaunsil]
n. 委员会，理事会,议会

unprecedented
[ʌnˈpresidəntid]
adj. 前所未有的，空前的
infrastructure
[ˈinfrəˈstrʌktʃə]
n. 基础设施，基础结构，基

Chapter 14 Internet of Things

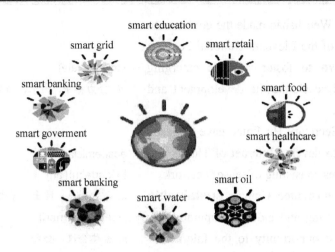

Fig. 14.4 The application field of Smart Planet

础建设

Sensing China

On August 7, 2009, Premier Wen Jiabao of the State Council **inspected** Wuxi Micro-nano and Sensing Engineering Technology Research and Development Center and brought forward the concept of "sensing China", as is shown in Fig. 14.5. He pointed, with the development of information technology and the virtual information space, the person-to-person interconnection has gradually entered into the material field and the real physical world. We should **vigorously** develop the sensor network, and master its core technology.

On November 3, 2009, Premier Wen Jiabao delivered a speech titled with *Make Technology Lead China in Sustainable Development* and instructed that breakthrough shall be made especially on key technologies of sensing network and internet of things.

inspect [inˈspekt]
vt. 进行检查，进行视察

vigorously [ˈvigərəsli]
adv. 精神旺盛地，活泼地

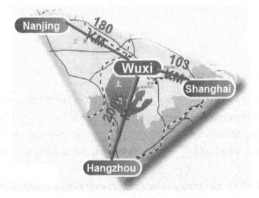

Fig. 14.5 Sensing China Center

On March 5, 2010, Premier Wen Jiabao made the government work report at the third session of the Eleventh National People's Congress and pointed to **strive** to foster strategic emerging industries, increase support and accelerate the development and application of Internet of Things.

On June 8, 2010, General Secretary Hu Jintao gave a speech at the **academician plenary** to develop Internet of Things and build the intelligent infrastructures consisting of sensor network.

In this post-crisis era, to guarantee China's **sustainable** development, economic restructuring and industrial upgrading is inevitable. This provides a good opportunity to the Internet of Things. The government pays much attention on Internet of Things, and the new policies have been taken to **promote** the development of the Internet of Thing since 2009. The local governments and businesses expressed keen interest to the Internet of Things, and promoted rapid development of Internet of Things and related industries in China. There are have advanced to the equipment manufacturing, network operations and the industrial applications for the internet of things. As an emerging high-tech industry, this progress itself is a result of industrial upgrading. Meanwhile, IoT **accelerates** the use of other high technologies, and thus improves product efficiency in many different industries. And it changes people's life style and stimulates their consumption which gives impetus to China's economic restructuring. The next development trend of Internet of Things lies in industrial applications and large-scale promotion in China, and the only way to achieve economies of scale.

strive [straiv]
vi. 努力奋斗，力求，力争

academician [ə,kædə'miʃən]
n. 学会会员，院士，学者

plenary ['pli:nəri]
n. 全体会议，全会

sustainable [sə'steɪnəbl]
adj. 合理利用的，可持续的

promote [prə'məut]
vt. 提升，提拔，促进，推动

accelerate [æk'seləreit]
vt. & vi. (使)加快，(使)增速

Exercises

Ⅰ. **Fill in the blanks with the information given in the text.**

1. The tide for the world information industry is respectively _____, Internet and mobile communication network, and _____ . These evokes scientific and economic tide again of the global _____ industry.

2. In what's called the Internet of Things, sensors and actuators _____ in physical objects——from roadways to pacemakers——are linked through wired and _____ networks, often using the same Internet Protocol (IP) that connects the Internet.

3. The biggest revolution which Internet of Things brings is to connect every objects and things together, that extends the internet of people to the more general internet which is the internet of all the things. This is the vision of a truly ubiquitous network—— "_____, anywhere, by anyone and _____".

4. Chinese Premier Wen Jiabao's proposal of the "_____" strategy in August 2009 has triggered the development of "sensory cities" around the country. Along with the development of new-generation information _____ technologies including the Internet of things and cloud computing, the development of sensory cities also focuses on the application of new technologies.

II. Translate the following passages from English into Chinese.

In the urban traffic field, advanced information technologies, data transmission technologies, electronic control technologies and computer processing technologies will be applied to traffic and transportation to establish an informatized, intelligentized and socialized system, which provides citizens with multiple services and enhance the security, energy-efficiency and effectiveness of urban traffic through the collection, processing, distribution, exchange, analysis and utilization of information.

The specific tasks include smart traffic signal control system, traffic video analysis and monitoring system, e-police system, automatic entry control monitoring system, dynamic traffic guidance information system, smart logistics information platform, goods tracing and positioning system, as well as process visualization and smart management system.

Section B   The Key Technology

Internet of Things is an important part of the new generation of the information technology. It **evokes** scientific and economic tide the global information industry after the Internet.

evoke [i'vəuk]
vt. 引起，唤起

Definition

Because the concept of IOT appears soon, its connotation is constantly developing and perfecting, and the **perspective** f academia and industry are different, so Internet of Things is not given a recognized unifying definition.

perspective [pə'spektiv]
n. 远景，希望，观点，想法
academia [ˌækə'diːmjə]
n. 学术界，学术环境

According to the **literal** meaning of explanation, IoT is also known as the sensor network, refers to a variety of information sensing devices combined with the Internet to form a huge network. It will connect all of the items to network to facilitate the identification and management.

literal ['litərəl]
adj. 照字面的，原义的

The ITU definition: from anytime, any place connectivity for anyone, we will now have connectivity for anything.

General definition: it is widely believed that Internet of Things is a **brand**-new information system, based on realizing intelligent identification, location, tracking, monitoring, management and service, deeply applied in economic society and nature field, improving the management level of production and

brand [brænd]
n. 商标，牌子

life of human beings, according to some agreement, linking up goods and Internet, exchanging, communicating and processing information. It bases on a new generation of information technologies, such as radio frequency identification (RFID), sensors, and smart phones. The purpose of the internet of things is connecting things to the internet and they can exchange information with each other. The basic of the internet of things is the internet, and IOT is an **extension** and the **expansion** of network which we are familiar with the Internet.

Architecture

As the Internet of Things is different from Internet and Telecommunications Network, the above two models are not suitable for IoT directly. But they have some similar feature in common. So through the technology **architecture** of the Internet and the **logical** structure of Telecommunications Management Network and combined with the specific features of the Internet of Things, the well-known 3-layer architecture of IoT is generally accepted. We believed that this architecture would better explain the features and connotation of the Internet of Things. We divided IoT into 3 layers, which are the **Perception** Layer, the Network Layer and the Application layer as shown in Fig. 14.6.

extension [iks'tenʃən]
n. 延伸，扩展
expansion [iks'pænʃən]
n. 扩大，扩张，扩展

architecture ['ɑ:kitektʃə]
n. 建筑风格，体系结构
logical ['lɔdʒikəl]
adj. 逻辑(上)的，合乎情理的

perception [pə'sepʃən]
n. 感知(能力)，觉察(力)，知觉

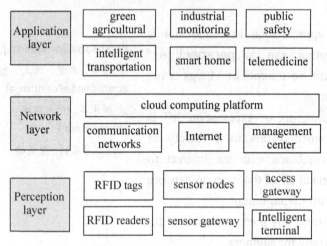

Fig. 14.6 3-layer architecture of the Internet of Things

The Perception layer is to perceive the physical properties of objects (such as temperature, location etc.) by various sensors (such as **infrared** sensors, RFID, **2-D barcode**), and convert these information to digital signals which is more convenient for

infrared ['infrə'red]
adj. 红外线的
2-D barcode
二维码

network transmission. The perception devices include **carbon dioxide** sensor, temperature sensor, humidity sensor, two-dimensional code labels, RFID tags and readers, cameras, GPS and other sensing devices. The role of perception layer is equivalent to the **ENT** and skin nerve endings of human, its main function is to identify objects, gather information.

The network layer is like the central nervous system and brain of IOT, its main function is to transmit and process information from the perception layer. The network layer is consisted of wired and wireless communication and Internet networks, network management center, information center and intelligent processing center, etc.

The Application layer is the interface of Internet of Things and users (including people, organizations and other systems), which combined with the industry needs, to realize the **intellectualized** industry, similar to person's social division of labor, eventually formed human society. Industry **Characteristics** of the Internet of Things are reflected in its applications like green agricultural, industrial monitoring, public safety, city management, telemedicine, smart home, intelligent transportation, and environmental monitoring, some industries have already accumulated a number of successful cases, as shown in Fig.14.7.

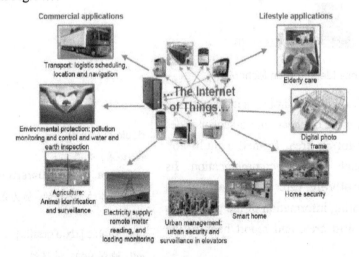

Fig. 14.7 The application of IOT

Core Technology

The Internet of Things is changing the way how people live

and work. IoT has a lot of benefits and it also brings great challenges to the IT industry. Its core technologies are RFID (Radio Frequency Identification) technology and WSN (Wireless Sensor Network) technology, MEMS (**Micro-Electro-Mechanical Systems**) technology and so on.

- Radio frequency identification(RFID): It is a kind of non-touching automatic identifying technique from the 1990s. It can identify target object automatically via radio frequency signal and obtain related data. It has high metrical **precision**, strong anti-interference and it is easy to control. The most basic RFID system consists of tags, readers and antennas in Fig.14.8. There is a widely applied prospect of RFID technology such as library management and mail processing program. RFID plays a very important role in the development of the internet of things.

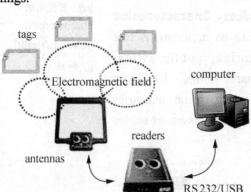

Fig. 14.8   Radio Frequency Identification technology

- Wireless sensor network (WSN): Wireless sensor network is consisted of a large number of cheap micro-sensor nodes **deployed** in the monitoring area, formed a multi-hop ad hoc networks through wireless communication. Its purpose is to **collaboratively** perceive, gather, process and transmit the monitoring information of the perception objects in the **geographic** area, and report back to the user.

As shown in Fig. 14.9, the data sensor nodes monitored are hop-by-hop transmitted along the other sensor nodes. During transmission, the Monitoring data may be processed by multiple nodes, and routed to the sink node after multi-hop, and finally sended to the management node through the Internet or satellite. The users **configure** and manage the sensor networks by the management node, issue the monitoring tasks and collect the monitoring data.

configure [kən'figə]

n. 配置，设定

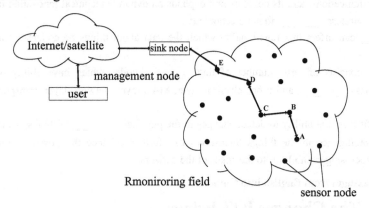

Fig. 14.9 The structure of wireless sensor network

- MEMS (Micro-Electro-Mechanical Systems): It refers to the system integrated of micro-sensors, actuators and signal processing and control circuits, interface circuits, communications and power. It can percept, identify, control and handle the natural information, such as sound, light, heat, **magnetic**, sports and so on, as shown in Fig.14.10. It is a very important achievement with the rapid development of micro/**nanotechnology**. Its sizes of the outline is below the millimeter level, and the sizes of its mechanical parts and semiconductor component are the **micron - nanometer** level ($10^{-6} \sim 10^{-9}$ meters), the micro-electromechanical system integrates micro-devices (micro-motors, micro-circuits, micro sensors, micro actuators and so on) into silicon. It can not only collect, proces and send informations, and independently operate according to the obtained information or the **external** action.

magnetic [mæg'netik]

adj. 有磁性的，有吸引力的

nanotechnology ['neinətɔ:]

n. 纳米技术

micron ['maikrɔn]

n. 微米

nanometer ['neinə,mi:tə]

n. 纳米

external [eks'tə:nl]

adj. 外面的，外部的

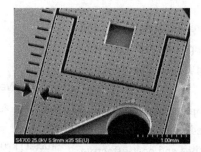

Fig. 14.10 Micro-Electro-Mechanical Systems

Exercises

I. Fill in the blanks with the information given in the text.

1. The Internet of Things is a technological _____ that represents the future of computing and communications, and its development depends on dynamic technical innovation in a number of important fields, from wireless _____ to nanotechnology.

2. Radio-frequency _____ can offers this functionality which the data about things be collected and processed.

3. Wireless sensor network consists of large number of tiny _____ nodes which have ability of apperceiving, computing and wireless _____, and it has physical layer, MAC layer, network layer, transport layer and _____ layer.

4. Data collection will benefit from the ability to detect changes in the physical _____ of things, using sensor technologies. Embedded intelligence in the things themselves can further enhance the power of the network by devolving _____ processing capabilities to the edges of the network.

II. Translate the following passages from English into Chinese.

The Changes IOT brings

Nowadays, Internet connects people together. People can send information across oceans and different time zones, through E-mail, instant messaging, SNS, blog and even twitter, within just a few seconds. However, in order to do so, you have to or sit in front of a PC or use handheld. At the same time, high-speed mobile networks such as 3Gb/s or 4Gb/s connects people from almost any location with their always-on handhelds. The biggest revolution which Internet of Things brings is to connect every objects and things together, that extends the internet of people to the more general internet which is the internet of all the things. This is the vision of a truly ubiquitous network—— "anytime, anywhere, by anyone and anything".

This ubiquitous network is enabled by technologies such as advanced sensor, chip and RFID. Everyday objects and things will be added into the internet by embedding chips and sensors into them. Therefore, all the things can send and receive data, process information and extract wisdom out of that information to help decision making process. Human's time communicating to machine will be leveraged by machine-to-machine intelligent communication which can take out automatically. Everything from cars to shoes will fall within communications range, turning to the chapter of a new era, one in which today's internet (of data and people) gives way to tomorrow's Internet of Things.

Section C Challenges and Concerns

Internet of Things represents the future of computing and communications, and its development depends on dynamic technical innovation in a number of important fields, from wireless sensors to nanotechnology.

First, in order to connect everyday objects and devices to large databases and networks——and indeed to the network of networks (the internet)——a simple, **unobtrusive** and cost-effective system of item identification is **crucial**. Only then can data about things be collected and processed. Radio-frequency identification

unobtrusive [ˌʌnəbˈtruːsiv]
adj. 不引人注目的，不显眼的
crucial [ˈkruːʃiəl, ˈkruːʃəl]
adj. 决定性的，紧要关头的，至关重要的

(RFID) offers this functionality.

Second, data collection will benefit from the ability to detect changes in the physical status of things, using sensor technologies. Embedded intelligence in the things themselves can further enhance the power of the network by devolving information processing capabilities to the edges of the network.

Finally, advances in **miniaturization** and nanotechnology mean that smaller and smaller things will have the ability to interact and connect (Fig. 14.11)

miniaturization

n. 小型化

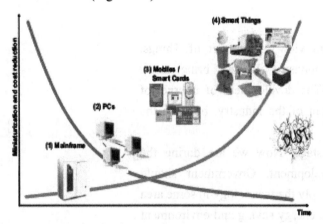

Fig. 14.11　Miniaturization towards the Internet of Things

A combination of all of these developments will create an Internet of Things that connects the world's objects in both a sensory and an intelligent manner. Indeed, with the benefit of integrated information processing, industrial products and everyday objects will take on smart characteristics and capabilities. They may also take on electronic identities that can be queried remotely, or be equipped with sensors for detecting physical changes around them. Eventually, even particles as small as dust might be **tagged** and networked. Such developments will turn the merely static objects of today into newly dynamic things, embedding intelligence in our environment, and stimulating the creation of innovative products and entirely new services.

tag [tæg]

vt. 加标签于

Characters

The core of Internet of Things is the information interaction between things and things, people and things. Its three important characters can be briefly **summarized** as the Table 14.1.

character ['kæriktə]

n. 特性，特色，特征

summarize ['sʌməraiz]

vt. 总结，概述

Table 14.1 Three characters of IOT

Comprehensive perception	Collecting and taking information of things at anywhere and anytime using RFID, sensors, two-dimension code and so on
Reliable delivery	Transmitting the information accurately and quickly by the mixture of internet
Intelligent processing	Using intelligent computing technologies to process the large amount of data so that we can realize the intelligent control of the things

The Future Development

We should take a long-term view of Internet of Things. Internet of Things is a new industry. It will bring many conveniences for our daily life. The development of internet of things is not only the development of the industry, but also the improvement of people's life.

- The industry formation stage. Now we are during the formation stage of development. Government should support the industry and apply the technology in some area like security management, energy saving and environment protection. As the expansion of the use of internet of things, it will become mature and drive the development of industrial chain.

- The standard formation stage. In 3 to 5 years, there should be a **mature** application standard and technology standard of the industry. After the **demonstration** effect in public area and the development of mobile internet, the application in company and industry will be the **focal** point of the development of Internet of Things. Some kinds of application plans are going to mature. The standard of industry will begin to take shape. With the expansion of industrial scale and the application of the **transducer** technology, the standard system will be a **nascent framework**.

- The industry developing stage. In 5 to 10 years, the business model of things of internet will be more active. The person market and family market are going mature. The standard of industry will be spread quickly and recognized widely. All kinds of companies providing

comprehensive [ˌkɔmpriˈhensiv]
adj. 广泛的，综合的

mature [məˈtjuə]
adj. 成熟的，深思的
demonstration [ˌdemənsˈtreiʃən]
n. 表明，证明，示范
focal [ˈfəukəl]
adj. 中心的，很重要的，焦点的
transducer [trænzˈdjuːsə]
n. 变频器，变换器
nascent [ˈnæsnt]
adj. 初期的，新生的
framework [ˈfreimwəːk]
n. 构架，结构

service about Internet of Things will be stars in the development of industry. The new type of business model will take the shape in the IOT industry.

Challenges and Concerns

Building on the potential benefits offered by the Internet of Things poses a number of challenges, not only due to the nature of the enabling technologies but also to the sheer scale of their deployment. Technological standardization in most areas is still in its **infancy**, or remains **fragmented**. Not surprisingly, managing and **fostering** rapid innovation is a challenge for governments and industry alike.

Standardization is essential for the mass deployment and diffusion of any technology. Nearly all **commercially** successful technologies have undergone some process of standardization to achieve mass market **penetration**. Today's internet and mobile phones would not have **thrived** without standards such as TCP/IP and IMT-2000.

Successful standardization in RFID was initially achieved through the Auto-ID Center and now by EPC Global. However, efforts are under way in different forums (ETSI, ISO, etc) and there have been calls for the increased involvement of ITU in the **harmonization** of RFID protocols. Wireless sensor networks have received a boost through the work of the ZigBee **Alliance**, among others. By contrast, standards in nanotechnology and robotics are far more fragmented, with a lack of common definitions and a wide variety of regulating bodies.

One of the most important challenges in **convincing** users to adopt emerging technologies is the protection of data and privacy, as shown in Fig.14.12. Concerns over privacy and data protection are widespread, particularly as sensors and smart tags can track users' movements, habits and **ongoing preferences**. When everyday items equipped with some or all of the five senses (such as sight and smell) combined with computing and communication capabilities, concepts of data request and data consent risk becom outdated. Invisible and constant data exchange between things and people, and between things and other things, will occur unknown to the owners and originators of such data. The sheer scale and capacity of the new technologies will

infancy ['infənsi]
n. 早期，初始阶段
fragmented [fræg`mentɪd, `frægməntɪd]
adj. 成碎片的，片断的
foster ['fɔstə]
vt. 促进，激励，鼓励
commercially [kə'mə:ʃəli]
adv. 商业上
penetration [peni'treiʃən]
n. 穿透，渗透，侵入
thrive [θraiv]
vi. 兴盛，兴隆
harmonization [,hɑ:mənai'zeiʃən]
n. 调和化，一致，融洽
alliance [ə'laiəns]
n. 联盟，同盟

convince [kən'vins]
vt. 使相信，使信服

ongoing ['ɔngəuiŋ]
adj. 继续进行的，不断前进中的
preference ['prefərəns]
n. 较喜欢的东西，偏爱，爱好，喜好

magnify ['mægnifai]

magnify this problem. Who will **ultimately** control the data collected by all the eyes and ears embedded in the environment surrounding us?

vt. 放大，增强，夸张
ultimately [ˈʌltɪmətlɪ]
adv. 最后，最终

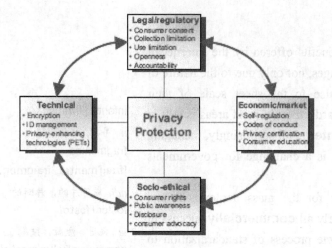

Fig. 14.12 The many facets of privacy protection

Public concerns and active campaigns by consumers have already **hampered** commercial trials of RFID by two well-known retailers. To promote a more widespread adoption of the technologies underlying the Internet of Things, principles of informed consent, data confidentiality and security must be safeguarded. Moreover, protecting privacy must not be limited to technical solutions, but **encompass** regulatory, market-based and socio-**ethical** considerations. Unless there are concerted efforts involving all government, civil society and private sector players to protect these values, the development of the Internet of Things will be hampered if not prevented. It is only through awareness of these technological advances, and the challenges they present, that we can seize the future benefits of a fair and user-centric Internet of Things.

hamper [ˈhæmpə]
vt. 妨碍，束缚，限制

encompass [inˈkʌmpəs]
vt. 围绕，包围，包含
ethical [ˈeθikəl]
adj. 伦理的，道德的

Exercises

Ⅰ. Fill in the blanks with the information given in the text.

1. The Internet of Things is a network of Internet-enabled objects which more objects are becoming embedded with sensors and gaining the ability to communicate, and its three important characters is comprehensive _____, Reliable _____, and Intelligent _____.

2. One of the most important challenges in convincing users to adopt emerging technologies is the _____ of data and _____.

3. In order to connect everyday objects and devices to large _____ and networks——and indeed to the

network of networks (the internet)——a simple, unobtrusive and cost-effective system of item identification is _____. Only then can data about things be collected and _____. Radio-frequency identification (RFID) offers this functionality.

4. As this document has described, IOT is not yet a tangible reality, but rather a prospective _____ of a number of technologies that, combined together, could in the _____ 5 to 15 years drastically modify the way our societies function.

5. Sensors play a pivotal _____ in bridging the gap between the physical and virtual worlds, and enabling things to respond to changes in their physical _____.

Sensors collect data from their environment, generating information and raising awareness about context.

Ⅱ. Translate the following passages from English into Chinese.

The internet as we know it is transforming radically. From an academic network for the chosen few, it became a mass-market, consumer-oriented network. Now, it is set to become fully pervasive, interactive and intelligent.

Real-time communications will be possible not only by humans but also by things at anytime and from anywhere. The advent of the Internet of Things will create a plethora of innovative applications and services, which will enhance quality of life and reduce inequalities whilst providing new revenue opportunities for a host of enterprising businesses.

Grammar 14　科技英语文体的基本特点

科技文体不同于文学类或其他形式的文体，它是与科学技术有关的一种独特的文体形式。科技文章有着其自身的特点和规律。了解和掌握科技英语文体的特点和规律对于阅读十分有益。

1. 无人称句和被动语态句多

无人称句是科技英语文体的一个特点之一。这是因为科技文章所涉及的范围多与科技事实、科学发现、研究结果等相关。人们更关注科技给人类带来的巨大影响，因此，科技文章往往没有人称，同时被动语态句在科技文章中也被广泛使用。

(1) A 15 ampere fuse melts if the current exceeds 15 amperes.
如果电流超过 15 安培，则 15 安培的保险丝就熔化。

(2) A combination of cushion blasting and line-drilling can be adopted to resolve our problem.
我们可以采取缓冲爆破和排钻采石法相结合的办法来解决问题。

很显然，以上两例中都没有使用人称句，第二句使用了被动语态。这正是因为科技英语的主旨在于阐述科技事实、科学发现、研究结果等，以陈述真实现象的客观性为目的，故在阅读中应考虑到这一特点，才能更好地理解科技英语文章。

2. 理论性和逻辑性强

科技英语文章与普通英文文学作品很大不同之处就在于它的理论性和逻辑性强，要求运用科学的原理和方法去阐明新的科学问题和现象，对客观事物的叙述必须实事求是、准确无误、客观真实、概念准确、逻辑严谨等。

(1) The area of electronics dealing with semi..conductors is called solid- state electronics, because the

electrons move through solids, especially crys..tals, rather than through a conductor or vacuum.

研究半导体的电子学领域称为固态电子学, 因为电子是在固态尤其是晶体中移动的而不是通过另段导体或真空管。

(2) As light energy can be converted into other forms of energy, so could the laser beam be converted to aircraft fuel.Such a breakthrough would greatly reduce the weight of aircraft and there by increase the probability of hypersonic travel——travel at speeds fiveormore times greater than the speed of sound. Planes could travel at 4000 to 5000 miles an hour and at a ltitudes of 150000 feet.

因为光能可以转化成其他形式的能量, 所以激光束可以被转化成飞行器的燃料。这项突破将大大减轻飞行器的质量, 从而增加特超音速飞机的可能性, 即以声速的五倍或五倍以上的速度飞行。飞机能够在150000 英尺的高度以每小时 4000~5000 英里的速度飞行。

从上面这两段文字可以看出, 文章中 so lid- state electronics (固态电子学), vacuum (真空管), light energy (光能), aircraft fuel(飞行器的燃料)等使用的专业词汇多, 对词语的定义表述准确, 推理严密, 逻辑、理论性强。阅读者需在概念明晰、语义变化的情况下, 来完成对所读材料的理解。因此, 在阅读中要注重科技英语文章的词、句和概念的表述具有科学性和规范性等特点。

 参考译文

Section A 物联网的历史

每一次危机都会催生一些新技术, 而新技术也是使经济, 特别是工业走出危机的巨大推动力。2008年, 席卷全球的金融危机也在催生新的经济驱动力诞生, 物联网就是众人最为推崇的动力。

在过去的几年中, 互联网已遍布世界各地。一个有创意的想法在移动设备和无线网络中迅速蔓延传播: 我们周围普遍存在的各种"物体"或"对象", 如 RFID、传感器、执行器、移动电话, 通过独特的解决方案能够互相交流, 并与邻近的"智能"部件合作, 实现共同的目标。这种小说的模式被命名为"物联网" (IOT)。它延续了智能环境的概念, 并使这些"物体"或"对象"随时随地接入互联网。物联网被认为是继计算机、互联网和移动通信网络之后全球信息产业的第三次浪潮。

应用场景

我们正处在一个新的全域计算和全域通信的时代, 它将彻底改变我们的企业、社区和我们自己。现在, 物联网是热点, 但物联网到底是什么?究竟能做什么?我们通过几个与人们生活密切相关的场景进行介绍。

场景 1: 这是一个冬天的早上 7 点。当你还睡在床上时, 你的传感器通过新陈代谢活动检测到你要起床。你的床通知厨房管理中心、汽车、PDA、闹钟等, 然后厨房开始给你热牛奶, 汽车开始启动引擎和预热, PDA 从谷歌日历中下载你今天的个人时间表, 闹钟开始叫醒你。

场景 2: 物联网冰箱可能是最常被引证的物联网例子之一。想象一下, 物联网冰箱可以监视冰箱里的食物, 并在我们去超市的时候告诉。它还可以跟踪美食网站, 为你收集食谱并在你的购物单里添加配料。根据你对每顿饭给出的评分, 这种冰箱知道你喜欢吃什么东西。他可以照顾你的身体, 因为他知道什么食物对你有好处。

场景 3: 当你想驾驶爱车外出度假时, 车上依法安装的 RFID 传感器在警告可能要出现的轮胎故障, 你需要到汽修厂进行检查。当你经过喜爱的汽修厂入口处的时候, 使用无线传感技术和无线传输技术的诊断工具对你的汽车进行检查, 并要求其驶向指定的维修台。这个维修台是由全自动的机器臂装备的。你可以离开自己的爱车去喝点咖啡。Orange Wall 饮料机知道你对加冰咖啡的喜好,当你利用自己的互联网手表安全付款之后立刻倒出饮料。等你喝完咖啡回来,一对新的轮胎已经安装完毕,并且安装了检测压力、温度和形变的集成式 RFID 标签。

以上描述的场景是物联网时代未来生活的一窥。今天,我们正处在开启信息技术新篇章的边缘:无处不在的计算和通信时代。我们的生活、商业和社会将会发生根本性地转变。

轻触一下计算机或者手机的按钮,即使千里之外,你也能了解到某件物品的状况、某个人的活动情况。发一个短信,你就能打开风扇;如果有人非法入侵你的住宅,你还会收到自动电话报警。如此智能的场景已不是好莱坞科幻大片中才有的情形了,物联网正在步步逼近我们的生活。

有专家预测 10 年内物联网就可能大规模普及,发展成为上万亿规模的高科技市场。届时,在个人健康、交通控制、环境保护、公共安全、平安家居、智能消防、工业监测、老人护理等几乎所有领域,物联网都将发挥作用。有专家表示,只需 3～5 年,物联网就会全面进入人们的生活,改变人们的生活方式。

历史沿革的物联网

作为新兴事物的物联网其实并不年轻,它的演变历史超过 15 年,如图 14.1 所示。

1995 年,Bill Gates 在出版的《未来之路》一书中就曾提及机器之间的通信。

1999 年,美国麻省理工学院的前身自动识别(Auto-ID)中心提出"物联网"的构想。物联网最初的含义是指把所有物品通过射频识别等信息传感设备与互联网连接起来,实现智能化识别和管理。

2005 年,在突尼斯的世界首脑会议上,国际电信联盟(ITU)发布了"物联网"的技术报告,该报告扩展了物联网的概念。信息和通信技术(ICT)的世界加入了新的维度:从任何时间、任何地点连接任何人,发展到连接任何物体(如图 14.2 所示)。各种连接将成倍增加,并创造出一个全新的动态网络——物联网。

2009 年,IBM 公司推出其智慧地球计划。物联网为其中不可或缺的一部分。Obama 总统对"智慧地球"的构想做出了积极回应,并将其提升为国家级的发展战略,从而引起全球的广泛关注。

智慧地球

2008 年 11 月 6 日,IBM 董事会主席兼 CEO Sam Palmisano 先生在纽约外交关系理事会上发表题为《一个智慧的地球:下一代领导人议程》的演讲,正式提出"智慧地球"的概念。他认为智慧地球的实现需要物联化、互连化和智能化,如图 14.3 所示。

对 IBM 而言,智慧地球是指将智慧嵌入系统和流程之中,将世界嵌入各类没人会看作计算机的物品中,如汽车、电器、铁路、电网、服装等,甚至是自然系统,如农业和水域中。其应用领域如图 14.4 所示。这些前所未有的"智慧"基础设施,为创新提供了无穷无尽的空间。

感知中国

2009 年 8 月 7 日,国务院总理温家宝考察无锡高新微纳传感网工程技术研发中心,并提出了"感知中国"的概念,如图 14.5 所示。他指出,随着信息技术和虚拟信息空间的发展,人与人的互连已逐渐进入到材料领域与真实的物理世界。我们要大力发展传感网,掌握核心技术。

2009 年 11 月 3 日,总理温家宝发表了《让科技引领中国可持续发展》的讲话,并指出要突破传感网和物联网的关键技术。

2010 年 3 月 5 日,温家宝总理在第十一届全国人民代表大会第三次会议上作了政府工作报告,其中强调要大力培育战略性新兴产业,加大支持和推进物联网的研发应用。

2010 年 6 月 8 日,胡锦涛总书记在院士全会上为此发表了讲话,努力发展物联网和建立由传感器网络组成的智能基础设施。

在这个后金融危机时代,中国可持续发展的目标表明中国经济的结构调整和产业升级势在必行,这为物联网的发展提供巨大的空间和良好的契机。2009 年以来,中国政府对于物联网的发展给予了高度的关注,不断出台新政策鼓励物联网的发展。地方政府和企业也对物联网表示了浓厚的兴趣,促使物联网及相关产业在我国迅猛发展,物联网产业的设备制造、网络运营和产业化应用方面已经取得了巨大进展。作为新兴高技术产业的代表,物联网本身的发展就代表着产业升级的成果。同时,物联网在各个领域的应用不仅促进了这些产业中其他高新技术的融合和应用,提高了生产效率,还改变了人们的生活方式,刺激了消费,为经济结构调整提供了动力。我国物联网下一步的发展趋势在于产业化应用和大规模推广,只有这样才能达到规模效益。

Section B 主要技术

物联网是新一代信息技术的重要组成部分,是继互联网之后全球信息产业的又一次科技与经济浪潮。

物联网的定义

由于物联网的概念出现不久,其内涵还在不断地发展和完善,并且学术界和工业界的视角各异,至今都没有给出一个公认的统一定义。

根据字面意思解释,物联网又名传感网,是指将各种信息传感设备与互联网结合起来而形成的一个巨大网络,可使所有的物品与网络连接,方便识别和管理。

国际电信联盟定义:任何时间、任何地点、任何人、任意物体之间互联。

一般定义:普遍认为,物联网就是按照约定协议,把物体与互联网等网络连接起来,进行信息交换、通信和处理,在实现智能化识别、定位、跟踪、监控、管理和服务的基础上,深度应用于经济社会和自然领域,提高人类生产生活管理水平的全新信息系统。它立足于新一代信息技术,如无线射频识别(RFID)技术、传感器和智能手机。物联网的目的是连接网络和事物,并且他们可以互相交换信息。物联网的基础是互联网,它是在我们所熟悉的互联网基础上延伸和扩展的网络。

物联网的结构

由于物联网不同于互联网和电信网,上述两种模型并不适合直接用于物联网,但他们有一些共同的类似功能。因此,利用互联网的技术架构和电信管理网络的逻辑结构,并结合物联网的具体特点,物联网的3层架构被普遍接受。我们相信此架构将更好地解释物联网的特点和内涵。我们将物联网分为3层,分别为感知层,网络层和应用层,如图14.6所示。

感知层是通过各种传感器(如红外传感器、RFID、二维条码)感知物体的物理性质(如温度、位置等),并将这些信息转换成更方便网络传输的数字信号。这些感知设备包括二氧化碳传感器、温度传感器、湿度传感器、二维码标签、RFID标签和读写器、照相机、GPS和其他传感装置。感知层的作用相当于耳鼻喉和人体皮肤的神经末梢,它的主要功能是识别物体和收集信息。

网络层就像物联网的中枢神经系统和大脑,其主要功能是传输和处理来自感知层的信息。网络层由有线/无线通信网络和互联网、网络管理中心、信息中心和智能处理中心等组成。

应用层是物联网和用户(包括个人、组织和其他系统)的接口,结合行业需求,以实现智能化行业,类似于人类的社会分工,最终形成人类社会。物联网的行业特点反映在像绿色农业、工业监控、公共安全、城市管理、远程医疗、智能家居、智能交通、环境监测等应用中,一些行业已经积累了一些成功案例,如图14.7所示。

物联网的核心技术

物联网正在给人们的生产和生活方式带来深刻的变革。物联网在带来诸多好处的同时,也给整个信息技术领域带来了前所未有的挑战。它的核心技术是射频识别(RFID)、无线传感器网络(WSN)和微机电系统(MEMS)等。

- 射频识别(RFID)：它是从20世纪90年代开始兴起的一种非接触式自动识别技术。它可以通过射频信号自动识别目标物体并获取相关数据。它具有测量精度高，抗干扰能力强，容易控制的特点。最基本的RFID系统由标签、读写器和天线所组成，如图14.8所示。射频识别技术有广泛的应用前景，如图书馆管理和邮件处理程序。RFID在物联网的发展中扮演一个非常重要的角色。
- 无线传感器网络(WSN)：它是由部署在监测区域内大量的廉价微型传感器结点，通过无线通信方式形成的一个多跳自组织网络。其目的是协作地感知、采集、处理和传输网络覆盖地理区域内感知对象的监测信息，并报告给用户。如图14.9所示，传感器结点监测的数据沿着其他传感器结点逐跳地进行传输。在传输过程中监测的数据可能被多个结点处理，经过多跳后路由到汇聚结点，最后通过互联网或卫星到达管理结点。用户通过管理结点对传感器网络进行配置和管理，发布监测任务以及收集监测数据。
- 微机电系统(MEMS)：是集微型传感器、执行器以及信号处理和控制电路、接口电路、通信和电源于一体的系统。此系统对声、光、热、磁、运动等自然信息进行感知、识别、控制和处理，如图14.10所示。它是正在飞跃发展的微米/纳米技术的一项十分重要的成果，外形轮廓尺寸在毫米量级以下，构成它的机械零件和半导体元器件尺寸在微米-纳米量级($10^{-6} \sim 10^{-9}$米)。这种微型机电系统将微型电机、微型电路、微型传感器、微型执行器等微型装置和器件集成在硅片上，不仅能够搜集、处理与发送信息或指令，还能够按照所获取的信息自主地或根据外部的指令采取行动。

Section C 挑战和关注

物联网揭示了计算和通信的未来，它的发展也依赖于一些重要领域的动态技术创新：从无线传感技术到纳米技术。

首先，为了将日常用品和设备连接到大型数据库和网络——实际是网络的网络(即互联网)，一个简单易用并有效的物体识别系统是至关重要的。只有那样，物体的数据才能够被收集和处理。无线射频识别(RFID)提供了这样的功能。

其次，数据收集受益于探测物体物理状态改变的能力，使用传感器技术就能满足这一点。物体中的嵌入式智能技术能够通过转移信息处理能力到网络边缘而进一步增强网络的威力。

最后，小型化技术和纳米技术的优势意味着体积越来越小的物体能够进行交互和连接(图14.11)。

所有这些技术的融合形成了将世界上的物体与感官和智能行为连接到一起的物联网。事实上，借助集成化信息处理的帮助，工业产品和日常用品将会获得智能化的特征和性能。它们还能满足远程查询的电子识别需要，并能通过传感器探测周围的物理变化。就这样，甚至于像灰尘这样的微粒都能被标记并纳入网络。这样的发展将使现在的静态物体变成未来的动态物件，在我们的环境中嵌入智能，刺激更多创新产品和服务的诞生。

特征

物联网的核心是物与物以及人与物之间的信息交互。其重要的3个特征可简要概括在表14.1中。

表14.1 物联网的3个特征

全面感知	利用射频识别、传感器、二维码等随时随地采集和获取物体的信息
可靠传送	通过网络融合将物体的信息适时准确地传递出去
智能处理	利用各种智能计算技术，对海量的感知数据和信息进行分析并处理，对物体进行实时智能化控制

未来发展

我们应该对物联网采用长远的眼光。物联网是一个新的产业,它会为我们的日常生活带来许多便利。物联网的发展不仅是行业的发展,而且是人民生活的改善。

- 产业形成阶段。现在我们正处在物联网发展的形成阶段。政府应该支持物联网行业,并将物联网技术应用到安全管理、节约能源和保护环境等领域。扩展物联网的用途,它会变得成熟起来,并带动产业链的发展。
- 标准形成阶段。在 3~5 年内,应该有一个成熟的应用标准和行业技术标准。在公共场所和移动互联网发展的示范效应后,在公司和行业的应用将是物联网发展的重点。某些类型的应用计划正在成熟。行业标准将开始初具规模。随着产业规模的扩大和活跃的传感器技术的应用,标准体系将是新生的框架。
- 行业发展阶段。在 5~10 年内,物联网的商业模式将更加活跃。人才市场和家庭市场正在走向成熟。行业标准将迅速蔓延,并得到广泛的认可。各种提供物联网服务的公司将成为行业发展的明星。新型的商业模式将形成。

挑战和关注

在物联网所带来的潜在利益的基础上,由于使能技术的成熟和部署规模的庞大,物联网也向我们提出一系列的挑战。大多数领域的技术标准化尚处于起步阶段,或者仍然支离破碎。这并不奇怪,管理和促进快速创新对各国政府和产业界都是挑战。

标准化对于任何技术的大规模部署和扩散都是至关重要的。几乎所有商业上成功的技术都经历了一些标准化的进程,以实现大规模的市场渗透。今天的互联网和移动电话如果没有像 TCP/IP 和 IMT-2000 标准也不会有今天的蓬勃发展。

RFID 的标准化通过 Auto-ID 中心和现在的 EPC Global 初步实现。然而,不同的论坛(ETSI、国际标准化组织等)正在努力,并一直呼吁在国际电信联盟参与 RFID 协议的协调统一。无线传感器网络通过 ZigBee 联盟的工作取得了进步。相比之下,纳米技术和机器人技术的标准更为零散,缺乏一个共同的定义和各种监管机构。

说服用户采用新兴技术的一个最重要的挑战是对数据和隐私的保护,如图 14.12 所示。对隐私和数据保护的关注是普遍的,尤其是可以跟踪用户的活动、习惯和持续喜好的传感器和智能标签。当日常用品配备了与计算和通信能力相结合的部分或全部五种感觉(如视觉和嗅觉),数据请求和数据应答风险的概念就成为过时的概念。物体和人之间、物体和物体之间无形而持续的数据交换将会给数据的所有者和组织者带来未知的隐患。新技术的大规模铺开将加剧这个问题。谁将最终控制嵌入到我们周围成千上万的"眼睛"和"耳朵"所收集的数据呢?

公众的关注和消费者的激进活动已经阻碍了两家知名的零售商的 RFID 的商用试用。为了更广泛地推广物联网相关技术的部署,用户知情权、数据保密和安全的原则必须得到维护。此外,保护个人隐私必须不局限于技术解决方案,还需要包含市场和社会伦理考虑的监管。如果政府、民间团体和私营部门参与者不做出共同努力,物联网的发展将受到阻碍甚至终结。只有意识到这些技术的进步和他们所提出的挑战,我们才能从未来公平的以用户为中心的物联网中受益。

Chapter 15 Cloud Computing
(云计算)

Section A What Cloud Computing Really Means

Cloud computing (Fig.15.1)is **all the rage**. "It's become the phrase **du jour**," says Gartner senior analyst Ben Pring, echoing many of his peers. The problem is that (as with Web 2.0) everyone seems to have a different definition.

all the rage
时尚，风行一时的事物
du jour
(法语)当今的

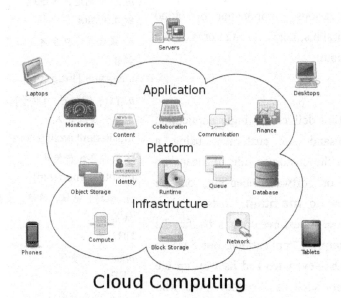

Fig.15.1 Cloud computing logical diagram

As a **metaphor** for the Internet, "the cloud" is a familiar **cliche**, but when combined with "computing", the meaning gets bigger and fuzzier. Some analysts and vendors define cloud computing narrowly as an updated version of utility computing: basically **virtual servers** available over the Internet. Others go very broad, arguing anything you consume outside the firewall is "in the cloud", including conventional **outsourcing**.

Cloud computing comes into focus only when you think about what IT always needs: a way to increase capacity or add capabilities on the fly without investing in new infrastructure, training new personnel, or licensing new software. Cloud

metaphor ['metəfə]
n. 暗喻，隐喻，比喻
cliche ['kli:ʃei; kli:'ʃei]
n. 陈词滥调，陈腐思想
virtual servers
虚拟服务器

outsourcing [aʊt,sɔːsɪŋ]
n. 外包，外购，外部采

computing encompasses any **subscription-based** or **pay-per-use** service that, in real time over the Internet, extends IT's existing capabilities.

Cloud computing is at an early stage, with a motley crew of providers large and small delivering a slew of **cloud-based** services, from **full-blown** applications to storage services to spam filtering. Yes, **utility-style infrastructure** providers are part of the mix, but so are SaaS (software as a service) providers such as Salesforce.com. Today, for the most part, IT must plug into cloud-based services **individually**, but cloud computing **aggregators** and **integrators** are already emerging.

InfoWorld talked to dozens of vendors, analysts, and IT customers to tease out the various components of cloud computing. Based on those discussions, here's a rough breakdown of what cloud computing is all about:

SaaS

This type of cloud computing delivers a single application through the browser to thousands of customers using a **multitenant architecture**. On the customer side, it means no upfront investment in servers or software licensing; on the provider side, with just one app to **maintain**, costs are low compared to conventional hosting. Salesforce.com is by far the best-known example among enterprise applications, but SaaS is also common for **HR** apps and has even worked its way up the food chain to **ERP**, with players such as Workday. And who could have **predicted** the sudden rise of SaaS "desktop" applications, such as Google Apps and Zoho Office?

Utility Computing

The idea is not new, but this form of cloud computing is getting new life from Amazon.com, Sun, IBM, and others who now offer storage and virtual servers that IT can access on **demand**. Early enterprise **adopters** mainly use utility computing for **supplemental**, **non-mission-critical** needs, but one day, they may replace parts of the datacenter. Other providers offer solutions that help IT create virtual datacenters from commodity servers, such as **3Tera's** AppLogic and Cohesive Flexible Technologies' Elastic Server on Demand. Liquid

---

subscription-based
订阅型，基于订购，订阅制
pay-per-use
付费，使用付费，量计价
cloud-based
基于云的
full-blown [ful'bləun]
adj. 成熟的，(花)盛开的，(帆等)张满的
utility-style infrastructure
公用计算基础架构
Individually [ɪndɪ'vɪdjuəlɪ]
adv. 个别地，单独地
aggregator
n. 聚合器，整合者，汇集者，聚合
integrator ['intigreitə]
n. [自] 积分器；[电子] 积分电路；整合之人
multitenant architecture
多重任务执行架构
maintain [men'tein]
vt. 维持，继续，维修，主张，供养
HR
abbr. 人力资源
ERP
abbr. 企业资源计划
predict [pri'dikt]
vi. 做出预言、做预料、做预报
vt. 预报，预言，预知
demand [di'mɑ:nd]
vi. 需要，请求，查问
n. [经] 需求，要求，需要
vt. 要求，需要，查询
adopter [ə'dɒptə(r)]
n. 养父母，[化工] 接受管
supplemental [,sʌpli'mentl]
adj. 补充的，追加的
non-mission-critical

Computing's LiquidQ offers similar capabilities, enabling IT to stitch together memory, I/O, storage, and computational capacity as a virtualized resource pool available over the network.

Web Services in the Cloud

Closely related to SaaS, Web service providers offer **APIs** that enable developers to exploit **functionality** over the Internet, rather than delivering full-blown applications. They range from providers offering discrete business services (such as Strike Iron and Xignite) to the full range of APIs offered by Google Maps, ADP payroll processing, the U.S. Postal Service, **Bloomberg**, and even conventional credit card processing services.

Platform as a Service

Another SaaS **variation**, this form of cloud computing delivers development environments as a service. You build your own applications that run on the provider's infrastructure and are delivered to your users **via** the Internet from the provider's servers. Like Legos, these services are **constrained** by the vendor's design and capabilities, so you don't get complete freedom, but you do get **predictability** and **pre-integration**. Prime examples include Salesforce.com's Force.com, Coghead and the new Google App Engine. For extremely lightweight development, cloud-based **mashup platforms** abound, such as Yahoo Pipes or Dapper.net.

MSP (managed service providers)

One of the oldest forms of cloud computing, a managed service is basically an application exposed to IT rather than to end-users, such as a virus scanning service for e-mail or an application **monitoring** service. Managed security services delivered by **SecureWorks**, IBM, and Verizon fall into this category, as do such cloud-based **anti-spam** services as Postini, recently acquired by Google. Other offerings include desktop management services, such as those offered by CenterBeam or Everdream.

Service Commerce Platforms

A hybrid of SaaS and MSP, this cloud computing service offers a service hub that users interact with. They're most common in trading environments, such as **expense** management systems that allow users to order travel or **secretarial** services from a common platform that then **coordinates** the service delivery and pricing within the **specifications** set by the user. Think of it as an automated service bureau. Well-known examples include Rearden Commerce and Ariba.

Internet Integration

The **integration** of cloud-based services is in its early days. OpSource, which mainly concerns itself with serving SaaS providers, recently introduced the OpSource Services Bus, which employs in-the-cloud integration technology from a little startup called Boomi. SaaS provider Workday recently acquired another player in this space, CapeClear, an ESB (enterprise service bus) provider that was edging toward B2B integration. Way ahead of its time, Grand Central —— which wanted to be a universal "bus in the cloud" to connect SaaS providers and provide integrated solutions to customers ——flamed out in 2005.

Today, with such cloud-based **interconnection** seldom in evidence, cloud computing might be more **accurately** described as "sky computing", with many isolated clouds of services which IT customers must plug into individually. On the other hand, as virtualization and SOA permeate the enterprise, the idea of loosely coupled services running on an **agile**, **scalable** infrastructure should eventually make every enterprise a node in the cloud. It's a **long-running** trend with a **far-out** horizon. But among big **megatrends**, cloud computing is the hardest one to argue with in the long term.

expense [ɪkˈspens]
n. 损失，代价，消费，开支
secretarial [ˌsekrəˈtɛəriəl]
adj. 秘书的，书记的
coordinate [kəʊˈɔːdinit]
vi. 协调
vt. 调整，整合
adj. 并列的，同等的
specification [ˌspesifiˈkeiʃən]
n. 规格，说明书，详述
integration [ˌintiˈgreiʃən]
n. 集成，综合
interconnection [ˌintə(ː)kəˈnekʃən]
n. [计] 互连，互相联络
accurately [ˈækjuritli]
adv. 精确地，准确地
agile [ˈædʒail]
adj. 敏捷的，机敏的，活泼的
scalable [ˈskeiləbl]
adj. 可攀登的，可去鳞的，可称量的
long-running
长期上演的，连续上演很长时间的
far-out
走在时代前端的，非常遥远的
megatrends [ˈmegətrɔn]
n. 大趋势，向信息社会发展的趋势

Exercises

Ⅰ. **Fill in the blanks with the information given in the text.**

1. At the foundation of cloud computing is the broader concept of infrastructure convergence (or Converged Infrastructure) and _____.

2. Cloud computing providers offer their services according to three fundamental models: Infrastructure as a service (IaaS), _____ as a service (PaaS), and software as a service (SaaS).

3. In IaaS model, cloud providers offer computers——as physical or more often as _____ machines, raw (block) storage, firewalls, load balancers, and networks.

4. In _____ model, cloud providers install and operate application software in the cloud and cloud users access the software from cloud clients.

5. A cloud-based application _____ working if you lose your connection.

II. Translate the following passages from English into Chinese.

Service Models of Cloud Computing

Cloud Software as a Service (SaaS). The capability provided to the consumer is to use the provider's applications running on a cloud infrastructure. The applications are accessible from various client devices through a thin client interface such as a Web browser (e.g., Web-based E-mail). The consumer does not manage or control the underlying cloud infrastructure including network, servers, operating systems, storage, or even individual application capabilities, with the possible exception of limited user-specific application configuration settings.

Cloud Platform as a Service (PaaS). The capability provided to the consumer is to deploy onto the cloud infrastructure consumer-created or acquired applications created using programming languages and tools supported by the provider. The consumer does not manage or control the underlying cloud infrastructure including network, servers, operating systems, or storage, but has control over the deployed applications and possibly application hosting environment configurations.

Cloud Infrastructure as a Service (IaaS). The capability provided to the consumer is to provision processing, storage, networks, and other fundamental computing resources where the consumer is able to deploy and run arbitrary software, which can include operating systems and applications. The consumer does not manage or control the underlying cloud infrastructure but has control over operating systems, storage, deployed applications, and possibly limited control of select networking components (e.g., host firewalls).

Section B   Mobile Cloud Computing

Mobile cloud computing is the usage of cloud computing in **combination** with mobile devices. Cloud computing exists when tasks and data are kept on the internet rather than on **individual** devices, providing **on-demand** access.

Applications are run on a remote server and then sent to the user. Because of the advanced improvement in mobile browsers thanks to Apple and Google over the past couple of years, nearly every mobile should have a suitable browser. This means developers will have a much wider market and they can **bypass** the **restrictions** created by mobile operating systems.

Mobile cloud computing gives new company chances for mobile network providers. Several operators such as Vodafone, Orange and Verizon have started to offer cloud computing services for companies.

Alibaba Group launched cloud-based operating system Aliyun on 29th July 2011. The Aliyun operating system will feature cloud services such as E-mail, Internet search and support

combination [ˌkɔmbi'neiʃən]
n. 结合，组合，联合
individual [ˌindi'vidjuəl]
adj. 个人的，个别的
n. 个人，个体
on-demand
按需要
bypass ['baipɑːs; (US) 'baipæs]
n. 旁路；[公路] 支路
vt. 绕开，忽视，设旁路；迂回
restriction [ris'trikʃən]
n. 限制，约束，束缚

for Web-based applications. Users are not required to download or install applications onto their mobile devices.

Definition

Mobile cloud computing is a combination between mobile network and cloud computing, thereby providing optimal services for mobile users. In mobile cloud computing, mobile devices do not need a powerful configuration (e.g., CPU speed and memory capacity) since all the data and complicated computing **modules** can be processed in the clouds.

Applications

Mobile applications are a rapidly developing segment of the global mobile market. They consist of software that runs on a mobile device and perform certain tasks for the user of the mobile phone. As reported by World Mobile Applications Market, about 7 billion (free and paid) application downloads were made globally in 2009 alone from both native and third-party application stores, generating **revenues** of $3.9 billion in the same year. The global mobile application market is **expected** to be worth $24.4 billion in 2015, growing at a CAGR of 64% from 2009 to 2015. Apple is a typical example for the **explosion** of mobile applications. Apple with a whopping more than 4 billion downloads to date commanded more than 90% of the application market share in 2009. The success of Apple's App Store has not only **established** the **scalability** of mobile applications, but has also shown that the best of these offer the **potential** to generate enormous revenues.

- Mobile Commerce. The explosion in the use of electronic commerce (e-commerce) by the business sector has been tremendous since its inception only a few years ago. E-commerce is known as buying and selling of products or services over electronic systems such as the Internet and other computer networks. From governments to **multinational** companies to one-person start-ups, e-commerce is **increasingly** viewed as a key business modality of the future. Ease of **transaction**, widening markets, and decreased overheads are factors that make e-commerce solutions more and more attractive, as evident

module ['mɔdju:l]
n. [计] 模块，组件，模数

revenue ['revinju:]
n. 税收，国家的收入，收益
expected [iks'pektid]
v. 预期，盼望（expect 的过去分词）
adj. 预期的，预料的
explosion [iks'pləuʒən]
n. 爆炸，爆发，激增
establish [is'tæbliʃ]
vi. 植物定植
vt. 建立，创办，安置
scalability [,skeilə'biliti]
n. 可扩展性，可伸缩性，可量测性
potential [pə'tenʃ(ə)l]
n. 潜能，可能性
adj. 潜在的，可能的，势的
multinational [mʌlti'næʃən(ə)l]
adj. 跨国公司的，多国的
n. 跨国公司
increasingly [in'kri:siŋli]
adv. 越来越多地，渐增地
transaction [træn'zækʃən]
n. 交易，事务，办理，会报，学报

with the growth of on-line sales.

- Mobile Learning. Mobile learning today is becoming more popular as there are many people using mobile devices to enhance their learning. Mobile learning (m-learning) is not only electronic learning (e-learning) but e-learning plus mobility. It is clear that learning via mobile brings many benefits for mobile users. It brings the **convenience** for them since they can learn anywhere they want in any convenient time from a **portable** device. However, there is some research pointing out restrictions of traditional mobile learning such as: expensive mobile devices, high cost of network, poor network transmission rate, and limited educational resources. As a result, it is difficult for mobile learning to take full advantage and to be popular as well.

- Mobile Healthcare. The development of telecommunication technology in the medical field helped **diagnosis** and treatment become easier for many people. This can helps patients regularly monitor their health and have timely treatment. Also, it leads to increase **accessibility** to healthcare providers, more efficient tasks and processes, and the improvement about quality of the healthcare services. Nevertheless it also has to face many **challenges** (e.g., physical storage issues, security and privacy, medical errors). Therefore cloud computing is introduced as a solution to address **aforementioned** issues. Cloud computing provides the convenience for users to help them access resources easily and quickly. Besides, it offers services on demand over the network to perform operation that meet changing needs in electronic healthcare applications.

- Mobile Computing. The analysis of the impact of mobile computing on the various services shows the mobile computing has changed each service. As mobile computing has become more popular over the past decade, it has been under continuous development with advances in hardware, software and network. Mobile computing has various applications in our everyday life. Use of this technology has become a **fundamental** skill. With

conveniences [kən'viːnjənsɪ]
n. 方便性
portable ['pɔːtəbl]
adj. 手提的，便携式的，轻便的
telecommunication ['telɪkəmjuːnɪ'keɪʃən]
n. 电信；[通信] 远程通信，无线电通信
diagnosis [ˌdaɪəg'nəʊsɪs]
n. 诊断
accessibility [ˌæksesɪ'bɪlɪti]
n. 易接近，可亲，可以得到

challenge ['tʃælɪndʒ]
n. 挑战，怀疑
vt. 向……挑战
aforementioned [ə'fɔːˌmenʃənd]
adj. 上述的，前面提及的

fundamental [ˌfʌndə'mentl]
adj. 基本的，根本的
n. 基本原理，基本原则

mobile computing we can check our email messages, our bills, our bank accounts and our other private information just by using a mobile phone or laptop anywhere. All the **functionalities obligate** each exchange data to make it safe and **immune** from any attack. Mobile computing services have simplified our lives. Every day we get attached to a new device that includes a lot of functionalities and is based on mobile computing, as examples, iPhone from Apple, Net-Book, etc.

For future research, there are still some challenging issues related to the models of mobile cloud computing and services. They are:

(1) Mobile devices are constrained in storage and processing capacity. How can efficient use be made of the limited resources for cloud computing?

(2) There are several operating systems for mobile devices, especially mobile **smartphones**. These include Android, Symbian, iOS, Chrome, and MeeGo. Is it possible to provide a general access platform for mobile cloud computing on top of these various OS platforms?

(3) Mobile devices act not only as clients but also as components of clouds. What is the impact of mobility of mobile devices on performance of the cloud? What are the benefits and **disadvantages**?

(4) Users in mobile clouds are still exposed to security threats both inside and outside the cloud. What is the best solution for such a mobile environment?

Demand and applications of mobile cloud computing will grow rapidly, and researchers and developers should pay more attention to this area of cloud computing research and development.

functionality
[ˌfʌŋkəʃəˈnæliti]
n. 功能；[数] 泛函性，函数性
obligate [ˈɔbligeit]
vt. 使负义务，强使，强迫，对施以恩惠
adj. 有责任的，有义务的，必须的
immune [iˈmjuːn]
n. 免疫者，免除者
adj. 免疫的，免于的，免除的

smartphone
n. 智能手机

disadvantage
[ˌdisədˈvɑːntidʒ]
n. 缺点，不利条件，损失

Exercises

I. Translate the following terms or phrases from English into Chinese and vice versa.

1. on-demand
2. Cloud-based
3. processed
4. Start-up
5. 移动云计算
6. 应用程序
7. 在线的，即时的
8. 智能型手机

Ⅱ. Translate the following passages from English into Chinese.

Deployment Models of Cloud Computing

Private cloud. The cloud infrastructure is operated solely for an organization. It may be managed by the organization or a third party and may exist on premise or off premise.

Community cloud. The cloud infrastructure is shared by several organizations and supports a specific community that has shared concerns (e.g., mission, security requirements, policy, and compliance considerations). It may be managed by the organizations or a third party and may exist on premise or off premise.

Public cloud. The cloud infrastructure is made available to the general public or a large industry group and is owned by an organization selling cloud services.

Hybrid cloud. The cloud infrastructure is a composition of two or more clouds (private, community, or public) that remain unique entities but are bound together by standardized or proprietary technology that enables data and application portability (e.g., cloud bursting for load-balancing between clouds).

Section C Clash of the Clouds

The **launch** of Windows 7 marks the end of an era in computing—and the beginning of an epic battle between Microsoft, Google, Apple and others.

Windows 7 is not just a sizeable step for Microsoft. It is also likely to mark the end of one era in information technology and the start of another. Much of computing will no longer be done on personal computers in homes and offices, but in the "cloud": huge data centres housing vast storage systems and hundreds of thousands of servers, the powerful machines that dish up data over the internet. Web-based E-mail, social networking and online games are all examples of what are increasingly called cloud services, and are accessible through browsers, smart-phones or other "client" devices. Because so many services can be downloaded or are available online, Windows 7 is Microsoft's first operating system to come with fewer features. Windows is not going to disappear soon, but cloud computing means it is no longer so important.

The rise of cloud computing is not just shifting Microsoft's centre of gravity. It is changing the nature of competition within the computer industry. Technological developments have hitherto pushed computing power away from **central hubs**: first from mainframes to minicomputers, and then to PCs. Now a combination of ever cheaper and more powerful processors, and ever faster and more ubiquitous networks, is pushing power back

launch [lɔːntʃ, lɑːntʃ]
vt. 发射(导弹、火箭等), 发起, 发动, 使下水
n. 发射, 发行, 投放市场, 下水, 汽艇
vi. 开始, 下水, 起飞

central hub
中央集线器

to the centre in some respects, and even further away in others. The cloud's data centres are, in effect, outsize public **mainframes**. At the same time, the PC is being pushed aside by a host of smaller, often wireless devices, such as smart-phones, **netbooks** (small laptops) and tablets (touch-screen computers the size of books).

Although Windows still runs 90% of PCs, the fading importance of the PC means that Microsoft is no longer an all-powerful **monopolist**. Others are also building big clouds, including Google, a giant of the internet, and Apple, renowned as a maker of hardware, with a market **capitalisation** that now exceeds those of both Google and IBM, its original arch-rival.

A Taxonomy of Giants

Despite the growing **similarities** among the three, each is a unique beast, says Michael Cusumano, a professor at **Massachusetts** Institute of Technology's Sloan School of Management. They can be classified according to how they approach the cloud, how they make money and how openly they approach the development of **intellectual property**.

Google, you might say, has been a cloud company since its birth in 1998. It is best known for its search service, but now offers all sorts of other products and services, too. It has built a global network of three dozen data centres with 2 millions servers, say some estimates. Among other things, it offers a suite of web-based applications, such as word processing and spreadsheets. Lately it has branched out, releasing Android for phones, and its Chrome web-browser and operating system for PCs.

It took Google a while to come up with a way of making money, but it found one in advertising, its main source of revenue. It handles more than 75% of **search-related** ads in America. Worldwide its share is even higher. Google is also trying to make money from selling services to companies. On October 12th it said that Rentokil Initial, a pest control to parcel delivery group, would roll out Google's online applications to its 35000 employees, making it the biggest company to do so.

Google's reliance on advertising explains its open approach to intellectual property. Giving Android and Chrome OS away as

mainframe ['meɪnfreɪm]
n. [计] 主机，大型机，大型主机
netbook
n. 上网本

monopolist [mə'nɒpəlɪst]
n. 垄断者，独占者，专利者
capitalisation
[ˌkæpɪtəlaɪ'zeɪʃən]
n. 市值
taxonomy [tæk'sɒnəmi]
n. 分类学；分类法
similarity [ˌsɪmɪ'lærɪti]
n. 类似；相似点
Massachusetts
[ˌmæsə'tʃuːsɪts]
n. 马萨诸塞州(美国)
intellectual property
[专利] 知识产权；著作权

search-related
搜索相关联的

open-source software not only makes life difficult for rivals' paid-for products but also increases demand for Google's services and the reach of its ads. Its openness has limits: Google says little about the architecture of its data centres and search algorithms, because they give the company its competitive edge. The way it organises **R&D** internally is open and **decentralised**: **self-organising** teams come up with ideas for most new services.

If Google was born in the sky, Microsoft started on the ground. Office, its bestselling suite of PC programs, is almost as **ubiquitous** as Windows. But the company is less a stranger to cloud computing than it may seem. It has built a network of data centres, and is starting to gain traction after losing billions developing online services. Its Xbox games console has powerful online features. Bing, its new search engine, has gained a shade in market share (though it is still miles behind Google). It is even preparing a **stripped-down** Web-based version of Office, and it now offers much of its business software as online services.

However, most of Microsoft's revenue and all of its profit still come from conventional **shrink-wrapped** software. But the company cannot leave online advertising to Google, because consumers expect cloud services to be free, financed by ads. Hence Microsoft's efforts to convince Yahoo, another online giant, to merge its search and part of its advertising business with Microsoft's. The deal, sealed in July, means that Microsoft will handle 10% of searches, against Google's 83%, says Net Applications, a market-research firm.

Given Microsoft's history, it is hardly surprising that its treatment of intellectual property differs from Google's. It gives other software firms the technical information they need to write programs that run on Windows. Otherwise, it guards the underlying recipes of its software jealously. That said, the firm now supports many open standards and has even started using bits of open-source software. Internally, its R&D is somewhat more centralised than Google, at least in its online division: teams are bigger, work with more **co-ordination** and get more guidance from above.

Apple, too, came from outside the cloud. Online services have always been a bit of an afterthought to what the company excels at: pricey but highly **innovative** bundles of hardware and

---

open-source
adj. 开放源代码
R&D
abbr. research & development
研究与开发
decentralise [ˌdiːˈsentrəlaɪz]
vt. (英)分散,分权(等于 decentra-lize)
self-organising
自我组织
ubiquitous [juːˈbɪkwɪtəs]
adj. 普遍存在的,无所不在的

stripped-down [ˈstrɪptˈdaʊn]
adj. (尤指车辆)无附件和附属设备的,仅具必要装置的,(机器等)拆散的,解体的
shrink-wrap [ˈʃrɪŋkræp]
n. 包装用的收缩胶膜
vt. 用收缩胶膜包装

co-ordination
[ˌkəʊprɔˈspərəti]
n. 协调,配合
innovative [ˈɪnəʊveɪtɪv]
adj. 革新的,创新的

software, of which the iPhone is only the latest example. Its online offerings——the iTunes store for music and video, the App Store for mobile applications, and MobileMe, a suite of online services——were all originally meant to drive demand for Apple's hardware, but the firm's interest in the cloud has grown. It is building a $1 billion data centre, possibly the world's largest, in North Carolina.

Still, Apple's financial health thus far has depended mainly on selling hardware. **Gadgets** generate most of the firm's revenue and profit. The firm does not reveal its revenue from services separately, but it is not to be **sneezed at**. Apple accounts for 69% of online music sales in America and 35% of all sales, more than Wal-Mart, reckons NPD Group, a market-research firm. Apple has so far forgone advertising revenue: its services are **ad-free**, but most of them require payment. Apple's services are aimed at consumers, not businesses.

Apple is also the odd one out when it comes to openness. The word does not appear in its vocabulary. It does not allow any other hardware-maker to build machines using its operating system. It blocks iPhone applications it does not approve of from appearing in the App Store. Apple is also secretive about the way it conducts its internal R&D. Mr Jobs clearly calls most of the shots. But insiders say that there is a system of teams that pitch projects to him.

How will this three-way contest play out? The last similar war was in the 1980s and early 1990s, when Apple, IBM and Microsoft fought for mastery of the PC. After much fire and smoke, Microsoft was victorious. Thanks to what economists call strong **network effects**, which allow winners to take almost all, Windows relegated its rival operating systems to mere sideshows, securing fat profits for its owner.

Such a **lopsided** result is unlikely this time. One reason is that the economics of the cloud may be different from those of the PC. Network effects are unlikely to be as strong. Much of the cloud is based on open standards, which should make it easier to switch providers. To underline this point and to counter arguments that it is trying to lock users in, Google has set up the **Data Liberation Front**, a team of engineers whose job is to

gadget ['gædʒit]
n. 小玩意，小器具，小配件，诡计

sneezed at
vt. 蔑视，轻视

ad-free
无广告

network effects
网络效应

lopsided ['lɔp'saidid]
adj. 不平衡的，倾向一方的

Data Liberation Front
数据自由前线，数据自由火线

Chapter 15　Cloud Computing

devise ways of allowing people to transfer their data.

Second, all three giants have reliable sources of cash to sustain them. Windows may be under attack, not least because of the boom in cheap netbooks, which has forced Microsoft to reduce prices, says Matt Rosoff of ***Directions on Microsoft***, a newsletter. Even so, the operating system will keep on giving for some time. Microsoft has other strong divisions too, including business and server software. Google may lose some market share in search (and some advertising) to the combination of Bing and Yahoo!, but it is unlikely to be dethroned. Apple is still able to command premium prices, although others make hardware just as **slick**.

Full War Chests

This means that all three will have ample resources to spend in the main areas of the fight: data centres, cloud services and the periphery. In data centres, Google is ahead, but Microsoft is catching up in size and **sophistication**. Apple has most to learn, but this, too, seems only a question of time and money. Just as much of hardware has become a **commodity**, knowing how to build huge data centres may not be a big competitive advantage for long. And data centres can get only so big before scale ceases to be an advantage.

In services too, Google is ahead. But in Bing Microsoft may at last have created a worthy rival. The "**decision engine**", to use the company's term, does a good job of helping people choose a new camera or book a holiday. The big question is whether Apple can catch up. Its iTunes and App stores are successes, to be sure, but for now they are highly specialised. Its broader suite of cloud services, Mobile Me, is nothing to write home about.

At the cloud's periphery, however, Apple has a strong position, thanks to the success of the iPhone. Its share of the American market is pushing 14%. The App Store now boasts 85,000 applications and a total of more than 2 billion downloads. But recently Google's Android has gained momentum. Several handset-makers have released smart-phones based on it, or will do so in the next few months. In early October it received the backing of Verizon, America's biggest mobile operator. At the

Directions on Microsoft
微软指南

slick [slɪk]
n. [机] 平滑器，修光工具，通俗杂志
adj. 光滑的，华而不实的，聪明的，熟练的，老套的
adv. 灵活地，聪明地
vt. 使光滑，使漂亮
vi. 打扮整洁
sophistication
[sə,fɪstɪ'keɪʃən]
n. 复杂，诡辩，老于世故，有教养
commodity [kə'mɔdɪti]
n. 商品，货物，日用品
decision engine
决策引擎，决定引擎，抉择引擎

end of 2012, predicts Gartner, a market-research firm, Android phones will have a bigger share of the market than iPhones.

Microsoft's mobile strategy, though, is in **disarray**. This could prove to be a serious weakness, as people increasingly use mobile devices to reach online services. Plans to build smart-phones of its own seem to be going nowhere. Its music player, Zune, will remain just that, Steve Ballmer, Microsoft's boss, said recently. Pink, a project to develop phones based on technology from Danger, a start-up acquired by Microsoft in 2008, is said to face death by **cancellation**——even more likely after Danger lost personal data belonging to tens of thousands of its customers earlier this month. And the latest version of Windows Mobile is no match for the iPhone and Android. Some **handset-makers**, including Motorola, have ditched the software.

Then there are market forces. One of the three may come up with something "insanely great", an expression used at Apple in times past to describe the original Macintosh computer. Apple itself may do so with a **tablet computer**, **rumoured** to be ready for release as early as January. Others have built such a dream device, but none has yet overcome the problem of input: typing on a screen is difficult and **handwriting recognition** has never really worked. If Apple has **cracked** it, it could upend the PC industry, as the iPhone did the handset market. If the tablet is also a good substitute for paper, the publishing and newspaper industries could be in for more upheaval. The **blogosphere** is abuzz with **rumours** that Apple is talking to publishers about offering their content on its device.

The final possibility is for another contender to emerge. The obvious candidates are Amazon, the world's biggest online **retailer**, and Facebook, the leading social network. Amazon already has a cloud of sorts. It offers cloud computing services to other online firms and has developed the Kindle, an electronic reader, which is due to be available worldwide from October 19th. Facebook runs what is arguably the most successful cloud service, with more than 300 millions registered users. It provides a platform for people to communicate, share information and **collaborate** online——all things that businesses want to do, too.

disarray [ˌdɪsəˈreɪ]
n. 无秩序，杂乱，衣冠不整
vt. 使混乱，弄乱，使脱去衣服

cancellation [ˌkænsəˈleɪʃən]
n. 取消，删除

handset-maker
手机生产商

tablet computer
平板计算机

rumoured [ˈruːməˈmʌŋɡə, -ŋɡm]
adj. 谣传的，传说的
v. 谣传(rumour 的过去式和过去分词)

handwriting recognition
手写识别

cracked [krækt]
v. 破裂，崩溃(crack 的过去分词)，发沙哑声，失败
adj. 破裂的，声音嘶哑的，精神失常的

blogosphere
n. 博客圈(网络上博客的总称)，博客世界，空间

rumour [ˈruːmə]
n. 谣言
vt. 传闻

retailer [riːˈteɪlə]
n. 零售商，传播的人

collaborate [kəˈlæbəreɪt]
vi. 合作，勾结，通敌

Only one thing seems sure about the future of the digital skies: the company or companies that **dominate** it will be American. European or Asian firms have yet to make much of an appearance in cloud computing. Nokia, the world's biggest handset-maker, is trying to form a cloud with its set of online services called Ovi, but its efforts are still in their infancy. Governments outside America may **harbour** ambitious plans for state-funded clouds. They would do better simply to let their citizens make the most of the competition among the American colossi.

dominate ['dɔmineit]
vt. 控制，支配，占优势；在其中占主要地位
vi. 占优势，处于支配地位
harbour ['hɑ:bə]
n. 海港(等于 harbor)，避难所
vt. 庇护，藏匿，入港停泊
vi. 藏匿，入港停泊，庇护

Exercises

Ⅰ. **Fill in the blanks with the information given in the text.**

1. Other products, some being _____ this autumn with less fanfare than Windows 7, represent Microsoft's future.

2. Microsoft has agreed to give Windows users in Europe a "ballot screen" that allows them to choose a rival _____ in place of its own Internet Explorer.

3. Having control over the software on the PC, smart-phones and other client _____, Microsoft can more easily create what it calls "seamless experiences".

4. Cloud _____ provides computation, software applications, data access, and storage resources without requiring cloud users to know the location and other details of the computing infrastructure.

5. End users access cloud based applications through a web browser or a light weight desktop or mobile app while the business software and data are stored on _____ at a remote location.

Ⅱ. **Translate the following passages from English into Chinese.**

Granted, there are hundreds if not thousands of firms offering cloud services——web-based applications living in data centres, such as music sites or social networks. But Microsoft, Google and Apple play in a different league. Each has its own global network of data centres. They intend to offer not just one or two services, but whole suites of them, with services including e-mail, address books, storage, collaboration tools and business applications. They are also vying to dominate the periphery, either by developing software for smart-phones and other small devices or by making such devices themselves.

Grammar 15 其他计算机英语文体的写作技巧

1. 软件产品广告的结构

软件产品广告主要是为了更好地销售软件而设计的简短的专业英语文章，为了达到销售的目的，除了用大量的术语来阐述其主要功能外，有的时候日常英语中常见的广告语言技巧也应用到这里面中。一则软件广告通常包含标题、该软件产品的说明（图片或者外观图等）、软件的主要新功能或者用途及特点、最后的销售该软件的客户信息等。

软件产品广告作为一类特殊的广告，常常有自己的语言特点，下面举几个常见的例子，

大家体会一下其中的特点。

例如：

Finally, the dBASE, you've been waiting IV.

Get the new dBASE IV, Now for just $ 449.

大家盼望已久的 dBASE 增强型版本 dBASE IV 终于问世了。该软件目前的售价仅为 449 美元。

Twice the performance at half the cost.

The New Ultra Graphics Accelerator from Metheus

"花一半的钱，却得双倍的性能，何乐而不为！"这是 Methus 公司为其图形加速器所做的广告。

有些广告为了吸引消费者，甚至采用夸张大胆的说法，或者为了让自己的广告语通俗易懂且能朗朗上口，常常是很风趣幽默的。下面给出一则广告，请读者自己尝试翻译。

Over 100 MB Removable Drives Fight it Out: Magnetic vs Optical Storage systems with removable disks and capacities of 100 MB or more are beginning to be mounted in personal computers. Within a few years floppy disks with capacities of over 100 MB and optical disks with capacities of 650 MB are expected to be standard storage devices. There types of high-density floppy disks have appeared in the US and Japan, with the Zip drive from Iomega Corp of the US leading in shipments. The LS-120 from Matsushita Industries, Ltd of Japan and the drive being developed by Mitsumi Electric Co, follow closely in second and third place. In optical disk drives, the CD-R drives are receiving high praise because it allows data to be read on a standard CD-ROM drive.

2. 计算机学术论文的写作

通常，一篇计算机学术论文是由 Title（标题）、Abstract（摘要）、Introduction（简介）、Method（方法）、Result（结果）、Discussion（讨论论证）、Conclusion（结论）和 Reference（参考文献）组成的八项内容是必不可少的，其他内容则根据具体需要而定。有些计算机学术论文还有 Table of contents(目录)、Nomenclature(术语表)和 Introduction(引言)等。

学术论文的正文写作部分是下面主要叙述的重点，这部分主要说明作者研究的主要内容、研究使用的方法和过程、研究的结论。它具有严密的科学性和客观性，反映一个研究课题的价值，同时提出以后的研究方向。事实上，为了更好更形象地表达问题，在论文中常常引用了大量的图形和数据，所以在引用过程中，要注意符合英文的写作规范。

结论部分是计算机学术论文的落点，这部分也可以是表达的建议等。常见的句子类型如下。

例如：

It can be concluded that ...(可以得出结论……)

We may conclude that...或 We come to the conclusion that...(我们得出如下结论……)

We think (consider, believe, feel) that...(我们认为……)(用于表示留有商量余地的结论)

也可以是以建议的形式出现。

例如：

It should be realized (emphasized, stressed, noted, pointed out) that ...

It is suggested (proposed, recommended, desirable) that ...

It would be better (helpful, advisable) that…

在文章的末尾部分，常常是作者的致谢。为了对曾给予支持与帮助或关心的人表示感谢，在论文之后，作者通常对有关人员致以简短的谢词，可用如下方式。

I am thankful to sb. for sth

I am grateful to sb. for sth

I am deeply indebted to sb. for sth

I would like to thank sb. for sth.

Thanks are due to sb. for sth

The author wishes to express his sincere appreciation to sb. for sth.

The author wishes to acknowledge sb.

The author wishes to express his gratitude for sth

 参考译文

Section A 云计算的真正含义

云计算正风靡一时。Gartner 公司高级分析员 Ben Pring 和他的许多同行一样认为："云计算是一句时髦的词"。问题是（类似于 Web 2.0 一样），每个人对于云计算似乎都有自己不同的定义。

作为对互联网的比喻，"云"是一个众所周知的陈词滥调，但是当"云"结合了"计算"以后，它的意义就变得庞杂而模糊了。一些分析师和厂商狭隘地将云计算定义为某种升级版的效用计算：由虚拟服务器在 Internet 上使用。而其他人定义的范围又太过于宽泛，他们坚持认为任何防火墙之外的操作都是"在云里"，这也包括传统的外包。

云计算的焦点只在于，当我们想到 IT 的实际需求：在没有新的投资，不培训新员工，或者不购买新软件的前提下还能够增加资源容量或者提高性能的一种方法。云计算在互联网上实时地包含任何的订阅模式或者按使用量付费的服务，扩展了 IT 行业现有的能力。

云计算还处于初级阶段，各种杂乱的大型或小型的供应商提供了一系列的云端服务，从全面的应用程序到存储服务，再到垃圾邮件过滤。并且，公用计算基础架构的供应商也是其中的一部分，所以如 Salesforce.com 这样的 SaaS（软件即服务）供应商也在提供云计算服务。现在，绝大多数 IT 部门都必须独立地参与到基于云的服务中来，云计算的聚合和集成已经出现。

美国媒体 InfoWorld 与数十家厂商、分析师和 IT 客户进行交流，整理出云计算的各个部分。基于这些讨论，对云计算进行了以下粗略的分类。

SaaS

这种类型的云计算提供了单一的应用程序,通过浏览器向数以千计的客户使用多重任务执行架构。对客户而言，这意味着没有关于服务器或软件授权的前期投资；对于厂商只需要保证一个应用程序持续可用即可，与传统的虚拟主机相比成本更低。Salesforce.com 是迄今为止在企业应用中最有名的例子。另外，SaaS 的人力资源应用程序也很常见，甚至已经开始向 ERP 领域拓展，如 Workday。而且，谁又可以预测像 Google Apps 和 Zoho Office 这种同样基于 SaaS "桌面"的应用会突然崛起？

公用/效用计算

这不是一个新的概念，但这种形式的云计算是从 Amazon.com、Sun、IBM 和其他人在存储和虚拟服

务器上所提的需求而来,使云计算获得新的生机。早期的企业采用公用/效用计算的方式作为补充手段,利用在非关键任务的需要,但有一天,他们可能会取代数据处理中心的一部分。其他供应商提供的解决方案是帮助 IT 企业创建虚拟数据中心服务器,如 3 兆的 AppLogic、Cohesive Flexible Technologies 的 Elastic Server on Demand。Liquid Computing 公司的 LiquidQ 也有类似的服务,能帮助企业将内存、I/O、存储容量和计算容量通过网络集成为一个虚拟的资源池来使用。

云计算领域的 Web 服务

和 SaaS 相类似,Web 服务供应商提供 API 让开发人员在互联网上进行应用开发,而不是提供完整成熟的应用程序。这种服务范围非常广泛,从分散的商业服务(如 Strike Iron 和 Xignite),到谷歌地图、ADP 薪资处理、美国邮政服务、彭博资讯和常规信用卡处理服务等全方位的 API 服务。

平台服务

平台服务是 SaaS 的变种,这种云计算将开发环境作为一种服务提供给用户。可以在供应商的基础设施上建立自己的应用程序来运行,并且可以通过网络从供应商的服务器上交付给用户,如 Legos。这些服务会受到厂商的设计以及能力的限制,所以用户不是完全自由的,但是可以获得可预见性和预集成。主要的例子包括 Salesforce.com 的 Force.com、Coghead 和全新的谷歌应用搜索引擎。基于极轻量级开发的云混合平台比比皆是,比如 Yahoo Pipes 和 Dapper.net。

MSP(管理服务供应商)

管理服务是云计算最古老的形式之一,它是面向 IT 人员的应用程序而不是最终用户,如电子邮件的病毒扫描服务或者应用程序监控服务。由 SecureWorks、IBM 和 Verizon 公司所提供的管理安全服务可以归入此类,还有近期被谷歌获得的 Postini 云基础上的反垃圾邮件服务,还有其他的桌面管理服务,如 CenterBeam 和 Everdream 提供的产品。

服务商业平台

这种云服务融合了 SaaS 和 MSP,为用户提供了一种交互性的服务平台。这是最常见的商业贸易环境,如某个消费管理系统可以让用户在一个网络平台上在线订购旅行或秘书类服务,并且服务的交付方式和价格也是由用户实现设置好的,可以把它想象成是一个自动服务机构。非常典型的例子是 Rearden Commerce 和 Ariba。

云计算集成

云计算的集成还只是初级阶段。SaaS 供应商 OpSource 最近推出了 OpSource Services Bus,它使用了一家新成立的叫 Boomi 的小公司的云计算集成技术。SaaS 供应商 Workday 最近也收购了一个在这个领域的一家公司 CapeClear。这个公司提供对于 B2B 集成的企业服务总线。在这之前,2005 年开始兴起的 Grand Central 想要成为一种通用的"云计算总线",通过这个总线把多家 SaaS 供应商联合起来一起为用户提供更加综合完善的服务。

如今,云计算的运用还不是很常见,因为很多云计算的服务相对于用户来说过于孤立,使云计算更可能被看成是"天空运算"。反过来说,随着虚拟化和 SOA 在企业中的影响,松散耦合灵活的服务、可扩展的基础构架最终可以使每一个企业成为"云"中的一个结点。这将是一个不同以往的长期趋势。但是在这个大趋势中,云计算在很长的时间内还将会是业内争论的焦点之一。

Section B 移动云计算

移动云计算是将云计算和移动设备相结合来使用。这种方式是将云计算相应的任务和数据存储在互联网上，而不是个人的设备上，并且按需访问。

应用程序运行在远程服务器上，然后发送给用户。因为在过去几年里，由于苹果和谷歌的移动浏览器进行了先进改善，因此几乎所有的手机中都有一个合适的浏览器。这意味着开发商可以绕过创建移动操作系统的限制，从而获得更广阔的市场。

移动云计算为新公司提供了成为移动网络供应商的机会。一些运营商，如 Vodafone(沃达丰，美国电信企业)、Orange 和 Verizon(威瑞森无线通信)已经开始为企业提供云计算服务。

2011 年 7 月 29 日，阿里巴巴集团推出基于云计算的操作系统 Aliyun。Aliyun 操作系统将采用云服务，如电子邮件、互联网搜索和基于网络的应用程序的支持。用户不需要下载或安装这些程序到自己的移动设备中。

定义

移动云计算是移动网络和云计算之间的结合，从而为移动用户提供最佳的服务。在移动云计算中，移动设备并不需要很高级的配置(如 CPU 速度和内存容量)，因为所有的数据和复杂的计算模块都可以在"云"中处理。

相关应用

移动应用是全球手机市场迅速发展的一部分。它们是由运行在移动设备和执行手机用户提出某些任务的软件所构成。按照世界移动应用市场报告，仅在 2009 年全球从本地和第三方的应用程序商店所下载的应用程序就达到了大约 7 亿(包括免费和付费的程序)，在同一年产生了 3.9 亿美元的收入。预计在 2015 年总值将达到 24.4 亿美元，从 2009 年到 2015 年，全球移动应用市场的复合年增长率将达到 64%。苹果公司就是一个典型移动应用程序的激增的例子。在 2009 年，苹果公司有高达超过 4 亿的数据下载命令，超过了整个应用程序市场份额的 90%。苹果公司 App Store 的成功不仅确立了移动应用程序的可扩展性，而且也表明，提供更好的移动应用程序可能产生巨大的收益。

- 移动商务。从电子商务出现以后仅仅几年的时间中，其在商务领域使用率的激增却是非常惊人的。电子商务被称为在互联网和其他计算机网络中买卖产品或服务的电子系统。从政府到跨国公司再到个人创业，电子商务正日益被视为未来的关键业务方式。方便交易、扩大市场，并减少开支的因素使电子商务解决方案越来越具有吸引力，因此在线销售量明显增加。
- 移动学习。今天的移动学习正变得越来越受欢迎，因为有许多人使用移动设备来提高他们的学识。移动学习并不仅仅是电子学习，而是电子学习附加可移动性。很显然，通过移动学习为手机用户带来了许多好处。这为他们带来了便利，因为他们可以随时随地在任何方便的时候从便携式设备中学习。然而，有一些研究指出一些常规移动学习所具有的一些限制条件，如移动设备价格昂贵、网络成本高、网络传输速率差、有限的教育资源。因此，移动学习是难以充分利用和流行起来的。
- 移动医疗。远程通信技术在医疗领域的发展，使许多人的诊断和治疗变得更加容易。这可以帮助患者定期监测他们的健康以便于及时治疗。此外，它会使辅助医疗服务供应商增加，进而可以提供更高效的过程和工作，改善医疗服务质量。尽管如此，它也面临诸多挑战如物理存储的问题、安全和隐私、医疗事故。因此，需要引入云计算作为一个解决方案来解决上述问题。云计算为用户提供了便利条件，帮助他们轻松快速地访问资源。此外，云计算还在网络上提供需求操作的服务，以满足电子医疗应用程序不断变化的需求。
- 移动计算。移动计算中各种服务的影响分析表明，移动计算已经改变了每一个服务。在过去十年中，移动计算变得越来越流行，它在硬件、软件和网络方面一直在不断地发展进步。移动计算已经有了我们的日常生活所需的各种应用程序。使用这项技术，已成为一项基本技能。在移动计算支持下，无论在任何地方只需要使用移动电话或笔记本式计算机，我们就可以检查电子邮件、账单、银行账户和其他私人信息。所有的功能迫使每一个数据交换必须是安全和免受任何攻击的。

移动计算服务简化了我们的生活。我们每天依赖着这个包含了很多基于移动计算功能的设备，如苹果公司的手机、网络预订等。

在今后的研究中，仍有一些具有挑战性的问题，涉及移动云计算和服务的模式。它们分别是：

(1) 移动设备存储和处理能力的限制。如何才能有效地利用有限资源来云计算？

(2) 有多个操作系统的移动设备，尤其是移动智能系统。这些措施包括安卓(Android)、塞班(Symbian)、IOS、谷歌浏览器(Chrome)和 MeeGo 系统。他们是否能够提供一个通用的接入平台，在不同的操作系统上进行移动云计算？

(3) 移动设备不仅仅是客户端而且是云中的组成部分。移动设备的移动性会对云的性能有什么影响？好处和坏处各是什么？

(4) 移动云层中的用户，对于内部和外部云来说还是同时具有安全威胁。对于这种移动环境最好的解决方案是什么？

移动云计算的需求和应用将迅速增长，研究人员和开发人员应该更加关注这一领域中云计算的研究和开发。

Section C 云计算大战

Windows 7 的发布标志着一个计算时代的结束，也标志着微软、谷歌、苹果等公司之间大战的开始。

Windows 7 不仅是微软坚实的一步，而且可能标志着信息技术一个时代的结束和另一个时代的开始。很多计算工作将不会在个人家庭计算机或办公室的计算机上完成，而是在"云"中：巨大的数据中心，它拥有庞大的存储系统和成百上千的服务器，这种强大的设备通过网络存储数据。基于网页的电子邮件、社交网络和在线游戏都是越来越多的被称做云服务的例子，它们都通过网页浏览器、智能手机和其他终端设备提供访问。由于有如此之多的服务可以下载或者在线使用，Windows 7 是微软第一个新功能较少的操作系统。Windows 不会很快消失，但是云计算意味着它不再那么重要了。

云计算的兴起不仅仅动摇了微软的重心地位，也改变了计算机工业竞争的本质。科技发展目前为止推动计算能力原理中央集线器：开始从大型机转向微机，然后到个人计算机。现在集合了更廉价更快的处理器和随处可见的更快的网络，在某些方面正在把计算能力推回中央处理的形式，甚至比其他方面推的更远。实际上，"云"的数据中心比公共的大型主机还要大。同时，个人计算机正在趋向成为大量越来越小而且可以经常无线的设备，如智能手机、上网本（小型笔记本式计算机），还有平板计算机（书本大小的触摸屏计算机）。

尽管 Windows 仍然运行在 90%以上的 PC 上，PC 重要性的衰落意味着微软不再是全能的垄断者。其他人也在建立"云"，包括因特网巨人谷歌、著名的硬件制造商苹果，苹果的市值已经超过谷歌和原来的竞争对手 IBM。

巨头公司的分类

尽管 3 家公司有越来越多的相似之处，每一家公司都是独一无二的野兽，麻省理工学院的斯隆管理学院的教授 Michael Cusumano 说。他们可以按照实现云计算的方式、盈利模式和对知识产权发展的开放程度来分类。

你可能会说，谷歌从 1998 年创建的时候就是云计算公司了。它最著名的就是它的搜索服务，但是现在也提供所有其他的产品和服务了。谷歌建立了一个估计拥有 30 多个数据中心超过 200 万台服务器的全球网络。其中，谷歌还提供了一套基于网络的应用程序，如文字处理和电子表格。最近，谷歌扩充出手机的 Andriod 系统、Chrome 网页浏览器与个人计算机的操作系统。

谷歌从创建到盈利，走了很长的一段路，但是它找到了一条在广告上面的道路，这成为了他们主要盈利方式。谷歌掌握美国市场超过 75%的搜索相关广告,其全球的份额更高一些。谷歌也在试图通过将服务卖给公司来赚钱。10 月 12 日,谷歌宣布,害虫防治快递公司 Rentokil Initial 集团将使 35000 员工都用上谷歌的在线程序,是目前应用人数最多的公司。

谷歌对广告的依赖解释了其对知识产权的开放态度。Android 和 Chrome OS 都使用开源软件,不仅使那些收费的竞争对手的日子更加难过,还会增加对谷歌服务的需求,从而也增加了谷歌自己的广告。但它的开放性也有界限:谷歌很少谈论到它的数据中心架构和搜索算法,因为这样会泄漏公司的竞争优势。内部的组织研发是公开并且分散的:大多数新的服务都是自我组织的团队提出的想法。

如果谷歌是诞生在空中,那么微软就是诞生在地面了。微软最畅销的个人计算机应用程序套件 Office,几乎有 Windows 的地方就有它。但是,微软看起来好像不知云计算为何物,实际上却不是如此。它已经建立了网络数据中心,在已经丢掉的数以亿计的发展中的在线服务后,正在开始增加吸引力。微软的 Xbox 游戏终端有强大的在线特点。新的搜索引擎 Bing,已经在市场份额中得到了一些栖息之所(尽管仍然与谷歌的市场份额相去甚远)。微软甚至正在准备一个具有基本功能的基于网页版本的 Office,并且,微软正在提供越来越多的其商业软件的在线服务版本。

但是,大部分微软的收入和总利润仍然来自于传统的盒装光盘套装的软件。但是微软相对谷歌来说不能离开在线广告业务,因为用户希望云计算服务是免费的,由广告资助。因此微软努力说服另一家网络巨头雅虎(Yahoo),与它的搜索和一部分广告业务合并。这笔七月达成的交易,意味着微软将会掌握 10%的市场份额,对抗谷歌的 83%,一家网络应用公司市场调研厂商说道。

从微软的历史看,微软的知识产权处理方式与谷歌的不同并不令人奇怪。微软也提供了其他软件公司需要的技术信息,以使他们能够写出在 Windows 上运行的软件。但是,微软谨慎地保护其软件的底层技术细节。就是说,微软目前支持很多开放标准,并且已经开始使用很少量的开源软件。在内部,微软的研发比谷歌更加集中一些,至少是它的网络部门是这样:团队更大,工作更多协调,并且上级主管那里还有很多规范。

从云外面进来的苹果公司也是一样。在线服务对苹果来说一直以来有点后知后觉,其擅长的领域:昂贵且很创意的软硬件打包销售,最近的例子就是 iPhone。苹果的在线服务——iTunes 商店,卖音乐、视频;应用程序商店(App Store),卖移动应用程序和 Mobile Me(一套原本打算推动苹果硬件需求的在线服务),总之,苹果对云计算的兴趣增加了。苹果正在北卡罗来纳州建造一座价值 10 亿美元的数据中心,可能是世界上最大的了。

不过,苹果的财务迄今为止,主要是依靠硬件销售。电子产品的销售构成该公司的绝大部分收入和利润。苹果没有分别列出来自各项服务的收入,但它不能轻视。一个市场研究公司 NPD 的统计,美国 69%的在线音乐销售,占有所有音乐销售的 35%,比沃尔玛还多。苹果公司至今已放弃的广告收入:它的服务都是没有广告的,但大多数都是收费服务。苹果公司的服务是面向消费者,而不是商业。

谈到开放,苹果也是一家很奇怪的公司。苹果的词典里面没有这个词。它不允许任何其他硬件制造商制造机器使用其操作系统。苹果通过不批准一些程序来封锁一些 iPhone 的应用,以使他们不能出现在应用程序商店(AppStore)里面。苹果公司的内部研发也是保密的。Jobs 显然发布大部分的号令,不过根据内部人员所说,有一个团队对他游说各种项目以求批准。

这三方的竞争将如何上演呢?上次类似的大战是在 20 世纪 80 年代末和 90 年代初,苹果、IBM 和微软为统治个人计算机作战。经过交战,微软获得了胜利。多亏了经济学家所谓的强大的网络效应,让获胜者几乎获得了百分之百的市场份额,Windows 将竞争对手的操作系统降低为"配角",保证其主人得到了丰厚的利润。

这次不太可能发生这种不平衡的结果。其中一个原因是,云计算的经济学可能与个人计算机的不同。网络效应不是那么强大了。大部分云计算是基于开放的标准,应该更容易更换服务商。为强调这一点,并反驳这是试图绑住用户,谷歌已经建立了数据自由前线,即一个工程师团队,他们的工作就是制定让人们的数据可以输出。

其次，巨头们都拥有可靠的资金来源以支撑自己。Windows 可能会受到抨击，尤其是因为越来越多的廉价上网本，迫使微软降低 Windows 的售价，一家报纸媒体《微软指南》的 Matt Rosoff 说。即便如此，操作系统将继续在一段时间内保持售价。微软还有其他强大的部门，包括商业和服务器软件。Bing 和雅虎可能会让谷歌在搜索上会丢失部分市场份额（和一些广告），但不太可能被拉下第一的位置。苹果也仍然能够叫卖出非凡的价格，尽管其他厂家的硬件一样运行流畅。

足够的战争基金

这意味着所有这三方都有足够的资金花费在战争的主要领域：数据中心、云服务和周边产物。在数据中心上，谷歌领先，但微软正在规模和复杂度方面紧追不舍。苹果需要学习的最多，但是这似乎也只是时间和金钱的问题。正如许多硬件已经成为一种日用品，从长远看来，知道如何建立庞大的数据中心可能不会是一个大的竞争优势了，并且数据中心扩大到了一定程度，其规模就会不再是竞争的优势。

在服务方面，也是谷歌领先。但是微软起码已经建立起来了一个配得上的竞争力，Bing。"决定引擎"（该公司团队使用的叫法）的确在帮助人们在选择一个新的相机或预订假期方面做了一个很好的工作。最大的问题是苹果公司是否可以迎头赶上。可以肯定，其 iTunes 商店和应用商店是成功的，但现在他们太专注局部了。其具有大局观的云服务，Mobile Me，没有什么可以引人入胜的地方。

但是，在云计算的周边，苹果公司拥有强大的优势，这多亏了 iPhone 的成功。其在美国市场的份额正在逼近 14%。在 AppStore 自称现拥有总计 85000 个应用程序和超过 20 亿的总下载量。但是，最近谷歌的 Android 也势头正猛。目前，几家手机制造商已经发布或在接下来的几个月内发布基于此系统的智能手机。10 月初，谷歌收到的美国最大的移动运营商 Verizon 支持。截至 2012 年底，据市场研究公司 Gartner 的预测，Android 手机将拥有比 iPhone 手机更大的市场份额。

但是，微软的移动战略目前处于混乱之中。这可能会被证明是一个严重的弱点，因为人们越来越多地使用移动设备来获得在线服务。计划自己建设的智能手机似乎陷入了僵局。其音乐播放器 Zune，一直就那样了。微软的老板 Steve Ballmer 最近说，Pink，一个基于 Danger（微软 2008 年年初收购的一家公司）的技术开发手机的项目，可能真的由于取消而面临终止，很有可能是由于这个月初 Danger 丢失了数以千计的用户信息，并且新版本的 Windows Mobile 是无法与 iPhone 和 Android 竞争的。一些手机制造商，包括摩托罗拉，已放弃该软件。

然后是市场的力量。三家中可能有一家搞出了某些"超级伟大"的东西，拿当年的苹果来形容，就是原始的 Macintosh 计算机。苹果自己可能会用平板计算机来实现，据说正在为一月的发布做准备。其他家虽然已经存在了这样一个梦幻产品，但迄今没有产品克服输入的问题：在屏幕上打字是困难的，手写识别从来没有真正好用过。如果苹果破获了它，它就能够颠覆个人计算机产业，就像 iPhone 在手机市场上曾经做过的那样。如果平板计算机还可以很好的替代纸张，报纸出版产业可能会有更大的波澜。而博客空间中则充斥着关于苹果的谣言：苹果正在和出版商讨论在它的设备上提供内容。

最后的可能性是其他竞争者的出现。显而易见，世界上最大的网上零售商亚马逊和领先的社会网络 Facebook 是候选的竞争者。亚马逊已经有某种形式的云计算了。它给其他在线公司提供云计算服务并且开发出了电子阅读器 Kindle，这款产品将于 10 月 19 日全球发行。Facebook 也许是运行的最成功的云服务了，超过 3 亿的注册用户。它为人们提供了沟通、共享信息和协作的网络平台，所有这些也是企业要去做的事情。

关于数字天空的未来，只有一件事似乎是肯定的：主宰它们的公司或公司们将是美国公司，欧洲或亚洲企业在云计算方面，还没有多少可以拿出来的东西。全球最大的手机制造商——诺基亚，试图用它那套叫做 Ovi 的在线服务构成一朵云彩，但其工作仍处于起步阶段。美国之外的各国政府正雄心勃勃地着手准备国家资助的云计划。他们其实只需要让国民们充分利用美国的云计算大战，坐收渔翁之利会更好。

参 考 文 献

[1] [美]Eckel Bruce. Java 编程思想(英文版)[M]. 3 版. 陈昊鹏译. 北京：机械工业出版社，2004.
[2] 刘艺，王春生. 计算机英语[M]. 2 版. 北京：机械工业出版社，2005.
[3] [英]Coulouris George，Dollimore Jean，Kingberg Tim. 分布式系统概念与设计[M]. 3 版. 金蓓弘，等译. 北京：机械工业出版社，2004.
[4] [美]Box Don, Sells Chris. .NET 本质论(影印版)[M]. 北京：中国电力出版社，2003.
[5] 冯燕奎，赵德奎. JSP 案例教程[M]. 北京：清华大学出版社，2004.
[6] [美] Rossand John，Murdock Kelly. PC User's Bible[M]. Indianapolis：Wiley Publishing，Inc，2007.
[7] [美]Kalback James. Designing Web Navigation[M]. Indianapolis：Wiley Publishing，Inc，2007.
[8] [美] Joyce Jerry, Moon Marianne. Windows Vista™ Plain & Simple[M]. Indianapolis：Wiley Publishing, Inc, 2007.
[9] [美] Brown L Eric. SQL Server 2005 Distilled[M]. Indianapolis：Wiley Publishing, Inc, 2007.
[10] [美] Gralla Preston, Troller Michael. How the Internet Works[M]. Indianapolis: Wiley Publishing, Inc, 2007.
[11] [美] Powell Gavin .Beginning XML Databases[M]. Indianapolis：Wiley Publishing, Inc, 2007.
[12] [美] Josuttis M Nicolai .C++ Standard Library: A Tutorial and Reference[M]. Indianapolis：Wiley Publishing, Inc, 2007.
[13] [美] Luger F George. 人工智能(英文版)[M]. 5 版. 北京：机械工业出版社，2005.
[14] [美] Russell Stuart，Norvig Peter. Artificial Intelligence: A Modern Approach(影印版)[M]. 2 版. 北京：清华大学出版社，2006.
[15] [美] O´Leary J Timothy，O´Leary I Linda. Computing Essentials(影印版)[M]. 北京：高等教育出版社，2003.
[16] [美] Han Jiawei，Kamber Micheline. 数据挖掘概念与技术(影印版)[M]. 北京：高等教育出版社，2001.
[17] 孙建忠. 计算机专业英语[M]. 2 版. 北京：中国水利水电出版社，2007.
[18] [美] Mazidi Ali Muhammad，Mazidi Gillispie Janiice. The 80x86 IBM PC and Compatible Computers :volumes Ⅰ & Ⅱ(影印版)[M]. 北京：清华大学出版社，2002.
[19] [美] O´Leary J Timothy, O´Leary I Linda. 计算机专业英语[M]. 北京：高等教育出版社，2001.
[20] [美] Brookshear J Glenn. 计算机科学概论(英文版)[M]. 6 版. 北京：人民邮电出版社，2004.
[21] [美] Rowe H Stanford, Schuh L Marsha. Computer Networking(影印版)[M]. 北京：清华大学出版社，2006.
[22] [美] Stallings William. Computer Networking with Internet Protocols and Technology(英文版)[M]. 北京：电子工业出版社，2006.
[23] [美] Knorr Eric Gruman Galen. What Cloud Computing Really Means[M]. InfoWorld. 2009.
[24] [美] Cloud Computing: Clash of the Clouds[J]. The Economist. 2009.
[25] [美] Fan Xiaopeng, Cao Jiannong, Mao Haixia. A Survey of Mobile Cloud Computing[J]. ZTE Communications Magazine, 2011, No.1.

[26] http://en.wikipedia.org/wiki/Mobile_Cloud_Computing.
[27] 李庆诚. 嵌入式系统原理[M]. 北京：北京航空航天大学出版社，2009.
[28] http://en.wikipedia.org/wiki/Embedded_system.
[29] http://baike.baidu.com/view/6115.htm.
[30] 黄桂田，龚六堂，张全升. 中国物联网发展报告(2011)[R]. 北京：社会科学文献出版社，2011.
[31] 王志良，石志国. 物联网工程导论[M]. 西安：西安电子科技大学出版社，2011.
[32] [美] ITU Internet Reports 2005: The Internet of Things[R], 2005.
[33] [美]European Commission, Internet of Things — An Action Plan for Europe[C], 2009.
[34] http://www.ibm.com/the smartercity.

北京大学出版社本科计算机系列实用规划教材

序号	标准书号	书名	主编	定价	序号	标准书号	书名	主编	定价
1	7-301-10511-5	离散数学	段禅伦	28	43	7-301-14506-7	Photoshop CS3 案例教程	李建芳	34
2	7-301-10457-X	线性代数	陈付贵	20	44	7-301-14510-4	C++程序设计基础案例教程	于永彦	33
3	7-301-10510-X	概率论与数理统计	陈荣江	26	45	7-301-14942-3	ASP .NET 网络应用案例教程 (C# .NET 版)	张登辉	33
4	7-301-10503-0	Visual Basic 程序设计	闵联营	22	46	7-301-12377-5	计算机硬件技术基础	石磊	26
5	7-301-10456-9	多媒体技术及其应用	张正兰	30	47	7-301-15208-9	计算机组成原理	娄国焕	24
6	7-301-10466-8	C++程序设计	刘天印	33	48	7-301-15463-2	网页设计与制作案例教程	房爱莲	36
7	7-301-10467-5	C++程序设计实验指导与习题解答	李兰	20	49	7-301-04852-8	线性代数	姚喜妍	22
8	7-301-10505-4	Visual C++程序设计教程与上机指导	高志伟	25	50	7-301-15461-8	计算机网络技术	陈代武	33
9	7-301-10462-0	XML 实用教程	丁跃潮	26	51	7-301-15697-1	计算机辅助设计二次开发案例教程	谢安俊	26
10	7-301-10463-7	计算机网络系统集成	斯桃枝	22	52	7-301-15740-4	Visual C# 程序开发案例教程	韩朝阳	30
11	7-301-10465-1	单片机原理及应用教程	范立南	30	53	7-301-16597-3	Visual C++程序设计实用案例教程	于永彦	32
12	7-5038-4421-3	ASP .NET 网络编程实用教程 (C#版)	崔良海	31	54	7-301-16850-9	Java 程序设计案例教程	胡巧多	32
13	7-5038-4427-2	C 语言程序设计	赵建锋	25	55	7-301-16842-4	数据库原理与应用 (SQL Server 版)	毛一梅	36
14	7-5038-4420-5	Delphi 程序设计基础教程	张世明	37	56	7-301-16910-0	计算机网络技术基础与应用	马秀峰	33
15	7-5038-4417-5	SQL Server 数据库设计与管理	姜力	31	57	7-301-15063-4	计算机网络基础与应用	刘远生	32
16	7-5038-4424-9	大学计算机基础	贾丽娟	34	58	7-301-15250-8	汇编语言程序设计	张光长	28
17	7-5038-4430-0	计算机科学与技术导论	王昆仑	30	59	7-301-15064-1	网络安全技术	骆耀祖	30
18	7-5038-4418-3	计算机网络应用实例教程	魏峥	25	60	7-301-15584-4	数据结构与算法	佟伟光	32
19	7-5038-4415-9	面向对象程序设计	冷英男	28	61	7-301-17087-8	操作系统实用教程	范立南	36
20	7-5038-4429-4	软件工程	赵春刚	22	62	7-301-16631-4	Visual Basic 2008 程序设计教程	隋晓红	34
21	7-5038-4431-0	数据结构(C++版)	秦锋	28	63	7-301-17537-8	C 语言基础案例教程	汪新民	31
22	7-5038-4423-2	微机应用基础	吕晓燕	33	64	7-301-17397-8	C++程序设计基础教程	郗亚辉	30
23	7-5038-4426-4	微型计算机原理与接口技术	刘彦文	26	65	7-301-17578-1	图论算法理论、实现及应用	王桂平	54
24	7-5038-4425-6	办公自动化教程	钱俊	30	66	7-301-17964-2	PHP 动态网页设计与制作案例教程	房爱莲	42
25	7-5038-4419-1	Java 语言程序设计实用教程	董迎红	33	67	7-301-18514-8	多媒体开发与编程	于永彦	35
26	7-5038-4428-0	计算机图形技术	龚声蓉	28	68	7-301-18538-4	实用计算方法	徐亚平	24
27	7-301-11501-5	计算机软件技术基础	高巍	25	69	7-301-18539-1	Visual FoxPro 数据库设计案例教程	谭红杨	35
28	7-301-11500-8	计算机组装与维护实用教程	崔明远	33	70	7-301-19313-6	Java 程序设计案例教程与实训	董迎红	45
29	7-301-12174-0	Visual FoxPro 实用教程	马秀峰	29	71	7-301-19389-1	Visual FoxPro 实用教程与上机指导（第 2 版）	马秀峰	40
30	7-301-11500-8	管理信息系统实用教程	杨月江	27	72	7-301-19435-5	计算方法	尹景本	28
31	7-301-11445-2	Photoshop CS 实用教程	张瑾	28	73	7-301-19388-4	Java 程序设计教程	张剑飞	35
32	7-301-12378-2	ASP .NET 课程设计指导	潘志红	35	74	7-301-19386-0	计算机图形技术(第 2 版)	许承东	44
33	7-301-12394-2	C# .NET 课程设计指导	龚自霞	32	75	7-301-15689-6	Photoshop CS5 案例教程 (第 2 版)	李建芳	39
34	7-301-13259-3	VisualBasic .NET 课程设计指导	潘志红	30	76	7-301-18395-3	概率论与数理统计	姚喜妍	29
35	7-301-12371-3	网络工程实用教程	汪新民	34	77	7-301-19980-0	3ds Max 2011 案例教程	李建芳	44
36	7-301-14132-8	J2EE 课程设计指导	王立丰	32	78	7-301-20052-0	数据结构与算法应用实践教程	李文书	36
37	7-301-21088-8	计算机专业英语(第 2 版)	张勇	42	79	7-301-12375-1	汇编语言程序设计	张宝剑	36

38	7-301-13684-3	单片机原理及应用	王新颖	25	80	7-301-20523-5	Visual C++程序设计教程与上机指导(第2版)	牛江川	40
39	7-301-14505-0	Visual C++程序设计案例教程	张荣梅	30	81	7-301-20630-0	C#程序开发案例教程	李挥剑	39
40	7-301-14259-2	多媒体技术应用案例教程	李建	30	82	7-301-20898-4	SQL Server 2008 数据库应用案例教程	钱哨	38
41	7-301-14503-6	ASP.NET 动态网页设计案例教程(Visual Basic .NET 版)	江红	35	83	7-301-21052-9	ASP.NET 程序设计与开发	张绍兵	39
42	7-301-14504-3	C++面向对象与 Visual C++程序设计案例教程	黄贤英	35					

北京大学出版社电气信息类教材书目(已出版)
欢迎选订

序号	标准书号	书名	主编	定价	序号	标准书号	书名	主编	定价
1	7-301-10759-1	DSP 技术及应用	吴冬梅	26	38	7-5038-4400-3	工厂供配电	王玉华	34
2	7-301-10760-7	单片机原理与应用技术	魏立峰	25	39	7-5038-4410-2	控制系统仿真	郑恩让	26
3	7-301-10765-2	电工学	蒋 中	29	40	7-5038-4398-3	数字电子技术	李 元	27
4	7-301-19183-5	电工与电子技术(上册)(第2版)	吴舒辞	30	41	7-5038-4412-6	现代控制理论	刘永信	22
5	7-301-19229-0	电工与电子技术(下册)(第2版)	徐卓农	32	42	7-5038-4401-0	自动化仪表	齐志才	27
6	7-301-10699-0	电子工艺实习	周春阳	19	43	7-5038-4408-9	自动化专业英语	李国厚	32
7	7-301-10744-7	电子工艺学教程	张立毅	32	44	7-5038-4406-5	集散控制系统	刘翠玲	25
8	7-301-10915-6	电子线路 CAD	吕建平	34	45	7-301-19174-3	传感器基础(第2版)	赵玉刚	30
9	7-301-10764-1	数据通信技术教程	吴延海	29	46	7-5038-4396-9	自动控制原理	潘 丰	32
10	7-301-18784-5	数字信号处理(第2版)	阎 毅	32	47	7-301-10512-2	现代控制理论基础(国家级十一五规划教材)	侯媛彬	20
11	7-301-18889-7	现代交换技术(第2版)	姚 军	36	48	7-301-11151-2	电路基础学习指导与典型题解	公茂法	32
12	7-301-10761-4	信号与系统	华 容	33	49	7-301-12326-3	过程控制与自动化仪表	张井岗	36
13	7-301-19318-1	信息与通信工程专业英语(第2版)	韩定定	32	50	7-301-12327-0	计算机控制系统	徐文尚	28
14	7-301-10757-7	自动控制原理	袁德成	29	51	7-5038-4414-0	微机原理及接口技术	赵志诚	38
15	7-301-16520-1	高频电子线路(第2版)	宋树祥	35	52	7-301-10465-1	单片机原理及应用教程	范立南	30
16	7-301-11507-7	微机原理与接口技术	陈光军	34	53	7-5038-4426-4	微型计算机原理与接口技术	刘彦文	26
17	7-301-11442-1	MATLAB 基础及其应用教程	周开利	24	54	7-301-12562-5	嵌入式基础实践教程	杨 刚	30
18	7-301-11508-4	计算机网络	郭银景	31	55	7-301-12530-4	嵌入式 ARM 系统原理与实例开发	杨宗德	25
19	7-301-12178-8	通信原理	隋晓红	32	56	7-301-13676-8	单片机原理与应用及 C51 程序设计	唐 颖	30
20	7-301-12175-7	电子系统综合设计	郭 勇	25	57	7-301-13577-8	电力电子技术及应用	张润和	38
21	7-301-11503-9	EDA 技术基础	赵明富	22	58	7-301-20508-2	电磁场与电磁波(第2版)	郄春明	30
22	7-301-12176-4	数字图像处理	曹茂永	23	59	7-301-12179-5	电路分析	王艳红	38
23	7-301-12177-1	现代通信系统	李白萍	27	60	7-301-12380-5	电子测量与传感技术	杨 雷	35
24	7-301-12340-9	模拟电子技术	陆秀令	28	61	7-301-14461-9	高电压技术	马永翔	28
25	7-301-13121-3	模拟电子技术实验教程	谭海曙	24	62	7-301-14472-5	生物医学数据分析及其 MATLAB 实现	尚志刚	25
26	7-301-11502-2	移动通信	郭俊强	22	63	7-301-14460-2	电力系统分析	曹 娜	35
27	7-301-11504-6	数字电子技术	梅开乡	30	64	7-301-14459-6	DSP 技术与应用基础	俞一彪	34
28	7-301-18860-6	运筹学(第2版)	吴亚丽	28	65	7-301-14994-2	综合布线系统基础教程	吴达金	24
29	7-5038-4407-2	传感器与检测技术	祝诗平	30	66	7-301-15168-6	信号处理 MATLAB 实验教程	李 杰	20
30	7-5038-4413-3	单片机原理及应用	刘 刚	24	67	7-301-15440-3	电工电子实验教程	魏 伟	26
31	7-5038-4409-6	电机与拖动	杨天明	27	68	7-301-15445-8	检测与控制实验教程	魏 伟	24
32	7-5038-4411-9	电力电子技术	樊立萍	25	69	7-301-04595-4	电路与模拟电子技术	张绪光	35
33	7-5038-4399-0	电力市场原理与实践	邹 斌	24	70	7-301-15458-8	信号、系统与控制理论(上、下册)	邱德润	70
34	7-5038-4405-8	电力系统继电保护	马永翔	27	71	7-301-15786-2	通信网的信令系统	张云麟	24
35	7-5038-4397-6	电力系统自动化	孟祥忠	25	72	7-301-16493-8	发电厂变电所电气部分	马永翔	35
36	7-5038-4404-1	电气控制技术	韩顺杰	22	73	7-301-16076-3	数字信号处理	王震宇	32
37	7-5038-4403-4	电器与PLC控制技术	陈志新	38	74	7-301-16931-5	微机原理及接口技术	肖洪兵	32

序号	标准书号	书　　名	主　编	定价	序号	标准书号	书　　名	主　编	定价
75	7-301-16932-2	数字电子技术	刘金华	30	94	7-301-18672-5	太阳能电池原理与应用	靳瑞敏	25
76	7-301-16933-9	自动控制原理	丁　红	32	95	7-301-18314-4	通信电子线路及仿真设计	王鲜芳	29
77	7-301-17540-8	单片机原理及应用教程	周广兴	40	96	7-301-19175-0	单片机原理与接口技术	李 升	46
78	7-301-17614-6	微机原理及接口技术实验指导书	李干林	22	97	7-301-19320-4	移动通信	刘维超	39
79	7-301-12379-3	光纤通信	卢志茂	28	98	7-301-19447-8	电气信息类专业英语	缪志农	40
80	7-301-17382-4	离散信息论基础	范九伦	25	99	7-301-19451-5	嵌入式系统设计及应用	邢吉生	44
81	7-301-17677-1	新能源与分布式发电技术	朱永强	32	100	7-301-19452-2	电子信息类专业MATLAB实验教程	李明明	42
82	7-301-17683-2	光纤通信	李丽君	26	101	7-301-16914-8	物理光学理论与应用	宋贵才	32
83	7-301-17700-6	模拟电子技术	张绪光	36	102	7-301-16598-0	综合布线系统管理教程	吴达金	39
84	7-301-17318-3	ARM 嵌入式系统基础与开发教程	丁文龙	36	103	7-301-20394-1	物联网基础与应用	李蔚田	44
85	7-301-17797-6	PLC原理及应用	缪志农	26	104	7-301-20339-2	数字图像处理	李云红	36
86	7-301-17986-4	数字信号处理	王玉德	32	105	7-301-20340-8	信号与系统	李云红	29
87	7-301-18131-5	集散控制系统	周荣富	36	106	7-301-20505-1	电路分析基础	吴舒辞	38
88	7-301-18285-7	电子线路CAD	周荣富	41	107	7-301-20506-8	编码调制技术	黄 平	26
89	7-301-16739-7	MATLAB基础及应用	李国朝	39	108	7-301-20763-5	网络工程与管理	谢 慧	39
90	7-301-18352-6	信息论与编码	隋晓红	24	109	7-301-20845-8	单片机原理与接口技术实验与课程设计	徐懂理	26
91	7-301-18260-4	控制电机与特种电机及其控制系统	孙冠群	42	110	301-20725-3	模拟电子线路	宋树祥	38
92	7-301-18493-6	电工技术	张　莉	26	111	7-301-21058-1	单片机原理与应用及其实验指导书	邵发森	44
93	7-301-18496-7	现代电子系统设计教程	宋晓梅	36	112	7-301-20918-9	Mathcad在信号与系统中的应用	郭仁春	30（估）

请登录www.pup6.cn免费下载本系列教材的电子书(PDF版)、电子课件和相关教学资源。
欢迎免费索取样书,并欢迎到北京大学出版社来出版您的著作,可在www.pup6.cn在线申请样书和进行选题登记,也可下载相关表格填写后发到我们的邮箱,我们将及时与您取得联系并做好全方位的服务。
联系方式：010-62750667，pup6_czq@163.com，szheng_pup6@163.com，linzhangbo@126.com，欢迎来电来信咨询。